More praise for *Captain James Cook*

"This is a fine solid book, the fruit of immense reading, of very close personal research by the author and by his most distinguished predecessors, above all by the honored but somewhat unwieldy Beaglehole. It is the kind of book that can be written only by a man wholly devoted to his subject and largely indifferent to the ordinary economics of writing: a most respectable accomplishment."   —Patrick O'Brian

"A vivid and well-documented account of the life and voyages of the famous 18th-century English navigator. . . . Hough has a keen eye for the pathos and absurdity of human nature, which enhances descriptions both of the high and mighty with whom Cook had to contend in England and of the natives whom he encountered in his amazing journeys."   —*Kirkus Reviews*

"An engaging, intelligent retelling of Cook's extraordinary life."   —Verlyn Klinkenborg, *Boston Globe*

"A highly readable narrative of the great 18th-century navigator, explorer, and cartographer, who 'shaped the shores' of the Pacific Ocean, including many of its islands and polar regions. . . . The author's travels in the wake of Cook's voyages and his scrutiny of the scattered archival sources give this work a fresh and lively quality."
     —*Library Journal*

"[Hough's writing] evokes the creak of canvas, the smells of a crowded wooden ship, the howl of a gale off Cape Horn, the fear of the unknown that every sailor felt. . . . Hough recreates for us how it must have felt for those hardy mariners to sail into uncharted waters and meet the tribes of New Zealand, Australia, Tahiti, and Hawaii."
     —Don Follmer, *Raleigh News and Observer*

CAPTAIN
JAMES COOK

Richard Hough

W. W. NORTON & COMPANY
New York   London

First published as a Norton paperback 1997
Copyright © 1994 by Richard Hough
First American Edition 1995

All rights reserved
Printed in the United States of America
Manufacturing by the Maple-Vail Manufacturing Group, Inc.

Library of Congress Cataloging-in-Publication Data
Hough, Richard Alexander, 1922–
    Captain James Cook : a biography / Richard Hough.
       p.   cm.
    Includes bibliographical references and index.
    ISBN 0–393–03680–4
    1. Cook, James, 1728-1779.   2. Explorers--Great Britain
    --Biography.   I. Title.
    G246.C7H615 1995
    910'.92--dc20
    [B]   94-35998
                                       CIP

ISBN 0-393-31519-3 pbk.

W. W. Norton & Company, Inc.
500 Fifth Avenue, New York, N.Y. 10110
W. W. Norton & Company Ltd.
10 Coptic Street, London WC1A 1PU

1 2 3 4 5 6 7 8 9 0

FOR JACK GARLAND

Contents

Illustrations

The sloop, *Resolution*, drawn by John Webber (1752–93) [The British Library]

Dusky Bay Maoris, engraving by Lerperniere after William Hodges (1744–97) [The British Library]

New Zealand war canoe with defiant Maori warriors, drawn by Sporing [The British Library]

BETWEEN PAGES 334 AND 335

Captain James Cook at the termination of his second voyage, by Willam Hodges (1744–97) [National Maritime Museum, London]

James Burney, son of musicologist Charles Burney and brother of the novelist and diarist, Fanny

Omai, the Polynesian from the Society Islands [National Maritime Museum, London]

Adventure Bay, Bruni Island by William Ellis (1747–unknown) [National Maritime Museum, London]

Sandwich (Prince William) Sound, drawn by John Webber (1752–93) [The British Library]

William Bligh's chart of the Sandwich Islands [The British Library]

Resolution and *Discovery* off Icy Cape, drawn by John Webber (1752–93) [Courtesy, Peabody & Essex Museum, Salem, Ma., USA]

Resolution and *Discovery* at anchor in Kealakekua Bay [Public Record Office, MPM 44]

Mrs Elizabeth Cook, artist unknown [Mitchell Library, State Library of New South Wales, Sydney]

The fight between Cook and his marines and the Hawaiian warriors of Kealakekua, by Johann Zoffany (1734/5–1810) [National Maritime Museum, London]

Maps and Drawings

The charts not otherwise acknowledged are reproduced by kind permission of the Hakluyt Society from *The Journals of Captain Cook* edited by Dr J. C. Beaglehole

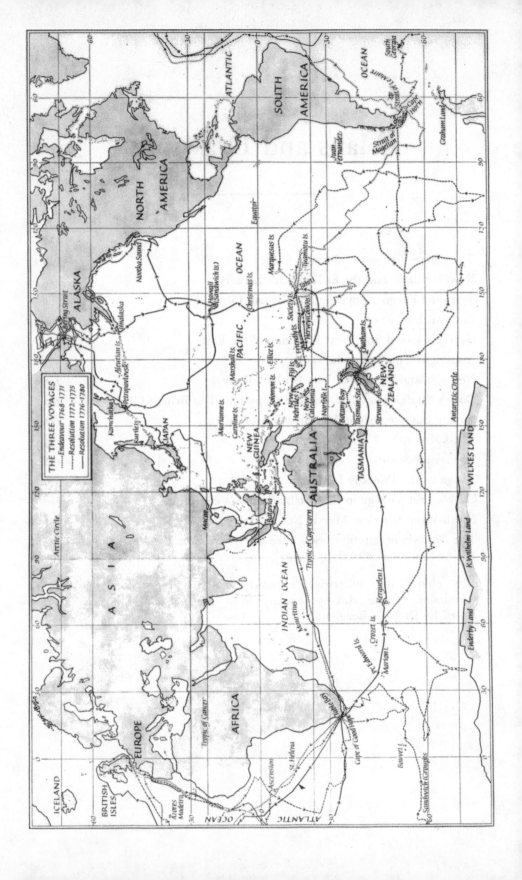

Foreword

SOME YEARS AGO I WROTE a short book entitled *The Murder of Captain James Cook* (*The Last Voyage of Captain James Cook* in the United States), its publication to coincide with the bicentenary celebrations of his death. Several critics at the time, including Sir Charles Snow, suggested that I should one day write a full-length biography. It is only recently that I have been able to undertake this challenging but wholly enjoyable task.

As with the earlier book, and for my *Captain Bligh and Mr Christian*, I benefited greatly from being able to travel in the wake of the eighteenth-century navigators, from Cape Horn and southern Tasmania in the southern hemisphere, to Vancouver and Alaska in the north, taking in certain parts of the eastern seaboard of Australia, especially the Great Barrier Reef, parts of the coastline of New Zealand, Easter Island, all the French Society Islands, and all the American Sandwich (Hawaiian) Islands.

Like so many of my predecessors in this field, I have sometimes, for readers' convenience, taken liberties with the original spelling, punctuation and, occasionally, the sentence construction of Cook's writing. The source references (pp. 374 to 384) make the original readily accessible. For example, on page 13 there is a log extract: 'Received on board from the *Esperance* 26 prisoners at 4 o'clock. *Esperance* on fire and there being no possibility of keeping her above water.' In the original, this reads: 'Recd on B^d from y^eEsperance 26 prisoners att 4 Esperance on fire . . .'

The late Dr J. C. Beaglehole himself, the incomparable authority on Cook's life and voyages, once wrote of Robert Molyneux's remarks on Tahiti (*Journals* I, p.551): 'A few obvious slips have been silently corrected, and a minimum of punctuation supplied where its absence would be confusing . . .' Again, in *Journals* II, p.238n: 'I print this paragraph in this place, rather than incorporate it in the foregoing general description of Tahiti . . . because it is so obviously not a part of the original journal but added during the later revision . . .'

James Cook was a great re-drafter, and as Beaglehole (again) defined, 'to chart the coasts and record the soundings' of his *Journal* in all its variations, 'the reader' should be warned 'that there are rocks and deceptive shallows, and even a quantity of fog' (*Journals* I, p. CXCIV). I have attemped to overcome these within the confines of acceptable editorship.

Then again, a brief extract from Beaglehole's long Textual Introduction to the *Journal* of the first voyage (p. CCXXIII) gives some hint of the complexities involved in authenticating details of what Cook himself might regard as the definitive manuscript. Here Beaglehole is discussing what he calls the Greenwich MS, which was probably once the property of King George III and presented to the National Maritime Museum at Greenwich by King George V in 1935:

One may suggest that the copy was made at different times, for it reflects different stages of the original. Some of its omissions are identical with those of the Mitchell MS [Mitchell Library, Sydney, New South Wales]; on the other hand it picks up some revisions and alterations which that MS does not have . . . The names Botany Bay and New South Wales are written without erasure, although the frequent use of *was* in place of *were* argues a copy made before some of Cook's own revision . . .

My thanks are due to Janet Horncy, Reader Education Librarian at the Alexander Turnbull Library, Wellington, and to Laura Garland who carried out additional research for me there; the Librarian at the City of Auckland Public Library; Janet Anderson of the State Library of New South Wales, and Martin Beckett, the Microfilms Manager there; the Librarian at the National Maritime Museum, Greenwich; Libby Joy for much work on my behalf at the Public Record Office, Kew; Dr N. A. M. Rodger; Professor Samuel Hynes of Princeton University and Eleanor C. Au, Head of Special Collections, University of Hawaii at Manoa, for additional information; Douglas Matthews for compiling the index; also to the Hakluyt Society and its publishers, the Cambridge University Press, for allowing me to draw freely on the four volumes of *The Journals of Captain James Cook*, edited by Dr Beaglehole, whose immense biography was published posthumously in 1974.

RICHARD HOUGH
November 1993

Chronology

1728	27 OCTOBER	James Cook born	
1745	SUMMER	Apprenticed to William Sanderson, shopkeeper, at Staithes, north Yorkshire	16 YEARS
1746	AUTUMN	Apprenticed to John Walker, shipowner, Whitby, north Yorkshire	18 YEARS
1755	17 JUNE	Volunteers for Royal Navy	26 YEARS
1757	30 MAY	First serious action against a French man o' war	28 YEARS
	SUMMER	Promoted master	
	27 OOCTOBER	Appointed to HMS *Pembroke* on his birthday	29 YEARS
1758	22 FEBRUARY	Sails for Canada under Admiral Boscawen	
	26 JULY	At the capture of the French fort, Louisburg	
1759	13 SEPTEMBER	Involved in the capture of Quebec	30 YEARS
1762	26 OCTOBER	At the conclusion of the Seven Years' War, arrives Spithead from Newfoundland	33 YEARS
	21 DECEMBER	Marries Elizabeth Batts	34 YEARS
1763	5 APRIL	Appointed surveyor of Newfoundland	
	29 NOVEMBER	Returns from first survey	35 YEARS
1764	6 AUGUST	Injured by explosion	
1766	11 NOVEMBER	Returns from final survey	38 YEARS
1768	5 MAY	Appointed to command an expedition to the Pacific to observe the transit of Venus in 1769	39 YEARS
	25 MAY	Promoted to rank of lieutenant RN	
	26 AUGUST	Departs from Plymouth in *Endeavour* bark	
	12 SEPTEMBER	Anchors at Madeira	
	3 NOVEMBER	Anchors at Rio de Janeiro	40 YEARS

xv

1769	15 JANUARY	Anchors in the Bay of Good Success, Tierra del Fuego	
	25 JANUARY	Doubles Cape Horn	
	11 APRIL	Sights Tahiti	
	3 JUNE	Transit of Venus observed	
	26 JUNE	Circumnavigates Tahiti	
	9 AUGUST	Departs from the Society Islands	
	2 SEPTEMBER	Fails to find Great Southern Continent and heads north	
	7 OCTOBER	Sights coast of North Island, New Zealand	
1770	16 JANUARY	Anchors in Queen Charlotte Sound, South Island	41 YEARS
	7 FEBRUARY	Departs from Queen Charlotte Sound	
	27 MARCH	Completes circumnavigation of South and North Islands, New Zealand	
	19 APRIL	Sights the coast of New Holland (Australia)	
	28 APRIL	Lands at Botany Bay	
	10 JUNE	The *Endeavour* strikes a coral reef and in great danger	
	13 AUGUST	Takes the repaired *Endeavour* to sea again	42 YEARS
	11 OCTOBER	Arrives at Batavia and anchors	
	26 DECEMBER	'My hospital ship' departs from Batavia	
1771	14 MARCH	Arrives at Table Bay, Cape Town	
	16 APRIL	Departs from Table Bay for England	
	13 JULY	Anchors off Deal, Kent	
	DECEMBER	Takes Elizabeth to Yorkshire and visits his father and John Walker at Whitby; stays there until January 1772	43 YEARS
1772	13 JULY	Departs from Plymouth on second voyage	
	22 NOVEMBER	Departs from Table Bay on first Antarctic sweep	44 YEARS
1773	17 JANUARY	Crosses Antarctic Circle for the first time	
	23 MARCH	Arrives Dusky Bay, New Zealand	
	19 MAY	Reunited with *Adventure* Queen Charlotte Sound	
	7 JUNE	Both ships depart from Ship Cove	
	17 AUGUST	At Vaitepiha Bay, Tahiti	
	18 SEPTEMBER	Departs from the Society Islands	
	30 OCTOBER	Ships separated again off New Zealand	45 YEARS

	25 NOVEMBER	*Resolution* embarks for Antarctic again on second sweep	
1774	23 FEBRUARY	Taken ill on approach to Easter Island	
	4 JUNE	Leaves Tahiti again on King George III's birthday	
	27 JUNE	*Resolution* anchors at Tasman's Rotterdam, in the Tongan, or Friendly, group	
	JULY–AUGUST	Deep among the Melanesian Islands	
	18 OCTOBER	Back at Ship Cove, New Zealand	
	10 NOVEMBER	Departs Ship Cove	46 YEARS
	25 DECEMBER	At Christmas Harbour, Tierra del Fuego	
1775	3 JANUARY	Embarks on last Antarctic sweep	
	21 MARCH	Table Mountain sighted again	
	27 APRIL	Leaves the Cape	
	30 JULY	Anchors at Spithead	
	9 AUGUST	Promoted post-captain, his commission personally handed to him by George III	
1776	9 JANUARY	Dinner with Palliser, Stephens and Sandwich to discuss command of new North Pacific expedition	47 YEARS
	25 JUNE	Sails from the Nore	
	18 OCTOBER	At Table Bay	
	1 DECEMBER	*Resolution* and *Discovery*, united, sail from Table Bay	48 YEARS
	25–31 DECEMBER	At Christmas Harbour, Kerguelen	
1777	27–30 JANUARY	At Adventure Bay, Van Diemen's Land (Tasmania)	
	12–25 FEBRUARY	Queen Charlotte Sound, New Zealand	
	1 MAY–17 JULY	Diverts to Friendly Islands	
	13 AUGUST	At Tahiti again	
	8 DECEMBER	Departs from the Society Islands	49 YEARS
	25 DECEMBER	At Christmas Island	
1778	18 JANUARY	First Hawaiian islands sighted	
	6 MARCH	West coast of North America sighted	
	29 MARCH–26 APRIL	At Nootka Sound, Vancouver Island	
	1 JUNE	Suffers disappointment at Turnagain River, Cook Inlet, Alaska	
	26 JUNE	Hazards his ships again	
	3 AUGUST	Suffers the death of Surgeon Anderson	

	17 AUGUST	Both ships halted by ice	
	26 OCTOBER	Departs from Unalaska	
	27 OCTOBER	Celebrates his fiftieth birthday	50 YEARS
	26 NOVEMBER	Back at the Hawaiian islands, sights Maui	
	30 NOVEMBER	Chief Terreeoboo on board, and later sights Owhyhee (Hawaii)	
1779	16 JANUARY	Kealakekua Bay sighted	
	4 FEBRUARY	Departs from Kealakekua Bay	
	8 FEBRUARY	*Resolution* loses her foremast and returns to Kealakekua Bay	
	14 FEBRUARY	Theft of a cutter by Hawaiians leads to an affray ashore, Cook's failure to kidnap the King, and to his death, along with four marines	
	15 FEBRUARY	Part of Cook's body returned	
	22 FEBRUARY	Remains of Cook buried in Kealakekua Bay	

1

The Young Yorkshireman

JAMES COOK, THE SECOND SON of James Senior and Grace Cook, was born on 27 October 1728 at Marton, north Yorkshire. His father was a labourer on the land. The son was to become the most famous navigator in the world, discovering and charting coastlines from the Arctic to the Antarctic, the east coast of Australia to the west coast of North America, and hundreds of islands between.

Cook first sailed the Pacific 250 years after Ferdinand Magellan, but it was Cook who shaped the shores of this vast ocean, picked out the islands, made its geography coherent and 'cultivated a friendship with the natives'. In a single coasting of North and South Island, New Zealand (2,400 miles), Cook gave the world a chart which mariners relied upon for many years. His discoveries in Australia led to the founding of the first colony there a mere eighteen years later.

Cook's voyages led to the identification and drawing of thousands of new plants, birds and mammals by his talented passengers and officers, and the astronomical and horological work advanced those sciences immeasurably. His dietary routine for his crews, at a time when fifty per cent losses from scurvy on long voyages were commonplace, not only preserved their lives, but also the lives of numberless sailors in the future. So highly valued was his work for the betterment of man in days of peace, that the French and Americans, at the height of a naval war against his country, gave Cook's ships immunity from interference.

There were geo-political motives behind all three Pacific voyages: the claiming by Britain of the Great Southern Continent, if it could ever be found; the possession of New Holland (Australia) and New Zealand, and other lands that might be discovered; and the opening of the much-sought North-West Passage to shorten the route to the East. But there were other and more disinterested reasons for these voyages, too, in a period of intense scientific and geographic curiosity. As one botanist has claimed, the *Endeavour* expedition was 'the first organized and thoroughly equipped voyage of biological exploration'.

Besides being 'thoroughly equipped', Cook exhibited an entirely new and refreshingly civilised attitude towards the natives of the lands he exposed to public view for the first time. To the Polynesians and Melanesians, the Aborigines of New Holland and Van Diemen's Land, the Indians of Vancouver and the Eskimos of Alaska, he presented the most tolerant aspect of Western man. He might, and did, claim their land for King George III, but those were his instructions, and in the context of his time his behaviour and attitudes were remarkable for their gentleness and understanding. He was, in the judgment of Fanny Burney, whose brother sailed with Cook, 'the most moderate, humane, and gentle circumnavigator that ever went upon discoveries'.

JAMES COOK'S FATHER was a Scotsman by birth, parish records revealing that he was baptised on 4 March 1694 in the kirk of Ednam, a village near Kelso and not many miles north of the border. James Senior grew up in a harsh climate and in troubled times. As soon as he had developed the muscles, he helped his father on the land, but there was great restlessness throughout Scotland and, with the bloody and abortive Jacobite uprising of 1715–16, there was much suffering and devastation. Of some areas 'there was nothing but an entire desolation' and villages with 'nothing earthly undestroyed'. As they were later to seek a new life in the United States and Canada, so in the early decades of the eighteenth century many young Scotsmen sought to better themselves in England. Among those who migrated south from Ednam was James Senior, like many others attracted by the profitable mining in north Yorkshire of alum, a double sulphate much used in the chemical and dyeing trades. Here, he was told, he was likely to find some of his fellow countrymen. Tradition has it that when this young man left home for the last time, his mother uttered the blessing, 'God send you Grace.'

James Senior penetrated no further south than Cleveland, where he found work as a day labourer in a hamlet called Marton, in the parish of Ormesby. Here he soon acquired a reputation for steadiness and industry. He was also tall, good-looking and strong, and attracted a young girl called Grace. No doubt seeing her as the fulfilment of his mother's prayer, the young man proposed and was accepted. They married in 1726 and he brought Grace back to the two-room 'clay biggin' he rented. Here Grace gave birth to a son, John, before the family moved to the nearby village of Marton, attracted by the offer of regular employment by a farmer. In a thatched cottage which was

later demolished, Grace gave birth to a second son, who was baptised
James in Marton church a week later.

The parish of Marton is historically described as being

from north to south five miles, and about two miles broad. The village is small,
situated about a quarter of a mile from the road leading from Stockton [seven
miles distant] to Guisborough; and consists chiefly of a few farm houses and
cottages, ranged irregularly on the summit of a gentle elevation . . .

Here James lived until the age of eight, when he was already helping
his father at work in the fields or ditching and hedging.

The father and two sons had, as a team, acquired an excellent local
reputation, which was rewarded by the offer by Thomas Skottowe,
the Lord of the Manor of Great Ayton, a few miles away, of the
position of bailiff, a highly respected role for James Senior in that
small world of Cleveland villages. Moreover, Skottowe was shrewd
and kind enough to recognise special qualities in James and paid
for him to attend the village school. As one of James's Victorian
biographers has pointed out,

If we were to have chosen an ancestry which in those days would have
given a boy the best chance of success, it would have been difficult to
choose a better stock on both sides – on the one hand the Scotch
patience, intelligence, and industry, and on the other hand the Yorkshire
independence and self-reliance.

By the time James was sixteen his father – and no doubt Grace, too –
wanted a more promising future for him than as a labourer, especially
as he had had the benefit of an education, no matter how sketchy
it might have been. The next improving stage, they decided, was
apprenticeship in a trade, and at this time James Senior learned, as
these opportunities became known in the country and probably over
a glass of ale, that William Sanderson, a shopkeeper in the village of
Staithes, had an opening for an apprenticeship behind the counter of
his shop.

South of the Tees estuary, as far as the town of Scarborough, the
north Yorkshire coast is studded with fishing villages and small
towns: Redcar, Saltburn, Brotton, Sandsend, Whitby, Robin Hood's
Bay, Ravenscar, Hayburn Wyke. Most of them are tucked into clefts
in the cliffs, fed by a stream or small river, invisible from the land until
you are almost on top of them. Staithes is one of these, some fifteen
miles distant from Great Ayton, approached by a steep winding road
which flanks a river and leads past red-roofed dwellings to the centre
of the village. Here there were the market-place, one or two pubs, a

scattering of shops and the harbour, the *raison d'être* of the place, with the sturdy little fishing vessels either drawn up on the hard or moored in line, each with its nets and other fishing gear. Their size ranged from white-painted cobles to much larger smacks, whose crews numbered as many as six or eight.

Like sentinels guarding this little community are the 400-foot-high cliffs of Coburn Nab and Piercey Nab; but more effective protection against the weather is the man-made staithe, the wooden sea wall which breaks the worst of the northerly winds whipping bitterly off the sea in winter and at the equinoxes.

At Ayton the first preoccupation and subject of conversation was the state of the crops and stock; here at Staithes it was fish and fishing – the wealth or paucity of the herring, plaice or cod, and a factor which was never distant, the dangers of the calling, with whole crews sometimes never returning to port.

It was in the summer of 1745, when James was approaching his seventeenth birthday, that he made his lonely journey on foot to Staithes, carrying a few spare clothes and little else. He was an unusually tall young man with a fine craggy face and prominent nose, muscular from inheritance and hard work. He had no knowledge of what his life would be like, only that it must be different from his old occupation. He was a young man who took things as they came and was ready for what life held for him. He also possessed the twin characteristics which would serve him well throughout his life – decisiveness and self-confidence. His friends as a boy had noticed that he went his own way when it came to games or country pursuits like bird's-nesting, and they were inclined to resent this, especially as he ignored their complaints or taunts. He was, as the saying went, 'his own man'.

The first thing that James recognised about this large village – or small town – was its prosperity by contrast with the farming villages inland in which he had grown up. The dwellings were better found and maintained, the streets were cobbled, the shops well stocked and the citizens better dressed. The reason for this, he was soon to learn, was that there was more profit in fishing than farming and that this trade was supplemented by smuggling, mostly of brandy and wines, scents and other goods carrying a high excise duty.

William Sanderson's shop was easy to find, situated on the front, close to the sea. The smell of fish had been in the air from the outskirts of Staithes; here, where the fishermen stood in groups or sat on the gunwales of their boats with a mug of ale and smoking clay pipes, the smell of fish was almost overwhelmingly heavy.

Sanderson's was a double shop, a single front door leading on one side to a grocery and on the other to a drapery. There was no display window, but the rolls of cloth and ready-made garments were clearly visible, as was the grocery with stock ranging from herbs and biscuits and cakes in clearly marked tins, to sides of smoked bacon and fresh poultry. Above the shop were the living quarters for Sanderson and his wife and two children, a boy and a girl. They were a friendly family, and James was well fed and paid the token wage of an apprentice. But an apprentice did not live with the family. He took his meals, and slept, under the counter of the shop, where he kept all his possessions – such as they were – and a straw palliasse and blanket.

For some eighteen months James carried out his duties, from sweeping out and opening the shop in the early morning, to serving in it all day, and closing it down in the evening. He was liked by the customers, and also by the fishermen he would join in the evening to drink ale and listen to the tales of their calling. Several times he went with them on short trips outside the bay, and found himself attracted to the skills, adventures and constant stimulus of a sailor's life. The sea might be harsh and dangerous, but the comradeship and excitement in handling a fishing boat were in sharp contrast with the drudgery and subservience of working in a shop.

There is no reason to doubt the truth of the tale resulting in James's decision to break his apprenticeship with William Sanderson. It appears that a woman customer included in her payment an unusually shiny shilling, in fact a South Sea shilling minted in the reign of George I with, on the verso, ssc for South Sea Company. Later, he could not resist the temptation of taking this shilling from the till and replacing it with one from his pocket. South Sea shilling: it was like a harbinger of his future achievements on the other side of the world. But his master had spotted the coin in the till and now accused James of stealing it. James hotly denied this and his explanation was finally accepted. But the incident scarred the young man and he decided to ask to be relieved of his indenture. Sanderson, being a realist as well as a kind man, told James that he would not hold him against his wishes, and asked him what he intended to do. 'To go to sea, sir,' James replied.

Sanderson acted with remarkable speed and success to bring about this new change of course in James's life. First he acquired the necessary authority of James's father and then contacted a friend of his in the nearby port of Whitby, John Walker, shipowner and master mariner, who was known to take on apprentice seamen. Walker was introduced to James, fancied the cut of his jib and agreed to take him on. James Cook was bound an apprentice for three years.

NOW THAT THE TANG OF THE SEA and the stench of fish had become familiar to Cook, he was able to visualise the nature of this ancient port on the twelve-mile undulating walk along the Yorkshire clifftops, through Hinderwell and Runswick, the lower village of Lyth, past the alum works where once he might have worked, and an hour later down the long incline to Whitby.

The seaport, then and now, is divided by the broad River Esk and linked by a bridge, a primitive wooden affair at that time, paid for by tolls. Tradition has it that the first voyage out of Whitby took place in 684, when the Abbess Eafleda, daughter of King Oswy, went to Coquet Island, to the north in Alnmouth Bay, 'to commune on important matters with holy Cuthbert'. An abbey was built high up on the southern cliffs, was destroyed by Norse raids and was rebuilt from the early twelfth century.* The abbey required coal, and so did the alum works when they were set up. Ever increasingly, so did London. At first the coal from the mines to the north was brought by 'fyve man cobles', which could double up as fishing boats, stout and strong to withstand east-coast gales. Shipbuilding became important to the town, which in turn became prosperous. 'In February, 1301, in the reign of Edward 1, the port was deemed to be of sufficient rank to be called upon to furnish a ship, well manned and otherwise equipped, ready to set out against the Scots.'

At the time Cook crossed that bridge over the River Esk in order to reach Walker's house and offices on the south-west bank, the coal trade to London was the first source of profit for Walker and his brother, and for most of the shipowners and shipbuilders of Whitby. In the late 1740s London needed a million tons of coal a year and it took 1,000 ships to satisfy this demand. Ten return voyages a year for a ship was possible if the weather was favourable. But both fishing and cargo boats voyaged further, to the Baltic and the Low Countries, and ports on the Channel.

The type of vessel most used for this traffic had to be robust, capacious and manageable under the most adverse conditions. It was called a cat, and had been developed over many years by the men who sailed them in the changeable and dangerous waters of the North Sea and the Baltic, and especially down the east coast of England where the tides and currents, the ever-varying winds, the shifting sandbanks and the uncharted reefs demanded skill of a crew and strength and responsiveness in a ship.

* Its skeletal remains dominate the town today.

A cat has been defined as 'a vessel generally built remarkably strong, and may carry six hundred tons; or in the language of their own mariners, from 20 to 30 keels of coals. A cat is distinguished by a narrow stern, projecting quarters, a deep waist, and no ornamental figure on the prow.' So this is no graceful clipper ship, no greyhound of the ocean, but a workaday practical carrier of goods, capable of being handled by a crew of a dozen or fewer, most of them young apprentices of varying experience.

The Walkers were a Quaker family, sober people without pretensions, high principled and, like the Sandersons, kind and considerate. But Cook's living arrangements were very different from those of the shopkeeper at Staithes. At Whitby he lived with the family and had a room of his own. His keenness to learn the fundamentals of seamanship was encouraged. A woman called Mary Prowd, 'a trusty old nurse or housekeeper, many years employed in Mr Walker's house', took a particular fancy to the eighteen-year-old young man, and in the long winter evenings saw to it that he had a table, chair and candle so that he could read and pursue his studies. At a school for apprentices in the town – and there were many of them – he was taught navigation, how to 'shoot' the sun, the meaning of latitude and longitude, how to read a chart, and much more.

Cook first went to sea in one of Walker's cats, the *Freelove* of 450 tons, with John Jefferson as master and Robert Watson as mate. It was February 1747, Cook was eighteen, and the cat had a full cargo of best Tyne coal. Records show a complement of nineteen, including cook, carpenter, five sailors and no fewer than ten apprentices. None could be more inexperienced than Cook, but his keenness as well as his 'bookwork' were soon evident. He had never been happier in his life. His period aboard was one month and twenty-five days, roughly the time it would take under normal circumstances for the cat to reach London, discharge the coal, make good any repairs before sailing down the Thames estuary and then north up the coast 275 miles to Whitby, where she paid off.

Walker expected much of his apprentices and moved them up swiftly to higher responsibilities. Those who failed were soon discharged, but Cook was not only among the eldest but also the most promising. Walker was rigging and fitting out a new large cat, the *Three Brothers*, in early 1748, and Cook took part in this work, which was valuable experience; he then became one of her apprentice crew. This cat, more than any other vessel, formed a lasting impression on Cook. In her, again with John Jefferson as captain, he gained mature experience over a period of eighteen months, some of the time in the coal trade, and then in government service carrying foreign mercenaries and their horses from Middleburg in Flanders to Dublin and Liverpool.

By April 1750 Cook had completed his three-year apprenticeship, and for the first time could call himself a seaman instead of a mere boy. He could confidently carry out all the many tasks demanded of a sailor, from the manual skills of close reefing a sail and holding a luff, to hauling off when facing a hazard or using a handspike when heaving on the windlass; and the more intellectual skills of taking a running fix, reading a barometer and predicting the weather, sometimes using weather jingles like 'When the rain's before the wind/Topsail halyards you must mind;/When the wind's before the rain/Hoist your topsails up again'. The mere vocabulary of life at sea was like learning a foreign language. Cook loved it.

Cook was also confident that, if put to the test, he could handle one of John Walker's 400-ton cats from Whitby to Wapping, and home again. By now, too, he knew the Baltic run, through the tricky Skagerrak, steering clear of the treacherous, island-studded waters off the east Danish coastline, to the ports of Kiel and Rostock, Danzig, Königsberg, Malmö and far north to Stockholm's great harbour. He did in fact still have much to learn, but he was buoyed up with the self-confidence of youth and the satisfaction that he enjoyed from being at sea.

Promotion came unusually swiftly and by December 1752 he had passed all his examinations to become mate; he enjoyed this rank for two-and-a-half years in the agreeably named cat, *Friendship*. By 1755, at the age of twenty-seven Cook could reasonably feel something of a veteran; and this was confirmed when Walker offered him a ship of his own, the same *Friendship*. To Walker's surprise and disappointment, Cook turned down the offer. He had another ambition. He had served for nine years in the North Sea, the Baltic, the Channel and the Irish Sea, but already, at this still early age, he had his eye on farther horizons.

He was experiencing a growing curiosity to see more distant shores, perhaps even the Pacific Ocean. He had read of the Dutchmen of the last century, Abel Janszoon Tasman and, even earlier, Olivier Van Noort;* of the Portuguese Pedro Fernandez de Quiros and Luis Vaes de Torres; and, above all, of his fellow countrymen, Francis Drake, William Dampier and, within his own lifetime, Commodore George Anson, who had given the Spaniards such a drubbing in the Pacific that they looked unlikely ever to regain their dominance.

---

* Van Noort's voyage to the Pacific took place from 1597 to 1600.

James Cook, mate, had never felt the waters of the Mediterranean or the North Atlantic under his keel. And he had ambitions above the North Sea coal trade. Of course he could enter the service of the East India Company, whose ships would take him to the romantic East, or other shipping lines, which would at least lead him to Boston and New York, or far south to New Orleans. But these were dangerous times at sea and, if war with France should break out again, the press gangs would soon be combing sea ports and even vessels at sea for sailors to man new ships, and ships would be brought out of reserve. He would be a prime target for sure: young, fit, experienced. It would be much better for him to volunteer, to offer his services and work hard for promotion, and, in the words of a much later clarion cry, 'Join the Navy and see the world'.

After, no doubt, informing his father, because he was a considerate and loving son – and no doubt alarming his mother, Grace – Cook volunteered for the Royal Navy at Wapping, London.

2

'An Ambition to Go into the Navy'

RUMOURS OF WAR WERE HEAVY throughout England in 1755, although technically Cook as a ship's master was immune from press-ganging, like every sailor he knew that legal niceties did not figure strongly in the minds of press-gang officers. What Cook could not know was that the Admiralty was already devising a form of Royal Navy Reserve, which would radically reduce the need for press-ganging; had he remained a merchant seaman, he would certainly have taken advantage of 'His Majesty's Royal Bounty'.*

John Walker, regretful at losing such a fine sailor whom he had nursed and then promoted for so many years, recognised the inevitability of this step in a young man of Cook's character, and provided him with a glowing letter of reference. 'He had always', Walker once observed, 'an ambition to go into the Navy.' But, at least in the short term, to sign on for the Royal Navy meant a position many rungs down the ladder, the food, pay and conditions all being worse. On the other hand, Winston Churchill's much quoted claim that the Royal Navy was governed by 'Rum, sodomy and the lash' was inaccurate. Admiral Vernon, whose sobriquet on every lower deck was 'Old Grog', had recently watered down the rum ration, sodomy was limited because it was a hanging offence – 'a crime of so vile a nature' – and the lashes a captain could award were limited to twelve under his own authority, though this was sometimes exceeded. It had been

* 'It will remove . . . the aversion seamen have at present to enter into His
Majesty's service, the great expenses the navy is often at to get able seamen, and
the unconstitutional practice (in a nation that boasts her liberty) of impressing for
seamen, which to the officers of that service is very disagreeable . . .' Public pamphlet,
1756, quoted in J. S. Bromley (ed.), *The Manning of the Royal Navy* (Navy Records
Society, 1974).

recognised officially that a man o' war commanded and officered with justice, also with absolute firmness, was a more successful fighting ship than one ruled by fear. Cook had no bad opinion of himself and his confidence remained as high as ever at the time he signed on in the Royal Navy. He believed that before long he would be commissioned, and in the event of war he would be entitled to a share of any prize money.*

On 17 June 1755 Cook signed on at Wapping into the big ship-of-the-line HMS *Eagle*, which was fitting out at Portsmouth. He made his way to the naval base by coach from London and his entry on a naval muster roll for the first time reads: '161. from London Rendezvous, James Cook, rating, AB [able seaman], date of entry June 17th, 1755, first appearance, June 25th, 1755.'

The *Eagle*'s commander, Captain Joseph Hamar, was at his wit's end: his ship was not ready for sea and yet was sorely needed for the imminent war with France; and not only was she under-manned, but also the men he was sent were the dregs of the Navy. 'I do not believe there is a worse man'd ship in the Navy,' he complained to the Admiralty. 'Yesterday I received from the *Bristol* twenty-five super-numerarys belonging to different ships, but not one seaman among them; but on the contrary, all very indifferent Landsmen.'

With so few 'thought worth having', Cook stood out like a diamond amidst junk jewellery; and it was no surprise to anyone but Cook himself that in less than a month he was rated master's mate, the rank he had held in the *Friendship*. But now, instead of twenty keels of coal, his ship carried sixty 24- and 42-pounder cannon and their ammunition.

The Seven Years' War was mainly fought in three widely separated areas, India, the Continent of Europe and North America. Britain and France had been more or less at peace since the Treaty of Aix-la-Chapelle in 1748. But when the alliance of France, Austria, Russia and the German princes fell upon Prussia and its monarch, Frederick II, Britain willy-nilly found herself on the side of Prussia though in no position to support her militarily. However, the fighting in India, peripherally in the Mediterranean, in British and French home waters, in the Caribbean and in North America was exclusively between France and Britain. The outcome was not only to create the genesis of the British Empire,

* Prize money, derived from a captured enemy ship and fixed by a Navy agent, was divided into eight parts, three to the captain, one to the commander-in-chief, one to the officers, one to the warrant officers and two to the men. Many a great estate was founded on a captain's prize money, while a lieutenant might receive a five-figure sum and an ordinary seaman £100 or more.

but also to form the foundation of a unified Germany a century hence.

There had been sporadic sparring between the British and French colonists in North America for years. The source of argument related to trade, territory, piracy and fishing rights, and by its very nature was bound to break out into full-scale warfare by sea and on land. War was formally declared in May 1756, but there had been fighting on land long before then, and at sea the Royal Navy was interfering with trade between metropolitan France and her colonies in New France, or what was to become Canada.

In July 1755, with the *Eagle* still under-manned and scarcely ready for sea, Captain Hamar was ordered to patrol between southern Ireland and the Scilly Islands and intercept and capture any French ships. It was a brief and abortive cruise, the main hazard – as so often – being the weather. This turned foul in the middle of August and on 1 September 'a Monstrous great Sea', according to Hamar, 'Carry'd away the Driver Boom in a deep roll'. At the same time he suspected that his mainmast was sprung (cracked, split) and he therefore headed for Plymouth for repairs.

The Admiralty was not pleased that the *Eagle*'s patrol line was broken; and was even less pleased when it heard that the mainmast was found to be undamaged but that Hamar had meanwhile decided to clean and tallow his ship's bottom, which was a long business. Captain Hamar was forthwith relieved of his command and replaced by Captain Palliser, an appointment that was to have far-reaching consequences for Cook. Hugh Palliser, born in 1723 and therefore five years older than his master's mate, came from good West Riding of Yorkshire stock, the son of an army captain. Palliser was an officer of great vigour and determination, impatient with authority and sharp with any sign of loss of courage in both his superiors and his own officers and men.

Palliser, like Hamar before him, recognised the special qualities in Cook and before long was giving him instruction in navigation, charting, drawing coastal profiles and other special maritime skills. For his part, Cook respected Palliser from the start and saw in him a possible future patron. He also quickly recognised the positive elements in his new commander by contrast with Captain Hamar. The *Eagle* had been ordered to patrol the western approaches to the Channel, examining every ship she met, a tiresome business as most belonged to neutrals and only a few French fishing vessels, returning from Newfoundland waters, were captured and sent in under prize crews to Plymouth.

The *Eagle* was operating as part of the squadron of Admiral John Byng* when they came across a single French ship-of-the-line, much battered by Atlantic storms, and soon battered into surrender by the superior British force. It was the first time that Cook had taken part in a fight at sea, and that evening of 15 November 1755 he registered in his log, 'Received on board from the *Espérance* 26 prisoners at 4 o'clock. *Espérance* on fire and there being no possibility of keeping her above water.'

So the first opportunity for prize money slipped into the depths of the Bay of Biscay, and for the greater part of the winter of 1755–6 the *Eagle* remained at Plymouth undergoing a much-needed refit. It was not until 30 May 1757 that the *Eagle* was in action again, and close and bitter action it was, too. She was two days out of Plymouth when, in company with HMS *Medway*, she sighted a big 50-gun French ship, the *Duc d'Aquitaine*. Palliser, with great skill, was first to come alongside and the first to put a broadside into the Frenchman.

She returned fire [ran the *Eagle*'s log]. We engaged about three-quarters of an hour at point-blank range. She then struck. The *Medway* then came up astern. We were employed getting prisoners onboard and securing our masts and rigging. We killed 50 men and wounded 30. Our casualties were 10 dead and 80 wounded.

The 'return of damage' to the *Eagle* paints a truer picture of the intensity of the action, with a shot through the middle of the foremast, several shots and bars of iron sticking in the main and mizzen masts, and 'Sails rent almost to rags'. Palliser was pleased with the conduct of the ship's company, and the Lords of the Admiralty indicated that they were 'highly pleased with his success and gallantry on this occasion'.

Aside from the prize money, Cook was promoted full master after a mere two years in the service. It reflected his confidence and that other priceless quality in a naval officer, the sense of being a veteran, which comes after successfully enduring not only every natural hazard at sea but also experiencing and surviving battle. To have your courage tested and found to be solid is an exhilaration which lasts for life, and combined with the knowledge that you are approved by your seniors form a recipe for advancement to the highest levels.

The warrant as master of his next ship was dated 18 October 1757,

---

* His next command was in the Mediterranean, where he was responsible for the loss of Port Mahon, Menorca, to the enemy. He was sent home in disgrace, court-martialled, found guilty and sentenced to death, *pour encourager les autres*, according to Voltaire.

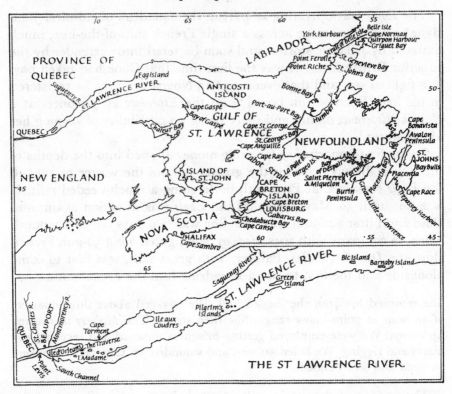

THE ST LAWRENCE RIVER

and his entry neatly coincided with his twenty-ninth birthday. The vessel was HMS *Pembroke*, a new 60-gun 4th rate* of 1,222 tons, which had been built at Plymouth dockyard that year. When Cook joined her, amidst the hurly-burly of the great naval port of Plymouth – such a contrast with the muted animation of Whitby – the *Pembroke* had just completed a shake-down cruise to Portugal and back and was re-provisioning for a much longer voyage across the Atlantic to places of which Cook had dreamed while carrying coals to London. All the talk was of the intensification of the war in North America, between the French in New France and the British in the colonies to the south.

Although the dimensions of the territories were vast, it was evident that there was no room for both French and British colonists. Even after the Treaty of 1748 the sniping between the two sides, with the intervention, mainly on the French side, of ferocious Indians, was

---

* The rating of men o' war had only recently been introduced by Admiral Anson as First Lord of the Admiralty. 1st rates carried more than 100 guns; 2nd rates 84–99; 3rd rates 70–83; 4th rates 50–69; 5th rates 32–49; and 6th rates up to 31 guns.

incessant and bitter. Authorised piracy against British shipping was commonplace.

The advent of William Pitt ('the Elder') as secretary of state and virtual prime minister, in 1756, led to a positive, skilful and more whole-hearted conduct of the war with France. Pitt determined to put an end to French interest in North America once and for all; and the warrant officer James Cook, master of HMS *Pembroke*, was to take his part in it, the small part of one individual in the epochal proceedings, but a highly influential part in the life of one of Britain's greatest sailors.

In this colonial war on the other side of the Atlantic for both protagonists, communications, and therefore sea power, must be the decisive factor. The French possessions were entirely dependent upon control of the St Lawrence River, a capillary penetrating deep into the continent and providing the outlet for the valuable French fur trade since the founding of Quebec in 1608. The conquest of French Canada depended first on control of this river; and second on the severance of seaborne supplies from France upon which the colonists depended for food, arms and other supplies.

In order to wrest control of the St Lawrence River from the French, Pitt knew, as did his generals and admirals, that two forts had to be stormed and attacked. The first was Louisburg, at the mouth of this great river, and then Quebec itself. For this formidable undertaking Pitt appointed General Jeffrey Amherst to command the land forces and the immensely experienced Admiral The Hon. Edward Boscawen as commander of the fleet.

Boscawen, 'Wry-neck'd Dick' as he was nicknamed after he suffered a serious neck injury in a famous victory against the French ten years earlier, was tough and ruthless and much admired by all who served under him; and by no means thought less of for being responsible for the court-martial and subsequent shooting of Byng.

The *Pembroke* was one of the eight ships-of-the-line Boscawen took to sea from Plymouth on 22 February 1758. This, at last for Cook, was no routine patrol. He was to cross the Atlantic for the first time, calling at the romantic-sounding islands of Tenerife and Bermuda. It was a long, slow passage with much bad weather and unfavourable winds. With his day-to-day management of the ship keeping him busy, he became increasingly concerned at the state of sickness of the lower deck. For the first time he was witnessing the effect of poor diet on the well-being of the crew on a long voyage. Scurvy, caused by Vitamin C deficiency, had for long been recognised as the almost inevitable price of lack of fresh vegetables and fruit. Anson, on his circumnavigation, at one time was scarcely able to man his ships, and even on long blockading duties off the French coast, many men were stricken with it: their teeth fell out, their skin became blotchy, and they descended into a state of lethargy which could lead to death.

Scurvy was such a commonplace affliction which could strike after about six weeks on salt rations that it was taken for granted even though it led to the total loss of hundreds of ships. On this, his first long voyage, Cook was an appalled witness of the decimation of the men, so great that it affected the working of the *Pembroke*. Twenty-six men died on the passage, most from scurvy, and many more were laid so low that on arrival at Halifax they had to be taken straight to hospital.

Cook had too much on his hands while the *Pembroke* came alongside the jetty in Halifax to spare any time to view the first North American town he had visited. But it was soon clear to his experienced eye why the British had established this fortress base ten years earlier. It was a deep, excellent natural harbour, well protected from the weather and, judging by the strength of the fortifications, from the French, too. It was also, he was told, ice-free the year round.

Halifax had never been so crowded with men o' war and transports as now; there were hundreds of them, bearing witness to Pitt's determination to clear the French out of Canada. From his captain, John Simcoe, Cook soon learned that Admiral Boscawen was so keen to get at the enemy at Louisburg that he would have to leave the *Pembroke* behind until sufficient of her company had recovered to man the ship safely. With a heavy heart Cook watched the fleet of 157 vessels slowly heading out of Halifax, a splendid sight which every citizen and serving man witnessed from the docks and the slopes rising above the town.

Louisburg is a little over 200 miles east of Halifax on the island of Cape Breton. The French fortress had been strategically sited to control the entrance to Cabot Strait and the Gulf of St Lawrence. It was known to be extremely heavily defended although neither Boscawen nor Amherst knew the number of guns they would have to face, nor the strength of the garrison. (It was discovered later that there were 419 guns and seventeen mortars.)

In fact, the French were in a very vulnerable condition. By cruel luck some ships returning to France the previous year had brought dreaded ship fever with them. Two thousand men died on the voyage; others took the disease ashore and no fewer than ten thousand died in Brest, crippling the fleet intended to supplement naval forces already at Louisburg. Back home the British had also hoodwinked the French into believing that invasion forces were poised to attack the French coast.

Before the arrival of Boscawen, five French ships-of-the-line managed to slip through Admiral Edward Hawke's blockade. But only one was armed, the others being stripped of their guns in order to bring sorely needed supplies to the French colonies.

While the *Pembroke* was still making her way up the Nova Scotia coast, the battle had begun. One of Amherst's brigadiers, James Wolfe, made a successful landing on the south side of Gabarus Bay close to Louisburg and set up batteries preparatory to a bombardment. A strong gale interrupted proceedings for two days, but after that the attack went ahead implacably, the Navy and the Army co-operating excellently. More and more naval guns and troops were ferried ashore at Gabarus Bay, at some cost, but most arrived safely and were soon in action. A French frigate managed to slip through the net and headed out to sea. No one cared. It was clearly on its way to France with the ominous news of the imminent loss of the fort.

Luck continued on the British side. A hit on one of the remaining French big ships found her magazine. There was a mighty explosion which utterly destroyed the vessel and led to fatal fires in the *Célèbre* and the *Capricieux*, both of 64 guns. Three days later, under cover of thick fog, the *Pembroke* and other big ships sent in boats to deal with two more French men o' war. One was captured, the other towed away and burnt. In his log Cook reported the vessels as 'Ben Fison of 64 guns' and 'the Prudon 74 guns'. It hardly mattered that they were the *Bienfaisant* and *Prudent*. The following day, 26 July 1758, the French Governor capitulated.

The St Lawrence River – St-Laurent – was now wide open, with no impediment all the way to Quebec.

THE INVESTMENT AND CAPTURE of Louisburg had been a triumph in all but one particular: they had taken longer than intended and the summer was now well advanced. In a latitude where military operations – and much else – depend on the weather, the second stage of the St Lawrence campaign, the capture of Quebec, had become urgent. Of all the commanders concerned, James Wolfe for the Army and Cook's captain, John Simcoe, were keenest to press on while they had the momentum and before General Louis de Montcalm, the French commander-in-chief, could further build up his defences.

Amherst for the Army and Boscawen and the other admirals considered the risk too great, and to Prime Minister Pitt's chagrin, it was decided to postpone the assault until the spring. But it was not to be an uneventful winter for Cook, John Simcoe and HMS *Pembroke*'s company. The shores of the Gulf of St Lawrence were studded with small French settlements, mostly fishing and hunting communities which contributed to the provisioning of the French colonists and their ships. The British high command decided that the *Pembroke* and other men o' war, with Wolfe and three battalions of infantry, should raid a number of these villages during the weeks of early autumn before the cold weather set in. Destroying these communities, sinking the small craft and capturing more worthwhile larger vessels was not very appetising work. Prisoners were taken and a few guns destroyed before the squadron returned to Louisburg on 2 October 1758.

More notable for Cook at this time, and more prescient of his future, was his first serious attempt at surveying. Shortly after the surrender of Louisburg, Cook found himself on the recently captured shoreline in conversation with an army lieutenant, Samuel Holland. This officer* was working with a plane table making a plan of the area by taking observations and making notes and drawings in a pocket-book. As Cook watched him and asked Holland questions, he became more and more excited at the seeming magic of the reproduction in miniature on paper of the environment.

Cook was keen on mathematics, had received a grounding in plain and spherical trigonometry from Palliser, and had been using charts since he first went to sea. But actually to create a chart, to record by triangulation every indentation, every point and cove, hazardous reefs and rocks – what a worthwhile and fascinating exercise! The two young men (they were born in the same year) took to one another and Holland promised to give Cook a short course with his instrument the next day. Captain Simcoe, told of this lieutenant and his work, wanted to join the course but was too indisposed to leave his cabin. However, Holland brought his plane table on board the *Pembroke* that evening, demonstrated it to the captain as far as he was able and spent the night in the ship.

The following day Cook joined Holland as he continued his survey of Gabarus Bay. As soon as he returned from the raiding operations, Cook applied to Simcoe for permission to work on a survey himself. Where he obtained his instrument he did not record, but most likely he borrowed Holland's and then worked with his delicate hand until he had completed his 'survey of Gaspé Bay and harbour' by 'James

---

* In 1791 he became the first 'surveyor of lands' in the first administration of Upper Canada under the lieutenant-governorship of John Simcoe's son, of the same name.

Cook Master of His Majesty's Ship the Pembroke'. This was sent to the Admiralty in London and, to Cook's delight, was officially published the following year.

Some fanciful claims have been made for Cook's further surveys during the winter of 1758–9 and early spring; even that he, alone, conducted a full survey, with soundings, of the 400-mile length of river to Quebec. This, it has been written, made it possible for the big British men o' war to make a safe passage to the Canadian capital and thus bring French resistance to an end.

In truth, before the 1759 attack, the British were in possession of some charts of the river of an unreliable nature, captured at Louisburg. There was also an English chart, published recently and inaccurately entitled an *Exact Chart of the River St Laurence*. What Cook and Holland did, encouraged and assisted by Simcoe, was to sail the *Pembroke* up the river from Cape Breton, as the weather permitted, and to correct and elaborate on the existing charts, taking precise soundings and 'sailing directions'. These last were defined as 'Descriptions for sailing in and out of Ports, with soundings, Marks for particular Rocks, Shoals, &c. with Latitude, Longitude, Tides and Variations of the Compass'. This survey work was especially valuable at the approaches to the Traverse down-river from Quebec because Montcalm had ordered the removal of all direction buoys.

This was a wearying but fascinating time for Cook, with the added burden of the weather, which was the coldest ever known in Canada. For a time ships could not get in or out of Louisburg, although the port itself remained ice-free, because of the ice floes in the surrounding sea.

THE ST LAWRENCE EXPEDITION OF 1759, one of the most momentous in British combined operations history, was under the joint command of Admiral Sir Edward Saunders and General James Wolfe, whose record at Louisburg had been warmly approved by Pitt. The fleet consisted of thirty-five ships-of-the-line, supported by another dozen smaller men o' war and numerous transports, an enormous armada which inched its way into the Gulf of St Lawrence through thick fog, guns and muskets sounding to reduce the risk of collisions.

Upon these vessels, the men who manned them, and the ten thousand or so soldiers on board the transports, lay the responsibility for the possession of North America. The risks were bayonet sharp, but the soldiers were of the highest quality, their morale was high, and the Royal Navy was, as usual, spoiling for a fight.

For Cook and the rest of the *Pembroke*'s company, the short voyage was sadly marked by the death of their captain. John Simcoe had been in poor health for some weeks and was confined to his cabin when they were at Louisburg. He never emerged from his bunk, and on the evening of 16 May he died. 'At 6 buried the corpse of Captain John Simcoe & fired 20 guns, half a minute between each gun,' his master wrote in his log.

Pausing cautiously at several of the river's islands, but assisted by a steady north-east wind, Admiral Saunders's armada at last, on 8 June 1759, came in sight of the Traverse. This narrowing of the St Lawrence corresponds to the cliffs which rise ever higher above the water, and the channel is divided in two by a scattering of islands. Here the hazards from shoals, rocks and shallows were complemented by the threat of cannon fire from high above.

Here Cook and the masters from other ships took on the hard task of sounding ahead from boats and marking the waters Cook and Holland had not charted earlier. It called for steady nerves and hands, but they were all experienced men and by 10 June Cook was able to report: 'Retired satisfied with being acquainted with the channel.'

To ensure further the safety of the armada, Admiral Saunders ordered the seizure of several French pilots who knew comprehensively the difficult Traverse waters. It was made clear to these unfortunate men that their lives were at stake, and never before had they exercised their skill and knowledge so determinedly.

On 27 June the last vessel got through safely to the basin below Quebec, the *Pembroke* among them, and anchored. Not a ship had been lost or even damaged. It had been a triumph of navigation and seamanship, appreciated even by the army officers and men, who were now taken ashore from their transports on to the large Ile d'Orléans. This was then fortified and became the site for a field hospital.

Cook and many other officers now experienced for the first time in their lives a weapon of naval war first perfected and used with decisive consequences against the Spanish Armada off Calais in 1588, the fireship. It had also been used at a number of actions during the Dutch wars of the seventeenth century. In its most refined form a daredevil crew sailed these small and mostly unneeded vessels, filled with combustibles, towards an anchored enemy. The men would attempt to grapple a ship, preferably the flagship which brought double the reward, ignite a slow match and train of powder, and leave as rapidly as possible by a boat towed astern.

The fireships now employed by the French were not in the least refined, and not even manned, but terrifying none the less. Suddenly at midnight, 27–28 June, seven of them and three fire rafts, with the wind behind them and already well ablaze, appeared from up-river like floating firedragons in the night. The two most vulnerable British ships-of-the-line cut their cables and just succeeded in avoiding the first fireships. Cook ordered boats equipped with grappling irons to be launched from the *Pembroke*, and with other boats, their crews exercising great skill and courage, succeeded in towing these blazing vessels clear.

Over the next weeks there was sporadic fighting on shore below the city, and bombardments between ships and from ship to shore. During this time, while Wolfe was attempting to devise a plan for an assault on Quebec and its well-placed forts, it is possible to obtain occasional glimpses of Cook, which confirm that he was extremely active and often in danger.

There was the day when he was out in one of the *Pembroke*'s boats sounding and laying buoys for a possible landing when he was surprised by a number of canoes manned by French infantry and ferocious Indians. Hopelessly outnumbered, Cook retreated to the shore of the Ile d'Orléans. Eyewitnesses described how the boat was rowed on to the beach, Cook and the crew leaping out at the bows while the Indians were already leaping into the stern. But the enemy got no farther because some of the guard of the hospital fortuitously turned up and drove the canoeists back into the river.

Then there was another day when the *Pembroke* was ordered to cover a major landing, including two cats, of troops and artillery at Beauport, just below Quebec. The landing was repulsed with heavy losses. The *Pembroke* kept up a steady fire with her 24-pounders in support of the cats, but they grounded too far from the shore for their men to land and, after suffering a severe defeat, the soldiers had to be taken off while Cook supervised the destruction by fire of the stranded cats.

This was only one of a number of setbacks and for a time it seemed as if Montcalm might still be in Quebec for another winter, in spite of his shortage of supplies. Then in early September, during a reconnaissance up-river from Quebec, Wolfe spotted a cove where a landing might succeed in darkness, and a possible way up the steep cliffs to the Heights of Abraham above.

While a feint attack, in which the *Pembroke* was involved, was made down-river, Wolfe conducted a successful landing under cover of darkness with some five thousand men, and sailors to haul up the guns and man them. By a superhuman effort, on the morning of 13 September Wolfe had his officers and men in position to attack the enemy. Montcalm appeared with a force twice the size of the

British, but the morale of his men was low. They were hungry as well as demoralised, and in a mainly hand-to-hand battle in which both Wolfe and Montcalm were killed, the French capitulated.

Although present and fully engaged during this critical battle, Cook was absent from the Heights of Abraham – where it could be said the British Empire was born – only noting in his log:

Moderate and cloudy weather at 6 p.m. Unmoored and hoved in to half a cable on the best bower anchor. At midnight all the rowboats in the fleet made a feint to land at Beauport in order to draw the enemy's attention that way to favour the landing of the troops above the town . . . At 10 o'clock [the next morning] the English army commanded by General Wolfe attacked the French under the command of General Montcalm in the field of Abraham behind Quebec and totally defeated them.

3

'Mr Cook's Genius and Capacity'

WITH THE FALL AND OCCUPATION OF QUEBEC and the end of
hostilities on the St Lawrence River,* there was much movement
of the ships of Admiral Saunders's fleet, and of personnel manning it.
Cook was transferred from the *Pembroke* to the 3rd-rate *Northumberland*,
a slightly larger ship, also built at Plymouth. She was under the
command of Captain Lord Colville, another officer who came to
admire Cook and became a great influence on his career.

Saunders returned to Britain, leaving two guardships at Quebec for
the winter and a substantial squadron, including the *Northumberland*, at
Halifax under the overall command of Colville. Apart from the routine
of maintenance and repairs, there was little to occupy the 3,500 or so
sailors at this chilly winter port. This, as always, led to drinking,
wenching and fighting, and the consequences were derating, flogging,
one or two hangings and 'the venereals'.

Cook had long since become hardened to the necessary disciplinary
processes of the Royal Navy, but like most officers of his time did not in
the least care for the inflicting of punishment and was sparing in his use
of the lash when he reached command rank. For him the long winter
months of inactivity provided the opportunity to continue his studies.

He employed his leisure hours in reading Euclid [according to his early
biographer, George Young] and studying astronomy, with other branches
of science connected with his profession. His books were few, and his
opportunities for improvement limited; yet by dint of application, and
vigour of intellect, he made uncommon progress.

* Fighting continued elsewhere, however, and it was not until General Amherst, after
advancing from New York, crossed Lake Ontario and occupied Montreal, that French
Canada surrendered on 7 September 1760.

Cook's practical surveying that winter was limited to Halifax harbour itself, in three exquisite manuscripts which in their accuracy and form are precursors of all those that were to follow, from New Zealand and Tasmania to the Hawaiian islands and Alaska.

Having decided that the worst of the winter was over, Colville sailed from Halifax to Quebec with his squadron on 22 April 1760. By coincidence, in London on that same day Admiral Saunders submitted to the Lords Commissioners of the Admiralty Cook's 'Draught of the River St Lawrence, with the Harbours, bays and Islands in that river . . . with all the Rocks, Shoals and Soundings . . .' No credit was given to Cook, nor should it have carried his name alone anyway because the contributions of Samuel Holland and John Simcoe were considerable. Permission was granted and it was published later in the year in what Dr J. C. Beaglehole, one of Cook's later biographers, conservatively describes as 'a large production': seven feet by three feet in twelve sheets, along with a quarto edition of 'sailing directions'.

For two-and-a-half years longer the *Northumberland* remained on the North American station,* though frequently on the move. Ill-health and ill-discipline were the two worst enemies, as always without the crisis of war. Once again Cook witnessed the ravages of a poor diet. 'The scurvy never fails to pull us down in great Numbers, upon our going to Sea in the Spring,' Colville reported to the Admiralty, but he praised the quality of the 'frozen Beef from Boston'.

Before the signing of the Peace of Paris on 10 February 1763 (at which Britain secured not only Canada but also Nova Scotia, Cape Breton, Florida, Senegal, St Vincent, Tobago, Dominica and Grenada), there was a short occupation by the French of St John's, Newfoundland. In the brief fighting which followed, the *Northumberland* experienced her last combat in the arduous, confused and occasionally very bloody Seven Years' War.

Every officer and man of the *Northumberland* was elated when it became known that they were soon to sail for home, and the end of a commission which had lasted for too long. She sailed from St John's on 7 October 1762 and made a good passage to Spithead in nineteen days. On 11 November Cook was discharged from the ship he had come to know so well, drawing accumulated pay of no less than £291 19s 3d.

It would be satisfactory at this point to record that James Cook, master, aged thirty-three, made his way to the North Riding of

---

* This naval station, as the North American and West Indies station, survived until 1914, with the main base still at Halifax.

Yorkshire to greet his family (his brother John had long since died). It would be in character for him to make this considerable effort, but there is no evidence. What is known, with ample evidence, is that Cook had now determined to find a wife.

On his arrival in London from Portsmouth, Cook sought lodgings close to the river, as did most sailors. Stepney, on the north bank, was a typical sailors' area, and Cook chose to live in the parish of Shadwell. It was a town with some eight thousand houses, mostly of wood frame and brick construction, those nearest the river of a basic nature, those more distant more refined. Your neighbours were likely to be men of the river and of the sea – lightermen, wharfingers, ferrymen and sailors awaiting the offer of a berth. The parish smelt of tanneries, breweries and rope, all associated with the industries of Shadwell.

Among the citizens of Shadwell was a Mrs Mary Blackburn, who had been married to John Batts before his death. She had a daughter, Elizabeth, by him, and this daughter lived not far away at Barking. Details are missing but Elizabeth Batts met James Cook probably while visiting her mother. The two suited one another well. Elizabeth was a comely girl of twenty-two, sensible and intelligent, Cook was a warrant officer in the Royal Navy clearly anxious for marriage, and as soon as possible, before he was sent to sea again.

Dispensing with banns, the marriage was fixed for 21 December 1762. Elizabeth later recounted how she and Cook walked together over the meadows outside Barking to the parish church of St Margaret's, where they were married. Relatives and those who knew the couple well invariably described the union as happy in every respect. Elizabeth knew that her husband would be away at sea for much – probably most – of the time.

LITTLE MORE THAN A WEEK after Cook's marriage, Admiral Lord Colville addressed this letter to the Secretary of the Admiralty:

London, 30 December 1762
Sir,

Mr Cook, late Master of the *Northumberland*, acquaints me that he has laid before their Lordships all his draughts and observations relating to the River St Lawrence, part of the coasts of Nova Scotia and Newfoundland.

On this occasion I beg to inform their Lordships that from my experience of Mr Cook's genius and capacity, I think him well qualified for the work he has performed and for greater undertakings of the same kind. These draughts being made under my own eye, I can venture to say they may be the means of directing many in the right way, but cannot mislead any—

I am, Sir, your most obedient and humble servant,

COLVILLE

This was not the sort of recommendation that authority could merely file away. A man of 'genius and capacity' who dealt ably with surveys and charts was a man unlikely to be idle for long. The vast new territories and coastlines the Treaty of Paris had granted Britain were now, more than ever before, in need of surveying, not only for their defence, but also for the safety of shipping of all kinds.

The St Lawrence, never a safe river, had been made as safe as could be expected by that immense chart. This arrow pointing to the heart of Canada, and its present and potential future riches, could be navigated now by the largest of ships, winter weather permitting. The two entrances to the St Lawrence, the Strait of Belle Isle north of Newfoundland and the Cabot Strait to the south, were much less precisely known. In fact, the whole triangular slab of Newfoundland was little understood, except by the canny French and British fishermen who were in the profitable cod trade, and worked from memory and experience rather than from charts. There were charts, British and French, but they were mainly old and unreliable, and by no means comprehensive. It was quite by chance, like so many coincidences in his life, that Cook's decision to marry was made at the same time as the Government's decision to survey the coast of Newfoundland and the southern coast of Labrador, ensuring Cook of a steady income. The juxtaposition could not have been neater.

This immense undertaking – Newfoundland is bigger than Ireland with a coastline of 6,000 miles – was a gesture of confirmation of the final control, following the Peace of Paris, of this valuable island. It was always referred to as England's oldest colony. It had first been claimed for England and King Henry VII in 1497 by John Cabot, whose name marks the southern entrance to the St Lawrence. Three years later the Portuguese made a similar claim. Then again, Sir Humphry Gilbert planted the English flag for Queen Elizabeth I on the shore in 1583.

By this time, swarms of English, French and Portuguese fishermen were crossing the Atlantic in the spring exploiting the cod-rich waters off the island; and it is recorded that some 150 fishing boats sailed from Devon annually by 1626, catching then salting and drying their cod on the shores before returning home in September. The interior of the island was scarcely given a thought, and no European nation encouraged settlement. But Britain was in nominal control, and the first Governor of the island was appointed in 1728. The Treaty of Paris confirmed British sovereignty, and, even before the signing of this treaty, Captain Thomas Graves had been reappointed Governor.

In his early days, while the French were still being troublesome about St John's, Graves had met and been much impressed by Cook and his work. Now, with peace confirmed, Graves, on leave in London, took steps to fulfil his many and complex instructions, among them to draw up 'Draughts of Coasts and Harbours'. The choice of surveyor was never seriously in doubt, in the minds of the Admiralty and of Captain Graves himself. Cook had proved himself an exceptional surveyor, and a steady and responsible warrant officer, who knew the waters and the coastline of Newfoundland, and Labrador, an undeveloped province now included in the Governor's territory.

On 5 April 1763, little more than three months after Cook's marriage, the matter of the appointment appears to have been settled. In a letter to Philip Stephens, the newly appointed Secretary of the Admiralty, Graves wrote:

Sir–

I have this moment seen Mr Cook and acquainted him he was to get himself ready to depart, the moment the Board was pleased to order him, and that he was to have 10 shillings a day while employed on this service . . .

There should be a Theodolite and drawing instruments, which will cost about £12 or £15 . . . The officers of the yard should be ordered to supply me with two or three azimuth compasses and a number of pendants of any colour to put as signals on different points for taking the angles as the survey goes on. I shall set out this afternoon for the ship [at Portsmouth] and hope to be there by tomorrow.

> I am, Sir, etc., etc.,
> [signed] Thomas Graves

Cook was as eager as his captain to be away, but there were still many more necessities to be issued from Admiralty stores or purchased privately, such as leads, compasses, lines and drawing tables. There was also the question of an assistant, the work being far too taxing to be conducted by one man. Graves found Mr Edward Smart, a Londoner from Lambeth and an ordnance draughtsman. Finally, as Graves pointed out to the Admiralty, 'The sending out of a draughtsman to survey the harbours seems to point out the necessity of their having a small vessel fit to use on that business.'

Graves's ship, which would also conduct Cook to Newfoundland for his first session of surveying work, was the 4th-rate *Antelope*, built as long before as 1703 but completely rebuilt more recently and well fitted out as a colonial governor's floating office as well as a fine man o' war. The *Antelope* made landfall at Cape Race on the south-east extremity of Newfoundland early in June 1763; and the surveying began without delay.

As a surveyor, Cook employed two methods. First was the running survey employed at sea, which he used later in the Pacific when time, circumstances or the hostility of the shore (human or geographical) prohibited working from the land. Second, and the more accurate and effectual, was the survey worked mainly on land but also from the sea when called for.

In this connection, Mr R. A. Skelton of the British Museum delivered the annual lecture of the Society for Nautical Research for 1953 entitled 'Captain James Cook as a Hydrographer'. Skelton made reference to the works of two pioneers published several years after Cook's Newfoundland survey but whose principles Cook certainly followed. These were Alexander Dalrymple's *Essay on the most Commodious Methods of Marine Surveying* (1771) and Murdoch Mackenzie's *A Treatise of Maritime Surveying* (1774). In such a survey,

A level base was measured by pole or chain. The primary triangles on land were observed by theodolite; and subsidiary stations, shoals, soundings and anchorages plotted by cross-rays with the compass or by angles taken with sextant or theodolite . . . Mackenzie recommended the sextant as being 'more portable . . . and generally more accurately . . . divided' than the theodolite. And Dalrymple remarked that Hadley's quadrant 'is used with equal facility at mast-head as upon Deck, and therefore the sphere of Observation is . . . much extended . . . taking angles from heights, as hills, or a ship's mast-head, is almost the only way of exactly describing the extent and figure of shoals.'

Cook's first and most urgent work was to survey two islands, St Pierre and Miquelon, off the southern coast of Newfoundland. By a clause in the Treaty of Paris, and the payment by France of £300,000, the British granted ownership of these islands to the ex-enemy, on condition that they were not fortified, in order that the French could continue to conduct their fishing, albeit under a set of complicated conditions, which were later to lead to much dissension.

Pitt wanted these islands thoroughly surveyed before handing them over, and by mid-June Cook was hard at work, operating from the smaller and more suitable HMS *Tweed*, going ashore by longboat, cutter or tender with his party, sometimes remaining ashore for several days in order to save time: 'Sent the longboat with 4 days provisions for the men with Mr Cook', runs the *Tweed*'s log.

The first island was ready to be handed over to the French by 31 July, the second by the end of August, thanks to the 'unwearied assiduity of Mr Cook', according to Captain Charles Douglas of the *Tweed*.

Back at St John's, Graves had meanwhile purchased a more convenient vessel from which Cook could continue his work, now with draughtsman Smart, newly arrived from England. She was the schooner *Sally*. She displaced 69 tons and had been built in a Massachusetts yard ten years earlier. Graves changed her name to *Grenville* in honour of the new Prime Minister and recent First Lord of the Admiralty. She was the ideal vessel for this work and Cook was delighted with her. This time he was sent to the north end of Newfoundland:

The moment the schooner was ready Mr Cook proceeded in her to survey Quirpoon and Noddy Harbours [Graves reported to the Admiralty] and from thence to York Harbour to take a compleat survey of that or any other good harbour he should fall in with on the Labrador coast.

'With indefatigable industry', as Graves described Cook's surveying, the programme was adhered to precisely, and by the end of September 1763 the *Grenville* was back at St John's, rich with the fruit of dawn-to-dusk surveying of unknown coastlines. Five weeks later Graves reported to Stephens at the Admiralty:

The *Tweed* sails with these dispatches and I hope to leave the country about the same time. As Mr Cook, whose pains and attention are beyond my description, can go no farther in surveying this year, I send him home in the *Tweed* in preference to keeping him on board, that he may have the more time to finish the difficult surveys already taken . . .

The *Tweed* suffered adverse winds and weather, and it was not until 29 November 1763 that she anchored at Spithead. A message to St John's before he left told Cook that he was now the father of a boy, which added to the haste with which he took the stage from Portsmouth to London, and then farther east to Shadwell. At the rooms in which Cook had left her, he greeted Elizabeth, who proudly showed him the seven-week-old baby.

After attending the baptism of his son – also named James – Cook set about finding a house. He could well afford one on his pay and with the amount of capital he had accumulated. He chose an end-of-terrace house, 7 Assembly Row, in the Mile End Road.* It was a modest little

---

* In spite of the blue commemorative plaque honouring Cook's name secured to the front of the house in 1907 (Beaglehole tells us), it was demolished some time after, though the rest of the terrace was saved.

two-up-two-down dwelling with a garden at the back and front and fields not far away. The only drawbacks were the weight of traffic along the Mile End Road and a gin distillery next door from which there emanated some foul odours, especially evident when the wind was in the east.

As soon as his family had settled in, Cook spent the winter like a commuting clerk, taking the horse bus in the morning to the Admiralty and home again in the evening, and working all day on the most recent charts he and Smart had brought back from Newfoundland and Labrador, assisted by Smart's brother. There were many details to fill in, and copies to be made, including 'a fair copy of St Peter's and Miquelong [the islands handed over to the French] to be laid before the King'. This information was included in a letter to Graves, who had just returned from Newfoundland for the last time for he was to be superseded by Cook's old patron, Palliser, 'a gentleman I have been long acquainted with'.

Though pleased to be working under Palliser again, Cook at this time suffered a grave loss, the death of Smart on 8 March, which deprived him of a man he worked well with and who understood his surveying practices.

THE ATLANTIC CROSSING was becoming a commonplace to Cook, although he was always glad to be away at sea and felt comfortable with a deck under his feet and the smell of salt spray in the air. After his relatively late start in his profession, he now felt himself to be the complete sailor, his heart, mind and soul conditioned to the maritime life; and especially the 'unpathed waters, undreamed shores'.

The passage to St John's took five weeks, the surveying party's ship anchoring on 14 June. They transferred on the same day to the *Grenville*, which had been refitted and overhauled in their absence, and were soon at work, according to Palliser's instructions, on the northern shore of Newfoundland.

Cook and his party quickly regained the routine and pace of the previous season, in spite of the absence of Smart. Cook had acquired as mate of his cutter a warrant officer called William Parker,* who was to remain as his number two until the completion of the survey. Parker tended to occupy himself offshore while Cook worked ashore with his theodolite, taking fixes and placing his flags, while the small

---

* Later Admiral Sir William Parker, friend and near contemporary of Nelson, who took a notable part in such famous battles as The Glorious First of June and Cape St Vincent.

boats kept up the monotonous cries of sounding as the men cast the lead and line.

This routine was broken on 6 August 1774 by a curious and unexplained accident:

2 p.m. Came on board the cutter with the Master [ran the *Grenville*'s log], who unfortunately had a large powder horn blown up and burst in his hand, which shattered it in a terrible manner. One of the people who stood hard by suffered greatly by the same accident. Having no surgeon on board bore away for Noddy Harbour where a French fishing ship lay. At 8 sent the boat in for the French surgeon. At 10 the boat returned with the surgeon.

It was Cook's right hand that was so damaged, resulting in a permanent scar from thumb and forefinger to high up his wrist, and it was a month before he could resume his work. During this enforced lull, he sent Parker away in a boat to survey Griguet Bay. That kept some of the men busy, but idleness among those in the *Grenville* led to the brewing of spruce essence – a potent form of wood-derived alcohol – and loss of discipline. From his temporary sickbed, Cook had some of the men punished. By 26 August he had returned to his duties, the *Grenville* was at sea, and there was no more leisure for drinking and fighting.

On 14 October they were all back at St John's with a surprisingly full set of rough charts considering the brevity and broken nature of the trip. Cook was home early in December 1774, just in time for the birth of his second son, Nathaniel. He rapidly (it had to be rapid considering the time available) adapted himself to the duties and pleasures of family life, but was soon at work every day, except the Sabbath, making fair copies of his charts and supervising the overhaul of his ship. The cutter was 'very much eat with worms', he informed the Admiralty, at the same time requesting permission to adapt the masts, sails and rigging to convert her into a brig. 'Schooners are the worst sort of vessel to go upon any discovery, for in meeting with any unexpected danger their staying cannot be depended upon, and for want of a sail to lay aback they run themselves ashore before they wear.' Cook had been on this surveying work for so long by this time that it is surprising that no earlier complaint was recorded.

Two more seasons lay ahead for Cook as, mile by mile, the indentations, the harbours and headlands, the shoals and hazardous rocks, and the sea depths of the coasts of Newfoundland and southern Labrador were recorded on board the *Grenville*. For the crew this was monotonous work, but for Cook and his assistant every mark on the fine hand-made paper was like a satisfactory note to the composer of a great symphony.

The log of the brig records a few of the events worthy of mention, like the picking up of two men lost in the forest and close to starvation. Then, on 23 July 1765, the *Grenville* ran on to a not-yet-recorded rock and had to unload her swivel guns and ammunition and most of her stores before she could be floated off at high tide. This was the only occasion when the little ship was close to being lost, which, considering the nature of the task in previously uncharted and dangerous waters with highly variable weather, was a remarkable record.

But there was another event the next season, not even recorded in the *Grenville*'s log, which indirectly was to lead to another sharp turn in Cook's career and to the road to fame. On 5 August 1766 he was engaged on surveying the Burgeo Islands on the south coast of Newfoundland. Because he had for long kept in touch with astronomical matters when at home, he knew that on this day there was to be an eclipse of the sun. He had brought on this survey 'a very good apparatus of instruments, among them a brass telescopic quadrant'.

The observations which followed were later transmitted to the Royal Society,* whose members were impressed to learn at a meeting on 30 April 1767:

Mr Cook, a good mathematician, and very expert in his business, having been appointed by the Lords Commissioners of the Admiralty to survey the sea coast of Newfoundland, Labrador, etc. . . . being, 5th August 1766, at one of the Burgeo Islands . . . and having rectified his quadrant, he waited for the eclipse of the sun: just a minute after the beginning of which he observed the zenith distance of the sun's upper limb, 31° 57′ 00″; and allowing for refraction and his semi-diameter . . .

Cook completed what was to be his last crossing of the North Atlantic when he picked up Cape Race on 9 May 1767. His final season as hydrographer of Newfoundland covered a greater length of coastline than any other, from Cape Anguille, almost at the uttermost south-west corner, to as far north as St Margaret's Bay at the inner mouth of the Strait of Belle Isle. Although not so indented as the east coast of the island, it was a prodigious achievement carried out in one brief summer season.

* The Royal Society for Improving Natural Knowledge, founded in 1645, its members at first wealthy and talented amateurs in search of practical knowledge in all spheres, and for 350 years a notable and prestigious body.

Captain Sir Hugh Palliser, who had supervised and encouraged Cook in his work for so long, and with increasing admiration, had already obtained authority for the publication of the early charts. After the completion of the 1767 season, he now wrote to the Secretary of the Admiralty:

Sir—

Mr Cook, appointed by the Right Honourable my Lords Commissioners of the Admiralty, to survey the sea coast of Newfoundland and Labrador, under my direction, having finished his chart of the south-east coast of Newfoundland . . . and upon a large scale of one inch to a mile, you will herewith receive the said chart, which be pleased to lay before the Right Honourable the Lords Commissioners of the Admiralty.

He having also, last year, delivered in to the Board his survey of the northern part of Newfoundland . . . likewise, another of the above mentioned survey of a part of the south coast of Newfoundland both upon a proper scale to the Trade and Navigation of His Majesty's subjects; therefore, as a publication of the same, I am of opinion, will be a great encouragement to new adventurers in the fisheries upon these coasts, be pleased to move their Lordships to permit Mr Cook to publish the same.

I remain, etc., etc.,

HUGH PALLISER

Another thirty years was to pass before the Admiralty set up a Department of Hydrography. One of the most eminent of the Admiralty's hydrographers (1884 – 1904), Rear-Admiral Sir William Wharton, was to note more than a century later, in the course of working in the same area as Cook: 'The charts he made during these years in the schooner *Grenville* were admirable. The best proof of their excellence is that they are not yet wholly superseded by the more detailed surveys of modern times . . . Their accuracy is truly astonishing.'

Now, with the personal recommendations of Cook's qualities – and especially that of Palliser – together with the material evidence of his charts, and above all the observations of the eclipse of the sun, carried out entirely on his own initiative, Cook was soon destined to embark on one of the great voyages of discovery, on the other side of the world. It was to be the fulfilment of the great dream he had enjoyed time and again during the years when he had carried coals from Whitby to London.

4

Appointment to the Endeavour Bark

GRACE COOK, JAMES'S MOTHER, had died, aged sixty-three, while he was away on his second season of surveying in Newfoundland. She had suffered the loss of two sons and three daughters, all at a heartbreakingly young age, but the survival of less than half the offspring of a marriage was not unusual at that time. James Cook Senior carved his wife's name, and those of their dead children, on the family tombstone in Ayton churchyard. In his loneliness, he later went to live with his surviving daughter Margaret, who was married to 'a respectable fisherman and shopkeeper', James Fleck of Redcar.

The strong, fit, tall, surviving son of this marriage returned to his wife and two growing sons at the Mile End Road. His life had many times been in danger during the four seasons in Newfoundland, but ironically he was never at greater risk than on his arrival in the Thames estuary on 10 November 1767. The *Grenville* anchored in very heavy weather off the Nore; it was found that the anchors would not hold, and at length one parted and she 'taild into shoal water', striking very hard. After a while she again struck very heavily and 'lay down on her larboard bilge'. Cook and his men took to the boats in the howling gale and succeeded at length in making Sheerness. It had been a close-run thing.

During the winter of 1767–8 Cook occupied himself as he had done previously on his return to London, making fair copies of his work, calling at the Admiralty many times, meeting Captain Palliser, the nearest figure to a patron in his life, making arrangements with the engravers and having his mathematical instruments repaired. But also, as before, he found time for his family and remained aware that his time at home was precious to his wife and two boys. Elizabeth was pregnant again.

Everything went forward as if he were to continue his surveying work, probably in late April. Certainly, Palliser gave no hint that he was to be sent elsewhere.

IN HIS NAVIGATION, in his surveying work, in his observation of the eclipse of the sun in 1766, and in his intense reading and desire for self-improvement, Cook had touched the edges of eighteenth-century science. What he had achieved virtually without formal education, without close association with the scientists of the time, was remarkable; remarkable enough to gain himself a small name among the grave, wise men of the Royal Society on the one hand, and the old sea dogs of the Admiralty on the other.

Especially in astronomy, great strides forward into the unknown had been made, mainly by the French and English, as the eighteenth century advanced, following the epochal discoveries in the sixteenth and seventeenth centuries of Copernicus, Kepler, Brahe and, in England, Newton and Halley among many others. The first requirement for accurately mapping the solar system was the calculation of distance – between the earth and the sun, between the earth and Venus, and so on.

It was Halley who most firmly believed that the rare and unevenly spaced transits of the planet Venus, the closest to the earth, across the face of the sun would offer the needed information on distance to the planets, and by a relatively simple calculation and observation. But the observations had to be widely taken across the earth in order to fulfil the needs of parallax observation, exactly as practised on a small scale by Cook in his marine surveying.

For the 1761 transit, the French took the lead, providing thirty-two widely spread observers; there were eighteen English, as well as Swedes, Italians, Russians, Spaniards and other nationalities with their instruments as widely spread as Siberia, China, St Helena in the South Atlantic and the Cape of Good Hope. However, the international exercise was not a success. Perhaps there were too many, perhaps the co-ordination was lacking, certainly cloudy skies ruined many of the observations.

This failure made it all the more important that the 1769 transit should succeed because the next one was not due to occur until 1874.* In 1765 Dr Thomas Hornsby, Professor of Astronomy at Oxford University (who observed the 1761 transit from sites in England),

---

* There would then be a transit in 1882, none in the twentieth century, but two more opportunities in the first decade of the twenty-first century.

pressed upon the Royal Society the need to prepare early for the 1769 transit and pursue the idea of making an observation from a site in the Pacific Ocean, which had not been attempted before, and where there was a good chance of clear skies.

The Royal Society, unaccustomed to haste, proceeded in its usual leisurely manner, and it was not until June 1766 that consideration was given to sites and observers – the most radical of which called for the professor of mathematics at the University of Pavia, a Jesuit priest named Boscovich, to go to California. There was also a resolution that a suggestion might be made to the Admiralty that if any men o' war happened to be in the Pacific they 'should be directed to make observations'.

A further five months elapsed before the Royal Society set up a committee 'to consider and report on the places where it would be advisable to take observations, the methods to be pursued, and the persons best fitted to carry out the work'. The committee consisted of the Astronomer Royal, Nevil Maskelyne, Dr John Bevis, another noted astronomer who had drawn the Society's attention to Cook's report on the eclipse of the sun in Newfoundland, Captain John Campbell RN and four more members.

The committee first met on 12 November 1767, at the time when Cook arrived back from Newfoundland, and a mere nineteen months before the transit was due to take place, 3 June 1769. It was first decided that two observers should be sent to three sites, North Cape, Hudson's Bay and – rather vaguely considering its area of seventy million square miles – the Pacific Ocean, though several known islands were suggested. By far the most radical and important of these sites was the last, and it was decided that the Government should be asked to supply a ship, which Captain Campbell, a highly experienced sailor, would command. As for the first observer on this voyage, Dr Maskelyne suggested the name of Alexander Dalrymple, 'a proper person to send to the South Seas, having a particular turn for discoveries, and being an able navigator and well skilled in observation'.

A memorial to the King was then drawn up, which included these paragraphs:

That the passage of the planet Venus over the disc of the Sun, which will happen on 3rd of June in the year 1769, is a phenomenon that must, if the same be accurately observed in proper places, contribute greatly to the improvement of Astronomy, on which Navigation so much depends.

That several of the Great Powers in Europe, particularly the French, Spaniards, Danes and Swedes are making the proper dispositions for the Observation thereof: and the Empress of Russia has given directions for having the same observed in many different places of her extensive Dominions . . .

That the British nation has been justly celebrated in the learned world, for their knowledge of astronomy, in which they are inferior to no nation upon earth, ancient or modern; and it would cast dishonour upon them should they neglect to have correct observations made of this important phenomenon . . .

That the expense of having the observations properly made . . . would amount to about £4,000, exclusive of the expense of the ship . . .

That the Royal Society are in no condition to defray this expense . . .

The appeal was answered favourably, and other arrangements went ahead successfully, the details dealt with. But Dalrymple proved to be a difficult fellow. He is one of those uneven figures in history who emerge with most frequency in maritime affairs. He was the youngest son of a notable Scottish family, and was still only thirty when he became involved in the plans for this voyage to the Pacific. At half this age he had gained employment in the East India Company, and his first voyage to Madras instilled in him the passion for travel, exploration and map-making which lasted all his life.*

Dalrymple became a young authority on Borneo and the East Indies, where he attempted to revive British trade lost to the Dutch in the previous century. His wider ambition was eventually to sail and explore the Pacific, and discover and chart the mythical *Terra Australis Incognita*, the Great Southern Continent. It was this experience, along with his enthusiasm, charm and energy, which had recommended him to Maskelyne.

Truth to tell, Dalrymple was not much interested in astronomy but saw the first purpose of this voyage as an opportunity to pursue his passion for discovery and charting distant shores, as he had done before. But this young hot-head also had an exaggerated opinion of himself, and when the Council of the Royal Society offered him the post of senior observer, he agreed but only on no other condition 'than that of having the management of the ship intended for the service'.

Whatever the Royal Society thought about this condition, there was an immediate and sharp response when it was put to the Admiralty. It was, came the answer, 'entirely repugnant to the regulations of the Navy'. They had made an exception to this principle in 1698, when Halley was granted command of a naval vessel, with dreadful and mutinous consequences; never again.

It is said that Sir E. Hawke [Admiral of the Fleet and First Lord of the

---

* He became the first official hydrographer to the Admiralty in 1795; and subsequently became involved in much contention.

Admiralty] . . . positively refused to sign any such commission, saying that he would rather cut off his right hand than permit anyone but a King's Officer to command one of the ships of His Majesty's Navy.

Dalrymple fought back, using his considerable influence in high places, and pointing out his experience in the East and his impeccable record when commanding ships of the East India Company. But other forces were at work within the Admiralty, and these were all-powerful. Philip Stephens, the Secretary, had already been much impressed by Cook's work in Canada and Newfoundland, knew him personally and, though for the present Cook was only a warrant officer, believed he would be ideal for the task. Backed by Palliser, the two making an undefeatable team, Hawke approved of the appointment, while Stephens made the Admiralty's decision known to the Royal Society. Dalrymple never forgave Cook and never missed an opportunity of traducing him and denying him credit for all his achievements.

On 5 May 1768 a meeting of the full Council of the Royal Society was convened, with Cook at the Society's headquarters awaiting a summons. The Minutes of the Society recorded that,

Captain John Campbell mentioned that Captain James Cook who now attended will be appointed by the Admiralty to the command of the vessel destined for the observation in the Southern Latitudes, and that he was a proper person to be one of the observers in the observation of the Transit of Venus, Mr Cook was called in, and accepted the employment in consideration of such gratuity as the Society shall think proper, and an allowance of £120 a year for victualling himself and the other observer in every particular.

Mr Green, attending, was also called in, and accepted the engagement of observer, and agreed to the allowance aforesaid, with a further gratuity to himself of 200 guineas for the voyage, and if the voyage should exceed two years, then at the rate of 100 guineas per ann.

Resolved that the instruments for the use of the observers in the Southern Latitudes be the following:

2 Reflecting telescopes of two feet focus, with a Dolland's micrometer to one of them and moveable wires for the other, now at Mr Shorts.

2 Wooden Stands for the telescopes with polar axes suited to the Equator; provided by Mr Short and now at his house.

An astronomical Clock and Alarm Clock, now at the Royal Observatory.

A Brass Hadley's sextant, bespoke by Mr Maskelyne of Mr Ramsden.

A Barometer, bespoke of Mr Ramsden.

A Journeyman Clock, bespoke of Mr Shelton.

2 Thermometers, of Mr Bird.

1 Stand for Bird's quadrant, now at the house of the Society.

A dipping needle, bespoke of Mr Ramsden.

The Minutes were incorrect in reporting Cook's rank, but he had just taken the King's commission and was now a lieutenant in the Royal Navy, with effect from 25 May, when he received these formal preliminary instructions:

Whereas we have appointed you First Lieutenant of His Majesty's Bark, the *Endeavour*, now at Deptford, and intend that you shall command her during her present intended voyage; and, whereas, we have ordered the said Bark to be fitted out and stored at that place for Foreign Service, manned with seventy men (agreeable to the scheme on the Back hereof) and victualled to Twelve months of all species of Provisions (for the said number of men at whole allowance) except Beer, of which she is to have only a proportion for one month and to be supplied with Brandy in lieu of the remainder; you are hereby required and directed to use the utmost despatch in getting her ready for the sea accordingly, and then falling down to Galleons Reach, take in her guns and gunners' stores at that place and proceed to the Nore for further orders.

Given etc., etc., 25th May 1768

ED HAWKE. C. TOWNSHEND. P. T. BRETT.

TO LIEUT. JAMES COOK.

ON 28 NOVEMBER 1520 the Portuguese-born Ferdinand Magellan sailed into the Pacific from the east for the first time. The sea was as calm as the proverbial millpond. The guns of his ship, the *Trinidad*, crashed out a celebratory cannonade, the silk banner of his command was held aloft, and Magellan himself sank to his knees in thankfulness, prayed that these waters might always be so calm and pronounced, 'I shall name this sea the *Mar Pacifico*.' As all the world knows, he crossed this ocean at terrible cost in the suffering and lives of his men. While one of his caravels continued to make the world's first circumnavigation, the great navigator was left dead on the shore of a small island in the Philippines after a fracas with hostile natives.

For the following two-and-a-half centuries the exploration and charting of the Pacific was a spasmodic business carried out by the Spaniards, Portuguese and Dutch and a handful of Englishmen and Frenchmen more concerned with plunder than discovery. After Magellan other Spaniards desultorily explored the Pacific. From their newly conquered land in South and Central America, they spread out in their colonial-built caravels and established a regular trading route between Acapulco in Mexico and Manila in the Spanish-held Philippines. Straying from their route, some of these vessels chanced upon New Guinea, the Caroline and Marshall islands among others. Enterprising Dutchmen, like Abel Tasman and Willem Cornelisz, and Portuguese mariners of whom Luis Vaez de Torres was the most notable, nibbled at the eastern and western fringes of the Pacific.

With the arrival of peace at the conclusion of the Seven Years' War, the minds of the defeated French as well as of the successful British turned towards distant horizons, leading from war in the North Atlantic, North America and the Mediterranean to peaceful and fruitful competition on the other side of the world in the Pacific. The thrust of scientific curiosity, colonial acquisitiveness and the need for trade were about equal in both countries. The first British expedition departed in 1764, two ships (one experimentally copper-bottomed) commanded by the Hon. John Byron (grandfather of the poet). As a midshipman 'Foul-weather' Jack Byron had sailed with Anson and suffered the shipwreck of his ship off the coast of Chile, returning home six years later after enduring unbelievable hardships. His brief was not very well thought-out, including as it did yet another search for *Terra Australis Incognita*, in the deepest south, and the much-sought North-West Passage from the east in the far north of New Albion. His ship was the *Dolphin*, a 6th-rate 500-ton frigate.

Byron was also briefed 'to ascertain the latitude and longitude in which such islands are situated, and to observe the height, direction and course of the tides and currents; the depth and soundings of the sea; the shoals and rocks; the bearings of headlands and variation of the needle; and also to survey and make plans and charts of such of the coasts, bays and harbours as you shall judge necessary' – which was quite a tall order. Nor was Byron the right man for the job as he lacked sufficient curiosity and energy. Perhaps those six years of suffering had drained him of both. He found almost nothing new in the Pacific and entirely ignored his instructions both in the far north and the far south. He was home in twenty-three months, the fastest circumnavigation to date.

Next there was Samuel Wallis, the key linking figure between all that had gone before and Cook's first voyage. Wallis was a much better navigator and explorer than Byron, and departed in his ship, the same frigate, *Dolphin*, within one month of Byron's return. His brief was roughly the same, which suggests the keenness of the British Government's desire to confirm or deny the existence of the Great Southern Continent.

Wallis was a Cornishman who possessed many of Cook's qualities: pertinacity combined with concern for his men, navigational skill and experience as well as a desire 'to cultivate a friendship with the natives', although he was not always successful in doing so. He took with him the small and somewhat worn-out sloop *Swallow*, commanded by Philip Carteret, who had also sailed with Byron. The two ships divided on emerging from the Magellan Strait after a severe drubbing from the elements. Carteret continued alone and, especially considering the inadequacy of his vessel, made some important discoveries in Melanesia and Polynesia, including Pitcairn Island, and conducted valuable surveys round the Philippines before returning home.

Wallis with the *Dolphin* at first followed the now traditional north-west course across the Pacific, but altered to west when the winds permitted. This took him south of Byron's track and, after several weeks, to a series of apparently uninhabited atolls, which led finally to a distant sight of towering peaks topped by the cloud that characterises Pacific volcanic islands. At the same time, far to the south, Wallis and his men thought that they saw higher and more extensive peaks stretching clear across the horizon. There at last, he noted, was the Great Southern Continent. 'This made us all rejoice and filled us with the greatest hopes imaginable.' Within minutes fog closed off this dramatic sight in the centre of the ocean.

Overnight they drifted towards the nearer land and at dawn found the ship surrounded by many canoes all packed with fine-looking men and women of remarkable beauty. They were curious but cautious at first, following the *Dolphin* from a safe distance as Wallis took her along parallel with the thunderous reef. At length he found a break through which he sailed into a protected anchorage.

It was a sensationally beautiful island, the woodland of palm and breadfruit,* bananas, yam and other fruit rising up the lower slopes of the mountains, which were scored with valleys bringing water tumbling down to the shoreline. 'It is impossible to describe the beautiful prospects we beheld in this charming spot,' wrote George Robertson, the *Dolphin*'s master. 'The verdure is as fine as that of England, there is great plenty of livestock, and it abounds with all the choicest productions of the earth.'

Here Wallis remained for six weeks, repairing his ship, stocking up with provisions and water, and, after an early dispute or two, 'cultivating a friendship with the natives' as instructed. There was no opportunity to make a study of the society these Polynesians had created although it was evidently complex and hierarchical, with no

* Breadfruit, *Artocarpus*, which was to figure so prominently in the Pacific diet of so many explorers, grows to about the size of a coconut and is very abundant and nutritious, but woolly and unpalatable. Banks asserted that 'they sometimes griped us', and found them inferior to plantains and yams. When at the second attempt (after the *Bounty* mutiny) the plants were shipped to the West Indies, the slaves refused to eat them.

sign of conflict between the communities (the *Dolphin* had arrived at a peaceful period), and every sign of contentment with the untroubled and easy life they lived.

Wallis named the island King George's Land and took possession of it in this sovereign's name. They never saw again those distant mountains of the continent to the south. No doubt the light had been unusually clear on the day of their arrival. Or had they been victims of an illusion? Wallis took his leave of these amiable people and arrived home on 20 May 1768. He then released a letter which he had written *en route*. It began:

We have discovered a large, fertile and extremely populous island in the south seas. The *Dolphin* came to an anchor in a safe, spacious and commodious harbour ... From the behaviour of the inhabitants, we had reason to believe she was the first and only ship they had ever seen ...

This was certainly the case, but more were to follow with increasing frequency, the second less than one year later. Tahiti's era of isolation and innocence was soon to end.

FIGHTING ON THE OPPOSITE SIDE to Cook at Quebec was a remarkable aristocratic Frenchman, Comte Louis Antoine de Bougainville, a close friend of Montcalm and his aide-de-camp. Of him Montcalm had written to his wife, 'He has talent, a warm head and a warm heart. He will ripen in time.' He was then thirty years old, one year younger than Cook. Bougainville did indeed mature quickly, and at the end of the war he was ready for new enterprises, freshened rather than exhausted by the fighting.

While primarily a soldier – and one who had shown great skill and courage on the battlefield, and tact in negotiation with the English – Bougainville was also an enterprising sailor. On his return to France he learned that his people, determined not to be upstaged by the British, were planning expeditions and colonising operations in the south. Bougainville volunteered to lead the first expedition, to the Falkland Islands, which, in their strategic situation, could secure all lines of communication between the South Atlantic and the South Pacific – or so it was calculated.

At his own expense Bougainville gathered together a settlement party of men, women and children, acquired a boat of sufficient size, and set sail south for these inhospitable islands. The English had long since made claim to the Falklands, by John Davis, the first to discover them, in 1592 and confirmed by Sir John Hawkins two years later. Lord Falkland was a later First Lord of the Admiralty. The French colony had a brief life. Learning of it, the Spanish authorities, allies of France, made their own claim to the islands and requested the removal of these unfortunate French men and women. Bougainville had the unhappy task of carrying this out. But he combined the operation with one of the greatest voyages in the early annals of Pacific exploration.

Bougainville chartered two ships for this voyage, the *Boudeuse* and the *Etoile*, and embarked in November 1766, shortly after Wallis. If he had not been delayed by his activities at the Falklands, he might have reached Tahiti first. But his second task further delayed him. Once again Western man entered the Pacific with the intention of finding the Great Southern Continent, and Bougainville deviated for this purpose, but, like all before him, found nothing. Always a sceptic about *Terra Australis Incognita*, and a man of sound commonsense, he wrote:

Upon the whole I know not on what grounds our geographers lay down, after these isles, a beginning of lands seen, as they say, by Quiros, to which they give seventy leagues of extent . . . If any considerable land existed hereabouts, we could not fail meeting with it . . . I agree that it is difficult to conceive such a number of low islands, and almost drowned lands, without supposing a continent near them. But geography is a science of facts . . .

A science of facts: no neater definition could be made. Here was a man you could sail round the world with, fearing nothing. In April 1768, while Cook was making his preparations before sailing for this recently discovered island, Bougainville arrived off Tahiti. The romantic aspect of his personality was captivated. He named it New Cythera, claimed it for France and, when he returned home, described the people and their way of life, and the beauty of their island, in such glowing terms that Tahiti seemed to express the ultimate in the contemporary fashionable Rousseauism.*

On leaving Tahiti Bougainville continued on his way, holding a due westerly course towards New Holland, which earlier explorers had avoided for its extremely hazardous navigation. At that time no navigator had noted the Great Barrier Reef. None had seen, let alone traced, the eastern coast of Australia, though Bougainville must have been the closest to doing so. He wrote graphically of a two-week-long fight to claw off the north-eastern coast of Australia and the east coast of New Guinea, low in provisions. For days the fog was so thick that the two ships were obliged to fire guns in order to keep company. 'In the dark, in the midst of a sea strewn with shoals, we were obliged to shut our eyes to all signs of danger.'

* Based on the romantic concept espoused by Jean-Jacques Rousseau (1712–78).

Bougainville was home by March 1769, a national hero who aroused a passionate enthusiasm for the great south seas in his native country, a fitting precursor to Cook, who at this time was about to double Cape Horn.

5

The People and the Gentlemen

BECAUSE OF THE RELAXED PROCEEDINGS of the Royal Society during 1767 and 1768, by the time Cook had received his instructions in late May 1768 his departure had become a matter of urgency. Wallis had returned, in the nick of time, to inform the Admiralty – and no doubt Cook personally – of the existence of an island that would make the ideal site for the observations. But King George's Land was on the other side of the world, separated from England by predictable and unpredictable hazards: both Cape Horn and Magellan's Strait could frustrate a vessel for several weeks. And if they were late, it would be another 100 years before the transit of Venus would again be available for observation.

Unlike the Royal Society, the Royal Navy was a service inspired when necessary with a spirit of urgency and decisiveness. Within three days of the Navy Board being told of the decision of the Admiralty and the Royal Society, with the blessings of the King, to mount the expedition to the Pacific, the Board was giving immediate attention to the choice of the vessel, replying: 'We are of the opinion the *Tryal*, sloop, lately taken into the dock at Deptford to be repaired, may when completed be a proper vessel for this purpose . . .'*

When they learned that the *Tryal* could not be fully refitted for this voyage before the end of May, other vessels were considered, among them the *Rose*, a 6th rate of 449 tons, the *Valentine* and *The Earl of Pembroke* of 368 tons. Of these the last was the preferred choice. It was, ran the Navy Yard's report, 'built at Whitby, her age three years nine months, square stern back, single bottom, full built . . . is a promising ship for sailing of this kind and fit to stow provisions and store as may be put on board her'.

---

* This and much else to follow is derived from C. Knight, 'H. M. Bark *Endeavour*', *The Mariner's Mirror*, vol. XIX, no. 3.

The Lords of the Admiralty approved the purchase of this vessel for £2,840 10s 11d and informed the Navy Board on 5 April 1768:

Whereas you have represented to us by your letter of the 29th. of last month that ... you have purchased a cat-built bark of the burthen of 368 tons, for conveying to the southward such persons as shall be thought proper for making observations on the passage of the planet Venus over the sun's disk, we do hereby desire and direct you to cause the said vessel to be sheathed,* filled, and fitted in all respects proper for that service, and to report to us when she will be ready to receive men. And you are to cause the said vessel to be registered on the list of the Royal Navy as a bark by the name of the *Endeavour*, and to cause her to be established with six carriage guns of four pounds each and eight swivels.

These instructions and exchanges took place several weeks before Cook's appointment to command the *Endeavour*. The Admiralty could not have chosen a more appropriate vessel for him: a cat built at Whitby by the company he knew so well and admired, Messrs Fishburn. When he was told about the vessel, he studied her statistics eagerly: 97 feet overall, 29-foot 3-inches beam, height between decks (an important consideration for a man of Cook's build) varying from 7 foot 11 inches to 7 foot 6 inches, with ample space for stores and provisions.

Compared with an equivalent frigate, she was a chunky little tub, built for the worst that the North Sea could do to her, which was just right for doubling Cape Horn or facing tropical storms. Considering that there might be trouble with natives on the Pacific islands, as experienced by both Byron and Wallis and many a Dutch *jacht* and Spanish caravel, Cook put in a request for four more swivels, making twelve in all, for the reason 'that four of these will be wanted to the longboat'.

Cook had only to cross the Thames by ferry and make his way down to Deptford to supervise the fitting out of the *Endeavour*. It was a time of intense and totally pleasurable work. Nothing gave him greater satisfaction than to have his sense of responsibility stretched to the utmost, and there was no more responsible task than preparing a ship which was to carry him and some one hundred souls to the other side of the world and back. He noted with satisfaction that the bark carried five anchors, three bower including one sheet, one

---

* Sheathed over the bottom planks with thin boards filled with nails with large, flat heads as protection against *teredo navalis*, a mollusc notorious for boring into wood, especially in warm waters.

stream and one kedge,* and that all were in good order. He noted also that of the three main boats carried, longboat, pinnace and yawl, the longboat was only varnished and under the varnish the bottom was badly eaten. He had a new bottom fitted and then painted with white lead, which, it seemed, had succeeded in protecting the pinnace constructed from the same wood.

There is no surviving record on Cook's domestic life during these active weeks, but it would be odd and uncharacteristic if he did not take a boat down-river to Deptford to show Elizabeth and the children the bark, moored in the dockyard with men putting the finishing touches to their work. Perhaps they met one or two of the officers who might be there, as keen as Cook to ensure that the fitting out was proceeding satisfactorily. The two boys, James aged six and Nathaniel only five, were registered as sailing with their father in ghostly guise as 'servants' to, respectively, the third lieutenant and the carpenter. Although bodily at home safely with their mother, by their names appearing on the muster book they gained several years' earning time towards sitting their lieutenant's examination, thus making possible their much earlier promotion. This reveals that their father was prepared to act outside the law but not of custom, and that Cook assumed that his sons would follow him into the Royal Navy.

The members of her husband's ship's company Elizabeth and her children did not meet were the most unusual and talented of them all, the 'supernumeraries'. Their inspiration and leader was Joseph Banks, aged twenty-five, whose family was typical gentry, with much land in Lincolnshire and excellent social connections. His home was Revesby Abbey, near Lincoln, and his father was an 'agricultural improver' and specialist in land drainage, for which there was plenty of scope in the midst of the Lincolnshire fens. The young man brought with him from Revesby four servants, two of them negroes, and two of his beautiful greyhounds, a dog and a bitch.

When Joseph Banks was growing up, his tutors had found him to be an agreeable boy without any pretensions to academic accomplishment. He enjoyed fishing and other country pursuits and, at the age

* Bower anchors: those at the bows and in constant working use. They are called best and small, not from a difference in size, but as to the bow on which they are placed; starboard being the best bower, and larboard (later port) the small bower. Stream anchor: a smaller one by two-thirds than the bowers, and larger than the kedges, used to ride steady, or moor with occasionally. In certain cases it is used for warping. Kedge anchor: a small anchor used to keep a ship steady and clear from her bower anchor while she rides in harbour, particularly at the turn of the tide. Also used to warp a ship from one part of a harbour to another. W. H. Smyth, *The Sailor's Word Book; An Alphabetical Digest of Nautical Terms*, 1867.)

of nine, was sent away to Harrow school. He enjoyed himself, was an enthusiastic games player and learnt very little. He was therefore packed off to Eton next in the hope that he might do better there. His most recent biographer stated that at this time 'he was big for his age, uncommonly strong, active and brave . . . Even though he was not of a particularly aggressive disposition, and even though there was a fair amount of gentleness in his nature, Eton suited him: he made many friends . . .'

As Cook's life was changed after his arrival at Staithes, at about the same age Banks took the turning, which was to bring him fame and accomplishment, one summer afternoon in 1759. The story is vouched for by a friend, a distinguished surgeon, Sir Everard Home, to whom Banks related how he had been left behind by some friends after a swim in a river, and as he was strolling back to the college along a country lane richly endowed with wild flowers, 'he stopped and looked round, involuntarily exclaimed, How beautiful! After some reflection, he said to himself, it is surely more natural that I should be taught to know all these productions of Nature, in preference to Greek and Latin . . .'

Banks had become in that one moment a happy, enthusiastic slave to botany, and later to the whole range of natural philosophy. His bible became Gerard's *Herbal*. When he went up to Oxford and discovered that there was no one to teach botany, he visited Cambridge, found a tutor there who suited him and brought him back, paying him handsomely. Meanwhile, Banks's father died in 1761, and his mother moved to London, to a house in Paradise Walk, Chelsea. This was coincidentally and conveniently close to both the Apothecaries' Garden and the London house of John Montagu, fourth Earl of Sandwich, a man who became his friend, and who became deeply involved in the lives of both Banks and Cook.

When Banks inherited his father's fortune, and responsibilities, in early 1764, he bought himself a house in New Burlington Street, and with his wealth and social standing, his charm, youth and enthusiasm, quickly became a man about town of the world of scientific philosophy and natural history. Among his new friends was Thomas Pennant, himself a friend of Gilbert White and of Carl Linnaeus of Uppsala University, the Swedish founder of modern botany and the creator of the system of classification of plants. For his increasing knowledge and beguiling manner rather than for any single achievement, Banks was elected a member of the Royal Society.

At this time Banks made numerous natural history tours of various parts of England and Wales, each lasting several weeks, and then returned to London with samples of plants, birds and mammals he had shot, geological specimens and much else. His home began to assume the character and appearance of a small natural history museum. But his ambitions extended far beyond his home country. With the coming of peace after so many years of war, the delights of travel again seized the nation. While others hastened south to the Mediterranean, and especially Italy, Banks's ambition lay to the west, to the scene of the recent fighting, specifically to Newfoundland and its unexplored natural history.

Banks made enquiries of the Admiralty through the best of all channels, his friend the Earl of Sandwich, now First Lord. He was told that HMS *Niger*, a 680-ton 5th rate, would be leaving for St John's some time in April 1766 and that a berth would be available if he wished it. He seized the opportunity, and throughout that summer, moving from harbour to harbour with the ship which was on fishery supervision duties, Banks botanised furiously, following in the wake of Cook's surveying, even enthusing members of the ship's company who helped in the sample gathering. He was not in the least put out by the infernal mosquitoes: 'He works night and day, and lets the mosquitoes eat more of him than he does of any kind of food, all through eagerness,' noted Lieutenant John Phipps of the *Niger*, who had become a friend.

Banks was back in London in January 1767 and was soon to learn through his new membership of the Royal Society of the plans to observe the transit of Venus. He was not in the least interested in astronomy, or in mathematics for that matter. To him these were subjects of distant observation and theory. But he was uncommonly interested in the subject of a voyage to the Pacific. At this date Wallis had not yet returned with news of the discovery of Tahiti, and Cook had received no hint that instead of returning to Newfoundland to continue his survey, he would be selected to command the expedition. A connection between the rich, buoyant young naturalist and the wise, experienced mariner had already been made, not only in St John's but also by reason of Cook being asked by Governor Palliser to take back with him on board the *Grenville* an Indian canoe, a gift from Palliser to Banks. Unfortunately, this had been washed, or thrown, overboard during the storm in the Thames while Cook lay anchored above the Nore light. There was the suggestion that it might have been washed up on the Essex shore, but this was never pursued and there is no further record of the incident, certainly not between Banks and Cook. In fact, there appears to be no personal contact between the two men until Banks and his entourage arrived on board the *Endeavour* on 26 August 1768.

The arrogant ease with which Banks secured accommodation on board the *Endeavour* for himself and his regime (as they were officially described) of seven reflects the contemporary power of wealth, position and connections, the functional influence of the Royal Society, to say nothing of the 4th Earl of Sandwich. Cook, in command of a small bark carrying an inflated muster of men already, together with guns, provisions, astronomical instruments and astronomers, on a voyage expected to last at least two years, was not even consulted. Desiring something, circumstances unfolded in Banks's favour, doors were opened, and his wishes were fulfilled without fuss or question.

Banks had chosen as companion and collaborator on the voyage Dr Daniel Carl Solander, a friend and fellow member of the Royal Society. Solander, born in northern Sweden in 1733, was ten years older than Banks, a short, already rather tubby fellow, with little of Banks's *joie de vivre* and charm but all his dedication to botany and the natural sciences. He had a great respect and liking for Banks, and, all round, a greater knowledge of the subjects they shared. Solander was one of the ablest pupils of Linnaeus and was held in high regard.

Solander's reputation spread far beyond Sweden, and in 1758 two English naturalists, Peter Collinson and John Ellis, for long two of Linnaeus's many correspondents, wrote to ask the master to 'lend' Solander to London as a botanist prophet who would spread his knowledge. It was a wonderfully successful appointment, and the Swede showed no wish to hurry home. This is Collinson writing to Linnaeus on 2 September 1762:

My dear Linnaeus cannot easily conceive the pleasure of this afternoon. There was our beloved Solander seated in my Museum, surrounded with tables covered with an infinite variety of sea-plants, the accumulation of many years. He was digesting and methodizing them into order, and for his pains shall be rewarded with a collection of them, which no doubt you will see ... Solander is very industrious in making all manner of observations to enrich himself and his country with knowledge in every branch of natural history.

For his part, Ellis added his own praise to the master a few weeks later: 'He is exceedingly sober, well-behaved and very diligent ... I can assure you the more he is known, the more he is liked.'

Banks first met Solander at a private dinner party in London shortly after he had completed his arrangements with the Royal Society and the Admiralty to accompany Cook to the Pacific. The two men took to one another, and the conversation warmed further as Banks told the table about his imminent voyage, at which Solander is said to have leapt to his feet and declared that he wished to come too. The Admiralty agreed the following day, and one of the great natural history partnerships of the eighteenth century had been sealed.

Ellis thought it suitable to tell Linnaeus of the arrangement so rapidly reached and wrote to him:

> I must now inform you that Joseph Banks, Esq., a gentleman of £6,000 per annum estate, has prevailed on your pupil, Dr Solander, to accompany him in the ship that carries the English astronomers to the new discovered country in the South Sea, where they are to collect all the natural curiosities of the place, and after the astronomers have finished their observations on the Transit of Venus, they are to proceed . . . by order of the Lords of the Admiralty, on further discoveries. No people ever went to sea better fitted out for the purpose of Natural History, nor more elegantly. They have got a fine library of Natural History: they have all sorts of machines for catching and preserving insects; all kinds of nets, trawls, drags and hooks for coral fishing; they have even a curious contrivance of a telescope, by which, put into the water, you can see the bottom at a great depth, where it is clear. They have many cases of bottles with ground stoppers, of several sizes, to preserve animals in spirits. They have the several sorts of salts to surround the seeds; and wax, both bees-wax and that of the myrica; besides, there are many people whose sole business it is to attend them for this very purpose. They have two painters and draughtsmen, several volunteers who have a tolerable notion of Natural History; in short, Solander assured me this expedition would cost Mr Banks £10,000.

'Mr Banks' natural history painter', as he was usually referred to, was a twenty-two-year-old artist of immense talent, Sydney Parkinson. The two men first met at that great rendezvous of botanists, the Vineyard Nursery on the London road in Hammersmith. This was set up in 1745 by two notable botanists, James Lee and Lewis Kennedy, one of a number of nursery gardens thriving in west London. From here Lee wrote *An Introduction to Botany*, a book for laymen and professional botanists which explained Linnaeus's classication for the first time. It brought him wealth and fame. Banks was often at the Vineyard, no doubt after visiting the Apothecaries' Garden *en route*, and was a close friend of Lee. Parkinson, like James Lee, came from an Edinburgh Quaker family. He was educated in that city, was apprenticed to a woollen draper and was simultaneously trained in draughtsmanship under the distinguished Frenchman, William de la Cour. With the death of his father, Parkinson sought his artistic fortune in London, where he soon became a minor celebrity for his paintings of plants and flowers. Banks was among his admirers and recruited him with the firmness of a sergeant-major in an alehouse.

Parkinson did not look the part of a circumnavigator. The impression that the young man first gave was that he might be blown overboard in the first heavy weather, being feather-light, with long, artistic fingers and a long, beaked nose. He was serious, intelligent and a delight to talk to, though there was not much laughter in the young Quaker. To a man, the *Endeavour's* company came to like and admire Parkinson.

Not content with a single talented artist in his retinue, Banks chose 'for figure and landskip' a draughtsman called Alexander Buchan, another Scot and another frail figure. He was an epileptic, but whether he concealed this weakness or Banks brushed the handicap aside is not known. He, too, was an intelligent young man, but he does not stand out as positively as Parkinson.

As secretary/writer and administrator of his little group, Banks took along Herman Diedrich Spöring, another rather solemn Swede – described by Banks as 'a grave thinking man'. He had sought to carve a career in London and became a watch-maker, an amateur natural historian and an artist. Solander, while working at the British Museum, sought his services as a clerk and no doubt recommended him to Banks for his pragmatism and good sense.

Charles Green was a key figure on this voyage, a skilled and experienced astronomer and assistant to Maskelyne, who admired but did not much approve of him. He was a heavy drinking man who cared nothing for his health, or other people for that matter. He had entered the Navy as a purser, but was soon back to his telescope when the Royal Society selected him.

Green attended the meeting of the Royal Society on 5 May 1768, at which Cook was present, in the role of fellow observer with him, accepting an allowance of '£120 a year for victualling', 'a further gratuity to himself of 200 guineas for the voyage' and, 'if the voyage should exceed two years, then at the rate of 100 guineas per ann.'. At the same meeting it was also agreed by the committee that the two observers should be equipped with two reflecting telescopes of 2-foot focus, 'with a Dolland's micrometer to one of them and moveable wires for the other'. With them came two wooden stands, an astronomical quadrant, an astronomical regulator clock, a sextant, a barometer, a journeyman clock, two thermometers and a dipping needle.

AMONG THE COMMISSIONED OFFICERS, midshipmen, warrant officers and men who sailed with Cook were a number who survived this voyage to sail with him again, and even on all three of his voyages. Worthy of first mention is the American-born John Gore. He had sailed with both Byron and Wallis, a double-circumnavigator already therefore. Here was a sailor who had shone under all circumstances, reliable and tireless in a gale, cheerful, idle only when off watch asleep in his swinging bed, enterprising and taking advantage of every moment ashore when opportunity allowed, shooting any bird and mammal in the sights of his gun. Gore had joined the Royal Navy in 1755 as a midshipman and was probably only a few years younger than Cook, whom he admired and respected from first meeting. He was no intellectual and possessed little imagination, but who wanted those characteristics as third lieutenant on a voyage like this? What he possessed in abundance was ability, skill and experience: in the Mediterranean, the Caribbean, the Atlantic and, above all, the Pacific. In fact, Wallis had been in such poor health that Gore virtually commanded the *Dolphin* across the Pacific.

Three more from the *Dolphin*, which suggested that Wallis had enjoyed a fine ship's company, were, first, Dick Pickersgill, nineteen years old, overfond of the liquor like most sailors, but with a good, clear head (when sober) and a talent for surveying and chart-making. Being a Yorkshireman further recommended him to Cook, and he was appointed to the responsible position of master's mate in spite of his youth.

Then there was Robert Molyneux, another heavy drinker, who was three years older than Pickersgill. He came from the other side of the Pennines, Hale in Lancashire, and became master of the *Endeavour*. The Welshman, Francis Wilkinson, was also promoted warrant officer before the ship sailed after being an AB in the *Dolphin*. All these ex-*Dolphin* men had enjoyed no more than a few weeks on dry land before embarking with Cook. None was worried about that, you can be sure, for employment was not easy with the return of peace.

The man with whom Cook had most contact for almost the entire voyage was Zachary Hicks, his second lieutenant, a man of great experience, a twenty-nine-year-old Londoner who had just come ashore from the sloop *Hornet* and had taken Cook's fancy as an agreeable, reliable fellow.

On a more personal basis, Cook probably saw as much of his young servant as his second lieutenant. Will Howson, another Londoner, was only sixteen but had satisfied Cook's needs on the last surveying expedition in the *Grenville*, and was to do so on this voyage, too. Of the same age was Elizabeth Cook's nephew, Isaac Smith, who had also proved himself a capable sailor and apprentice surveyor in the *Grenville*. 'Very expert', his relation described him, justifying his later promotion from AB to midshipman. He was a lively lad, liked and teased by even the roughest crew members.

There are few more responsible trades than that of carpenter on a long voyage, and on this one the crew's lives were to depend on their skills. Cook's chief carpenter was John Satterley, 'a man much esteemed by me and every gentleman on board', was Cook's judgment. Among his crew were Richard Hughes, George Nowell and Francis Haite, an 'elderly' gentleman of forty-two, who had been with Byron in the *Dolphin*. Haite was already a veteran; William Peckover AB was to become one. At the age of twenty-one on this voyage, he was to sail twice more with Cook and continued to lead an active sea-going life until sailing under William Bligh in 1786. As a loyalist at the mutiny of the *Bounty*, he survived his captain's incredible open-boat voyage.

Another sailor who was less satisfactory than Pickersgill but sailed with Cook on all three voyages was the quartermaster, Robert Anderson, a Scot from Inverness, who became very tiresome when with liquor, having to be flogged at Rio de Janeiro and again at Tahiti. The boatswain's mate, John Reading, was so drunk at Rio that he could not be trusted to flog Anderson and others, as was his duty, and was himself given a dozen lashes.

The ship's surgeon, upon whom a number were to depend for their life, was William Monkhouse from Penrith, Cumberland, who was highly regarded by Cook. When Monkhouse died, Cook promoted Surgeon's mate William Perry from Chiswick as surgeon. He was well up to the job and Cook also thought highly of him.

Equally important for the men's welfare was the ship's cook. The first one the Board offered Cook seemed so frail that he asked for another. John Thompson was sent in his place. Was it the Board's rather sick joke that Thompson had only one hand? Cook complained vehemently, but could not persuade them a second time. In the event, Thompson did an excellent job.

There were three young midshipmen on Cook's muster roll, John Bootie, Jonathan Monkhouse, brother of the surgeon, and Patrick Saunders. Monkhouse proved much the most satisfactory in this difficult 'in-between' rank and came to be 'much trusted' by Cook. The youngest on board, who was later to be promoted midshipman, was Isaac Manley, aged twelve, a servant and, surprisingly, the son of a Middle Temple bencher.

Surely the most colourful and intriguing of all the ship's company was Charles Clerke, aged twenty-five, master's mate from Weathersfield in Essex. Clerke proved to be irrepressibly cheerful, fearless and able. At the same time, at sea there was nothing he enjoyed more than yarning over a bottle. His anecdotes were limitless, so it seemed, and many of them hair-raising; others were prurient even by sailors' standards. He came to the ship with a considerable reputation as a womaniser, and even in the most unlikely places on the voyage, and with the most unlikely natives, pursued his seductions. Cook predicted that life on board the *Endeavour* would not be dull for long with Clerke as company for the men. He was right.

And what of these men, the 'people' of the lower deck? Did they have any common characteristic? They did not. They were a polyglot crowd, originating from many different parts of the world. The Britons came from places as widely separated as Cork in Ireland, Fife in Scotland, and even farther north, the Orkneys; and hundreds of miles south, Guernsey. There was the oldest, John Ravenhill from Hull, whom Cook estimated was seventy or eighty. 'Generally more or less drunk every day.' Antonio Ponto was a twenty-four-year-old Venetian. John Dozey was from Brazil, and another Brazilian joined him later. There were two ABS from New York, one a volunteer, James Magra, and a second was impressed at Madeira.

These people made up a rough, tough crowd of some seventy-five men, most of them with experience of crowded, confined quarters for months at a time. There was fighting, starting from drink rather than argument, and there was certainly some buggery and sharing of hammocks, a capital offence, 'a crime of so black a nature' but so widely practised on long voyages that it was taken for granted if reasonable discretion was observed. It certainly in no way affected the heterosexuality of those who practised it when opportunity occurred on shore or for those married when they returned home.

Buggery certainly did less harm than drink. Heavy drinking was widespread, even among the youngsters, and led to more accidents (and on this voyage several deaths) than any other cause. Rum had been the standard issue drink in the Royal Navy since the conquest of Jamaica a hundred years earlier, when it had replaced brandy. Concerned at the degree of drunkenness in the Navy, the daily issue of one pint a day and half a pint for boys was spread over two sessions, at noon and 6 p.m., and, to the outrage of the men when it was first introduced, diluted with a quart of water. It was full-strength rum that they drank, about ninety-four proof, and it may seem a sufficiency but the most wily and daring means were used to supplement the ration. Ships' logs were peppered with records of flogging for stealing rum.*

Men o' war crews did not vary widely in quality, but Cook could consider himself fortunate in the six dozen or so men who were sent to the *Endeavour*. There were one or two who had to be discharged before

---

* The rum, or 'grog', ration continued in the Royal Navy until 1970.

sailing and a number of them 'ran', which was probably a good thing for the ship, but they were mostly a decent group of young men – there were only a couple over thirty – boisterous and sentimental, especially about their pet animals, of which there were many (and a goat for the officers' milk).

COOK'S FINAL INSTRUCTIONS from the Lords of the Admiralty, signed on 30 July 1768, were formally described as secret and were in two parts, the second part to remain sealed until he was at sea. These were concerned with the aftermath of the observation of the transit and the departure from Tahiti. Cook had, like Bougainville, for long suspected that *Terra Australis Incognita* was a myth, but the received opinion of scientific bodies, of the Royal Society, of Joseph Banks himself and of the Admiralty was that it existed, and this was supported by Wallis's supposed sighting of those distant peaks. So,

Whereas there is reason to imagine that there is a Continent or Land of great extent, may be found to the southward of the Tract lately made by Captn Wallis or the Tract of any former Navigators in Pursuits of the like kind . . . You are to proceed to the southward in order to make discovery of the Continent above mentioned . . .

On discovering this continent he was to explore as much of the coast as practicable, to land, take possession 'with the consent of the natives' of 'convenient situations', and take notes and samples of the soil and its products, 'beasts, birds, fishes and minerals, seeds of trees, fruits and grains'.

If he failed in this quest, Cook was 'to fall in with the Eastern side of the Land discover'd by Tasman and now called New Zealand'. Cook, too, had read of Tasman's remarkable voyage 126 years earlier and his conclusion (which Cook did not share) that the land he briefly touched was the western coast of the Great Southern Continent, the eastern end being Staten Land, noted by his fellow Dutchman, Willem Schouten. After all this he was to proceed home by way of the Cape of Good Hope, or Cape Horn, according to his judgment.

Today, in the closing years of the twentieth century, with two world wars and countless lesser conflicts behind us, when man has walked on the moon and contrived numberless devices and inventions which have transformed life on earth, we can still stand back in wonder at the dimensions of these orders, at the sheer effrontery of asking nearly one hundred men to embark in a wooden vessel, scarcely more than one hundred feet in length, and dependent for its mobility upon the whim of winds, and currents and tides, to sail to the other side of a world only dimly charted, there to carry out an exacting observation, and then to discover a completely uncharted continent, survey its coastline and take note of its characteristics. Perhaps an even greater wonder was that men of experience and wisdom were prepared to take on this undertaking and with pleasure and excitement.

So it was that Cook took leave of his anxious wife Elizabeth, heavy with child,* and three children at the Mile End Road on Saturday, 6 August 1768. His luggage had gone ahead of him, stowed in the *Endeavour*, which the pilot sailed first from Deptford down-river to Galleons Reach, and thence to the Downs. Cook arrived at Deal by coach at noon on 7 August with Green the astronomer, went aboard and discharged the pilot, who, obligatorily, had conned the bark through the hazards of the lower Thames and the estuary of sandbanks. At 10 a.m. the next day, 'weighed and came to sail', Cook noted in his journal on the first day at sea under his command. There was a fresh breeze from the north-west, and by noon they were some six miles from the South Foreland, which bore north-east.

But even now their voyage had not yet begun in earnest. There was still much to do at Plymouth. It took five days' sailing along the south coast, in sight of Dungeness and Beachy Head, south of the Isle of Wight, to reach Plymouth Sound. The weather was mainly calm with winds veering from north-west to north-east. The passage was useful in allowing time for the men to become acquainted with one another and to assess the merits and demerits of the warrant officers and commissioned officers. Cook did the same thing and on the whole was satisfied with his men, a number of whom had sailed with him before. Of their arrival at Plymouth Midshipman Jonathan Monkhouse† wrote of 14 August:

Got the ship into a proper berth betimes this morning – had a boat from Hammoaze [river] to enquire who we were. Captain Cook and I went ashore before breakfast to send an express to Mr Banks acquainting him of our arrival here. We found the postmistress extremely pert. Went to dock. C. C. [Cook] dined with the Commissioner and I with Mr N—n whose wife was then in the straw [childbirth]. Received my father's last letter . . .

---

* Elizabeth had living with her Frances Wardale, one of her husband's Yorkshire cousins, who was a great comfort to her, especially at this time.
† Although this is a fragment of a few surviving pages of an anonymous journal in the Alexander Turnbull Library, Wellington, New Zealand, there is little doubt of the identity. He was clearly a well-educated young man, scion of a good Cumberland family, and Cook in writing to the father tails the letter, 'My respects to all the family'.

There were other pleasant days at Plymouth, but everyone worked hard stowing provisions for eighteen months: four tons of beer, 185 pounds of great Devonshire cheeses, fresh meat by the hundredweight, salt beef by the ton, biscuits and vinegar, healthy sauerkraut and fruit against scurvy, six bags of freshly baked bread for the first days, 604 gallons of rum, four more guns received on board and stowed, twelve barrels of powder with round shot and pellets for the ship's guns and muskets and pistols, spare sails, trinkets for the natives – the list seemed endless.

On 15 August Cook received orders to increase the number of sailors from seventy to eighty-five, which entailed much work ashore checking them for suitability. 'Several shipwrights and joiners from the yard employed on board refitting the gentlemen's cabins and making a platform over the tiller . . . ' This last was to permit exercise for the gentlemen.

On another day, to the surprise of some of the men and dismay of others, 'Received on board . . . a sergeant, corporal, a drummer and nine private marines'. They were a mixed bunch, rough, tough, heavy drinking like the men of the lower deck, and more susceptible to crime and punishment than they were. But Sergeant John Edgcumbe ('A good soldier, very much of a gentleman') and Corporal John Truslove ('A man much esteemed by everyone on board') offset the poor expectations of their charges.

On 19 August, when the *Endeavour* was almost ready to sail, Cook assembled the ship's company and, according to custom and duty, read to them the Articles of War. This related to thirty-six clauses concerned with discipline, punishment and 'for the provision for the public worship of Almighty God', and took some time; the men were rewarded by the payment of two months' wages in advance. 'I also told them', wrote Cook, 'that they were not to expect any additional pay for the performance of our intended voyage.' Cook also noted thankfully that 'they were well satisfied and expressed great cheerfulness and readiness to prosecute the voyage'.

Joseph Banks endorsed this view: 'All in excellent health and spirits perfectly prepared (in mind at least) to undergo with cheerfulness any fatigues or dangers that may occur in our intended voyage.'

Banks had been at the opera in London when he received an urgent message from Cook to join the ship. With him were an old friend, a rich Swiss with pretensions to science, Horace de Saussure, and Banks's fiancée, Miss Harriet Blosset. Afterwards they had dinner together, but Banks did not divulge to them the contents of the message from Cook and, according to de Saussure,

Miss Blosset 'was quite gay', while Banks drank heavily 'to hide his feelings'.

The next morning, 16 August, Banks was early on the road with Dr Solander, arriving at Plymouth by post-chaise two days later. His servants and luggage were already on board, and their arrival created a minor sensation among the men. Who were these gentlemen with their excessive luggage and servants, their expansive accommodation and their fine clothes?

THE *Endeavour* WAS READY to put to sea by the afternoon of Saturday, 20 August, but the wind suddenly got up, from the south-west, with driving rain. For three days and nights the foul weather continued as if, after all the man-made delays, the fates still conspired to prevent their sailing. At last, on 26 August, Cook was able to write:

At 2 p.m. got under sail and put to sea having on board 94 persons including officers, seamen, gentlemen and their servants, near 18 months provisions, 10 carriage guns, 12 swivels with good store of ammunition and stores of all kinds. At 6 a.m. the Lizard bore WNW½W* 5 or 6 leagues distant.

Banks and Solander were already taking notes while still in sight of land. *Delphinus Phocaena*, or common porpoise, were seen in abundance: 'Their noses are very blunt.'

But Banks, never a good sailor, was soon feeling seedy and took it out on the *Endeavour*:

Found the ship to be but a heavy sailer, indeed we could not expect to be any other from her build, so are obliged to set down with this inconvenience as a necessary consequence of her form, which is more calculated for stowage than for sailing.

The wind remained 'foul' for several more days, the ship's motion so violent that 'Mr Parkinson could not set to his pencil', according to Banks. The artist was trying to draw a tiny sea insect, *Medusa Pelagica*, which they had taken with a small casting net. 'The different motions in swimming amused us very much.' Parkinson's finished drawing was a gem, a foretaste of so many more brilliant drawings in the months to come.

* The compass circle was divided into thirty-two points, each of 11¼°. The *cardinal points* are north, south, east and west. The *inter-cardinal* or *half-cardinal* or *quadrantal points* are those midway between: NE, SE, SW, NW. The *intermediate points* are those between cardinals and intercardinals: NNE, ESE, and so on. The remaining sixteen points are called *by-points*, all containing the word 'by': NW by N, S by E, and so on. Points are further divided into *quarter* (2° 48′ 45″ each) and *half points* (5° 37′ 30″ each): NE by E½E, SE, and so on.

Banks found the nights particularly uncomfortable even though he had such superior accommodation – or so he thought – with his swinging bunk in the main cabin, cheek by jowl with the other gentlemen and the officers. It was not until the afternoon of 30 August that 'for the first time my sickness left me and I was sufficiently well to write'.

The remission was brief, however. Early the following morning a full gale set in and the Bay of Biscay lived up to its reputation. Cook ordered the topsails close reefed and the top-gallant yards got down. Through the spume and low cloud brushing the wave tops he caught sight of the 6th-rate 587-ton HMS *Guadeloupe* and spoke with her. The men were too busy to do more than note with a fleeting sense of solidarity that others were sharing their suffering. Banks was not interested in this man o' war, but instead noted many Mother Carey's Chickens. They were traditionally supposed to warn sailors of an imminent gale, but on this occasion they were too late. Banks retired to his cabin and was very sick.

Cook was not in the least concerned with Banks's seasickness, or with the other gentlemen's condition. He was entirely preoccupied with the ferocity of the gale and the state of his ship. The 'very hard gale', as he defined it, had broken one of the main topmast puttock plates (iron plates with dead-eyes in the topmast rigging), washed overboard the boatswain's small boat and 'between 3 and 4 dozen of our poultry, which was worst of all'.

Once again the weather eased overnight, and when he came on deck at dawn on 2 September he was able to order two reefs loosed out of the two topsails. By midday land was in sight for the first time since the Lizard. It was Cape Ortegal, the northernmost point of Spain, the land bearing away towards Cape Finisterre. Between were the city of Corunna and the coastline so often pillaged by Francis Drake and his fellow privateers. But that was long ago and now – for the time being at least – there was peace between the two empires. The *Endeavour* was making progress, 130 leagues or 390 nautical miles in the first ten days.

6

'A Nursery for Desperation'

THE *Endeavour*'S FIRST PORT OF CALL was Funchal, the capital of the beautiful Portuguese island of Madeira. With its benign climate and rich soil, it had for years been a favourite port of call for ships heading for the southern hemisphere, be it 'the Brazils', the Spanish colonies of South America, India and the East Indies or the Dutch colonies at the Cape and the Indies. The ten-day-long passage was mercifully uneventful and the weather relatively fair. Banks had more to report than his captain. Now spared from further seasickness, he recorded with characteristic enthusiasm the birds he sighted and the sea life brought on board. European wheatears *en route* to their winter quarters in Africa rested in the rigging for a while to the delight of the two scientists. Crabs were brought up with the fine net and were drawn by Buchan because Parkinson was busy on other work.

On 10 September Banks noted: 'Today for the first time we dined in Africa [meaning in an African latitude] and took our leave of Europe for heaven alone knows how long, perhaps for ever.' He added philosophically: 'That thought demands a sign as a tribute due to the memory of friends left behind and they have it.'

Two mornings later, 12 September, Madeira in its full precipitous glory was in view, together with its smaller satellite of Porto Santo. During that day they swung south of the two islands and approached Madeira's southern tip, Porto de S. Lourenco, and north of the strip-like islets, the Desertas. The town of Funchal, tucked into the southern coast below the terraced vineyards which are such a feature of the island, was evidently busy with a number of ships in the roads taking in stores in the last light of the day. These included merchantmen and, always a welcoming sight, a British man o' war, HMS *Rose*. She was a Hull-built 450-ton 6th rate, to whom Cook spoke before anchoring at 8 p.m.

Everyone agreed that it was paradoxical as well as sad that their first serious mishap should occur in warm sunny weather in the calm conditions of Funchal roads. During the night the stream anchor had slipped 'due to the carelessness of the person who had made it fast'. The Scottish quartermaster, Alex Weir, a most experienced man, launched a boat to find the anchor. He and his crew were retrieving it when somehow Weir became entangled with the buoy rope and the anchor itself. The weight of the anchor pulled him overboard and before anyone could help he was carried to the bottom of the harbour. By the time the anchor and Weir were recovered, he had long since drowned.

The Portuguese authorities, well used to dealing with newly arrived ships, sent a medical team on board to conduct a cursory examination of the men before allowing anyone ashore. The first to disembark were Banks and his party, complete with instruments and tools carried by the servants. Their first call was on the British Consul, a most agreeable and hospitable Mr Cheap, who was also a prominent merchant of the island. 'He insisted upon our taking possession of his house and living entirely with him during our stay, which we did,' Banks reported gladly. For the five days they were on the island Cheap obliged by meeting Banks's every need, procuring permission for the scientists to travel wherever they wanted, together with horses and guides.

Banks and Solander wasted no time in taking advantage of this generosity and off they went, arousing curiosity among the islanders as they dug up wild plants and shrubs, from jasmine to veronica, salvia to rosemary, nearly seven hundred species in all. This figure indicates the extent of their industry, especially as it was the worst possible time of the year, with the grape harvest in full swing and most plants confined to the banks of streams and irrigation channels.

The crew were working almost as hard. It would be some two months before they could hope to reach Rio de Janeiro, their next port of call, and Cook took on board stores to the extent of 20 pounds of onions a man, 270 pounds of fresh beef and a live bullock for future slaughter, 3,032 gallons of wine, 10 tons of water, sweetmeats, poultry and much else. There was more work to do on the ship, including caulking and painting, the repair of sails and rigging. Not everyone fancied the fresh meat issued while they were at anchor. Cook was outraged at this choosiness. If he was going to run a healthy, scurvy-free ship, his men must follow his dietary orders. John Gore recorded that these men received '1 doz each for mutiny', which by strict definition included refusal to obey orders. The rest of the lower deck, who were obliged to witness the punishment, took it with typical sailors' stoicism. One can even assume that the victims received some caustic ribbing about being the first of many more to come, a reasonable assumption on a voyage as long as this was likely to be.

Banks did not care for the use of the cat and kept to his quarters whenever it was applied, but he accepted the necessity of punishment to keep order and discipline at sea: it was, after all, the only punishment Cook was permitted to apply, except *in extremis* the death penalty for murder or for mutiny. Banks wrote a long report on the island as if no Englishman had ever before visited Madeira and he was compiling a guidebook.

Before leaving, Cook impressed a seaman, John Thurman, from an American sloop that lay at anchor, a seemingly arbitrary action but legitimate, the poor fellow being a British citizen if only a mere colonial. He no doubt enjoyed great gossip with his fellow New Yorker, Jim Magra.

At noon on 18 September, a soft, balmy day with almost no wind, Banks and Solander bade their host farewell and left his house on horseback (there were no wheeled vehicles on the island) and, with the servants following behind, wound down the track to the harbour where a boat from the *Endeavour* awaited them. Cook greeted them at the head of the ladder and told them that he planned to sail at midnight.

There is no more memorable and evocative experience than leaving a beautiful island in moonlight with a long voyage ahead. Those in the ship most likely to feel the emotion, if only because they were without occupation, were Banks, Solander, Charles Green, Parkinson and the other artist, Alex Buchan. In the near windless conditions the towering peaks remained in view until the moon set at 5.25 a.m. and then reappeared distantly and mistily at dawn. Not until the horizon was clear* did they begin to feel that they were on their way, for most of the ship's company in new waters, and for many of them warmer than they had ever known before.

The passage to Brazil was largely uneventful. There were several storms and during one of them the sky was filled with lightning and roaring thunder, 'as if the end of the world was nigh'. But the *Endeavour* was never in any danger.

Following the naval belief that Satan finds mischief for idle hands,

---

* A few days later there appeared in the far distance and above a cloud bank the tip of the immense peak of Pico de Teide ('the Pike') on Tenerife, 'so faint', Banks wrote, 'that no man who was not used to the appearance of land at a great distance could tell it from a cloud' (see p. 126).

Cook kept his men busy and his ship scrupulously clean. One memorable day he exercised the mates and midshipmen at small arms drill, which gave spectators some amusement at their incompetency. Green the astronomer likened them to 'the London Trane Band* with their muskets on one shoulder then on the other'. After they had been at sea for some two-and-a-half weeks, Cook issued sauerkraut and portable soup, a meat essence that was boiled with pease or oatmeal, as a precaution against scurvy. Neither was much appreciated by the notoriously conservative sailors, but knowing that their captain would not hesitate to use the lash they managed to get them down. Fresh fish was quite a different matter. 'Served out fishing hooks and lines,' noted Stephen Forwood, gunner; and on the same day, 'Served out pipes and tobacco'. What could be nicer than casting a line while enjoying a good smoke?

Cook and his two lieutenants and astronomer were particular about keeping track of their position as they sailed farther south. We can be sure that the computation on the equator on 26 October 1768 was accurate, and it was celebrated in the traditional robust manner. Every one of the ship's company, including Banks and the other supernumeraries, qualified, and those who could not prove with the aid of a chart that they had crossed the line on an earlier voyage found their name on the blacklist of twenty-five in all. The only alternative to being ducked was the sacrifice of four days' ration of grog, which Banks and Solander were the first to agree to.

An elaborate frame was contrived to which in turn the victims were held fast and hoisted on a long rope through a block at the end of the main yard. He was then dropped from this height deep into the sea three times. The noise of jeering, cheering and shouting continued with scarcely a break through the afternoon until dusk.

Sufficiently diverting it certainly was [wrote Banks] to see the different faces that were made on this occasion, some grinning and exulting in their hardiness whilst others were almost suffocated and came up ready enough to have compounded after the first or second duck, had such proceeding been allowable.

Banks omitted to add that there was scarcely a sober man on board the *Endeavour* when the tropical night closed in.

Immediately south of the equator on the following day they were all conscious of a fundamental change in the weather. The temperature climbed into the 80s, the barometer fell to the 70s and

---

* London Trained Bands were formed in Henry VIII's reign as volunteer militia.

the humidity soared. Banks's books became mouldy so that they all had to be wiped dry; leather also became mouldy, and everything iron became immediately covered in rust, even to the knives in the men's pockets. These uncanny conditions were a prelude to 'the calms'. This unpleasantness continued for several days, and men like John Gore, who had twice experienced the doldrums, warned that it could last a week or more.

In the last days of October the wind got up from the east, to everyone's relief, and Banks was the first to perceive, and admire, the change that came over the ocean. 'This evening the sea appeared uncommonly beautiful, flashes of light coming from it perfectly resembling small flashes of lightning,' he noted. The men who had observed this phenomenon on previous voyages into the tropics were divided in their opinions, some claiming it was caused by the agitation of the water by small fish, while others believed that they were only 'blubbers', or fragments of whale fat. Banks's servants managed to get some of them on deck with the aid of his landing net. He decided that they were small *Lepas*, or barnacle. Parkinson sketched them, and also the crabs that were in the net with them.

Shortly after dawn on 8 November land was sighted to the west, distant, misty and mountainous. Two hours later someone spotted a fishing vessel and Cook spoke with it. They learned that they were just south of Santo Espiritu and about 350 miles from Rio de Janeiro, which matched Cook's reckoning. Banks expressed his customary excitement at the sight of this boat and insisted on boarding it with Solander. They were greeted by eleven fishermen, nine of them blacks, all of them fishing with lines, and to good effect so it seemed. There were recently landed bream, dolphins, 'Welshmen' and others, almost the whole catch being bought by Banks on the spot for 19s 6d. To his surprise they preferred English coinage to the Spanish currency. They were also offered, again to Banks's wonder, fish salted in a special compartment amidships. But Banks and Solander were interested only in fresh fish, which was presented to the *Endeavour*'s entire company of ninety-six, who fully approved and set to with gusto that evening.

No one could have been friendlier than these Portuguese, like those who had been so hospitable at Madeira. Cook therefore expected a similar warm welcome at Rio de Janeiro; indeed, he wrote on 6 November, 'From the reception former ships had met with here, I doubted not but we should be well received.' They doubled Cape Frio, east of Rio, on the night of 11–12 November, and in the morning coasted along that magical beach of white sand, mile after mile of it, which continues without a break from the Cape clear to

the city. Forests flanked this beach, rapidly rising with the mountains
to what Banks, enchanted by the spectacular scenery, described as
'immensely high'. Rio de Janeiro's famous Sugar Loaf Mountain stood
like a castle, visible during the long, slow day's sailing, but they were
still short of the river mouth and harbour at dusk.

Dawn revealed the full wonders of the most spectacular port and
city in the world. Parkinson emulated his master by making his own
observation:

The country adjacent to the city of Rio de Janeiro is mountainous, full of
wood, but a very little part of it appears to be cultivated. The soil near the
river is a kind of loam, mixed with sand; but further up in the country we
found a fine black mould. All the tropical fruits such as melons, oranges,
mangoes, lemons, limes, cocoa nuts and plantains, are to be met with here
in great plenty. The air, it seems, is but seldom extremely hot, as they have
a breeze of wind from the sea every morning; and generally a land wind
at night.

Three peaks guarded the narrow entrance to the Baia de Guanabara
and its numerous islands, while inland the peaks rose above 9,000
feet, their summits lost in cloud. Cook sent Zachary Hicks and Charles
Clerke ashore in a boat to make themselves known and to ask for a
pilot. The trouble began when, after a reasonable length of time,
they failed to reappear. Instead, the boat set off from the distant
landing stage with a Brazilian army officer in the place of Hicks and
Clerke. The boat's cox explained to Cook that the two men would
be released only when Cook himself came ashore. Cook, becoming
both apprehensive and angry, ordered anchors cast. 'Almost at the
same time,' he wrote, 'a ten-oared boat, full of soldiers, came up and
kept rowing round the ship, without exchanging a word; in less than
a quarter of an hour, another boat[load] came on board with several
of the Viceroy's officers, who asked, whence we came; what was our
cargo; the number of men and guns on board; the object of our voyage,
and several other questions, which we directly and truly answered'.

The senior officer, 'the Disembarkadore' as John Gore described
him, also 'requested that there should be no illicit trade carried on
between us and their people either on shore or on board'.

It was the custom, Cook was told, to detain the first officer to come
ashore until the Viceroy's representative had visited the ship and was
satisfied that all was well. Lieutenant Hicks would be returned as soon
as they got back to their office. When this promise was fulfilled, Cook
appeared mollified and made plans to go ashore the next morning, 15
November.

His Excellency Don Antonio Rolim de Moura, sixty-one years old, had spent his life in the Portuguese diplomatic service and followed the full traditional courtesies when Cook visited his palace. But it became immediately evident that Cook and the *Endeavour* and the entire ship's company were under suspicion. Relations between the two nations were excellent, but English privateers had enjoyed a poor reputation since the days of Drake's raids and Portuguese Brazil had suffered much from spying and smuggling over the years. Brazil was the jewel in the Portuguese crown and the people were proud of their rich possession. Little more than a year earlier Bougainville had suffered such difficulties at Rio de Janeiro that soon after his return a protest had been issued from Paris to Lisbon.

The trouble appears to have been that this responsible Viceroy lacked the intellectual capacity to credit that both Bougainville's and Cook's scientists could be curious about the plant life, geology and general natural history of his country. As for the scientific instruments and Cook's explanation of the importance of observing the transit of Venus, that must surely be a blind for some mischief-making. Why sail thousands of miles to dig up plants? Why sail thousands more miles to study a planet?

John Gore learned

that one suspicion of us among many others is that our ship is a trading spy and that Mr Banks and the Doctor [Solander] are both supercargoes and engineers and not naturalists, for the business of such being so very abstruse and unprofitable that they cannot believe gentlemen would come as far as Brazil on that account only.

At the end of this protracted and highly unsatisfactory meeting, Cook learned that he and no one else would be allowed ashore, that he could purchase provisions but only through an agent at five per cent, and that an officer would accompany him at all times, 'as a compliment' he was told. (As it transpired, he was really a guard.) In vain, Cook underlined how important it was that his aristocratic scientists be allowed to make their studies; and, more practically, that he needed to attend to the underside of his ship and that he could hardly heel the boat with the entire ship's company and the supernumeraries on board.

He had one answer for everything I could say [wrote Cook in exasperation]. The restrictions under which he had laid us, were in obedience to the King of Portugal's commands, and therefore indispensable. In this situation I determined, rather than be made a prisoner in my own boat, to go on shore no more.

On his return to the *Endeavour* and informing Banks, Solander and Parkinson of his failure, he and Banks both drew up individual memorials. They were wasting their time. When Hicks went ashore with the papers, and with orders not to allow a guard to be put on his boat, inevitably this led to a row. The Viceroy refused to receive the memorials and, when the lieutenant returned to his boat, guards had taken over, Hicks was forced to return to his ship in a Portuguese boat, and his crew were carted off to prison, where they were 'vilely treated'.

The men were soon released, but this marked the start of what Cook described as 'a paper war between me and his Excellency wherein I had no other advantage than the racking his invention to find reasons for treating us in this manner for he never would relax the least from any one point'. The Viceroy's suspicions could not be allayed. He would not believe that this was a ship in the service of His Majesty King George. Because Cook had described the voyage from Madeira as a 'happy' one lasting only eight weeks, why was it necessary to call for further supplies? 'Why did you want so soon water and provisions? It could only proceed from not having loaded a sufficiency of those articles in that island,' he declared. This kind of 'dissimulation' renewed his doubts 'that your ship belongs to the Crown because it is not possible that His Britannic Majesty could consent that his ships should practise such like artifices with a nation so many years so strictly her ally'.

Banks and Solander did not bother themselves too much with this war of words. With no diplomatic or captaincy responsibilities, and the days ticking by, they had decided on action, at the same time relishing the notion of outwitting these 'illiterate impolite gentry', as Banks called them. At first Banks sent only his servants ashore under cover of darkness, and they brought back large numbers of plants, which he and Solander spent the daylight hours identifying. Their success only inflamed further Banks's curiosity and determination to explore the countryside himself.

Parkinson, who accompanied the two naturalists along with the servants, gave an account of their experiences over several nights:

Having obtained a sufficient knowledge of the river and harbour by the surveys we had made of the country, we frequently, unknown to the sentinel, stole out of the cabin window at midnight, letting ourselves down into a boat by a rope; and, driving away with the tide until we were out of hearing, we then rowed to some unfrequented part of the shore, where we landed, and made excursions up into the country.

On 26 November Banks went ashore alone with his servants before daylight, spent the whole day there and returned when darkness fell again. 'I met several of the inhabitants who were very civil to me, taking me to their houses where I bought of them stock for the ship tolerably cheap, a porker middlingly fat for 11 shillings, a muscovy duck something under two shillings &c.'

On this expedition Banks also feasted his eye on many exotic birds, several with 'most elegant plumage', shooting what he called *Loxia Brasiliensis*. He also spent part of this busy day examining some fruit and vegetable patches, tasting melons, bananas, pineapples, beans, turnips, cabbage and much else, but all inferior to what he grew or could buy at home. Cook, on the other hand, had more admiring words for the flowers: 'the wildest spots being varied with a greater luxuriance of flowers, both as to number and beauty, than the best gardens in England'.

The last days in Rio de Janeiro were no more comfortable than the first days, especially for two men who got twelve lashes and the boatswain's mate, who refused to inflict the punishment. Cook took the opportunity of sending to the Secretary of the Admiralty, care of a Spanish ship leaving for home, copies of all the sharp-worded memorials and other exchanges between himself and the Viceroy, just for the record.

Cook now experienced a tragedy, which if he could not blame the Portuguese for the cause was in keeping with the dour inhospitality of this place. 'In turning down the harbour,' he wrote in his log, 'Peter Flower seaman fell overboard and before any assistance could be given him was drowned. He was a good hardy seaman and had sailed with me above five years.' He had, it seemed, made a clumsy slip in the rigging. If it had been occasioned by rum – the usual cause – no one bothered to record it. At the last minute Cook managed to replace him with Manoel Pereira, a local Portuguese sailor, keen for the pay and the adventure.

However, Rio de Janeiro had not finished with the *Endeavour* yet. As they towed down the harbour with the pilot on board, the fort at the entrance suddenly opened fire, two shots across the bows. Cook was furious and sent the cutter to protest to the commander. He claimed that he had received no instructions to let the vessel pass. It took a last angry message to the Viceroy to get this corrected.

With enormous relief for the entire ship's company, they were now able to drop the pilot, recover their cutter and make their own way with the help of an easterly breeze out into the open sea. It was 7 December 1768. The *Endeavour* was well found, thoroughly caulked, the sails and rigging in good repair, and they had water, rum and provisions – fresh for the first days – to last them for three or four months.

'We are got fairly to sea and have entirely got rid of these troublesome people,' Banks noted with satisfaction, and settled down to summarise them and their city, and more usefully to sort, identify and note his collection of plants. He was not to know it, but one of the most significant and beautiful of them was a vividly coloured climber unknown anywhere else but Brazil, and named by Dr Solander *Calyxis ternaria*. It was not introduced into Europe until the 1820s, when it was named Bougainvillea after the French explorer rather than Dr Solander, or Parkinson who drew it as they sailed south down the Brazil coast towards Patagonia.

DAY BY DAY as they bore south towards higher latitudes the temperature fell. The weather varied from crystal-clear skies to wicked gales with thunder and lightning. The *Endeavour* was tested to the utmost but was never found wanting, and it was further proof of the qualities of the tubby cat-built design with origins in the Norsemen of the northern hemisphere and the short waves of the North Sea that it demonstrated the same excellence and security in the long rollers of the South Atlantic.

On 17 December Cook put his men on watch and watch, which meant no more than four hours' continuous rest but made more men available for any emergency. On the same day, he 'distributed the fearnoughts to the ship's company, enough to make each a jacket', as Stephen Forwood recorded.*

Disdaining the legendary superstition of ill luck for those killing an albatross (established long before Coleridge's *The Rime of the Ancient Mariner*), Banks shot a giant wandering albatross, *Diomedea exulans*, on 23 December; the only immediate consequence was calm weather for Christmas Day, of which Banks observed:

Christmas Day; all good Christians that is to say all hands get abominably drunk so that at night there was scarce a sober man in the ship, wind thank god very moderate or the Lord knows what would have become of us.

A day never went by without Banks and Solander catching some creature of the sea, or a bird:

Dr Solander and I went out in the boat and shot one species of Mother

---

* Fearnoughts, or dreadnoughts, were stout felt woollen jackets and trousers: the predecessor of duffle coats.

Carey's chickens and two shearwaters ... a very large shoal of porpoises came close to the ship, they are of a different kind from any I have ever seen but so large that I dared not throw the gig [multi-hook line] into any of them ... This morn took a shark who cast up his stomach when hooked or at least appears so to do. It proves to be a female and on being opened six young ones were taken out of her, five of which were alive and swam briskly in a tub of water ...

Cook was now accustomed to the ways of the 'gentlemen' and became increasingly interested in their finds and observations. Time and again he had to resist Banks's pleas to land – on the smallest sandbank or on large islands, which, aside from being surveyed and sometimes drawn, were of no concern of this voyage. Never for one moment did he allow the priority to slip of reaching Tahiti in good time. But Banks's determination never ceased to impress Cook. When thousands of insects and butterflies were thick about the ship, doubtless blown from the land, Banks thought nothing of spending four hours in the chains dipping for them with his special net. Later that same day, 30 December, with swarms of butterflies, moths and other insects clinging to the decks and rigging, he persuaded some of the men to gather armfuls of them to ensure that he would not miss any new species – and most of them were new. 'He gave them some bottles of rum for their trouble,' Parkinson noted.

Equally interested in the activities of the professionals was John Gore, whose enquiring mind and enthusiasm are reflected in the admirable journal this American kept. On this same day (30 December), he wrote:

The colour of the sea very white, contrary to that of the bottom which is black. Mr Banks and the Doctor employed some time today taking a variety of land inverts from the surface of the sea, some of them alive. Saw today a sealion, numbers of birds sitting on the water and some schools of fish like Borettoes in pursuit of small fish like spratts.

And again, a few days later: 'Passed by a great number of small red fish shaped like lobsters. They were in large shoals swimming on the surface of the sea ... In the morning a great number of small silver coloured birds about; they have a black streak upon each shoulder ...

On New Year's Day, 1769, they were in latitude 43°45' s, longitude 61° 8' 8" w, some 175 land miles south-east of the Valdes Peninsula on the Patagonia coast. The day 'made us pass many compliments and talk much of our hopes for success in the year 69', Banks recorded. Few people on board the *Endeavour* were immune to the emotion of entering the last year of this decade so far from home, with much already accomplished and so much more to look forward to, including the hazards of the Horn and the wastes of the Pacific. They could well have sent up some prayers of thankfulness that they had such an able and agreeable commander and that the company was as compatible as it had so far proved to be.

A few days later, with the thermometer still falling, 48°F at noon, Banks donned a flannel jacket, a waistcoat and thick trousers. Appropriately, they also saw their first penguins. They were south of the Falkland Islands now, to Banks's regret, because he had hoped to land there though it was never his captain's intention to do so.

In calm, warm weather, as it can be in these latitudes in mid-summer, the coast of Tierra del Fuego was in sight at dawn. They were six miles off the largest and most easterly of all the multitude of islands of this sub-Antarctic region, now called Isla Grande. 'Its appearance was not near so barren as the writer of Lord Anson's voyage has represented it* . . . we could see trees distinctly through our glasses and observe several smokes made probably by the natives as a signal to us.' Clearly this style of greeting had led Magellan to name these islands 'Land of Fire'. The reason why, later, Pedro Sarmiento, the Spanish explorer, had attempted to set up a colony here also became evident the following day when Cook coasted close inshore and saw through his glass patches of flowers and a hill covered with 'a beautiful verdure'. Banks also noted the rich forest land, the trees being between 30 or 40 feet high 'with flat bushy tops'. They were the evergreen Antarctic beech, the only tree of Tierra del Fuego, as it is today. Banks thought that they might be usable as topmasts.

At daybreak on 13 January they were close to Cape San Diego with the Straits of le Maire opening before them and leading them in to the Pacific. John Gore noted:

* 'The land on the south side of these straits is called Staten Land, and makes the most horrid appearance of anything I ever saw. It is very high, broken, rocky land, seems to be the vast ruins of some prodigious edifice, and is a proper nursery for desperation. Terra Fuego, which is the land on the other side, yields but an unpleasing prospect, but being in sight of the other it seems a perfect paradise, though it really is no more than a huge chain of monstrous mountains whose tops are continually covered with snow or hid in the clouds, and affords neither bush, tree, or shrub, nor indeed but little verdure of any kind.' (*Documents relating to Anson's voyage round the world 1740–1744*, Navy Records Society, 1967.)

The point Diego is a long low point without trees marking the north entry of the Straits le Maire. On the west side about three leagues to the westward of it were the 3 Brothers being 3 hummocks of land of a moderate height not far from each other and a little in the country . . . There is a good deal of low country without woods, which seems to form a deep bay . . .

Cook tells of their attempts to enter this strait:

Kept under an easy sail until day light at which time we were abreast of Cape St Diego at the west entrance of Strait le Maire East distance about five leagues . . . but the tide soon turned against us and obliged us to haul under the Cape again and wait until 9 am when it shifted in our favour. Put into the Straits again with a moderate breeze at sw which soon grew boisterous, with very heavy squalls with rain and hail and obliged us to close reef our topsails . . .

Cook knew that there was a 'Westerly current which comes round Cape Horn and through Strait le Maire', but he had not anticipated having to make three frustrated attempts to get through le Maire. While awaiting the fourth and successful attempt, Banks managed to persuade Cook to let him and Solander go ashore. For four hours they collected upwards of one hundred plants, every one new to them. There were no natives, but they found crude huts with traces of fire at the entrance where, in this climate, a door might have suited better.

At last, on the morning of Sunday, 15 January, with a more favourable and temperate wind, Cook got the *Endeavour* through, the shores on either beam appearing as dour and hostile as earlier Portuguese, Spanish, Dutch and English navigators had described this land.

At two o'clock [wrote Cook in his journal] we anchored in the bay of Good Success; and after dinner I went on shore, accompanied by Mr Banks and Dr Solander, to look for a watering place, and speak to the Indians, several of whom had come in sight. We landed on the starboard side of the bay near some rocks, which made smooth water and good landing; thirty or forty of the Indians soon made their appearance at the end of a sandy beach on the other side of the bay, but seeing our number which was ten or twelve, they retreated.

If the landing party numbered a dozen, it suggests that there could have been only one or two escorting marines, for Banks was rarely without his four servants or his greyhounds, and Spöring. Parkinson and his fellow artist, Buchan, were likely to have gone ashore, too, and Gore was certainly among them. But, fortunately, the natives proved to be friendly. Armed only with trinkets and coloured ribbon, Banks and Solander boldly advanced towards the

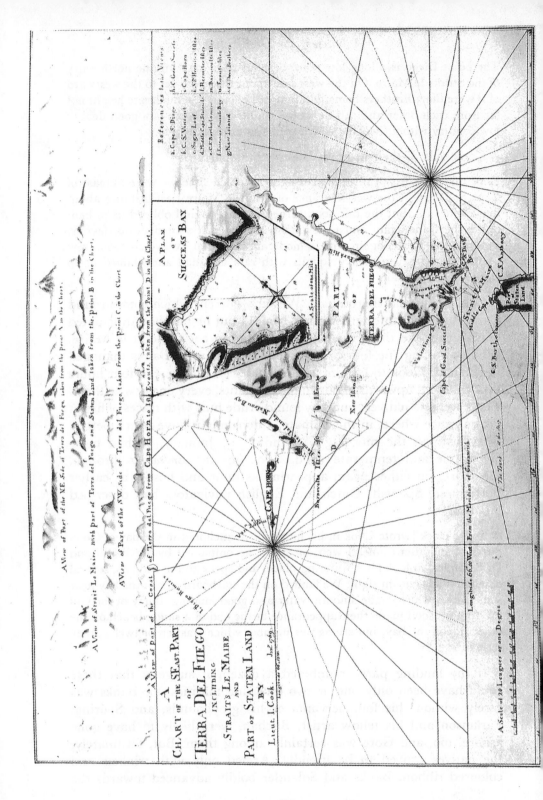

A View of Part of the NE Side of Terra del Fuego taken from the Point A in the Chart.

A View of Strait Le Maire, with Part of Terra del Fuego and Staten Land taken from the Point B in the Chart.

A View of Part of the SW Side of Terra del Fuego taken from the Point C in the Chart.

A View of Part of the Coast of Terra del Fuego from Cape Horn to 10 Leagues taken from the Point D in the Chart.

A PLAN
OF
SUCCESS BAY

A Scale of one Mile

References to the Views.
a Cape S. Diego.   h.d. Good Success
b. C. S. Vincent   k. Cape Horn
c. Sugar Loaf   k. N.ᵗ Hermite Isles
d. Middle Cape. Staten L. L.Hermite Isles
e. C.Bartholomew   m.Barnevelt Ile.
f. Entrance Success Bay n. Evouts Isles
g New Island   o.d Thee. Brothers

A
CHART of the SEast PART
OF
TERRA DEL FUEGO
INCLUDING
STRAIT'S LE MAIRE
AND
PART of STATEN LAND
BY
Lieut. I. Cook.   Jan.ʸ 1769.
Longit.ᵈ 66.19W.

PART
AND
OF

PART
OF
TERRA DEL FUEGO

TERRA DEL FUEGO

CAPE HORN

Cape of Good Success

Strait Le Maire

C.S. Anthony

Part
OF
Staten
Land

Middle Cape

C.S. Barth. or Aman.

Barnevelts Isles

New Island

Nassau Bay

Maurice Islands,

Longitude 66.19 West From the Meridian of Greenwich

A Scale of 20 Leagues or one Degree

74

Fuegians, two of whom stepped forward, advanced a few paces and then sat down. In a moment they rose again to their feet, displaying sticks with which they gestured and, evidently to renounce violence, ostentatiously threw them away.

Next the two natives, by gesture and by retreating towards the main party, invited Banks and Solander to join them. They were received 'with many uncouth signs of friendship', Banks confides to his readers without specifying what these were, though it may refer to the naked male Fuegians making much play with their penises, especially when greeting one another.

Banks and Solander replied by presenting them with their gifts, which were received with delight. 'A mutual confidence being thus produced, our parties joined; the conversation, such as it was, became general, and three of them came with us and went aboard the ship.'

One of the Fuegians was evidently a priest who was also, so it seemed, an exorcist. When anything caught his attention or when he was escorted to another part of the ship on this long and detailed tour, he shouted at the top of his voice for some minutes, addressing this outburst to no one in particular. What the crew made of this performance no one recorded, though we can assume that they were at first alarmed, and later unable to control their laughter.

These Fuegians were given some bread and beef, part of which they ate without evident pleasure, though they held on to what was left over. The drink was even less liked. Both wine and spirits got no farther than their lips and then were returned with 'strong expressions of disgust'. After two hours the Fuegians indicated that they wished to return to the shore. Cook escorted them to the waiting boat, and Banks accompanied them, anxious to see how they would be received by their friends. He noted 'the same vacant indifference, as in those who had been on board; for as on one side there appeared no eagerness to relate, so on the other there seemed no curiosity to hear how they had been received, or what they had seen'.

As a sort of celebration of their safe return, one of the three men produced the leather cover of a globe which he had stolen. He had 'carried it ashore, undiscovered, where he had no sooner arrived', Parkinson recalled, 'then he shewed his prize to the very person it belonged to, and seemed to exult upon the occasion, placing it upon his head, and was delighted with it'. Forwood noted: 'These people are of a middle stature, clothed with a skin [seal or guanaco] which they wrap round their bodies.' Later, he wrote: 'The Indians are of a copper colour with long black hair hanging over their shoulder';

their shoes were of sealskin, 'with the hair on the outside and tied in several places round their feet'.

John Gore gave the most succinct account of the Bay of Good Success:

Success Bay is roomy and with good anchoring all over it at moderate depths. But it has troublesome shores to land on by reason of a great surf, and that with the wind off the land. There is good water and wood, some clams, mussels, limpets and wild celery, with now and then a wild duck and seal. Every day we were on shore the Indians were with us (sometimes with their women and children). They behaved peaceably but were very thievish, and knew the power of firearms. They had among them French woollen cloth and English rings. Likewise bits of glass. They have a great dislike to seeing anyone smoke tobacco.

These people appear to me the same in every respect as those I formerly saw in the western ports of the Straits of Magellan.* That is their manner of living, stature, colour, dress, voice and arms, are the same, except that these have no canoes, probably from the winds being here too boisterous for them . . .

Cook was to spend the next day, 16 January, wooding and watering in the Bay of Good Success, and the men went ashore early with barrels and axes. Banks determined to take advantage of this free day by organising an expedition inland, through the forest and up into the hills, hoping to obtain a high view of the land – and seascape – and, as always, to gather plants. There was to be a full representation of the supernumeraries – Solander, Spöring, Green, surgeon Monkhouse, Buchan to draw the landscape, astronomer Green, Banks's four servants and two seamen 'to assist in carrying the luggage'. It was an ill-conceived expedition, which took no account of the possible hazards of the country and of the treacherous climate. They should have been warned of how deceitful the weather could be by the experiences of many earlier travellers in Tierra del Fuego since Pedro Sarmiento's fatal attempt to colonise the area. Banks in his innocence described the weather as 'vastly fine' when they set out, 'like a sunshiny day in May, so that neither heat nor cold was troublesome to us'. Both Banks and Cook had experienced similar conditions in Newfoundland, but here there was not even the inconvenience of insects. The air was still, the sky cloudless. The greyhounds raced about as if in a public park.

Their troubles began when they emerged from the forest and saw ahead of them what appeared to be smooth grassland. It was nothing

* Wallis had chosen the northern route through Tierra del Fuego in April 1769, following Magellan.

of the kind. It was a solid mass of beech saplings as if ready in one of West London's nursery gardens for planting out. On penetrating this vast area of green, they discovered that the close-packed saplings could not be bent aside to assist progress and that the ground itself was bog. 'No travelling could be worse than this,' Banks recalled, 'which seemed to last about a mile.'

They had not yet reached the other side of this area, sodden and almost exhausted, when poor Buchan suffered an epileptic fit. Those who could go no farther did what they could for him, and actually succeeded in lighting a fire. Solander, Green, Monkhouse and Banks pressed on with the four servants, soon emerging on to open rocky ground where the alpine plants fulfilled all Banks's expectations. At the same time, the weather changed from an amiable spring day to the depths of winter. The temperature dropped like a stone and the wind got up, bringing snow flurries. By now, Banks recounted, 'I had entirely given over all thoughts of reaching the ship that night'. This was a fearful prospect to face. They had brought with them no more food than a cold lunch, long since consumed, no tent, no blankets, nothing but what they stood up in, and just one bottle of brandy to keep them refreshed. Banks had it in mind to return to the others, regain the forest, build a wigwam and light a fire to save them from freezing to death.

They found Buchan in a much better condition than they had expected and, with Banks and Solander taking up the rear with Tom Richmond and George Dorlton, Banks's black servants, struggled back again through the accursed small beech. It was becoming dark and the cold suddenly became much worse – 'infinitely beyond what I have ever experienced', and that included winters in Canada. Solander was the first to succumb to it. 'I must lie down!' he kept pleading. Banks did his utmost to rally him, but failed, and the strong Swede lay down in the snow and at once fell asleep. Tom Richmond did the same. Banks told him that he would be frozen to death if he did not keep going, and Richmond answered simply, 'I will lie and die here.'

Banks succeeded in waking up Solander after shaking and cajoling him for fifteen minutes, but he could do nothing with Richmond. Leaving Dorlton and a sailor with him, promising to relieve them as soon as possible, Banks and the doctor struggled on, directed in the darkness by the flames of the fire the rest of the party had succeeded in lighting, in spite of the snow which was falling like a white curtain and which continued to do so for the rest of the night.

The surviving members of the expedition huddled round the fire, sodden, frozen and desperately hungry. Even the bottle of brandy could not be found. At midnight Banks heard a voice shouting in the night, located the man and helped him to the fire. It was the missing sailor in a pitiable condition. Then, with four of the least weak men, Banks ventured forth in the hope of rescuing alive his two black servants. When they were at last located, Richmond, to Banks's surprise, was on his feet, but quite unable to walk. 'We immediately called all hands from the fire and attempted by all the means we could contrive to bring them down but finding it absolutely impossible, the road was so bad and the night so dark,' Banks wrote later.

There was no possibility of lighting a fire beside the two men so hard was the snow still falling. All they could do was to lay out Richmond and Dorlton on a bed of boughs, placing more boughs over them, as some form of insulation from the snow and cold. Even as they did so, Banks discovered that one of these black servants had acquired the bottle of brandy and between them they had drunk the lot. They were, he knew, dying as much of drink as of cold, the one unable to offset the effects of the other. Banks's greyhounds, who were mostly looked after by the two men, lay down beside them and refused to move.

'Now might our situation truly be called terrible: of twelve our original number 2 were already past all hope.' But somehow the rest of the party, not daring to lie down, lived through the night, the snow sometimes easing and then whipping down again in flurries. Shortly after six o'clock, however, the snow finally stopped and the sun came out. Banks sent three men to see if Richmond and Dorlton had somehow survived the night. They returned soon with the news that they had not, but they persuaded the greyhounds, clearly affected as much by the loss of their friends as by the cold and wet, to return with them.

A vulture had been shot the previous evening and Banks now ordered this to be skinned and divided into ten equal parts and individually cooked. This was done, providing three mouthfuls for each of them.

On board the *Endeavour* Cook had had a troubled night, knowing that the party was not equipped for sleeping in the open, and certainly not in the terrible weather of the past twelve hours. 'However, about noon they returned, in no very comfortable condition.' 'Mr Banks etc. returned very much fatigued,' confirmed Forwood. Bob Molyneux added, 'As soon as they came on board they refreshed themselves and were put into warm beds. The only exception was Banks, who on hearing that they would soon be sailing away from this bay, after the briefest pause and with undiminished enthusiasm, began combing the water about the ship with his seine, to add sea life to what Molyneux described as his recent 'valuable collection of alpine and other plants hitherto unknown in natural history'.

As it turned out, bad weather delayed their departure and Banks was able to go ashore again and gather shellfish ('disappointing') and more plants; and, by penetrating deeper in another direction, he came across the nearest thing to a village, with some fifty inhabitants, men, women and children. He was as unimpressed by their huts as by the inhabitants. The former 'consisted of a few poles set up and meeting together at top in a conical figure, these were covered on the weather side with a few boughs and a little grass'. Facetiously, he added that they had no furniture, 'very little grass laid round the edges of the circle furnished both beds and chairs'. There were no eating or cooking utensils, of course, just what must have been a guanaco's bladder for water storage.

These Fuegians had, of necessity, contrived quite sophisticated weapons in the form of bows and arrows. Midshipman John Bootie wrote: 'Their arms are bows and arrows neatly made and headed with glass* or flint cut in the shape of a dragon's tongue. These are loose to remain in the wound.' Cook noted that their favourite colour was red, and best of all they liked red beads, strings of beads formed of shells or bones being their 'whole pride'. He was unable to discover 'that they had any head or chief, or form of government,' and concluded that these Fuegians 'are perhaps as miserable a set of people as are this day upon earth'.

Banks took a more detailed and on the whole more charitable view of them. He wrote of the simplicity of their clothing, such as it was – a loosely worn cloak of guanaco or seal thrown carelessly over their shoulders, and nothing else. He also went into great detail about the painting of their faces with some sort of oil and dust:

When we went to their town there came two out to meet us who were daubed with black lines all manner of ways so as to form a most diabolical countenance imaginable, and these two seemed to exorcise us or at least made a loud and long harangue which did not seem to be addressed either to us or any of their countrymen.

None of these early accounts of the Oona people mentions the seal oil with which their skin was covered from birth to death and was the reason why they survived this climate.*

---

* Evidently a gift from Bougainville when he was in this bay. One of the natives tried eating it and died as a consequence, in spite of the ministrations of the surgeon.

On 20 January Cook ordered some last wooding and watering, and, as Parkinson wrote, 'we let down our guns and lumber below deck to be better prepared for the high gales which we expected in going round Cape Horn'. At the last minute an accident led to the loss of the kedge anchor, hawser and buoy, which for the men, and especially Cook, set the seal of dissatisfaction with this ill-named Bay of Good Success.

Banks, who greatly missed his two black servants, wrote his last journal entry as they faced the rigours of the next few days:

Sailed this morn, the wind foul, but our keeping boxes being full of new plants we little regarded any wind provided it was but moderate enough to let the draughtsmen work, who to do them justice are now so used to the sea that it must blow a gale of wind before they leave off.

* When missionaries arrived in Tierra del Fuego at the end of the nineteenth century and insisted on their wearing Western clothing, the Oona tribe was almost wiped out by pneumonia.

7

Mar del Pacifico

EARLY MORNING, 21 JANUARY 1769, with anchors stowed, the *Endeavour* sailed smoothly out of the Bay of Good Success with its incurious, primitive inhabitants. In alternating rain, mist and clear skies Cook took them on a south-westerly heading, with the shattered coastline of the southernmost Fuegian islands to starboard. The first three of these small and heavily wooded islands,* Lennox, Picton and Nueva (New), were all unnamed at this time except for the nearest which Cook prosaically called New Island because it was new to his chart.

Cook determined to take advantage of the smooth seas and press on, overriding his instinct to survey this coast with its numerous islands and dangerous rocky islets and inlets.

When he sighted Woolaston and behind it Isla Hermite, he knew that on the next day, however poor the visibility, they were certain to sight Horn island itself and the cape. As expected, on the morning of 25 January, several of his men thought that they could see the island. 'I am of a contrary opinion,' Cook wrote. 'The thick hazy weather which came on a little before noon put a stop to all observations.'

But the sharp-eyed men – Hicks among them – had been right. '. . . at 8 a.m. saw a remarkable sugar loaf like an island,' he wrote. '. . . it is the south-easternmost of several islands, large islands with many rocks at the extremity and I believe it to be Cape Horn.' The 1,400-foot-high bluff wedge, like some triangular granite headstone to the grave of a continent, was indeed Cape Horn. In these unsatisfactory conditions, Cook and Green fixed it at 55° 59' s, 68° 13' w, which was remarkably close to its real position of 55° 58' s, 67° 16' w. Parkinson was moved to comment, 'We doubled it with as little danger as the North Foreland on the Kentish coast.' So now, surely beyond dispute, they had logged

---

* They guard the entrance to the Beagle Channel, which runs approximately parallel with the Magellan Strait into the Pacific. The Chilean flag flies on all three and, although uninhabited, they are disputed with Argentina in view of the potential oil reserves in these seas.

the end of the American continent and could claim that they were sailing the waters of Magellan's Mar del Pacifico. But Cook was, as always, first concerned with the record and his judgment for future navigators in these parts. Comparing their passage into the Pacific with Wallis's he wrote: The *Dolphin* in her last voyage, which she performed at the same season of the year with ours, was three months in getting through the Strait of Magellan, exclusive of the time that she lay in Port Famine; and I am persuaded, from the winds we had, that if we had come by that passage, we should not at this time have been in these seas; that our people would have been fatigued, and our anchors, cables, sails and rigging much damaged.

At the same time he also denied Anson's contention that it was better to avoid the Straits of le Maire and 'constantly pass to the eastward of Staten Land'. If the winds were favourable, as they had been for him, Cook claimed, it saved a great amount of time to follow his route. 'We were not once brought under our close-reefed topsails after we left the Strait of le Maire,' he emphasised. His luck may have been wonderful and rare, but that is as much a navigator's ingredient for success as for a general in battle.

Cook took no chances and continued far to the south of Cape Horn in mainly foul weather and negligible visibility, until, by his reckoning, the *Endeavour* was in latitude 69° s, where he swung on to a more westerly heading. But Cape Horn had deceived him, as it had so many mariners, for at 2 p.m. on Saturday, 28 January, he 'saw land bearing north distant about 8 leagues. It made in two hummocks, which I take to be the Isles of Diego Ramírez . . .' It was South America's final act of trickery which has led to many a shipwreck since these islets were charted by the cosmographer of that name on 12 February 1619, when the Portuguese Nodal brothers were doubling the Horn. 'Although it was high summer,' the Nodals wrote, 'there were strong gales every day, with furious squalls, much cold and snow.' A landing was out of the question. These islets are the end beyond the end, the last emergence of the Andes.

The Diego Ramírez islets stretch north-south over three miles, from Roca Norte, mere rocks as the name suggests, to Isla Bartolomé and Isla Gonzalo, after the brothers. Both are beaten by perpetual surf breaking against the west side, sending spray clear over them.*

THERE WAS NOT A MAN in the *Endeavour*'s company who was not surprised at the calm of these Cape Horn waters, even those who

---

* The author made a brief landing on Bartolomé, which boasts a minute sheltered beach, in 1969. The vegetation is tussock grass and the birds include three breeds of penguin, ferocious black corvids – 'Johnny Rooks' – and grey-headed albatrosses, all amazing to behold and unafraid, except the aggressive corvids.

had been here before. But it also meant that they made very little progress and the Diego Ramírez islets remained in sight for two days. On the last day of January, Banks reported 'very fine weather'; and on the following day he had a boat lowered and shot birds for identification and for drawing by Parkinson. They included a sooty albatross, *Phoebetria palpebrata*, and a black-billed albatross, *Diomedia antarctica*. He composed a little essay on these beautiful great birds, and the Mother Carey's Dove, which also became a victim of his gun.

Banks had no compunction about eating these albatrosses, pronouncing them excellent. He added a recipe for his readers, even if there might be little opportunity for finding any in London's Billingsgate market: 'Skin them overnight and soak their carcasses in salt water till morn, then parboil them and throw away the water, then stew them well with very little water and when sufficiently tender serve them up with savoury sauce.' Was it *Diomedia*'s revenge that led to Banks's severe bilious attack which laid him low for four days, the only time he was sick of the stomach on the voyage?

For the next eight weeks the *Endeavour* maintained a north-westerly heading, not always with favourable winds (at one point, Banks notes, 'we have not had the name of East in the wind since 31st January'); on other days the ship was almost without motion, whilst on 24 February she was logged at seven knots, 'no very usual thing with Mrs Endeavour'.

Day by day as the latitude lessened – 35° on 9 March – and the temperature rose, the men discarded their fearnoughts. Banks 'began the new month [March] by pulling off an under-waistcoat'. A few days later the temperature hit 70° F for the first time since they had left Brazilian waters. The old hands who had been to Tahiti before began retelling their experiences, especially with the lusty native women, stirring dormant libidos.

These men had little to complain about. Food and rum were ample. Even the water from Tierra del Fuego had not deteriorated as it usually did when 'brought from a cold climate into a hot one', as Banks remarked. 'It is now as clear as any English spring water.'

This long and pleasant passage was, however, marked by one tragedy which contained a poignant and affecting note quite out of proportion to the loss of one of the men. He was a twenty-one-year-old marine named William Greenslade, a quiet, withdrawn lad who had given no cause for complaint in his duties. At noon on 25 March he was on sentry duty at the door of the great cabin, which Cook shared with Banks and the other gentlemen, and, it seemed, had been entrusted with the safekeeping of a piece of sealskin which was to be cut up and made into tobacco pouches. Why this skin was deposited with Greenslade, who had begged unsuccessfully for a share, cannot be answered, but it seems likely that there was some mischievous plot behind it. Anyway, as soon as he was alone, this marine cut himself enough of the skin for his purpose and was, of course, found out later by its owner.

This unnamed fellow marine was extremely angry, but declared that the crime was too petty to be reported. Unhappily the other marines got wind of the incident and upbraided Greenslade mercilessly. Banks learnt later what had followed:

Sergeant John Edgcumbe particularly declared that if the person aggrieved would not complain he would, for people should not suffer scandal from the ill behaviour of one. This affected the young fellow much, he went to his hammock. Soon after, the sergeant . . . told him to follow him upon deck. He got up and, slipping the sergeant, went forward. It was dusk and the people thought he was gone to the head [lavatory] and were not convinced that he was gone overboard till half an hour after it happened.

Of all the wonderful Pacific seabirds they saw, and often shot, on this voyage, none caused greater wonder than the red-tailed tropic bird, named by Banks *Phaeton erubescens* (today *Phaeton rubricauda*), a beautiful bird, all white but for an orange beak and two long, scarlet feathers extending from the singular divided tail, likened to a boatswain's marlin, thus its later slang name bo's'n-birds. The men on deck watched in admiration at the way these big, graceful birds could wheel so nimbly in the air and then drop like a stone to the sea. Banks took out a boat and shot one, along with several petrels.

Land-based birds began to appear in the early days of April as the *Endeavour* approached the Tuamotus, the archipelago which stretches north-west by west between latitudes 19° and 15°s. Not surprisingly, many had been sighted and charted by earlier voyagers, but as the first appeared like a small smudge on the horizon after weeks of empty seas, it created great excitement. Alerted by his servant, Peter Briscoe, Banks left his cabin.

We stood towards it [he noted] and found it to be a small island about 1½ or 2 miles in length. Those who were upon the topmast head distinguished it to be nearly circular and to have a lagoon or pool of water in the middle which occupied much the largest part of the island.

Cook named it Lagoon Island and carefully drew it. From a mile distant he could distinguish a gathering of natives, tall, dark and stark naked. They held twelve-foot-long pikes in their hands, perhaps as a gesture of defiance at the sudden appearance of this vast canoe manned by white men. Banks and Solander would gladly have landed, as always, defying any hostile reception, but Cook was now hell-bent for Tahiti, not more than ten days' sailing time distant, in order to allow comfortable time for preparing the observatory.

Later Cook attracted the venomous pen of Dalrymple for failing to explore and chart these islands, some of which had been mentioned by Quiros back in 1606. But Cook, ever the explorer at heart and by instinct, kept his priorities intact. There would be plenty of time to linger and search later.

As for Banks and Solander, their interest in these little islands and islets never wavered. They recorded how the natives of several islands put off in canoes but came no closer than the reefs which almost surrounded most of the islands; how they gestured with their weapons, in greeting or defiance it was impossible to tell; how fires were lit as if in celebration at one island, while at another the natives disdainfully affected not even to glance towards the ship. At another, Cook brought the *Endeavour* close enough in so that Banks could even describe their hair-styles: 'tied back with a fillet which passed round their head and kept it sticking out behind like a bush'.

On one evening, as they approached a larger island than they had seen before although just as low and densely wooded, Banks left the dinner table when he heard of its sighting. He climbed the mainmast 'and remained at the mast head the whole evening admiring its extraordinary structure: in shape it appeared to be like a longbow, the wood and string of which was land and the parts within occupied by a large lake of water'.

Cook closed the land, and Hicks 'affirmed that he saw from the deck many inhabitants in the first clump of trees, that they were walking to and fro as if on their ordinary business without taking the least notice of the ship'. His fellow lieutenant, John Gore, noted in his journal: 'We saw inhabitants and their houses, proas* hauled up near them . . . The island is covered in trees and has a beautiful grove of coconuts on the east end.' Cook, of course, called it Bow Island; it is Hao today.

And so the *Endeavour*'s passage continued through the Tuamotos, no day without interest, more especially human interest. Except at what Cook named Bird Island – there were no natives but many birds – Banks for once gave more attention to the islands than the

* A double-ended canoe with an outrigger.

sky and sea, though two large fish attracted his attention. One was what the men called a King Fish, which they caught on a towing line baited with pork rind. Then, on the evening of 10 April, some of the men caught a Blew shark, *Prionace glauca*. It was attacking their next day's dinner which was being 'freshened' by being towed astern in a net. They had seen few fish for many days, but at dawn the following morning two more sharks were caught under the stern. These were common grey sharks, unlike the Blew with its 'abominably strong' smell, and were edible, making a welcome change in their diet.

Later that same morning, through rain squalls, the towering peaks of Tahiti were intermittently and dimly seen. At the same time the sky was suddenly full of birds, best of all tropic birds, swooping about the *Endeavour* in joyous welcome.

IT WAS ALMOST TWO YEARS since John Gore and others who had sailed with Wallis in the *Dolphin* made the first sighting of Tahiti on 19 June 1767. They had caught glimpses, through thick mist, of what they thought were high mountains the evening before, and on this day at 3 p.m., 'thanks be to the Almighty, we were not disappointed in our hopes ... We saw the land bearing w½s. It appeared to be a great high mountain [7,273 feet] covered with cloud ... This made us all rejoice', wrote the *Dolphin*'s master, George Robertson, 'and filled us with the greatest hopes imaginable ... We now supposed we saw the long wished-for Southern Continent which has often been talked of but never before seen by any Europeans.'

Thanks partly to the weather being thick and hazy and partly to their need to give attention to the excited natives and to provisioning, wooding and watering their ship, the illusion that Tahiti – King George's Land – was a northern extension of *Terra Australis Incognita* was retained for most of their brief stay at the island.

On that earlier voyage John Gore had experienced trouble with the natives and, although their intentions may have been innocent, their numbers were so great and their excitement so pressing that, in defending his little rowing boat, he had ordered shots to be fired, resulting in the death of one Tahitian and injury to another. But during the following four weeks relations were mainly cordial, and they had been begged to stay for longer. It was easier for Cook. The islanders knew now the destructive power of the white men in their great canoe and also the benefits of trading.

Banks saw early evidence of this:

13 April 1769

This morn early came to anchor in Port Royal [Matavai] Bay ... Before the anchor was down we were surrounded by a large number of canoes who traded very quietly and civilly, for beads chiefly, in exchange for which they gave coconuts, breadfruit, both roasted and raw, small fish and apples ... As soon as the anchors were well down the boats were hoisted out and we all went ashore, where we were met by some hundreds of the inhabitants whose faces at least gave evident signs that we were not unwelcome guests.

Parkinson, too, was pleasantly surprised by the warm welcome:

The 12th, the sea being mostly calm in the forenoon, we could get very little nearer land; but many of the Indians came off to us in canoes (one of which was double, and had much carved work on it) bringing with them cocoa nuts, and apples to truck for nails, buttons, and beads. These canoes were but just wide enough for one person to sit in the breadth: to prevent them from over-setting, they place out riggers, upon the top of which is fixed a bamboo fishing rod. The people in the canoes

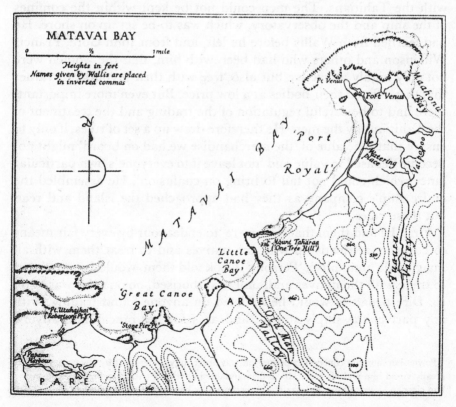

were of a pale, tawny complexion, and had long black hair. They seemed
to be very good natured, and not of a covetous disposition [but see below];
giving us a couple of cocoa nuts, or a basket of apples, for a button,
or a nail.

. . . Toward night we opened the NW point, and discovered the island
named by the *Dolphin*'s people, York Island, and called by the natives,
Eimayo [today Moorea]. A breeze springing up, we lay off and on all
that night; and, on the 13th, we made the island of Otaheite, called
by the *Dolphin*'s people George's Island . . . We entered Port Royal
harbour and anchored in nine fathoms of water, within half a mile of
the shore. The land appeared as uneven as a piece of crumpled paper,
being divided irregularly into hills and valleys; but a beautiful verdure
covered both, even to the tops of the highest peaks. A great number
of natives came off to us in canoes, and brought with them bananas,
cocoas, breadfruit, apples, and some pigs; but they were errant thieves;
and, while I was busied in the forenoon in trucking with them for
some of their cloth one of them pilfered* an earthen vessel out of my
cabin . . .

Long before his arrival at Tahiti, where they were to remain for
many weeks, Cook had recognised that there would be difficulties
with the Tahitians. The men could not be kept within the confines
of the ship and the observatory, which was to be set up on shore. He
had learned from Wallis before he left, and from John Gore, Francis
Wilkinson and others who had been with him, that the women were
not only highly attractive but also 'free with their favours', or rather
that they offered their bodies at a low price. But even more important,
there had to be careful regulation of the trading and the treatment of
the Tahitians by the men. He therefore drew up a set of rules, if only to
ensure that the value of 'the merchandise we had on board' might not
become debased in value and 'not leave it to everyone's own particular
fancy which could not fail to bring on confusion'. He assembled the
entire ship's company as they had approached the island and read
out these rules.

First, he told them that they were 'to endeavour by every fair means
to cultivate a friendship with the natives and to treat them with all
imaginable humanity'. 'Persons', Cook told them, would be appointed
to trade with the natives and, unless authorised, no one else was to do
so. Dire penalties would be inflicted on anyone found trading 'with
any part of the ship's stores'; and as a further precaution, anyone

---

* Polynesian morality concerning possession was never fully understood by Cook, and
greatly vexed him and his men. His understandable impatience with thieving was to bring
him close to violence time and again, and occasionally he was known to resort to it.

suffering loss of tools or arms or any other property would have it charged against his pay 'and suffer such further punishment as the nature of the offence may deserve'.

On the following morning, 14 April, Sydney Parkinson was on deck early, casting his artist's eye over the extraordinary scene presented to him: to the south the Pacific rollers sounded a continuous thunder on the reef, which, with few breaks, surrounded the island like a white bracelet; on the land side the wavelets reduced to puny proportions by this reef broke on the shore of black volcanic sand; then, behind the beach, the rising forests of breadfruit, coconut and other trees folded into valleys but still rose more and more steeply to the soaring, cloud-topped peaks.

By contrast with these masses of volcanic mountains, and less than a mile south of the anchored *Endeavour*, was an isolated hillock called by the natives Mount Taharaa, and by Wallis One Tree Hill for its single breadfruit on its summit. Then, to complete this panorama of enchantment, there were the rivers tumbling down the ravines, the nearest and biggest, the River Vaipopoo, which ran parallel with the black beach for more than half a mile, emerged at the headland marking the conclusion of Matavai Bay.

The sun had only recently risen, the temperature soaring with it, and before Parkinson descended to the cabin he saw a great number of canoes approaching from the south-east and heading swiftly towards the *Endeavour*. The natives, all male, did not behave in a hostile manner when they came alongside, but they exhibited a determination of purpose which caused Parkinson, and the men on watch, a certain anxiety. As they clambered on board they 'were very troublesome, attempting to steal everything they could lay their hands on'. There were dozens of them milling about and there were several scuffles with the sailors on watch.

The situation was saved by the arrival soon after of several more canoes, double ones this time, containing men who appeared to be of a different caste. 'Their clothes, carriage and behaviour evinced their superiority,' Parkinson noted. He also commented on their stateliness, 'having a pleasant countenance, large black eyes, black hair, and white teeth'. At this point Cook appeared on deck, singled out at once these elite Tahitians by their more elaborate dress – fine cloaks and turbans – as well as by their bearing, and invited them down to the cabin. Here these chieftains were entertained by Cook, Hicks and Gore as well as the 'gentlemen'.

With a singular lack of self-consciousness and with much gravitas, these chieftains took the social initiative, each chieftain selecting one of the officers and gentlemen as his own. Then, patting their breasts, they uttered several times the word *tao*, or 'friend', to which the *Endeavour*'s men responded in kind. Then the natives began undressing and slipping their cloaks over the shoulders of their *tao*. 'In return for this,' Banks noted, 'we presented them each [with] a hatchet and some beads.' It was altogether a pleasant occasion, and a promising start.

Meanwhile, up on deck the rough mob, whose behaviour was evidently much deplored by the chieftains, were prevailed upon to return to their canoes. They were from a different tribe from the locals, and with long, sweeping strokes with their paddles soon thankfully disappeared round a headland to the south-west.

The men took their dinner as usual on the mess deck, the officers in their cabin. The menu was the same as if they were still at sea, and Cook and his two lieutenants agreed that one of their first priorities must be to obtain fresh fruit and fresh meat – Wallis had waxed lyrical about the island's pork. So Cook ventured ashore for the first time that afternoon, hoping for some trade and also, as he put it, 'to try the disposition of the natives' and to confirm that the ship was anchored in the most favourable position. Cook was rowed in one boat with Banks and his party, while the officers, supported by Royal Marines, followed in another boat. Even before the stems of these two boats pierced the black, soft sand, some natives who had emerged from the trees swarmed around them with every sign of welcome and friendship.

John Gore, however, who remembered this bay from his last visit when Wallis named it Great Canoe Bay, was dismayed by the lack of numbers and the virtual disappearance of the community as he had known it:

I now expected to see the natives come off in their canoes [he wrote later] and among them some of our old acquaintances, but was disappointed in all except one, who is a man who first entered among the *Dolphin*'s people after their skirmish ... We then went into the woods [he continued, referring to the present] where almost everything was altered for the worse ... For instance, of a number of fine houses dispersed among the trees, many inhabitants of the better sort, a large number of large canoes lying round the bay in sheds, and others building among the trees ... hogs and fowls about the houses; instead of all this found a few temporary huts with a few of the inferior sort of inhabitants.

Cook was equally disappointed at 'the great number of houses raiz'd ... and not so much as a hog or fowl to be seen – no very agreeable discovery to us whose ideas of plenty upon our arrival at this island [from the report of the *Dolphin*] was carried to the very highest pitch'.

Had there been a war? Or a plague? Gore noticed that the natives here had 'an inveterate itch or yaws* & on account of this we imagine the principle people have abandoned the place'. Whatever the cause, it was deeply disturbing to return to the ship, after a brief walk through the woods, without so much as a single breadfruit or coconut to supplement the ship's rations.

NOW, SUDDENLY, the *Endeavour's* company were the guests of a people with ways alien to their experience and, to a large degree, to their understanding. Their lives, willy-nilly, were governed overall by the behaviour of their hosts. Militarily, they were infinitely more powerful than the Tahitians. And, as the visitors were soon to learn, their hosts were an exceedingly volatile people with a morality and with customs quite different from their own, as the events of the next day were to confirm.

The second day in Matavai Bay began well. The same chiefs from the nearest settlement were paddled out to the *Endeavour* and welcomed on board by Cook and Banks. As if now aware of the first needs of their visitors, they brought with them hogs, breadfruit and other fruit and vegetables. Cook made clear by sign and expression how much these were appreciated, and in his turn was lavish in his offer of 'hatchets, linen and such things as they valued'.

After these exchanges of goods and friendly gestures, the chieftains again indicated that they should come ashore. Banks wrote, 'the boats were hoisted out and we took them with us and immediately proceeded according to their directions'. After rowing a league and, escorted by many excited natives, walking some distance into the woods, they arrived at what Banks called 'a long house'. This was the *ario*-house at Point Utuhaihai, at the extreme south of Matavai Bay. It was the throne room for a very aged and very grand chief, to whom Banks gave the name Hercules 'for the large size of his body'.

After greetings of the warmest nature, mats were spread by attendants and the visitors encouraged to sit upon them. At once a cock and a hen were brought in and given, respectively, to Cook and Banks.

Then a piece of cloth was presented to each of us [Banks recorded], perfumed after their manner not disagreeably ... My piece was 11 yards long and 2 wide: for this I made return by presenting him with a large laced silk neckcloth I had on and a linen pocket handkerchief, these he immediately put on him and seemed to be much pleased with.

---

* Yaws, also known as framboesia, caused the eruption of tumours covered with yellow spots over any part of the body.

Banks was inclined to describe the next stage of their welcome rather coyly, while Cook left no record of it:

We walked freely about several large houses attended by the ladies who shewed us all kind of civilities our situation could admit of, but as there were no places of retirement, the houses being entirely without walls, we had not an opportunity of putting their politeness to every test that maybe some of us would not have failed to have done had circumstances been more favourable; indeed we had no reason to doubt any part of their politeness, as by their frequently pointing to the mats on the ground and sometimes by force seating themselves and us upon them they plainly showed that they were much less jealous of observation than we were.

These Tahitians were more successful in their hospitality with food, for in a few minutes the officers and gentlemen found themselves sitting cross-legged on fresh mats before a feast, including fish both raw and cooked, plantains and breadfruit. Banks was placed next to Hercules's aged wife – 'ugly enough in conscience' – who personally fed him with fish and coconut milk, even after Banks had given all his attention to 'a very pretty girl with a fire in her eyes that I had not before seen in this country' whom he bribed with beads to come and sit close to him on the other side.

This pleasant but bizarre scene was suddenly ended when Dr Solander and surgeon Monkhouse found that their pockets had been picked and that they had lost an opera glass in its case and a snuffbox. The complaint was addressed with some emphasis to Hercules. When Banks heard of the loss, he leapt to his feet, ignoring his hostesses, and 'striking the butt of my gun made a rattling noise which I had before used to frighten the people and keep them at a distance'.

The threat worked again and in a trice everyone, including Banks's fiery girl, ran out of sight, leaving only Hercules, his three wives and one or two cronies. This chief tried to make amends by indicating that Banks should help himself to any quantity he wished from a pile of cloth. Banks angrily refused, indicating that all he wanted were the stolen items. It was all sorted out amicably in the end, Hercules himself marching off and recovering them from the culprit whose petty crime he had no doubt witnessed.

There were still more than six weeks before the observation of the transit of Venus, but Cook and Green had determined to set up their observatory in good time. They had also decided that it should be incorporated within a fort, well armed with some of the ship's guns. Although these people seemed peaceable enough, they had learned – as had Wallis before them – that the island was subject to tribal warfare. They had already heard of a king who lived at the far end of Tahiti, at Little Tahiti, or Tahiti-iti, King Tiarreboo, who waged war from time to time and was much feared. Cook was determined to take every precaution against a surprise attack by him and his people, or even by Hercules and another chief Banks had named Lycurgus, after the mythical god of Sparta, who might turn against their guests and treat them as invaders. Cook and Banks had already witnessed the volatility of their immediate hosts, and this was to be confirmed by the events of the following day, only the third since their arrival.

Cook had settled on the provisional site of his fort/observatory from calculations made on board the *Endeavour*. It was a sandy spit marking both the north-eastern tip of Matavai Bay and the estuary of the River Vaipopoo. The trees thinned out here leaving a sky open to the telescopes and on a beach of no possible value to the natives. He had already marked it on his chart Point Venus, a name that is retained to this day. (A monument is placed there, albeit inaccurately, and the river is now reduced to a doubtful stream.)

On Saturday morning, 15 April, with the weather fine and clouds confined to the mountain tops, Cook went ashore again to take possession of Point Venus, knowing that this occasion demanded tact and firmness. In his party were Banks, Dr Solander, Green, Parkinson, young Midshipman Jonathan Monkhouse and all the marines, led by Sergeant John Edgcumbe. They were met on the beach by a large gathering of natives, who had evidently recovered their nerve from the previous day and showed every sign of friendliness and interest in what they were about. 'Not one of them had any weapon either offensive or defensive,' Cook noted.

Amongst them, and treated deferentially, was a very old chief, who was remembered by John Gore, Bob Molyneux and the other *Dolphin* people. Molyneux was also looking forward to meeting Queen Obadia, a woman of some importance whom he remembered affectionately. Wasting no time, Cook took his musket as a marker and drew a long line in the sand, indicating to the natives that they must never cross it. As an emollient, he also attempted to tell them in sign language that men from the big ship would sleep here for a number of nights, and then leave for ever. The natives still showed no signs of hostility although Cook was not at all certain that they had understood his message. He then ordered the tent they had brought with them to be erected.

Leaving young Monkhouse and the marines to guard this territory, Cook led the others on a search for trade, more especially for hogs and hens for which they had a great need. The expedition started off startlingly well. Shortly after wading across the river, some ducks arose in alarm. Banks swiftly raised his musket, which was loaded with birdshot, fired and killed three at once. This led to many congratulations, but to the natives who were following them it came as a miracle and many of them fell to the ground 'as though they had been shot likewise', Cook commented.

Later, and just as Cook was about to reverse their course and return, they heard the ominous, distant sound of musket fire. They ran back in a state of anxiety. What a start to their enterprise! Everything depended on maintaining good relations with the natives. What on earth had happened?

It seemed that a single (corpulent) Tahitian had crossed the line, had made a dash at one of the marines, knocked him over, seized his musket and run off. Monkhouse had immediately ordered all the marines to open fire on the fleeing crowd. Many were injured and the culprit shot dead, although another native picked up the musket and got away. Only courageous old Hercules had remained behind.

Banks judged the action taken as imprudent. 'If we quarrelled with those Indians,' he was heard to remark, 'we should not agree with angels.' Parkinson exclaimed, 'What a pity that such brutality should be exercised by civilized people upon unarmed ignorant Indians!'

Cook now rather desperately set about repairing broken fences. With Hercules's co-operation, he managed to persuade some twenty Tahitians to return. Using sign language he then got them with their chief to sit down by the tent, where we 'endeavoured by every means in our power to convince them that the man was killed for taking away the musket and that we would be friends with them. At sunset they left us, seemingly satisfied, and we struck our tent and went on board.'

For Parkinson it had been a miserable and disappointing day. He was a sensitive and gentle young man, and this was not the first occasion when he had been shocked by his shipmates' attitude and behaviour to the natives. He was fearful that a killing like that might blow up into full-scale warfare. This would result in making impossible the astronomical observations, the *raison d'être* of this expedition. More important from this artist's point of view, it would put an end to the comprehensive plan to draw all the flora and fauna of the island.

Parkinson was seized with even greater anxiety when he came back on board the *Endeavour*. Alex Buchan had suffered another epileptic fit, a more serious one this time, and had been unconscious all day. He never recovered consciousness. The surgeon could do nothing for him and he soon died.

This was a dreadful blow. Not only did Parkinson like and admire his fellow artist, but it also meant that he would have to do the drawings for both of them, 'figure and landscape', as well as take over all his botanical responsibilities. Fearing trouble with the Tahitians if Buchan's body were buried ashore, Cook conducted an immediate service, 'and we went out in the pinnace and longboat to the offing, and buried him'.

For Cook this was the lowest point of the voyage so far, and he went to bed that night deeply disturbed.

8

Venus Observed

THE MORNING AFTER THE BURIAL AT SEA of Alex Buchan was dour with intermittent showers. Cook, casting aside his gloom, determined to start work on the fort/observatory. He took ashore as many men as could be spared, equipped with spades, saws, axes and bill hooks for digging and cutting wood.*

By midday Point Venus, viewed from the anchored *Endeavour*, resembled the proverbial ants' nest, alive with figures darting to and fro, bringing wood from the forest, digging trenches, throwing up a bank of mixed black sand and soil and erecting a stout fence with pointed uprights. This scene of industry was enhanced by the increasing number of Tahitians who, 'so far from hindering us', enthusiastically joined in the activities, regarding the whole business as tremendous fun. Cook encouraged this participation and, at the same time, was punctilious in all his arrangements with them, never failing to ask permission before cutting down a tree and then offering gifts in payment.

At noon he decreed that fresh pork should be cooked for his men as a reward for their labours. It had already become clear that pigs were few and small and those available commanded the price of an axe. But it was also evident that the *Endeavour* had chosen to arrive at the height of one of the three annual breadfruit seasons. Nor was there any shortage of coconuts, yams and plantains.

Although they could not understand what was going on, the curiosity of the Tahitians increased with the advance of construction, and Chief Lycurgus turned up one day with his entire extensive family. Cook understood that he had come 'to live near us [bringing] with him the covering of a house with several other materials for building one.'

* Molyneux remarks: 'A party of men was now mustered to go on shore to do duty consisting of 50 men (including the Marines who were to do duty as sentinels) to erect a fort for the defence of the observatory . . .'

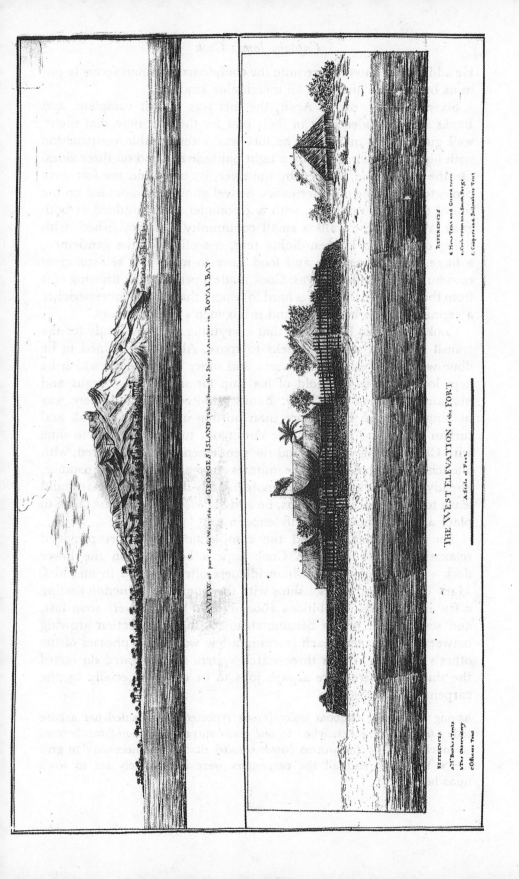

A VIEW of part of the West side of GEORGE'S ISLAND taken from the Ship at Anchor in ROYAL BAY

REFERENCES
a N.º Banks's Tents
b The Observatory
c Officers Tent

THE WEST ELEVATION of the FORT
A Scale of Feet.

REFERENCES
d Mess Tent and Guard room
e Cook room and Smith Forge
f Coopers and Sailmakers Tent

He added: 'We intend to requite the confidence this man seems to put in us by treating him with all imaginable kindness.'

Six days later, on 22 April, the fort was almost complete, and Banks and Solander slept in their tent for the first time that night, well guarded by marines. The fort was a remarkable construction with high walls supported by a tight palisade of wood on three sides. On the fourth side, flanked by the river, its bank and the fort were protected by a line of water casks. Swivel guns were mounted on the top of the castle ramparts, with a 4-pounder cannon added at both ends. Within these walls a small community was established, with living quarters, a kitchen-dining tent, a section for the gentlemen, a forge, and a magazine and food store to make it a self-sufficient community, all under canvas. Cook made a pen-and-ink drawing of it from the deck of his ship. It is hard to believe that he did not experience a certain pride in his design and in his men's achievements.

Cook could also be pleased that everything was now ready for the transit of Venus with six weeks to spare. All that remained to be done was to set up the telescopes and other instruments, which he kept locked up in the hold of his ship for security. Lycurgus and his family enjoyed their stay. Banks admired him; and there was nothing Lycurgus liked more than putting on his finest cloak and turban and being rowed in the cutter out to the *Endeavour* to dine with Cook and his officers, and the gentlemen. Banks observed, with a touch of xenophobia, that 'he imitates our manners in every instance, already holding a knife and fork more handily than a Frenchman could learn to do in years'. Lycurgus, he added, 'seems in every instance to place a most unbounded confidence in us'.

The weeks that followed the completion of the fort provided relaxation for all although Cook kept a keen eye on the lower deck – the 'people' – for whom idleness often resulted in mischief. Many of them had relationships with the women, a seduction costing a few illegal nails. Inhibitions about lack of privacy were soon lost, and some of the affairs became steady with real affection growing between the partners, each learning a few words and phrases of the other's language. But a three-watch system still operated on board the ship and there were always jobs to be done, especially by the carpenters. For example,

having found the longboat leaky [Cook reported], we hauled her ashore today to stop the leaks, when to our great surprise we found her bottom so much eaten by the worms [*teredo navalis*] that it was necessary to give her a new one, and all the carpenters were immediately set to work upon her.

Suitably, Sunday brought the visitors and Tahitians together. On 14 May, for example, Molyneux tells us that one of the ship's tents within the fort was fitted out for a service. The officiation was a duty Cook was happy to pass on to one of his officers, though he occasionally conducted it himself:

Divine Service was performed by Mr Monkhouse the surgeon; as many of the principal natives were admitted as we conveniently could and there was a vast concourse of people without the fort. The whole thing was conducted very quietly, those in the tent doing as we did, kneeling, standing or sitting. They understood perfectly that we were speaking to our God . . . as they themselves worship an invisible and omnipotent being.

Only occasionally were there difficulties in relations with the Tahitians. Unfortunately, one isolated case involved Lycurgus. After dining with Banks and the other gentlemen one evening and leaving the fort in his usual amiable temper, he returned 'with fire in his eyes', as Banks described him; 'he seized my arm and signalled to me to follow him'. It appeared that Henry Jeffs, the ship's butcher, who was no doubt drunk, had indicated to his wife that he wanted to purchase the chief's stone hatchet, offering a nail in payment. When this was refused, Jeffs threw down the nail, seized the axe and 'threatened to cut her throat if she attempted to hinder him'.

Banks intercepted the butcher, who scarcely bothered to defend himself, and Lycurgus was mollified, but still angry, until Banks promised that the butcher would 'tomorrow be punished'. Molyneux now takes up this curious tale:

The Captain invited the offended parties [Lycurgus's large family] on board who were ignorant of his intention. All hands being called and the prisoner brought aft, the Captain explained the nature of his crime in the most lively manner and made a very pathetic [emotional] speech to the ship's company. During his [lashing], the women were in the greatest agonies and strongly interceded for him.

'This is a good example of Cook's even-handed justice,' was Beaglehole's comment on the affair.

This was the only serious incident between Tahitians and ship's crew for which Cook's men could be held responsible, which says much for their conduct, especially as they were in daily and often intimate contact with them. Perhaps this was the reason why Queen Obadia, with whom the *Dolphin*'s men had formed a good relationship two years earlier, now made herself known.

On the morning of 28 April a middle-aged woman arrived at the fort with her entourage. Banks welcomed her into his tent. Almost immediately, Molyneux arrived from the ship and, as he stepped inside, recognised the Queen from his previous visit. 'I was overjoyed and introduced her to all the gentlemen present.' She, as instantly, recognised the ship's master and was evidently happy to see him again. He introduced her to Banks, who was relieved that he had offered her hospitality as soon as he had set eyes upon her. He later wrote of this meeting with Molyneux's one-time mistress:

Our attention was now entirely diverted from every other object to the examination of a personage we had heard so much spoken of in Europe: she appeared to be about 40, tall and very lusty, her skin white and her eyes full of meaning. She might have been handsome when young, but now few or no traces of it were left.

Banks then intimated that she might like to go on board the *Endeavour* and she seemed pleased at the suggestion, bringing with her two men and six women of her family/entourage. Cook was on deck when the cutter headed for his ship, and, sizing up the situation, was at the gangway when the Queen climbed the steps. He greeted her as if she were George III's Queen Charlotte, piling gifts on her and offering her finally 'a child's doll which I made her understand was a picture of my wife. As soon as we came ashore she fastened it to her breast, took my hand and led me first this way and then that, her people all the while crowding about us to get a sight of the doll.'

Both Cook and Banks were puzzled about her real standing with the Tahitians. She was certainly chief of her tribe and unrelated to Lycurgus, but she did not appear to have authority over other tribes and was not queen of the island. Nor did they understand whether or not she was queen consort to Hercules. A curious incident which occurred when Cook went ashore did not clarify the relationship. Both Hercules and the Queen were with Banks in the fort's main tent and there was tension in the air. Hercules was looking highly displeased as the Queen continued to flaunt her gifts. The only remedy, it seemed to Cook, was to offer equal gifts to Hercules, so he took the chief – or king? – back to the *Endeavour*. Hercules was offered a wide range of gifts, but he ignored everything, even axes, until he caught sight of a doll similar to the Queen's. He now returned to the shore a happy man.

Banks adds a footnote to this incident, informing us that, like spoilt children, very soon neither doll owner took any further interest in them, and we can assume that some fortunate members of the entourage took possession of them instead. He also mentions an incident which further clouds the Queen's relationship with Hercules. Judging it desirable to make a courtesy call on her the following day, Banks was directed to her canoe, which was drawn up on the beach. He

was surprised to find her in bed [under the awning] with a handsome lusty young man ... I however soon understood that he was her gallant, a circumstance which she made not the least secret of. Upon my arrival her majesty proceeded to put on her skirt, which done she clothed me in fine cloth and proceeded with me to the tents.

What Molyneux made of this incident is not recorded.

Three weeks later, it seemed, the Queen wearied of her gallant and Banks himself was offered the role in his place. Referring to his status at home, he reminded his readers, 'I am at present otherwise engaged; indeed was I free as air, her majesty's person is not the most desirable.'

Banks was evidently considered as a 'catch' among the better class of women. He was indeed young and good looking and, besides, was a man of evident authority. By the middle of May Banks had as a more or less constant companion and aide a bright young man called Tupia. He was a one-time priest who had been driven from his native island of nearby Raiatea when it was invaded by the fierce neighbouring warriors of Bora-Bora. He had prospered in Tahiti and, because of his intelligence and fetching ways, was promoted to become the Queen's chief priest.

Banks was glad to have Tupia at his side when, as was his custom, after breakfast he was at the entrance to the fort in the hope of conducting trade, for which he was the authorised official. A grand double canoe came into sight in Matavai Bay with a man and three young women under the awning. The quality of the canoe, its size, its carvings at the prow and the elegance of its sail were as sure a guide to the status of its occupants as a carriage in St James's, London. This was a very grand one. The nearest natives about the fort indicated to Banks that he should go out to meet these dignitaries, and he did so, with Tupia at his side. Banks greeted them respectfully and ordered his oarsmen to follow the canoe to the shore. Once landed again, the locals gathered and quickly formed a lane between the two parties on the beach.

It was clear to Banks that he faced another wearisome ceremony. He had suffered several already, and though not without interest, they were very long. This was no exception. The man who had been under the awning with the women now advanced down the passage clutching a bunch of boughs, which he formally presented to Banks, who received them with matching formality, handing them to Tupia, who in turn placed them in the drawn-up boat. Six times this was conducted, while Banks kept his impatience at bay. He was rewarded (up to a point) when a second man advanced with a number of lengths of cloth. Three of these he placed in a line on the ground towards Banks.

'The foremost of the women, who seemed to be the principal,' Banks noted, then stepped forward, 'quickly unveiling all her charms' and turned round slowly so that nothing could be missed. Three more lengths of cloth were then laid and the same procedure followed, until finally, while the man lifted the cloths behind her as she advanced, she stood before Banks. After a moment, and a last pirouette, she presented all the cloth to Banks. Followed by Tupia carrying the phallic boughs and lengths of cloth, Banks took her by the hand and led her to his tent. Another girl followed. Banks told how he lavished presents on both of them, but then added enigmatically, 'I could not prevail upon them to stay more than an hour.' Readers were presumably expected to draw their own conclusions, in spite of his 'engagement' at home.

The various ways in which the gentlemen and officers occupied themselves reflected their personalities. After three weeks Banks had exhausted the botanical range of the island, although he would still take long walks with Dr Solander, bringing back improved specimens of what he had already. Bob Molyneux enjoyed nothing more than to go out shooting, especially at a large swamp

that abounds with duck and teal and some birds like snipe; we frequently go shooting there and never fail of success, besides, shooting of rats is not only a pleasant but a profitable amusement as they are also good eating and it is easy to kill 1,000 in a day as the ground swarms and the inhabitants never disturb them . . . in eating rats we quite outdid the Indians who abhor them as food.

Parkinson was never idle, but was seriously inconvenienced by the flies of all sorts and sizes which can make life miserable on Tahiti, even today, especially after heavy rain. Cook commented:

Our residence on shore would by no means have been disagreeable if we had not been incessantly tormented by the flies, which among other mischief, made it almost impossible for Mr Parkinson . . . to work; for they not only covered his subject so that no part of its surface could be seen, but even ate the colour off the paper as fast as he could lay it on. We had recourse to mosquito nets and fly traps, which, though they made the inconvenience tolerable, were very far from removing it.

When not working on his drawings, of people, canoes, dwellings and landscapes, this gentle young genius made a thorough examination of the manners and customs of the people he depicted, usually in pen and ink. He made a special study of their methods of cooking. He noted, for example, how Lycurgus's family brought a small quantity of what looked like flour, mixed it with coconut and then dropped two or three hot stones into it. It was then stirred vigorously until it formed a strong jelly. 'On tasting it,' he told his readers, 'we found it had an agreeable flavour, not unlike very good blancmange.' Cooking hot dishes was a laborious business, he recounted, requiring first the making of fire by rubbing one stick up and down a groove in another stick until the sawdust caught fire. The fire was built up over stones sunk into a shallow pit, the embers eventually being brushed away. Then they placed on the hot stones prepared hogs, fowl, fish or dog, the last being bred for food, and very nice, too, most agreed. Banks kept a close eye on his greyhounds.

Whenever Cook and his officers and gentlemen were invited to feed with the native chiefs, which was quite as frequent as they dined with them, they could not prevail upon the women to join them. Evidently the sexes were strictly segregated at meals, although the better class allowed their wives to sit beside them during meals, feeding their men mouthful by mouthful, and when indicated holding a coconut to their lips to slake their thirst.

Parkinson recorded every aspect of the lives of these people: how they joyously played music on primitive flutes, with voice accompaniment; how they cried with joy on meeting a friend after a long absence; how the women exposed their breasts as a form of welcome; and how they expressed their grief at the loss of a friend, a child or husband:

[One wife] after weeping, and expressing some emotions of sorrow, took a shark's tooth from under her clothes, and struck it against her head several times, which produced a copious discharge of blood; then, lamenting most bitterly, she articulated some words in a mournful tone, and covered the blood with some pieces of cloth, and, having bled about a pint, she gathered up as much of it as she could, threw it into the sea, and then assumed a cheerful countenance, as if nothing had happened.

Relations between visitors and islanders remained remarkably cordial throughout the *Endeavour*'s stay at Tahiti. Lycurgus and Hercules, or their wives, occasionally took offence over some trivial matter. When this happened, they simply folded up their houses and made off somewhere else. Banks or Cook would then track them down, present them with gifts, and in a few days they would be back again with their families.

It is unlikely that Sydney Parkinson took what he called a 'temporary wife', especially after commenting rather censoriously:

Most of our ship's company procured temporary wives amongst the natives, with whom they occasionally cohabited; an indulgence which even many reputed virtuous Europeans allow themselves, in uncivilized parts of the world, with impunity; as if a change of place altered the moral turpitude of fornication: and what is a sin in Europe, is only a simple innocent gratification in America; which is to suppose that the obligation to chastity is local, and restricted only to particular parts of the globe.

An uncomfortable discovery after a few weeks at the island, although Cook had had earlier suspicions, was that venereal disease was apparently rife among his men, no fewer than twenty-four seamen and nine out of eleven marines being afflicted. This followed an examination of the entire ship's company by the surgeon. His men had been free from infection when they arrived, and Wallis had reported a clean bill of health among his men.

Cook was by now convinced that two ships had visited the island after Wallis. He had been informed where they had anchored, and all the evidence pointed to their being Spanish. Therefore, the only possible source for the infection of the natives with the venereals was the Spanish sailors.

This, as we now know, was a canard. It was Cook's old adversary from the Quebec days, Bougainville, who was last at Tahiti. No Spaniards had yet come. Moreover, it was the Frenchmen who were infected by the islanders. Nor was it a venereal disease but yaws, an endemic disease all over the Pacific. Yaws was highly infectious and it was treated at that time in the same manner as venereal disease, with arsenic injections.

During the second half of May the weather at Tahiti seriously deteriorated, and Cook became increasingly anxious about their imminent astronomic observation, which naturally called for clear skies. 'Morning cloudy with heavy showers', 'Thick cloudy weather and excessive hard showers of rain and very much thunder and lightning', was followed three days later with 'most part of these 24 hours cloudy with frequent showers of rain'.

As an insurance against failure or an obscured sky on 3 June, Cook ordered two separate parties, properly equipped by Green with instruments, to set up their own small observatories elsewhere. On 1 June John Gore led a party consisting of Banks, Dr Monkhouse and his brother, Jonathan, Spöring and a small party of natives to York Island, Tahiti's spectacular satellite island to the west. After landing they went 'in search of a proper place to fix for making the observation', Gore recorded. 'Hauled the boat off to a sound rocky island within the surf and about a hundred yards from the mainland, this being a convenient place . . .' Early the next morning a similarly equipped party led by

Hicks sailed east in the pinnace to an islet called Puaru off the bay where Bougainville had anchored.

Meanwhile, everything was made ready at the fort, the telescopes unpacked from the *Endeavour*'s hold and transported under heavy guard to the Point Venus beach. Molyneux noted that 'everything very quiet and all hands anxious for tomorrow'. Cook reported in detail on the completed arrangements for the observation:

The astronomical clock . . . furnished with a gridiron pendulum was set up in the middle of one end of a large tent, in a frame of wood made for the purpose at Greenwich, fixed firm and as low in the ground as the door of the clock-case would admit . . . The pendulum was adjusted to exactly the same length as it had been at Greenwich . . . Facing the clock and 12 feet from it stood the observatory, in which were set up the journeyman clock and astronomical quadrant [standing] upon the head of a large cask fixed firm in the ground. . . . The telescopes made use of in the observations were two reflecting ones of two feet focus each . . . one of which was furnished with an object glass micrometer.

The morning of 3 June dawned crystal clear, 'as favourable to our purpose as we could wish'. From horizon to horizon there was not a cloud to be seen so that Cook could be satisfied that his two lieutenants were equally favoured. Dick Pickersgill, master's mate and one-time servant to Cook, sardonically, but as it turned out inaccurately, remarked: 'If the observation is not well made it is entirely owing to the observers.'

It was not until around 9 a.m. that all those with eyes to the telescopes recognised that, whatever the weather might be like over the Pacific, conditions were not so good on the surface of Venus, sixty-seven million miles distant, where the edges of the planet were obscured.

'We all saw an atmosphere or dusky cloud round the body of the planet, which very much disturbed the times of contact, especially of the internal ones; and we differed from each other in our accounts of the times of the contacts much more than might have been expected,' Cook reported. But they fixed on the time of 9 hours, 25 minutes and 42 seconds a.m. for the first external contact, with total immersion nineteen minutes later. Throughout that long hot morning, with the temperature rising to 119°F, the little black dot could be clearly discerned moving across the face of the sun until it touched the far side at 3 hours, 14 minutes and 8 seconds p.m.

It had been an arduous six hours for all the observers, and though Cook and Green could not claim complete accuracy, they had done as good a job as circumstances allowed. But before Cook could settle back to rest and take some refreshment, he was informed of a serious break-in to one of his ship's stores by his own men, who had taken advantage of the distraction of all the officers. No less than 120 pounds of nails had been stolen. 'If circulated by the people among the Indians it would do us untold injury by reducing the value of iron, our staple commodity,' he commented angrily. One of the culprits was discovered, with his pocket full of nails, but refused to name any of his co-conspirators, which might have reduced his punishment. For this he was secured and given two dozen lashes, the worst punishment of the voyage so far.

Cook was now anxious to get away as soon as possible in order to carry out the next stage of his instructions: 'Proceed to the southward in order to make discovery of the continent . . . until you arrive in the latitude of 40°.' But there was still work to be carried out on the *Endeavour* before she was ready for the long journey home via the sub-Antarctic.

'Heel'd and bootop'd the larboard side. The coat consisted of pitch and brimstone; found the ship's bottom very foul and the sheathing damaged a little in several places,' Molyneux reported; and later: 'Scraped the masts and painted them with varnish of pine.'

Cook planted in a cleared patch of land a variety of vegetable seeds, which he had bought in a shop in the Mile End Road. He was also anxious to carry out a complete circumnavigation of the island, following the coastline by boat or on foot; in addition, he felt that it was his duty to locate and chart the other islands of the archipelago of which he had heard a great deal from the Tahitians.

But before embarking on these explorations a new bout of thieving by Tahitians broke out: they always seemed to come in waves. It culminated in the theft of an iron rake used for the oven fire ashore. This was taken from inside the fort with a crook stick, which was manipulated by an athletic native when the sentry's back was turned. Also recently lost were a musket, Banks's pair of pistols, one of the petty officers' swords, a water cask and sundry other items.

Cook took the radical step – disapproved of by Banks – of rounding up no fewer than twenty-two canoes of all sizes and quality; he then informed the owners 'that I would burn them every one unless the principal things they had stolen from us were restored'. This led to the recovery of the rake, but that was all, and Cook eventually reconciled himself to failure, returning the canoes.

Some of his men, but certainly not Parkinson, favoured the use of firearms, 'but I would not suffer them to be fired upon', Cook noted, reflecting the humanitarian policy he followed almost to the end of his voyaging.

At three o'clock on the morning of 26 June, Cook and Banks, with a boat's crew and accompanied by Tupia as a guide, set out in the pinnace on their expedition 'in order to examine and draw a sketch of the coast and harbours', as Cook defined his intentions. Although they were armed with muskets and pistols, it was a remarkably courageous thing to do, and it is a wonder that Cook did not bring along half-a-dozen marines who had come on this voyage for just this purpose. The survey was carried out with Cook's usual thoroughness, by boat when the coastline made this necessary, otherwise by walking rough, meeting tribes of natives from time to time, all of them very friendly and some of whom they greeted as old friends who had earlier visited the fort.

Here and there they found evidence of European visitors, like a 12-pound shot marked with the English broad arrow, which was likely to have been recovered after an unfortunate bombardment by the *Dolphin*. More happily they were shown a goose and a turkey, gifts from Wallis two years earlier. The local natives also pointed out to Cook and Banks where the crews of two ships (Cook still insisted that they were Spanish) had pitched their tents and wooded and watered at a stream.

As they worked their way south along the eastern coast, they were warned of what lay ahead: the kingdom of Taiarapu, or Tahiti-iti, where lived the feared tribe ruled by King Tiarreboo. In the event, they were received most cordially and hospitably, except that the King made off with a cloak he borrowed from Cook. The only evidence of possible past hostilities was what Cook described as a 'board of a semi-circular figure to which was fastened 15 lower jawbones of men, all seemingly firm and in good condition with scarce a tooth wanting among them'.

Returning by land along the west coast of the island they chanced upon 'the seat of [Queen] Obarea', or Obadia. She was not at home, but presuming upon her hospitality, they all settled down for the night in her house. Nearby, the next morning they found the biggest *marae* they had yet seen,*

---

* This *marae*, it was later established, was the finest and biggest place of worship not just in Tahiti but in all Polynesia; see Dr J. C. Beaglehole (ed.), *The Journals of Captain James Cook*, vol. 1 (1968), p. 112n.

a wonderful piece of Indian architecture and far exceeds everything of its kind upon the whole island. It is a long square of stonework built pyramadically. On the middle of the top stood the figure of a bird carved in wood and near it lay the broken one of a fish carved in stone . . . Near to this *marae* were several small ones, all going to decay, and on the beach between them and the sea lay great quantities of human bones . . .

This site provided confirmation – if it were needed – of the recent decay of Queen Obadia's reign. Banks later learned that about a year earlier, King Tiarreboo had led a large force of his people in a raid on this part of the island, killing great numbers of the Queen's subjects, burning the houses, stealing all the livestock and forcing the royal family to flee into the mountains. This assault accounted for the decorative jawbones, the presence of Wallis's turkey and goose in the Tiarreboo territory and the thick scattering of human bones along the seashore.

Cook and his party arrived back at the fort on the evening of the first day of July 1769. They were all tired and thankful for the prospect of a square meal. They had taken few provisions, relying upon local produce. But this was a poor season for fruit, and they were now between the breadfruit harvests.

For the following week all the *Endeavour*'s crew were occupied in giving the final scraping and painting of the ship's hull, examining all their original food stores and stocking up with water, sixty-five tons of it in all. Then, during their last days at Tahiti an event occurred which brought them nearer to armed conflict with the natives than at any other time. Cook's entry for Sunday, 9 July, recounts the opening circumstances:

Sometime in the middle watch Clement Webb and Sam Gibson, both Marines and young men, found means to get away from the fort . . . & in the morning were not to be found, as it was known to everybody that all hands were to go on board on the Monday morning & that the ship would sail in a day or two, there was reason to think that these two men intended to stay behind. However, I was willing to wait one day to see if they would return before I took any steps to find them.

But the next morning Cook learned from the local natives 'that they were gone to the mountains & that they had each of them a wife & would not return'. He consulted with his two lieutenants, and they agreed that it was essential to recover the two men. They also agreed that drastic measures must be taken to bring this about.

Queen Obadia and three other chiefs were therefore detained on board the ship. But, recognising that Hercules 'would have more weight with the natives than all these put together', Hicks volunteered to lead a party to capture him, a mission which he accomplished 'without the least disturbance'. Molyneux reported that 'this struck a general terror through the island, and the prisoners (though very well treated) were inconsolable'. All these kidnapped grandees were now taken on board the *Endeavour* for greater security, while Midshipman Monkhouse, the marines corporal, Jack Truslove, and three more marines marched off to inform the natives of the situation and to secure the release of the two deserters.

Unfortunately, when the news of this armed party spread with its usual electric speed, a group of natives had ample time to set up an ambush. The party was overwhelmed by sheer numbers and disarmed. Cook and John Gore learned of this setback when, at nine in the evening, Clement Webb was brought to the ship by a group of natives to appraise Cook of the situation.

This game of kidnap and counter-kidnap was brought to an end when, the following morning, Hicks led a strong force of marines to the place where Monkhouse and the other captives were held. Telling the party that their 'chiefs would suffer' unless they were immediately released, 'he recovered the men [including the two marines, who were later flogged] without the least opposition and returned with them about 7 o'clock in the morning,' Cook reported with evident relief.

The last thing that Cook wanted was to leave the island with relations under a cloud. He, Banks and Solander therefore paid a last visit to Queen Obadia to reassure her 'of our friendly disposition'. This evidently had the result they sought, for towards midday on 13 July, as they were getting under sail, the stout, illustrious figure of the Queen, with whom they had established closer relations than with anyone else on the island, appeared in her grand double canoe. She and her entourage had come to say good-bye. It was a tearful occasion, not only for the Queen and her retinue but also for Tupia, who was to join Banks's party, along with his own servant, the boy Tiata. It had tickled Banks's vanity to bring this young man to London, in order to show him off to his friends.

At the time, Banks wrote in defensive justification of this decision:

Thank heaven I have a sufficiency [of wealth] and I do not know why I may not keep him as a curiosity, as well as some of my neighbours do lions and tigers at a larger expense than he will probably ever put me to; the amusement I shall have in his future conversation and the benefit he will be to this ship, as well as what he may be if another [ship] be sent into these seas, will I think fully repay me.

There were broken hearts on both sides as the *Endeavour* under full sail edged out of Matavai Bay under a light easterly breeze, surrounded by canoes with their packed, lamenting natives. Banks as Tupia's patron climbed to the head of the topmast with him 'where we stood a long time waving to the canoes as they went off'. It will never be known whether this adventurous Polynesian expected to see his homeland again. Certainly, for the present he was eager to show off his knowledge. Even before nightfall the first of Tahiti's neighbours was in sight, a low, small island of this archipelago which came to be known as the Society Islands. Tupia told Banks that it was uninhabited, but that fishing parties occasionally went there.*

Before noon the following day two islands came into view, both with a dramatic silhouette, like Tahiti, saw-tooth mountains rising high, their summits hidden by cloud. The first, Huahine, was almost a double island, the two halves connected by the narrowest of isthmuses. Sounding cautiously round the north side of the island, Cook suddenly chanced upon a wonderfully sheltered bay, Owharre. With Tupia reassuring the natives, whose canoes soon surrounded the *Endeavour*, they came on board, to Banks's great satisfaction. Cook had been somewhat disapproving of Banks's decision to bring Tupia, but from this point he began increasingly to accept the advantages of having a native who understood and could interpret the manners and mores of Polynesians.

Nevertheless, at Raiatea, the next island, the presence of Tupia could not at first allay the fears or tame the aggression of the natives. All the young man could do, when a native alone on the shore and armed with a long lance 'began to dance and shake his weapon calling out in a very shrill voice', was to warn Banks of the danger, which was scarcely necessary under the circumstances.

But evidently the mood of the people suddenly changed, in the unsettling manner of these Polynesians. Before they left, John Gore became quite lyrical about Raiatea:

The people of this island [he wrote] appear to me to be in general the same as those of George's Island, except in this: they are less thievish and more courteous, otherwise their customs, language and manners are the same, fruits, roots and animals the same as the Georgeonians. The island is a

---

* After three months at Tahiti, Banks had become fluent in the language and the unusually bright Tupia had acquired a modest English vocabulary.

This portrait, painted by Nathaniel Dance shortly before Cook embarked on his third, and fatal, voyage, shows Cook as the fully matured, self-confident sea captain who has twice encircled the globe, penetrated deep into the Antarctic and charted coastlines from Newfoundland to South Island, New Zealand.

The Yorkshire port of Whitby where Cook began his seafaring life.

Twenty-seven years later in June 1769, the days of seafaring for Cook and all the *Endeavour*'s company nearly came to an end off the eastern seaboard of Australia at present-day Cooktown.

Lieutenant James King,
the intellectual and aesthete.

The indomitable American John Gore,
Cook's lieutenant on two of
his voyages.

Sir Hugh Palliser, who
discerned Cook's genius as a
navigator and surveyor.

John Montagu, 4th Earl of Sandwich,
rake, gambler but also an effective
First Lord of the Admiralty and
sponsor of Cook.

RIGHT Sydney Parkinson, the brilliant young man from Edinburgh and the *Endeavour*'s artist, who tragically died at sea on the way home in January 1771.

BELOW Joseph Banks, botanist and friend of all at sea, but he accepted too much of the credit for the success of the first voyage to the Pacific.

Phaëton. erubescens.

Sydney Parkinson pinx 1769

Banks could, however, rightly take full credit for the unprecedented collection of flora and fauna brought back from the *Endeavour* voyage, all drawn by Sydney Parkinson, like this spectacular tropic bird (ABOVE) and the Bougainvillea (RIGHT) found for the first time on an illicit trip ashore at Rio de Janeiro.

ABOVE Two Antarctic activities are shown in this drawing by the artist on the second voyage, William Hodges. The shooting of birds supplemented their food rations, and the collection and melting of ice produced, to their surprise, tons of sweet-tasting water, which was sorely needed.

LEFT Charles Clerke, lusty wag and extrovert, captured in a rare thoughtful mood which appears to puzzle the much-tattooed Maori.

OPPOSITE John Webber's drawing of Cook's sloop *Resolution*, which served him so well on his second voyage, but proved fatally flawed on the third voyage.

Dusky Bay Maoris, drawn by William Hodges.

New Zealand war canoe with defiant Maori warriors, drawn by Spöring.

beautiful spot, well clothed with fruit trees in many places, amongst which their houses are dispersed . . .

The natives of Bora-Bora, the next island to the west, proved enthusiastic, friendly and keen to trade, contrary to what had been said of them. Banks and Solander, with Tupia as interpreter, went ashore whenever they could to take plants for identifying and for Parkinson to draw, but there was no question of landing at this most spectacular of all the Society Islands, even if they had succeeded in finding a way through the pounding reef, for Cook was 'now fully resolved to stand directly to the southward in search of the continent'.

However, they were not yet finished with the Society Islands, and on the afternoon of 13 August their course took them close to Rurutu. Banks, as usual, was enthusiastic to land. Although Cook had no intention of anchoring, he agreed to a party, led by Gore, going ashore to find out if the natives knew of land to the south.

There being no convenient place for landing in the bay [Gore wrote later] we rode out along the shore . . . to windward, but not far, there being no prospect of landing with safety that we could see. Two or three of the natives followed on the shore flourishing their pikes, using many ridiculous gestures and calling to us in an affected swearing tone. We then rowed as near the shore as the surf would permit. Tupia called to one of them . . .

But it was a futile exercise, and Gore soon brought the pinnace back to the *Endeavour*, having learned nothing, while Banks was equally frustrated.

Cook was no less doubtful than before about the existence of the reputed *Terra Australis Incognita*, but he felt no satisfaction at the prospect of proving that it was a mere myth, least of all to the one man in the ship who had no doubts of its existence, Joseph Banks. In fact, they were scarcely clear of the Society Islands than Banks was commenting on the deep Pacific rollers indicating, he wrongly concluded, the imminence of their discovery. On 15 August he noted that they had crossed the line of the Tropic of Capricorn, and on the following morning he recorded that 'soon after we rose this morn we were told that land was in sight'. It proved, as he was obliged to add, to be a cloud, which in no way dimmed his confidence and enthusiasm.

In spite of Banks's cheerfulness, most of the ship's company found this southerly leg of the voyage disagreeable. Day by day the temperature fell, and one by one their live stock – the hens and pigs particularly – succumbed to the cold and lack of food, the fodder soon deteriorating and proving inedible. There was a break on

25 August, the anniversary of their departure from England. 'A piece of cheshire cheese was taken from a locker,' Banks recounted, 'where it had been reserved for this occasion, and a cask of porter tapped which proved excellently good, so that we lived like Englishmen and drank the health of our friends in England.'

A few days later the boatswain's mate, who was notorious as a drunk, consumed three half-pints of raw rum which the boatswain had given him 'out of mere good nature'. John Reading, of Kinsale, Co. Cork, died shortly after.

Cook took the *Endeavour* as far south as he had been instructed, and no farther. The weather was foul, as Banks, now less cheerful, reported: 'Blows very fresh with a heavy sea; the ship was very troublesome all last night and is not less so today [1 September 1769].' With the instinct of a true explorer, Cook knew that it was futile to continue on this course and that his destiny lay to the west and the north. At 4 p.m. on 2 September, with 'very strong gales, and heavy squalls of rain . . . and having not the least visible signs of land, we wore and brought to'. From s 29° E, the *Endeavour* was set on a course N 54° 3′ E.

9

'These People are Much Given to War'

SYDNEY PARKINSON, WRITING ON 5 October,* observed:

We had light breezes from the NE and pleasant weather: about two o'clock in the afternoon one of our people, Nicholas Young, Surgeon's boy, descried a point of land from the starboard bow at about nine leagues distance, bearing w and by N. We bore up to it and at sunset we had a good view of it . . . We regaled ourselves in the evening upon the occasion; the land was called Young Nick's Head, and the boy received his reward.

Cook, more austerely and accurately, entered in his log at 2 p.m.: 'Saw the land appearing in low hummocks, bearing w and N, distance 8 or 9 leagues. Same time altered the course for the land. The people employed in unbending the new foresail . . .'

Nick Young's reward was a gallon of rum, which, along with the daily ration, meant plenty for everyone. The officers and gentlemen, too, celebrated that evening. Banks especially was delighted at their discovery, justifying at last his long-held belief: 'All hands seem to agree that this is certainly the continent we are in search of.' Dick Pickersgill, who loved drawing charts, captioned his 'A Chart of the So. Continent between . . .'

Cook knew better but kept his counsel, not even confiding in his wife's nephew, Isaac Smith, whose schooling gave him so much pleasure. Cook was certain that this was the eastern coast of the land Tasman had sailed up in 1642 and had called Staten Land, the most easterly of the Fuegian islands, wrongly believing that it was part of the southern continent which le Maire and Schouten had discovered nearly thirty years earlier. When another Dutchman

* This is incorrect; it should read 7 October.

exploded this theory only months later by proving that Staten Land was an island, and a small and wretched island at that, Tasman's discovery was renamed New Zealand.

Cook had long admired this Dutchman, who had been dead now for 110 years. 'If you should fail of discovering the Continent . . .', Cook's secret instructions ran, 'you will upon falling in with New Zealand carefully observe the latitude and longitude in which the land is situated . . .' He knew his latitude. It was 38° 57' s, fewer than six degrees at variance with Tasman's calculation. This was New Zealand all right. And now, again according to Admiralty instructions, he must 'explore as much of the coast as the condition of the bark, the health of her crew and the state of your provisions will admit of'. All three were in good order; and so to work.

It took almost three days and nights to close this coast, so unfavourable were the winds. But at last, on the afternoon of 9 October, Cook manœuvred the *Endeavour* into a wide bay and was able to report:

We saw in the bay several canoes, people upon the shore and some houses in the country. The land on the sea coast is high with white steep cliffs, and inland are very high mountains. The face of the country is of a hilly surface and appears to be clothed with wood and verdure.

It all looked so promising, almost as if they were off the chalky Sussex coast, with the South Downs beyond. The weather, too, seemed to favour them and enhance their first impressions of this new land. In clear conditions and with gentle breezes, Cook tells us, he anchored the *Endeavour* on the north-east side of this bay and beside a river which appeared favourable for watering.

For their part, the Maoris were astonished at this sudden appearance of what they first identified as a bird of great size and beauty.

Upon seeing a smaller bird unfledged (without sails) descending into the water, and a number of parti-coloured beings, but apparently in the human shape, also descend, they regarded the larger bird as a houseful of divinities . . . The astonishment of the people . . . on seeing Cook's ship was so great that they were benumbed with fear, but presently, recollecting themselves, they felt determined to find out if the gods . . . were as pugnacious as themselves . . .

Cook ordered the pinnace and the yawl to be launched and headed for the shore with Banks, Solander and a party of sailors and marines, the 'parti-coloured beings'. Soon after they landed on the river bank, they saw a small party of Maoris on the other side, so they re-embarked and crossed over to confront them. The Maoris retreated and then

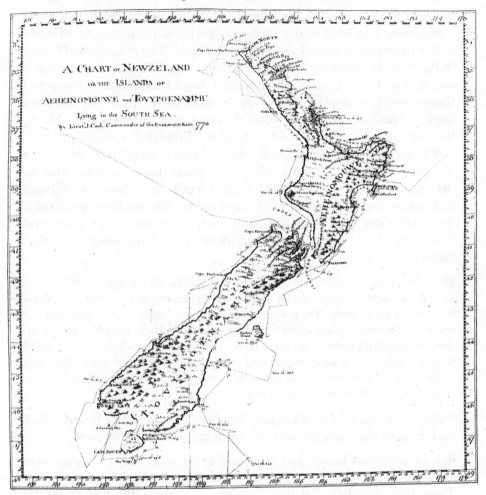

made off speedily into the woodland. Cook, Banks, Solander and Midshipman John Bootie followed them as far as a collection of huts, all empty. 'We then went up and examined one of their houses,' Bootie recalled, 'which we found to be low and very close and warm, thatched after the same manner as our houses in England.' While they were among these dwellings, they heard the sound of shooting and hastened back to the river.

On the way they came across the dead body of a Maori, clearly the victim of a musket ball, and the very last thing Cook wanted to find. It appeared that the cox in charge of the boats, which had become the object of the sudden reappearance of the Maoris, had ordered two

115

muskets to be fired over their heads. But this did not deter them and a third shot was fired at the leading Maori who continued to advance with a threatening spear raised above his head. The others stood frozen in their tracks, 'seemingly quite surprised, wondering no doubt what it was that had thus killed their comrade'. But as soon as they recovered themselves, they made off dragging the dead body a little way and then left it. It was later established that the dead man's name was Te Maro, the first Maori to die at the hands of the English.*

The following morning Cook was told that a large party of natives had assembled on the spot where the death had occurred, and he determined to convince them of his friendly intentions, a difficult task under the circumstances. Supported by the marines, he, Banks, Solander, Gore and Tupia, as translator, embarked in the boats and landed on the opposite side of the river. John Gore described what followed:

We landed at the place we left overnight, when about a hundred of the natives, all armed, came down on the opposite side of the river and drew themselves up in lines. Then with a regular jump from left to right and the reverse, they brandished their weapons, distorted their mouths, lolling up their tongues and turning up the whites of their eyes, the whole accompanied with a strong hoarse song, calculated in my opinion to cheer each other and intimidate their enemies, and may be called with propriety a dancing war song. It lasted three or four minutes.

After the row had finished and Tupia's voice might be heard, Cook took him to the bank of the river in order to tell the natives

that we were their friends and only come to get water and trade with them and that if they offered to insult us we could with ease kill them all. But Tupia told us plainly that they were not our friends and told us several times to take care of ourselves.

At length one of the natives stripped off his cloak and dived into the river, swimming the forty yards to the eastern bank. He was unarmed, but the two who followed him swam with their spears. Many more dived in after this, all carrying arms, which in no way impeded their swift swimming.

It was the first time on this voyage that Cook was aware that he, and all the men with him, were in acute danger. A dozen natives might be killed in a charge, but the others could come on and overwhelm them in seconds, either bludgeoning them to death or piercing them with their spears. But Banks and Cook advanced boldly towards them,

* Some two thousand Maoris died in the wars between 1843 and 1869.

passing nails and beads to those at the front. 'They seemed to set little value upon either,' Banks noted, 'but especially upon the iron the use of which they certainly were totally ignorant of. They caught at whatever was offered them but would part with nothing but a few feathers.'

All they seemed to want were muskets, these magical weapons which could kill a man instantly from afar. Cook ordered extreme vigilance while he, with Tupia still translating, continued to attempt trading. Unfortunately, astronomer Green, while turning about, exposed his hanger, the short, curved sword secured to his waist, and a Maori made off with it.

'We cannot allow them to succeed,' declared Banks; and Cook and the others in the isolated party of five agreed. Banks was the first to open fire on the retreating figure. His musket was loaded with small shot for birds. These struck the man all over his back. It momentarily silenced him, 'but instead of quitting his prize he continued to wave it over his head, retreating as gently as before'.

Surgeon Monkhouse now opened fire on the culprit, this time with ball, which fatally wounded him. Monkhouse grabbed Green's hanger just in time as the other Maoris returned. Cook, Green and finally Tupia fired at them, causing no more deaths but wounding three of them, and making them retreat into the river and swim across.

With typical *sang-froid* after this encounter, Cook now re-embarked in his boat, with the other two boats with which they were now joined following behind. He intended to row around the bay in search of another anchorage on the south side, and water that was not as brackish as the river water they had thankfully left behind them.

The day's adventures were not yet over, however. While crossing the bay they encountered two canoes. Cook calculated that the only way of convincing these Maoris of their friendly intentions was to capture some and ply them with kindness and gifts on board the *Endeavour*. The first of these canoes, which Cook reckoned had been fishing, caught sight of them in time to change course and speed towards the shore. The second one with some seven men at the paddles was caught as if by one of their own seine nets between the three boats. When the Maoris attempted to escape, Cook ordered shots to be fired over their heads. Banks describes the fatal outcome:

She immediately ceased paddling and the people in her . . . made all possible haste to strip as we thought to leap into the water. But no sooner did our boat come up with her than they began with stones, paddles &c. to make a brisk resistance that we were obliged to fire into her by which four were killed. The other three who were boys leaped overboard. One of them swam with great agility and when taken made every effort in his power to prevent [this] . . . The other two were more easily prevailed upon. As soon as they were in they squatted down expecting no doubt instant death. But on finding themselves well used and that clothes were given them they recovered their spirits in a very short time, and before we got to the ship appeared almost totally insensible of the loss of their fellows.

To kill more than half of a canoe-load of intended detainees in order to 'cultivate a friendship with the natives' appears to be an unbalanced calculation.

The tender-hearted Parkinson makes no mention of the affair. Most other references are simple and factual, and we can assume that the ship's company felt little compunction about firing on 'savages'. Midshipman John Bootie is strictly factual in his description:

The boats had been attacked by the natives in a very bold manner, those in their canoes fighting to the very last thing they had in their canoes . . . and though several lay dead . . . did not submit till all their ammunition was spent which consisted of spikes and spears from 8 to 10 feet long, paddles and their fish and ballast.

There was certainly regret, and remorse is implicit in Cook's journal. As for Banks, he wrote: 'Thus ended the most disagreeable day my life has yet seen that such may never return to embitter future reflections.' Meanwhile, the three boys were being treated to an immense dinner (their appetites appeared insatiable) and tucked down comfortably for the night. Tupia was particularly concerned for their welfare, comforting them in the night and listening to them singing a Polynesian lament.

Master's mate Frank Wilkinson concluded his account of this eventful day: 'I observe these people tie their hair on the top of their heads and put white feathers in it . . . They are all of a dark copper colour and wear the teeth of some of their dead friends in their ears. They are well made and numerous.' Numerous they certainly were.

With typical pragmatism, John Gore presented a different view:

The reason for the above proceedings with respect to the natives was this: that from the methods already taken it was found impracticable to bring them to any intercourse with us. Therefore Mr Cook determined at the first opportunity (meeting with any of the natives in their caves) to take some of them, treat them well and set them on shore among their countrymen as a means to bring them to friendly intercourse with us. The which a laudable proceeding in my opinion.

On the following morning, 11 October, Cook made one more

attempt to come to terms with the Maoris, but was not in the least surprised to be met with another mass hostile demonstration; so hostile indeed that the three captive boys begged to return on board and remain with these white men in the great canoe. However, in the afternoon, Cook insisted that they be put ashore, 'seemingly very much against their inclination'. Watching their arrival on shore through a glass, he 'saw them carried across a river in a catamaran and walk leisurely off with the other natives'.

Regretfully, Cook ordered preparations to be made to sail at dawn. It had been a catastrophic visit, discreditable to all. Having earlier determined to call this bay, their first landfall in New Zealand, Endeavour Bay, Molyneux noted that his captain named this 'Poverty Bay as it neither furnished us with provisions nor water', and only a small quantity of wood. However, at the last moment, with anchors already stowed, a canoe came alongside manned by a small party of Maoris, who, it seemed, had heard of the good treatment enjoyed by the boys. They all appeared anxious to trade though all they had were their paddles, which were eagerly exchanged for Tahitian cloth, which was to prove popular everywhere in New Zealand. Cook noted that they so deprived themselves that he wondered if they would be able to return home. In the event, three of them were found hiding on board long after all the canoes had left. Nor were they in the least concerned; they were rather pleased with themselves, in fact. Cook ordered a copper of wheat to be boiled for them, and sugared, and with all this hot cereal inside them, according to Frank Wilkinson, they then 'went to sleep on a steering sail under the forecastle'.

As the *Endeavour* continued to sail south very slowly in a near calm, canoes put off from the shore, and Cook determined that one of them should carry his unwanted guests back home. By this time, they were keen to leave, too, and when the men in the nearest canoe showed signs of nervousness, the guests beseeched them to come alongside. Tupia was engaged in translating this exchange, and we can presume that he hesitated, with shock or embarrassment, as he told Cook assurances of safety included the fact that his hosts were not cannibals. Thus Cook and his men learned for the first time the revolting truth that the people of this new land ate their enemies. Feeling more secure now, the canoeists came alongside, and the three young men shinned down a rope to drop into it.

Cook had determined to explore this coast down as far as the 41st parallel and then 'to return to the northward in case we meet with nothing to encourage us to proceed farther'. This course brought the *Endeavour* first to a prominent headland, which he named Portland

Point for its similarity with the Dorset headland of southern England. The bay which it commanded was immense and they could only just make out the continuation of the coast southward of it.

This bay Cook named Hawke's after his hero, Admiral Sir Edward Hawke, the creator of new aggressive tactics, a hero of the Battle of Quiberon Bay and First Lord of the Admiralty until shortly before they sailed. Cook was much pleased with this discovery, describing it,

The land near the shore is of a moderate height with white cliffs and sandy beaches – inland are several pretty high mountains, and the whole face of the country appears with a very hilly surface and for the most part covered with wood, and hath all the appearances of a very pleasant and fertile country.*

There was only one contact with the Maoris on this leg south before Cook put over the helm at prosaically named Cape Turnagain. They had just passed the southernmost point of Hawke's Bay when canoes put off and came alongside. One of the men was wearing a most elegant black cloak, to which Cook took a great fancy and especially wanted in order to establish what sort of animal had provided it. Offering a piece of red cloth in exchange, and foolishly trusting the honesty of the man, the canoe made off swiftly with Cook's cloth, the exchange unfulfilled.

The serious trouble began when one of the canoes came back in a few minutes when Tiata, Tupia's servant, happened to be over the side of the ship attempting to trade for some fish. Suddenly, the natives deftly grabbed the boy and made off. Molyneux now takes up the narrative:

We immediately wore the ship and in the interim fired upon the canoe, with an equal chance of killing the boy or the thieves. Other canoes joined the one poor Tiata was in, and a four-pounder [cannon] being fired they made for the shore, leaving the boy to shift for himself . . . we sent a boat to take the boy up who was brought on board half dead with fright and the fatigue of swimming.

'This affair', Cook noted, 'occasioned my giving this point of land the name of Cape Kidnappers.'

The *Endeavour* sailed back past Poverty Bay, with mainly favourable winds, and this time contacts with the Maoris were of an entirely friendly nature. At a promising cove, Tologa Bay, John Gore took a strong party of men and all the Marines to wood and water, acquiring in all two boatloads of wood and twelve tons of badly needed water.

* Today many of New Zealand's finest wines come from this beautiful area.

At one point, Hicks noted that 'the two canoes came up with about 50 men each, threatened us with their lances and dared us to fight. Fired two four-pounders over their heads and so frightened them to the shore.'

The land between Poverty Bay and what proved to be the most easterly point of New Zealand was rich and attractive. Cook went ashore while the wooding and watering was taking place, and climbed high into the hills. He was unable to see far inland because of the ever rising land, 'but the valleys and sides of many of the hills', he reported, 'were luxuriously clothed with woods and verdure and little plantations of the natives lying dispersed up and down the country . . . The country abounds with a great number of plants and the woods with as great a variety of very beautiful birds . . .'

Before the end of October they had doubled East Cape and found the land beyond even richer, with much cultivation and numerous settlements. Some very hostile canoes set off after the *Endeavour*. Cook ordered first grapeshot and then ball to be fired over their heads, which sent them home again. For this reason he, rather crudely, named the land Cape Runaway; the finding of names became increasingly tiresome as the voyage continued. Lieutenant Hicks, not for the first or last time, found his name appearing on Cook's chart when he discovered a little cove on the last day of October: Hicks Bay, still so-called today.

A mountain came into sight, standing in the middle of a plain, which 'makes it the more conspicuous'. Cook named it Mount Edgcumbe, failing to tell anyone whether it was in honour of his marines sergeant, the hill behind Plymouth, which was probably their last sight of the home country, or Lord Edgcumbe, the Admiral c-in-c Plymouth at the time of their departure.

It was at about this time that Charles Green reminded Cook that on the 9th of the month they could observe the transit of the planet Mercury. The weather on this northerly leg had been intermittently foul, and at best with hazy sunshine which would preclude any accurate observation. There had been several days when Banks and his party failed to emerge on-deck, and even the natives' canoes remained ashore because of the heavy and continuous rain.

However, after 'hazy, rainy weather' on 8 November, the 9th dawned clear at the anchorage Cook had selected, and at 8 a.m. he went ashore with Green and Hicks and all the necessary instruments. These they set up at the eastern end of the beach, some three hundred yards (Beaglehole tells us) from the river – named Oyster for obvious reasons, the bay being named after himself.

Cook Bay remained serenely fine all day, and the observation was faultless. There was no serenity on board the *Endeavour* that day, however. John Gore was in command and felt responsible not only for the ship but also for the vulnerable party ashore. A number of canoes made their almost inevitable appearance, the Maoris armed with pikes, darts and stones, but were prevailed upon not to attack by the Maoris already enjoying good trading of fish and Tahitian cloth. Instead, they assumed a more friendly demeanour and offered to trade themselves, indicating that their arms were for exchange. Gore himself took a fancy to one man's woven cloak, and it was agreed to exchange it for a length of cloth. Gore handed over his trade, but as soon as it was in the canoe the man retained his coat and infuriated Gore by making off while all his party waved their paddles and sang out a boisterous war chant.

This was too much for Gore, who levelled his musket, took careful aim and shot the culprit dead. (He was buried in Gore's cloak, it was learned later.) Neither Cook, Parkinson nor Banks approved of this rather hasty action. After Gore recounted the incident to his captain, Cook wrote: 'I must own that it did not meet with my approbation because I thought the punishment a little too severe for the crime, and we had now been long enough acquainted with these people to know how to chastise trifling faults like this without taking lives.'

A few days after leaving Mercury Bay, the *Endeavour* doubled a prominent headland, which Cook named after his old commodore, Lord Colville, and entered a deep bay, which he named the Firth of Thames and the river running into it after London's river. Here, while Cook was ashore, it was Hicks's turn to experience trouble with the Maoris when they came on board to trade. Both he and Gore as lieutenants felt keenly their responsibility when in temporary command of the ship, especially with the captain ashore and the upper deck swarming with excited Maoris. On this occasion one of them was seen to open and pillage the binnacle, removing the half-hour glass and making off with it. He was caught before he could escape over the side, and to make an example of him Hicks had him lashed to the gangway and given a dozen lashes with the cat. This caused something of a sensation, amongst the crew and the natives. But no one thought the action unjust, and 'one old man beat the fellow after he had got into the canoe'.

The lack of any form of Western morality on theft among these natives was as difficult to deal with here as it had been at Tahiti. To hope that the crew of a passing ship could correct the practices of generations of Maoris was absurd, and yet mild punishment to discourage 'cheating as usual by offering to trade and keeping what they had got' could only be countered in this way. 'Our usual punishment', Banks continued, 'was inflicted with small shot, which made the offender immediately relinquish his prize.'

On 26 November, close to what they named The Bay of Islands, with a party of Maoris behaving unusually boldly and in the crew's eyes disgracefully, one of the midshipmen, who had experienced a particular loss,

suffered upon a droll though rather mischievous revenge. He got a fishing line and when the canoe was close to the ship hove the lead at the man who had cheated, with so good success that he fastened the hook into his backside, on which he pulled with all his might and the Indian kept back, so the hook soon broke in the shank leaving its beard in his backside, no very agreeable legacy.

In the early days of December, as they approached the northern tip of this coast, the weather was particularly foul and the zig-zag course marked on Cook's chart underlines the trouble they experienced in making any progress. On the few occasions when they could go ashore, Banks was still writing about visiting 'the Continent'. In spite of the difficulties of charting this coastline, especially when out of sight of land for many hours, and of checking their own positions, Cook was almost certain that they were close not only to what he named North Cape, but also to the north-west tip of land. This had been Tasman's last landfall before sailing north into the Pacific, naming it Cape Maria van Diemen, after the wife of the Governor-General of Batavia who had sent him on the voyage.

At this doubling of the northernmost point of New Zealand, we see Cook the navigator at his finest. In fearsomely high seas, the rollers pounding in from the west, in gales and for a while a full hurricane the like of which he had never before experienced, with the rain driving horizontally, and with so many torn sails that the sailmakers could scarcely keep up with the arduous repair work, it took all Cook's skills to keep the *Endeavour* from foundering. But with no more than glimpses of the coastline, he continued with his running survey, fixing Cape Maria at 34° 30' s, 187° 25' w, a mere 2 degrees out in latitude and longitude. Was there ever such an achievement in the history of hydrography?

By Christmas the *Endeavour* was some twenty leagues west of the Cape, the weather suddenly quiet with hazy sunshine. Cook was too busy even to acknowledge Christmas in his journal, but Banks went out in a boat and shot some gannets for Christmas dinner. On the 25th, 'Our goose pie was eaten with great approbation,' he recorded, 'and in the evening all hands were as drunk as our grandfathers used to be upon like occasions.' Or as they all had been just one year earlier, in similar blessedly calm seas far away in the South Atlantic.

The fact that they were steering east for two days from 28 December, and then south along the coast, in no way disturbed Banks's confidence that they were following the coast of the continent. At the same time he pondered on the conversation Tupia had translated between himself and a group of Maoris in a canoe under the stern of the ship the last time they had had any contact with them before they had reached North Cape.

After some friendly trading, Tupia had enquired about the lie of the country. After three days' canoeing, he was told, from the northernmost land, the coast would extend no more to the west and instead turned south. Failing to understand this fully, Banks asked Tupia to enquire further. Did these Indians travel to any other country but their own, or had they heard of other lands? Tupia received a positive and unexpected response to this question. Many years ago some of his people had sailed away in a great canoe, steering (their informants indicated) NW by NNW or NNW. Of this number, some had returned to report that they had found another country where the people ate hogs – *booah* in Tahiti and other Polynesian islands, though no one on board the *Endeavour* had seen any since striking this coast.

This was confirmed when Tupia demanded to know if they had any, and received a negative answer. 'None of your ancestors brought any back with them?' Again there was a negative answer, provoking Tupia to exclaim, 'You must be a parcel of liars and your story a great lie for your ancestors would never have been such fools as to come back without them.'

The Maoris evidently took no offence, and Tupia may have spoken jokingly, for the conversation continued on other subjects in a friendly fashion, and the Maoris returned in the evening with some fish to trade. Banks certainly wondered on the meaning of this geographical conversation. He does not surmise in his journal, but it is likely that he saw these revelations as further evidence of the continent, with this reported land an extension of it.

We can do no better today, except that we know what vast distances the Polynesians could sail, guided by the stars and the immense clouds that hang over these volcanic islands and sometimes identifiable for hundreds of miles: New Zealand to Tahiti is about 2,500 miles, the same distance as from Tahiti to Hawaii, or, eastwards to Easter Island; while the Tasman Sea between New Zealand and New South Wales is a mere 1,800 miles at its narrowest point. If Banks is to be believed –

and why should he fabricate such a tale? – these Maoris of what Cook called (and is still named today) the Bay of Islands were pointing vaguely towards Australia, or possibly New Caledonia.

While the men off watch were carousing on Christmas Day, Cook saw through his glass land to the north-east, where none should be. The weather was 'a little hazy', which perhaps accounts for this brief misidentification. Soon he could see that he was looking at a small group of islands and realised that they were what the Dutchman had named the Three Kings. Even for a navigator whose discoveries over the 1770s were to be legion, there were two responses to the knowledge that Western man had been here before: disappointment at not being first, and comfort in the knowledge that a ship had been here before and survived.

But it is doubtful if Cook would have been pleased had he known that at this very moment the French navigator, Jean-François-Marie de Surville in the *Saint Jean Baptiste*, had just doubled North Cape and was only a few hours' sailing away. He was even nearer to Cook than Bougainville had been to Wallis in discovering Tahiti. At this time there was strong rivalry between the French, Spanish and British in the Pacific. Only the Spanish claimed the entire ocean, but the other two nations were fearful that the other would make as grandiose claims. Cook had already declared part of New Zealand for the crown and marked the occasion by hoisting the union flag. Surville's crew were suffering terribly from scurvy, and the French commander himself was drowned off Callao in his attempt to return home.

Cook continued to navigate down this western coast, exercising the caution necessary considering how the occasionally wild prevailing westerlies could so easily (and nearly did once) hurl him on this lee shore. However, he managed to keep close enough to continue his running survey, although too far out to sea most of the time to check the nature of the land and the density of habitation, if any.

The weather turned for the better on 10 January and 'put us all into high spirits'. On the previous day the land had been scarcely visible. Now the *Endeavour* ran seven leagues between noon and 8 p.m., bringing them within a league or two from the shore. Banks judged the land to be fertile, 'more so I think than any part of this country I have seen, rising in gentle slopes, not over-wooded but what trees there were well grown'. Before nightfall a high mountain could just be discerned to the south.

The great dome of the mountain bore straight ahead, much clothed in snow in mid-summer. There was speculation about its height, when the summit was clear of cloud, and many of the company thought it to be as high as the Pike of Tenerife (12,180 feet for the Pike, against 8,230 feet). The next day Cook named the mountain, and the Cape they doubled later, after Sir John Perceval, Earl of Egmont, First Lord of the Admiralty from 1763 to 1766.

On 14 January Cook ordered an eight-point turn to starboard, in order to conform to the coastline which tended more to the south-west than to the south-east. In the afternoon, between showers of rain and heavy cloud, they noted that the extremity of the land they had been following bore s 63° w. But more revealing and exciting than this was 'some high land which makes like an island* lying under the main bore sse distant 5 leagues'.

Of the number of inviting coves ahead, Cook named one Port Gore, which he planned to use for a thorough overhaul of his ship, a break for his men and livestock, and replenishment of supplies if possible. But overnight they were driven east and at dawn found themselves opposite a much wider inlet, which might serve their needs even better. Cook called at the first inlet on the north-west side of this sound, naming it Ship Cove. The sound beyond he named after the consort of his sovereign, Queen Charlotte.

At 2 o'clock [on Tuesday, 16 January 1770] we anchored in a very snug cove which is on the nw side of the bay . . . in 11 fathoms of water, soft ground and moored with the stream anchor. By this time several of the natives had come off to the ship in their canoes, and after heaving a few stones at us, and having some conversation with Tupia, some of them ventured on board . . .

The canoes were more primitive than any they had seen before and boasted none of the elaborate carvings they had earlier admired. Although these natives understood Tupia as well as the others, there were differences. These Ship Cove Maoris were rather darker in complexion and more simply dressed. As Tasman had drawn them, 'two corners of the cloth they wore were passed over their shoulders and fastened to the rest of it just below their breast'. None had the standard feathers attached to their hair which they had observed all along the coast. By contrast, Banks recorded that the women and some of the men sported 'a bunch of black feathers made round and tied upon the top of their heads which it entirely covered, making them look twice as large as they really were'.

But these Maoris were quite as fierce and aggressive as the others, throwing stones and threatening to hurl a spear at the slightest – or

---

* Was this remarkable percipience, or simply a supreme navigator's instinct?

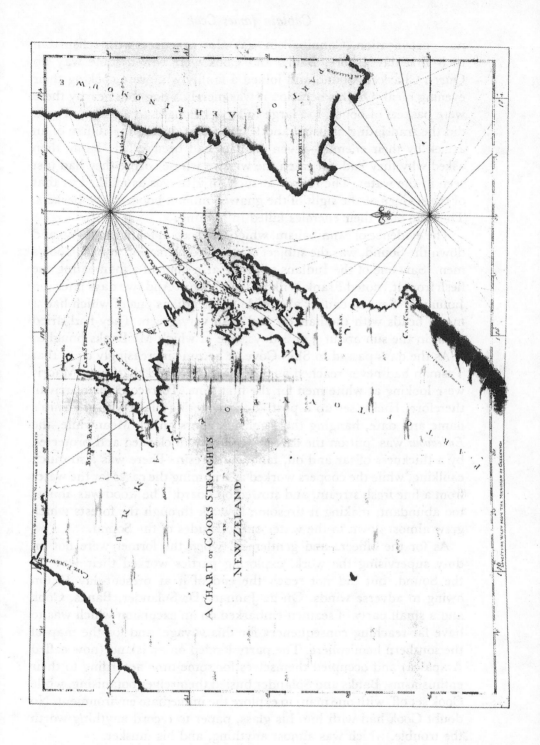

A CHART OF COOKS STRAIGHTS IN NEW ZELAND

no – provocation. Cannibalism was also practised with relish. On their first day ashore, Banks and Cook were rowed some way up Queen Charlotte Sound and joined a family who were cooking their evening meal. On this occasion it was merely a dog, but nearby there were baskets of bones, too large to have belonged to any dog. Tupia did the translating as usual and learned that during the course of an attack by their enemies, seven of them had been killed. Tupia then asked why they had not eaten the woman whose corpse they had just seen in the water. The horror at such an idea was as marked as that of the seamen at the sight of the gnawed human bones in the baskets. They ate only their enemies killed in fighting.

The evidence of cannibalism, which was seen in many places up and down the Sound, was the subject of much conversation among Cook's men. 'Saw one of the Indians with the arm bone of a man eating the flesh from it,' noted Frank Wilkinson in horror. And two days later (20 January): 'Several canoes alongside with Indians one of which had 4 men's heads with the hair on and flesh very green. They had dried them in the sun about 3 or 4 days, one of which Mr Banks bought.'

As the days passed in Ship Cove, it became increasingly clear that Tasman had never reached as far east as this, and that these Maoris were looking at white men for the first time. To record their arrival, therefore, Hicks 'set up a post at the watering place with the ship's name and date, hanging the English colours on it'. Meanwhile, the *Endeavour* was 'put on the careen', her bottom cleaned and protected by a thickness of tar and oil, tallow and resin. There was also much caulking, while the coopers worked at trimming the casks for the water from a fine fresh stream, and stowed on board. The wood was almost too abundant, making it tiresome to walk through the forests which grew almost down to the water on both sides of the Sound.

As for the officers and gentlemen, when the former were not on duty supervising the work, exploring parties worked their way up the Sound, but did not reach the end of it at present-day Picton owing to adverse winds. On 22 January Dr Solander, Banks, Cook and a small party of seamen embarked on an excursion which was to have far-reaching consequences for this voyage, and for the map of the southern hemisphere. The party landed on an island (now called Arapawa) and occupied themselves for some time according to their enthusiasms: Banks and Solander busied themselves botanising, while Cook set off, with one man, to explore the immediate environment. No doubt Cook had with him his glass, paper to record anything worth the trouble, which was almost anything, and his musket.

The climb cost only half an hour, through near impenetrable forest, but the dividend was immense. His view from the summit looking up the Sound, which he had hoped for, was obstructed by forest. But to the east, 'I saw what I took to be the Eastern Sea, and a strait or passage from it into the Western Sea . . .' The truth was now clear. They had all but circumnavigated this northern island over the past weeks. In order to conform to Admiralty orders, they must now work the *Endeavour* south and complete the survey of what Cook increasingly believed was another island.

When he rejoined the botanisers, he was, according to Banks, 'in high spirits', a condition he seldom exposed. They then 'refreshed themselves' before returning to the ship.

10

'The First Discoverer'

THE LAST DAYS OF JANUARY and the first days of February 1770 were occupied with preparations for departure, and formalities and farewells to the local people. On 29 January Cook and Banks with a party of five sailors formed an expedition to an island on the west side of the entrance to the Sound. After landing, they climbed to the summit of a hill and set about building a cairn of stones in which Cook buried some silver coins, musket balls and beads in order to demonstrate beyond doubt, he hoped, that this was not the work of local people. Two days later he returned with a stout post made by one of the carpenters and had it thrust firmly in the ground beside the pile of rocks. He 'hoisted thereon the Union flag and I dignified this inlet with the name of Queen Charlotte Sound and took formal possession of it in the name and for the use of His Majesty'. A bottle of wine was produced and they all drank Queen Charlotte's health. The empty bottle was then solemnly handed to an old man who had accompanied them to the summit and had witnessed this curious ceremony. He was delighted with his gift.

Tupia had already explained to the people who lived on the island what they were doing and had extracted a promise from them that they would not interfere with or demolish the cairn and flag. Cook had then distributed presents to all of them, silver threepenny pieces dated 1763 or spike nails with the King's broad arrow cut deep in them, 'things that I thought were most likely to remain long among them'.

Hicks noted with satisfaction in his log, shortly before their departure, that 'in this port the ship's company has been supplied with fish either from the seine or hook for neither beef, pork or flour has been served, and very few peas; for breakfast we boiled portable broth with celery'. Their first port of call here certainly contrasted favourably with North Island's Poverty Bay. But the natives were equally skilful at stealing, and the next day Hicks 'detected one stealing a pistol and a half-hour glass'. He recovered both.

After several false starts, the *Endeavour* 'made the signal for all boats and hoisted sail. Hoisted the pinnace in and the longboat up alongside. Made sail . . .' At last, on that evening of 7 February, they got out of the sound and very soon, owing to an unexpectedly fierce tide, almost came to grief on some rocks. As they worked their way through the strait,* then south, Cook named the cape to starboard after Captain John Campbell, a member of the Transit Committee who, like Cook, had begun his sea-going career in the coal trade. (He was also responsible for developing the quadrant into the modern sextant.)

Shortly after passing this cape, it was made clear to Cook that some of his officers were still in doubt that the land they had all but circumnavigated was in truth an island. 'No such supposition ever entered my thoughts,' he wrote, 'but being resolved to clear up every doubt that might arise on so important an object I took the opportunity of the shifting of the wind to stand to the eastward and accordingly steered NEBE all night.' One can almost hear his sigh of weariness at the obstinacy of his officers with their undimmed faith in the existence of the Great Southern Continent, when he knew that Cape Turnagain, where they had reversed course the previous year on 27 October, was just twenty-six leagues distant. He must even have been close to anger when the weather closed in and it was not until 10 February that the visibility allowed sight of the cape at 11 a.m., now a mere seven leagues away. 'I then called the officers upon deck and asked them if they were now satisfied that this land was an island, to which they answered in the affirmative and we hauled our wind to the eastward.'

With three days wasted, the *Endeavour* soon bore away to the south, to continue her coasting of what Cook was increasingly certain was another island. By sunset on 12 February they were passing the southernmost point of North Island, which he named after Hugh Palliser. A south-westerly course kept the *Endeavour* sailing parallel with the land, which appeared to be thinly populated and marked by high mountains inland, mostly snow-capped even in mid-summer. But several times the tide and wind forced them out to sea and out of sight of the coast. John Gore had another cove named after him; and Banks, though he makes no mention of it, gave his name to a large 'island'.

This was first sighted early on the morning of 15 February. 'At noon we were in the latitude of 43° 19' s, the peak on the snowy mountain bore N 20° E 27 leagues. The southern extremity we could see of that

---

* Banks declares casually: 'The strait itself was called Cook's Strait, the name of the Captain,' but gives neither the date nor the namer.

land bore west, and the land discovered in the morning making like an island . . .' And at sunrise the following day, 'being very clear', Cook was more certain: 'We plainly discovered that the last mentioned land was an island.' Anyone who has sailed these waters off present-day Christchurch will appreciate how easy it was for Cook to misidentify Banks Peninsula for an island.

Farther south they were driven out to sea, and then again on 25 February, off Cape Saunders, even farther. They were approaching the high 40°s and the weather was damnable. 'The wind whistling all round the compass, sometimes blowing a fresh gale and at other times almost calm.' The foresail was ripped to pieces, another being got up with the greatest difficulty. Soon after daylight the next morning, the gale increased to a storm.

Day after day the wind blew from sw to nw, and it was not until noon on 4 March that Cape Saunders was again sighted in the far distance to the north-west. The following day Cook saw that there was 'no land farther to the south' and was 'in hopes that this would prove the southern point' of what he now knew for certain was another island, South Island, New Zealand. The last substantial bay on this east coast Cook named Port Molyneux after his popular, if rather alcoholic, ship's master.

Here, deep down in New Zealand's highest latitudes, where they all suffered a good deal from the cold, Cook made another altogether forgivable surveying error. He had got so much right on this double running survey of these two large New Zealand islands, sometimes under appalling conditions, that it almost seems unjust to record, first that Banks Island was no island at all, and that now at this southern extremity, 'when I came to lay this land down upon paper from the several bearings I had taken, it appeared that there was little reason to suppose it [Stewart Island] an island; on the contrary, I hardly have a doubt but what it joins to and makes a part of the mainland'.

Now, as they approached the southern end of South Island, and the *Endeavour*, after several difficulties with dreadful weather again, bore south-west, the old controversy reasserted itself. The believers who still contended that this was part of the Great Southern Continent, *Terra Australis Incognita*, were now few in number, and even Banks was having his doubts.

We were now on board two parties [he wrote on 24 February], one who wished that the land in sight might, the other that it might not, be a continent. Myself have always been most firmly for the former, though sorry I am to say that in the ship my party is so small that I firmly believe that there are no more heartily of it than myself and one poor midshipman.

Then Banks sensed the mood of the homesick men and accurately added, 'The rest begin to sigh for roast beef.'

Banks now referred to the 'one poor midshipman' and himself as 'we Continents' as opposed to Cook and almost everyone else as 'no Continents', two parties gambling with the shape of the world's geography. But the contest was not yet over. On 5 March, in thick misty weather, the only land seen in the morning 'inclined much to the westward'. However, in the evening when visibility improved, the 'we Continents' had the pleasure to see more land to the southward. And, as always, Banks's hopes rose and he indulged himself in dreams of recounting to his social and scientific friends back home the events leading up to one of the great discoveries in history, in which he would take such a major part.

Hopes ebbed and flowed for several days of calm. Then the land to the southward turned out to be 'nothing but clouds'. They were close to South Cape on 9 March. Banks's hopes became as 'uncommonly barren' as the South Cape scenery, only a few miles distant. The next day it was all over. The *Endeavour* doubled the Cape, 'to the total demolition', as Banks quaintly and sadly put it, 'of our aerial fabrick called continent'.

Now the powerful south-westerlies drove them north almost into a wide bay, flanked by present-day Sand Hill Point. It was not until 12 March that they could resume their coasting, which was as difficult and hazardous as it had been all those weeks ago at North Cape. They were approaching that area of south-west South Island where the skyline is as fractured as the coast, the mountains in many places rising without a break from the sea. Cook writes of the face of the country bearing a 'very rugged aspect being full of high, craggy hills, on the summits of which were several patches of snow'.

For different reasons, both Cook and Banks were anxious to find a sheltered bay where the men could rest and repair, wood and water the *Endeavour*. Meanwhile, the gentlemen could go ashore to collect specimens of minerals which had appeared to be unusually interesting when they had been close to the shore. However, most of the bays they passed were distinctly inhospitable; one or two were easy to enter, but how would they get out again in this wild weather from the west and south-west?

At last, during the afternoon of 14 March, they found a bay which looked promising: deep, with an entrance three to four miles wide. Cook noted the coastal strip of level woodlands adjacent to this bay, quite different from what they had so far seen on this coast. He also noted that the north point of the bay was marked by five singular high-peaked rocks, like the raised hand of a man. He named it Point Five Fingers. But he could not get the *Endeavour* into this inviting bay before darkness closed about them, and fierce winds drove them north in the night. For this reason he named this lost haven, perhaps with some bitterness, Dusky Bay.

The *Endeavour* passed many more bays as they swept along this rugged coastline, to Banks's chagrin, as he longed to get ashore and sample the plant life as well as the geology. He never quite forgave Cook for what he regarded as his stubbornness. But had Banks had his way, he and all the ship's company may never have returned, ending their days on this bleak, uninhabited land. In a rare period of clear weather, north of Point Five Fingers, Cook writes uncompromisingly of the landscape:

Close behind these [coastal] hills lies the ridge of mountains which are of a prodigious height and appear to consist of nothing but barren rocks, covered in many places with large patches of snow which perhaps have laid there since the creation. No country upon earth can appear with a more rugged and barren aspect than this doth from the sea. As far inland as the eye can reach nothing can be seen but the summits of these rocky mountains, which seem to lie so near one another as not to admit any valleys between them ...

The land mellowed as they drove north, but not the weather, and there are few entries in any of the logs or journals referring to the weather as fair and only one or two telling of calm winds. Several times out of sight of the land altogether, Cook's running survey of parts of this west coast was the least accurate of the whole double circumnavigation of New Zealand's islands. Ironically, from Cape Foulwind north to Cape Farewell, the only length of this west coast where the charts made by Tasman and Cook overlap, the Dutchman's is more accurate. But then he had had excellent, clear weather, while Cook saw little of the land for the length of Karamea Bight.

However, this seems the appropriate place to quote the tribute of Julien Marie Crozet, the notable French navigator, who wrote of his time in New Zealand in 1772:

As soon as I obtained information of the voyage of the Englishman, I carefully compared the chart I had prepared for that part of the coast of New Zealand along which we had coasted with that prepared by Captain Cook and his officers. I found it of an exactitude and of a thoroughness of detail which astonished me beyond all powers of expression, and I doubt much whether the charts of our own French coasts are laid down with greater precision. I think therefore that I cannot do better than to lay down our track off New Zealand on the chart prepared by this celebrated English navigator. We landed at the foot of the high mountain named on this chart Mount Egmont . . .

North of the most northerly point of South Island, Cook knew that he was again at the western opening of the great strait that was to carry his own name and where the *Endeavour* had last been more than three months earlier. This time it was not so welcoming. For many hours, with the wind from the east, they 'gained nothing to windward', and it was not until the morning of 27 March that the wind backed to the north and they could make headway towards the island he had earlier named Stephens Island. Now, at last, Cook knew that he could find a satisfactory anchorage and, among much else, fill the empty water casks in the hold. The cove he chose, close to the entrance to Queen Charlotte Sound, he named after the Admiralty, which had ordered him here. He anchored at 6 p.m. and at daylight the following morning he had the ship moored conveniently for sending ashore all the empty casks.

Banks went ashore at once, as always with his greyhounds, his fellow scientists and surviving servants. He found the land much like that of Ship Cove, which was only a few miles distant, and they discovered only one new plant. Nor were there any Maoris about, only a small, neglected settlement. Tupia and Tiata took a boat and went fishing with a seine, catching enough and more for the ship's company in no time. Those not employed in wooding and watering fished with lines from the *Endeavour*'s ports. Cook explored the hinterland, with some difficulty as the hills were thick with ferns and shrubs under the trees. And it rained and rained. Once the full casks were on board and stowed, and the carpenters had felled and sawn enough wood, there was nothing further to delay their departure.

There were two ways home: by way of the Horn, which Cook would have preferred if the season were not so far advanced that he would have to double it at the worst time of the year, or he could sail west. Due west would be to follow Tasman's passage in reverse, taking the *Endeavour* south of what the Dutchman had named Van Diemen's Land, later renamed Tasmania. This was not yet known to be an island south of the great land mass, the continent which the Dutch had named New Holland.

New Holland was not this continent's first name. There is a vast confusion surrounding the origins of the name Australia, but in Spanish interpretations it long ante-dated the Dutch New Holland. Quiros, the Portuguese navigator, 'In the memorial which he addressed to the King of Spain in 1607, says that he named the land *Austrialia* "in happy memory of Your Majesty, whose dynastic name is *Austria*" . . . In a later Memorial of 1610 Quiros wrote that the King had ordered him to discover land "en la parte *Austrialia* Incognita".'* G. A. Wood, in his *The Discovery of Australia*, also notes that the British navigator, Matthew Flinders (1774–1814), favoured *Australia* over *Terra Australis* because it was 'more agreeable to the ear, and an assimilation to the names of other great portions of the earth'.

The Dutch had every right to sound a proprietorial note about New Holland, and to leave their Dutch names where their ships touched its coastline. Chinese merchantmen may have known the northern coast of this continent, and Malay prows were believed to have collected the prized *bêche-de-mer*, or sea cucumber, in the Gulf of Carpentaria, but it was the Dutch who first brought coherency to parts of the north, the west and south of New Holland.

This came about originally when the mariner Hendrik Brouwer in 1611 decided to experiment with a new route from the Cape of Good Hope to the rich Dutch possessions in the East Indies. Brouwer sailed on an easterly heading for 4,000 miles before turning north, instead of hugging the east coast of Africa, and in so doing cut weeks from the tiresome voyage.

When this new route became accepted as superior, it was only a matter of time before this new continent was discovered by chance, or by holding an easterly course for too long. First contacts were not encouraging. The few inhabitants were savage, the country sterile by contrast with the spice islands to the north. None the less, Dutch curiosity was aroused, if only to forestall any other power's claims. This eventually led to Tasman's two remarkable voyages of 1642 and 1644, in the course of which he circumnavigated the entire continent, proving it to be a vast island, and charting the greater part of the north-west and northern coasts.

After touching New Zealand's west coast and proceeding north from it, Tasman had later recovered the coast of New Holland at its northernmost tip, leaving unseen and uncharted the whole eastern coast of the continent, at least 2,000 miles of it, Cook calculated. Cook now therefore determined to fill this enormous gap in New Holland geography, sail NW, fall in with this coast and sail up it, charting every bay and headland, every river and every shoal. He could not know what he was letting himself in for, but it was an

* See G. A. Wood, *The Discovery of Australia* (1922), pp. 174–5, n. 1.

historic decision, typically enterprising and daring. Then he would pass through Torres's Strait and make for Batavia, thence home by the Cape.

THE NAME CAPE FAREWELL sounds a melancholy note and Cook was glad enough to see this cliff astern of the *Endeavour*. Cape Farewell is a black mass of shapeless rock, pounded white at the base by the rollers of the Tasman Sea. It was raining hard, hazy and with a favourable wind from the east, and this northernmost point of New Zealand's South Island disappeared from sight soon after 6 p.m.

The day was 31 March 1770. It was two years since they had left England. Now they could record, indisputably, that they were on their way home. The *Endeavour* continued on a NW by W course, suffering strange variations in weather. For days it was calm and fine with tropical temperatures and heavy dews at night, 'a kind of invisible spray or mist which thoroughly wetted my hair as I walked the deck,' noted Banks. Two mornings later he wrote in his journal: 'During last night and this morn the weather was most variable with continual squalls and winds shifting all round the compass.'

Two weeks from Cape Farewell the signs of land came, as so often, from the birds about the ship, first a small strayed land bird, thankful for a rest in the rigging, and then a gannet, 'which flew towards the NW with a steady uninterrupted flight as if he knew the road that he was going led to the shore'. Next, on 18 April, a shoal of porpoises greeted them, leaping out of the water like salmon, 'often throwing their whole bodies several feet high above the surface.'

Heavy weather still lay ahead: a hard gale with squalls on 17 April, and no improvement the following morning when Cook ordered the topsails to be taken in. Later in the day, as the wind eased, he had the topsails close reefed while the *Endeavour* sped through the rough seas.

Early the next morning, 19 April, Zachary Hicks climbed up high in the foremast rigging, keen as always to be the first to sight land. At 6 a.m. he had his reward, his moment of triumph, letting out that cry which has sent tremors of joy amongst those who have heard the words since the beginning of seafaring: 'Land ahoy!'

The land, according to Cook, extended from north-east to west at a distance of five or six leagues, and the southernmost point he named Point Hicks. But on bearing away south he was puzzled to find no further sign of land. According to his calculations he was still far north of the southern coast of New Holland, charted by Tasman 125 years earlier. What Tasman had not learned was that Tasmania, as it was to be named, was an island.

Cook put over the *Endeavour*'s helm and steered north again, determined to follow this land, and thus hoping to chart for the first time the eastern coastline of New Holland. He was to rename it New South Wales and take it into the possession of Britain and His Majesty King George III, raising the union flag on shore. For the present, and when the weather cleared to give him a good view of the coast, he expressed himself pleased with what he saw. It has, he wrote, 'a very agreeable and promising aspect. The land is of a moderate height, diversified with hills, ridges, plains and valleys, with some grass but for the most part the whole was covered with wood.'

Such a land must surely be populated; and on the next afternoon, in weather still fine and clear, they saw smoke rising from a number of fires, 'certain sign that the country is inhabited'. Soon they must go ashore for, as always, they needed wood and water. Then they would meet these people who had never set eyes upon anything afloat larger than their own canoes, nor seen a white man.

THE CHARTING OF NEW ZEALAND, the adventures and dangers they had experienced there, were stirring enough. But Abel Tasman had got there first, had for a while sailed along the same coast and had had relations with the natives (in fact, had been unfortunate enough to lose four of his men to cannibalism). But this coast was entirely new, and what they were looking at, with or without the aid of a glass, was the opening of a chapter in the history of exploration.

All that Cook was prepared to yield in his account of this coasting up the 2,000 miles of the east coast of this continent, one of the few moments when 'in the journals he opens the door just a little and lets us look through', was an admission of 'the very jaws of destruction' at one point and of 'the vicissitudes [which] . . . must always attend an unknown navigation', as well as 'the pleasure which naturally results to a man from being the first discoverer'.

On the morning of 20 April, on sighting a great cape, he named it after Richard (Earl) Howe, who at the age of thirty-three had led the line at Hawke's great victory at the Battle of Quiberon Bay and was currently Treasurer of the Navy. After the summer cold and the tearing wind and rain of New Zealand, the *Endeavour*'s men gloried in the warmth and relative serenity of this coastline. 'The country this morn', wrote Banks, 'rose in gently sloping hills which had the appearance of the highest fertility. Every hill seemed to be clothed with trees of no mean size . . . This east coast of New Holland might not be as spectacular as the west coast of New Zealand with its towering snow-clad peaks, but they all appreciated the warmth in the air, as well as sensing warmer hospitality here than during their last coasting, where the natives they met were mainly hostile. This increased the longing to find an anchorage and go ashore, especially by Banks and his colleagues, eager for plants from the new land.

Two days later – days of gentle breeze from the south and clear weather – they were able to sail close enough to shore to be able to examine the natives whose presence had been indicated if not proven by the numerous fires Cook and his men had seen. 'The people appeared to be of a very dark colour, or black colour,' Cook wrote, 'but whether this was the real colour of their skins or the clothes they might have on I know not.'

The *Endeavour* was now approaching a deep bay, today's Jervis Bay, and Cook at first thought that it might make a comfortable anchorage, until he tried and failed to take a closer look. 'Clear, serene weather' continued to prevail. 'Clear and pleasant weather on 26 April.' Yet they still could not get ashore, and as Banks had earlier observed – doubtless several times – this was a business requiring patience.

On the 27th Cook ordered the ship to be hove to and determined to go ashore by boat. He had seen a number of natives, four of whom were carrying a canoe as if to launch it and paddle the two miles to the *Endeavour*. But it was the ship's yawl that was first into the water with Cook, Banks, Solander and Tupia as translator. This little party was disappointed, however. The surf was too high, and Cook had to be content with observing more canoes drawn up, and trees 'of the palm kind' – doubtless Cabbage Palm, and later identified by Banks as *Livistona australis*.

This land of New Holland was, day by day, becoming more exasperating. The west coast of South Island, New Zealand, at least offered numerous harbours, even if the wild weather had prohibited their use. But overnight a blessing fell on the *Endeavour*, and at first light 'we discovered a bay', Cook was able to write with satisfaction, 'which appeared to be tolerably well sheltered from all winds, into which I resolved to go with the ship . . . sent the Master in the pinnace to sound the entrance'.

Bob Molyneux's report being favourable, on that afternoon of Saturday, 28 April 1770, Cook had the *Endeavour* brought through the entrance of this bay, with the wind from the south and the weather fine and clear. They saw scattered groups of natives as they sailed slowly along the shore, men, women and children, all stark naked, some of the men spear-fishing and not even bothering to raise their heads in acknowledgment of their arrival, although some followed their progress on foot, occasionally glancing in their direction.

Cook anchored the ship on this south side of the bay, two miles from its entrance, and half a mile from a group of huts in front of trees.

Soon after this [Banks recounted] an old woman followed by three children came out of the wood. She carried several pieces of stick, and the children also had their little burthens . . . She often looked at the ship but expressed neither surprise nor concern . . . She lit a fire and [at the same time] four canoes came in from fishing. They landed, hauled up their canoes and began to dress their fish for dinner, to all appearance totally unmoved at us.

The *Endeavour*'s men took their own midday dinner at the same time, some of the men sitting on deck, glancing at the black naked people on shore, which added a domestic and intimate note to this first contact between eastern Aborigines and Europeans. After this, the boats were lowered and nearly half the *Endeavour*'s company prepared to go ashore, as always well protected by the marines, even though Cook expected little trouble after the morning's demonstration of indifference.

Cook's boat led the way in. We can imagine him standing at the prow, with his wife's young nephew Isaac at his side, and Banks, Solander and Tupia waiting to leap out as soon as the keel cut into the sandy shore flanked by rocks. Those Aborigines who had been enjoying dinner by the fire, and others who had been drawn to the huts, retreated into the trees as the first boat approached. But two men stood their ground, both armed with long lances and both assuming hostile stances. Cook at once ordered his men to rest on their oars while he attempted to reassure the Aborigines of his peaceful intentions. Tupia called out that all they wanted was water, but 'They called us very loudly', Banks described, 'in a harsh sounding language, of which neither us nor Tupia understood a word.'

Sydney Parkinson, with his artist's eye, has left the most graphic account of this first meeting with the Aborigines:

Their countenance bespoke displeasure; they threatened us, and discovered hostile intentions, often crying to us Warra warra wai. We made signs to them to be peaceable, and threw them some trinkets; but they kept aloof and dared us to come ashore. We attempted to frighten them by firing off a gun loaded with small shot, but attempted it in vain. One of them repaired to a house* immediately and brought out a shield, of an oval figure, painted

* Cook calls them 'small huts made of the bark of trees'.

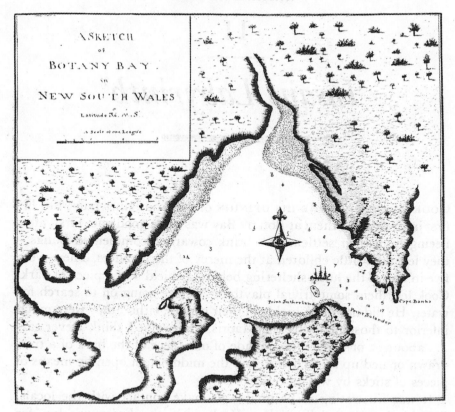

white in the middle, with two holes in the middle to see through, and also a wooden sword, and then they advanced boldly, gathering up stones as they came along, which they threw at us . . .'

Cook now ordered his boat forward and the prow dug hard into the sandy beach. At this point, with characteristic thoughtfulness, Cook turned to his wife's young nephew and, indicating his wish with a gesture, called to him, 'Isaac, you shall land first.' And so he did, with great eagerness.*

* Isaac Smith, who later became an admiral (and a very good one, too), could not claim to be the first Englishman to land on Australian soil, as Dampier several times went ashore on the west and north-west coast in January 1688, but that was 2,150 miles distant at Cygnet's Bay, King's Sound, north-west Australia, and Isaac Smith was certainly first ashore on the east coast of the continent.

11

'Insane Labyrinth'

COOK WAS TO CHANGE HIS OPINION of the Aborigines later, but his first impression of them at Botany Bay was not a good one. First, after fleeing from their settlement – 'rank cowards,' commented Banks – they left their little children at the mercy of the invaders. There were five in one of the huts, sheltering behind a shield and a piece of bark. Cook left them some trivial playthings before going off to search for water. He did not think highly of their canoes, either; they were much inferior to those made by the Maoris: 'the worst I think I ever saw ... about 12 or 14 feet long, made of one piece of the bark of a tree, drawn or tied up at each end, and the middle kept open by means of pieces of sticks by way of thwarts'.

It was frustrating to be unable to make contact with the locals, but this bay, called Sting Ray Harbour in the *Endeavour*'s log, for the obvious reason, and Botany Bay in Cook's journal, had much to commend it. The botany, as can be imagined, satisfied Banks and his friends, with the additional bonus of animal life. He and Solander spotted the tracks of a dog – doubtless a dingo; the brief sight of a small animal 'like a rabbit' (a pest yet to be introduced); and a herbivore 'in size not less than a deer', almost certainly their first sight of a kangaroo.

With peerless accuracy, Green placed the south entrance to Botany Bay at 34° 0′ s. Cook's and Banks's observations on the quality of the surrounding land were to have profound consequences.* An excursion into the country led Cook to remark on its diversity, with woods, grassland and marshes: 'The woods are free from undergrowth of every kind and the trees are at such a distance from one another

---

* 'In 1779 Banks was examined by a committee of the House of Commons [considering] what shall we do with our convicts? If it was thought expedient to establish a colony of convicted felons in a distant part whence escape would be difficult, and where from the fertility of the soil they might be enabled to maintain themselves after the first year ... what place did Mr Banks think best? His answer was – Botany Bay!'

that the whole country or at least a great part of it might be cultivated . . .'

On the last day of April Cook made a tour of the entire bay,* and at one point had his men cast the seine, hauling in 300 pounds of fish in no time, further evidence of the abundance of this place. Even oysters and clams were in free supply, and the water for the casks was as pure as that of Tierra del Fuego. Apart from their failure to establish any relations with the Aborigines, the only sadness associated with Botany Bay was the death of the thirty-year-old Orcadian, Forby Sutherland, who had contracted consumption shortly after they had left the Straits of le Maire, the first Briton to die in Australia. A point on the south side of the bay was given his name.

Before leaving this 'capacious, safe and commodious' bay, where the union flag had been flown every day, Cook ordered an inscription to be cut on a tree close to where they had watered, setting forth the ship's name and date, 6 May 1770. With all sail set and with a light southerly wind 'and serene pleasant weather', the *Endeavour* continued her coasting, a league or two offshore. Almost at once they sighted what 'appeared to be safe anchorage'. It was indeed, though Cook had no need of it. Peering through the heads, he named this harbour, one of the largest and most beautiful in the world, Port Jackson.** Today we know the city built upon it as Sydney.

After the hazards and wildness of the west coast of New Zealand, this northerly coasting of New Holland appeared relatively simple and safe. But night and day, at first with a faint moon and southerly breezes, decisions had to be made, hauling the wind, hoisting sail, heaving the lead when shoal water threatened, watching for breakers by day, listening for them at night, and standing off and on in the darkness when danger threatened. Bearings on the coast had to be taken, a full-time job for one man at least, and headlands and bays noted and named: Point Stephens, Broken Bay, Smoky Cape where the Aborigines' fires were notable, Cape Byron, Cape Morton, Indian Head and Sandy Cape.

'At 10 o'clock in the PM we passed at the distance of four miles having 17 fathoms of water [according to the lead], a black bluff, head, or point of land, which occasioned my naming it Indian Head . . .' Sometimes, because of poor visibility and after the *Endeavour* had been

---

* Today much of the north/south runway of Sydney international airport has been built over the north side of Botany Bay.
** After Sir George Jackson, second secretary of the Admiralty, and brother of Mrs Skottowe of Great Ayton.

forced farther from the shore than Cook would have preferred, islands are confused with a point, or a peninsula for an island, as on the east coast of New Zealand. But the detail and accuracy of the charts were otherwise superb.

Given time and opportunity, Cook would have wished to go ashore and take land bearings as well as sea bearings. But landing places were few and far between, and it was still a long way to Batavia, even if they were successful in finding the northern passage of Charles de Brosses's chart.*

Meanwhile, Banks busied himself in the cabin with his samples, his greyhounds beside him like twin sentinels: they wanted to go ashore as keenly as their master. Nearby, day after day, Parkinson produced his brilliant drawings. A week out of Botany Bay, Banks, after giving a favourable report on the land – 'fertile . . . varying . . . well clothed with trees' – tells his readers: 'Drawing the plants got in the last harbour [Botany Bay], which had been kept fresh till this time by means of tin chests and wet cloths . . . [Parkinson] has made 94 sketch drawings, so quick a hand has he acquired by use.'

For many days the land looked decidedly infertile, just rocks and sand, and lightly undulant. But it was as variable as the wind. On the afternoon of 22 May they saw much woodland and a generally fertile land; moreover, breaking into it was an 'inviting bay' where Cook made the sudden decision to anchor for the night and go ashore the following day. No one was happier about this than Banks.

There was a lot of drinking among the people that night, to celebrate idleness, no doubt, though there could be a lot of drinking any night off watch. One who had crawled into his hammock dead drunk was Dick Orton, Cook's able clerk. Orton was not known either for his violence, or for having enemies, but you could never tell on shipboard what the devil alcohol could do. It did badly for the clerk that night. First his clothes were cut off his back, and then his assailant returned and cut a piece off both his ears. We are not told whether this succeeded in awakening him, but it certainly must have caused much blood.

When Cook heard of this assault, he fell into a fearful rage. At a heated enquiry the next morning suspicion fell on Jim Magra, the midshipman from New York, who, Cook learned, had cut off Orton's clothes more than once before. Under interrogation, Magra gave evidence, albeit slim and inconclusive, of guilt. In a previous incident Magra had come close to murdering the unfortunate Orton, for what reason was not known, at least not to Cook. 'I therefore, for

* In that Frenchman's *Histoire des Navigations aux Terres Australes* (1756).

the present, dismissed him the quarterdeck and suspended him from doing any duty,' Cook reported, 'he being one of those gentlemen . . . that can very well be spared, or to speak more plainly, a good for nothing.'

Midshipman Magra was soon restored to his duties, and Cook's belief in his guilt began to fade. However, that was not the end of the affair as the truth behind the bloody event nagged at Cook.*

The *Endeavour* was in a bay close to the present-day town of Gladstone in southern Queensland. Cook, Banks and his gentlemen and greyhounds, with Tupia and a boat's crew, went ashore on the morning of 23 May 'to examine the country'. At first they saw no one, only much smoke inland, which Cook was increasingly certain, as they sailed north, was a form of warning signal from one community to another. But this was a poor place in which to settle. 'The country is visibly worse than the last place we were at, the soil is dry and sandy and the woods are free from underwood of any kind.' Most of these trees were mangroves or grey birch, yet in spite of the poverty of the soil, Banks was able to collect many plants which he had not found at Botany Bay.

It was also disagreeably cold when they first went ashore – it was near mid-winter – which made it all the more remarkable that when they came upon evidence of a community, marked by old fires and cockleshells, Cook concluded that the small amount of bark lying about 'were all the covering [the Aborigines] had in the night'. He continued: 'Many of them I firmly believe have not this but are naked as they sleep in the open air.' Tupia despisingly, and with his usual air of authority, claimed that they were *Taata Eno*'s, bad or poor people.

One of the party shot a bustard, 'such as we have in England', which weighed 17½ pounds. The next day they had it for dinner. 'It turned out an excellent bird,' Banks commented, 'far the best we all agreed we have eaten since we left England.'

After gathering as many oysters, mussels and cockles as the time allowed, Cook weighed from what he named Bustard Bay at 4 a.m. on 24 May, soon noting ominously at the break of dawn, 'breakers stretching out . . . NNE two or three miles'. They were approaching the Tropic of Capricorn, which led him to give that name to a prominent cape. The land was becoming mountainous, with the appearance 'more of barrenness than fertility', but none the less inhabited. Inland, smoke from fires followed their progress with uncanny, and somewhat unsettling, accuracy. Were there coastwatchers? Was a great army

* See Appendix 1 on page 371.

being assembled inland to await another landing by these white men in their monstrous canoe? By night the flames lit the western sky.

At sea, navigation was daily becoming trickier. Islands (one inhabited by naked dancing black figures), breakers, shoals, and protruding and threatening half-concealed rocks appeared with increasing frequency. Cook hoped for clear seas ahead. He could have no knowledge of the Great Barrier Reef, but that is what was closing in on the *Endeavour*.

A typical entry in Cook's journal for 28 May reads:

Fresh gales between the SSE and ESE. Hazy weather with some showers of rain in the PM. Having sounded about the ship and found that there was sufficient water for her over the shoal, we at 3 o'clock weighed and came to sail . . . At 6 o'clock we anchored in 10 fathoms of water, a sandy bottom about two miles from the mainland . . . At 5 o'clock a.m. I sent away the Master with two boats to sound the entrance to an inlet.

Here they anchored briefly, hoping both for water and a sight of the conditions ahead at sea. They found neither, nor 'signs of fertility'. As usual, fires broke out inland and a few Aborigines were seen distantly; certainly, there were no barbarian hordes armed with the long lances and wooden swords they had seen at Botany Bay.

Impatient with himself for wasting time on an unproductive landing, Cook named the place Thirsty Bay, although Banks and his gentlemen, who rarely failed to find something for their record or collection, noted a number of new plants, as well as shells, butterflies and a fish that could travel over dry land, the mud skipper or *Periophthalmus australis*. Progress north became slow, not from unfavourable winds but because of the islands and shoals all around them, and these continued for as far as could be seen from the top of the mainmast. Phrases like 'I was not sure there was a passage this way' and 'again embarrassed with shoal water' appear in Cook's journal, Hicks noting on 8 June, 'sailing between an island and the main, distance from each one mile'. The lead was kept going all of the night of the 3–4 June and continuously thereafter.

The weather was pleasant, the winds gentle and favourable. Pickersgill recorded: 'Running through a strait formed by a chain of very pleasant islands, on one of which we saw people who had canoes with outriggers, the first we have seen in the country.' They could have enjoyed everything that was to make this Great Barrier Reef coastline one of the most popular vacation areas in the world 200 years later – the benign winter weather, the beaches, the glorious islands and the warm sea – but Cook and his company were in uncharted waters, without power, in a ship which in size and unhandiness should not have been there.

Never before had the strains and stresses of command borne down more heavily on Cook. On the evening of 10 June, close to a point he was to name Cape Tribulation 'because here began all our troubles', they were approaching two small islands, or reefs, as some of his men correctly believed them to be:

At this time we shortened sail [Cook wrote] and hauled off shore ENE and NEBE close upon a wind. My intention was to stretch off all night as well to avoid the dangers we saw ahead as to see if any islands lay in the offing . . . having the advantage of a fine breeze of wind and a clear moonlight night. In standing off from 6 until almost 9 o'clock we deepened our water from 14 to 21 fathoms, when all at once we fell into 12, 10 and 8 fathoms. At this time I had everybody at their stations to put about and come to anchor, but in this I was not so fortunate, for meeting again with deep water I thought there could be no danger in standing on. Before 10 o'clock we had 20 and 21 fathoms and continued in that depth until a few minutes before 11 o'clock, when we had 17. Before the man at the lead could heave another cast, the ship struck and stuck fast.

Hicks's log baldly states: 'Before the leadsman could get another cast, the ship struck on some sunken rocks and stuck fast.'

Banks, as can be expected, paints a more colourful picture of the scene:

Scarce were we warm in our beds when we were called up with the alarming news of the ship being fast ashore upon a rock, which she in a few moments convinced us by beating very violently against the rocks. Our situation now became greatly alarming . . . we were little less than certain that we were upon sunken coral rocks, the most dreadful of all others on account of their sharp points and grinding quality, which cut through a ship's bottom almost immediately . . .

The sensible Parkinson summed up their position: 'We were at this period many thousand leagues from our native land, and on a barbarous coast, where, if the ship were wrecked and we had escaped the perils of the sea, we should have fallen into the rapacious hands of savages.' Sensible he may have been, but when his narrative was published it became evident, perhaps under the anxieties of the time, that he recorded the p.m. hours as a.m., the *Endeavour*'s striking before noon, and thus in full daylight.

Cook reacted swiftly and with characteristic coolness. All the sails were taken in within minutes, the boats launched to sound round the ship. They found the depth varied from three to four fathoms to three to four feet on the port side, a good deal more to starboard, the *Endeavour*'s head lying the north-east. They were, it was now clear, stuck on the south-east edge of a coral reef, with deep water astern.

They had struck at high water, so if they were going to haul her off they must be quick about it. Cable and anchor were therefore put into the longboat and carried to the starboard quarter, the cable being fed back to the ship. But no amount of pressure on the capstan and windlass could move the ship an inch – 'the ship being quite fast, upon which we went to look to lighten her as fast as possible, which seemed to be the only means we had left to get her off'.

For two hours, from 4 a.m. to 6 a.m., everyone 'heav[ed] overboard empty casks, . . . iron ballast', Hicks logged. The six carriage guns went over the side, along with decayed stores, stone ballast, staves, hoops and all their water – fifty tons by noon the next day. 'As this was not found sufficient,' Cook noted, 'we continued to lighten her by every method we could think of.'

The *Endeavour* had four pumps, one of which was unserviceable, and as the tide fell two pumps were needed to keep pace with the water they were taking in. Luckily, the sea remained calm, there was little wind and the afternoon of 11 June remained fine. But the next few hours were critical for their survival.

Carried out the two bower anchors, the one on the starboard quarter and the other right astern [Cook wrote of this fearful time]. Got blocks and tackles upon the cables, brought the falls in abaft, and hove taut. By this time it was 5 o'clock in the p.m. . . . The tide now began to rise and the leak increased upon us which obliged us to set the third pump to work . . . At 9 o'clock the ship righted and the leak gained upon the pumps considerably. This was an alarming and I may say terrible circumstance, and threatened immediate destruction to us as soon as the ship was afloat.

Cook was not a man to exaggerate or to use such language lightly. Their dilemma was as acute as it could be. If they remained as they were, the *Endeavour* would in time grind herself to pieces, they would lose her and all their remaining stores, and be forced to land from their boats on a barren shore without any expectation of rescue. If they got her off the reef, there was every likelihood of her sinking before she could be beached, the shore being seven to eight leagues distant.

Cook's decision was swift and decisive:

I resolved to risk all [he recounted] and heave her off . . . and accordingly turned as many hands to the capstan and windlass as could be spared from the pumps. About twenty minutes past 10 o'clock in the evening the ship floated and we hove her off into deep water.

'This desirable event gave us spirits,' wrote Parkinson with a touch of sententiousness, 'which, however, proved but the transient gleam of sunshine in a tempestuous day.' The reason was that the leak rate now increased greatly. There was already 3 foot 9 inches of water in the hold, and there were two men down there measuring it – the only men in the ship except the sick – who were not pumping for their lives in fifteen-minute shifts.

One of the men below made a measuring error which suggested that they were losing the battle even faster than in fact they were. The mistake was soon corrected and, after the despair it caused, the discovery put new heart into the panting and exhausted men. A while later they were further encouraged when Cook decided to

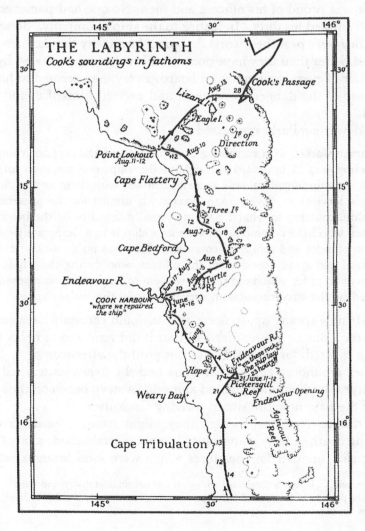

THE LABYRINTH
Cook's soundings in fathoms

fother* the injury. Midshipman Jonathan Monkhouse had been put in charge of this operation because he had once, in his short time at sea, been in a ship which was saved in mid-ocean by this ingenious method of plugging a leak, which could not be resorted to with the ship aground. 'He executed it very much to my satisfaction,' Cook recorded in a rare resort to praise.

This fothering was so effective that a single pump could gain on the leak; and this was just as well, for it took several dangerous days among the damnable rocks and shoals to find an anchorage and then, with needle-sharp care, edge the *Endeavour* into a bay and anchor her alongside a river and a beach. Mercifully, it was almost perfect for their needs.

Cook was proud of his officers and men. No one had panicked, no one had shirked his duty. 'In justice to the ship's company,' he wrote, when they were past their worst dangers, 'I must say that no men ever behaved better than they have done on this occasion, animated by the behaviour of every gentleman on board. Every man seemed to have a just sense of the danger we were in and exerted himself to the very utmost.'

Banks was similarly impressed:

The seamen worked with surprising cheerfulness and alacrity; no grumbling or growling was to be heard throughout the ship; no, not even an oath (though the ship in general was as well furnished with them as most in His Majesty's service) . . . Every man exerted his utmost for the preservation of the ship, contrary to what I have universally heard to be the behaviour of seamen who have commonly as soon as a ship is in a desperate situation begun to plunder and refuse all command. This was no doubt due entirely to the cool and steady conduct of the officers, who during the whole time never gave an order which did not show them to be perfectly composed and unmoved by the circumstances, however dreadful they might appear.

A gale now sprang up, so fierce that it would certainly have caused a disaster a day or two earlier. All that it did now was to delay their landing to a tedious extent. It was not until the afternoon of 17 June, and after grounding again, that Cook had the *Endeavour* warped into this natural harbour and moored alongside a steep beach on the south side of the bay, now the site of thriving Cooktown.

On this barren shore, where they might have so easily faced a lingering death, a busy community was soon established: a large tent for the sick, another for the stores which were soon brought ashore,

* 'A heavy sail . . . is closely thrummed with yarn and oakum, and drawn under the bottom; the pressure of the water drives the thrumming into the apertures.' (*The Sailor's Word Book, op. cit.*)

and a forge for the armourer, the carpenters' tools and equipment. The weather remained pretty miserable, but the men were not depressed by the gales and driving rain, still enjoying the exhilaration of being alive with their ship lying offshore, seemingly unaffected by her ordeal.

The *Endeavour*'s injuries were found to be much more serious than Cook had expected. After getting out all her coal, a laborious job indeed, Cook chose a spot higher up the harbour. He hauled her bow ashore at high tide, with her stern still in the water. The tide was at its lowest at the inconvenient hour of 2 a.m., but this did not prevent Cook from making a comprehensive examination. On the starboard side before the fore chains, 'Here the rocks [i.e. coral] had made their way through four planks quite to and even into the timbers and damaged three more.' He had never seen coral damage before and was amazed at the absence of any splinters, 'as if the damage had been done by the hands of man with a blunt edge tool'.

At first Cook could not understand why they had not foundered at once, but then he discovered a large piece of coral jammed into the worst hole, effectively part-sealing it; while elsewhere 'several pieces of the fothering, small stones, sand, etc., had made its way in and lodged between the timbers which had stopped the water from forcing its way in in great quantities'. Amazing good luck, supported by their own ingenuity, had saved them.

There was much more damage than this – part of the false keel had gone, for instance – but not of a fatal nature. By 9 a.m. the carpenters were at work, and the blacksmiths at the forge were busy making the great number of bolts and nails that would be required.

While all this sawing and hammering, on nails and anvil, continued at high speed, some of the men formed a digging party for fresh water. The river, which they named after their ship, had only brackish water. Others, under John Gore, went inland in search of food, shooting pigeon but failing at first to kill a kangaroo, which were to be found in numbers but proved elusive. Later, Banks's greyhound bitch, Lady, had no difficulty in taking a small kangaroo, but when they were fully grown these beasts could easily outstrip her. Others went out fishing with the seine and at first caught little. But turtles were found, three weighing 791 pounds, and provided a welcome change in the rations.

Cook climbed a 500-foot hill and did not care for what he saw. At low tide 'were a number of sandbanks or shoals lying all along the coast'. Two days later he sent Bob Molyneux out of the bay in the pinnace to reconnoitre the shoals and attempt to find a passage through to the north. He found nothing to reassure Cook about their future when the ship was repaired.

Cook was equally disappointed at first in their failure again to make any useful contact with the Aborigines. They had glimpses of them from time to time, and intermittently there were distant fires inland. On one day a sailor from a party out searching for food became detached and, alone and unarmed, chanced on a family of Aborigines eating round a fire. Sensibly, instead of running off, no doubt pursued by lances, he sat down with them in a companionable sort of way, remained a few minutes and then sauntered off.

On the morning of 10 July, when they had already been there for a month, Cook spotted a group of Aborigines on the other side of the bay. They had evidently intended to spear fish from a canoe with outriggers, but were soon distracted by the strange sight of the *Endeavour* lying half in the water, and the sight and sound of those working on her.

To Cook's delight, two of the Aborigines canoed across the bay and rested on their paddles close enough to the ship for them 'to take such trifles as we gave them'. They then paddled back to the other two and returned, all four landing on the beach close to the ship. They had their lances with them, but seemed happy to lay them down when Tupia, if no longer the interpreter but still the intermediary, suggested by gestures that they should do so.

Cook and several of the gentlemen then approached the Aborigines, taking care not to go between them and their weapons, sat down beside them and handed over more presents:

We continued together, with the utmost cordiality, till dinner time, and then giving them to understand that we were going to eat, we invited them by signs to go with us. However, they declined, and as soon as we left them they went away in their canoe. One of these men was somewhat above the middle age, the other three were young. They were of the common stature, but their limbs were remarkably small. Their skin was . . . a dark chocolate colour; their hair was black, but not woolly. It was short-cropped, in some lank, in others curled . . . Some parts of their bodies had been painted red, and the upper lip and breast of one of them was painted with streaks of white . . . Their features were far from disagreeable, their eyes were lively, and their teeth even and white. Their voices were soft and tuneable, and they repeated many words after us with great facility.

Nine days later, as the repairs to the *Endeavour* neared completion, there was another meeting with the locals, this time of a more hectic nature. A party of mixed men and women came to the ship, the men armed and all exuding a sense of purpose. It soon became clear that what they were after were the live turtles on the *Endeavour*'s deck, which they had probably seen earlier being brought back in one of the boats. They were evidently a delicacy for them, as they were for Cook's men, and these locals set about dragging several to the side of the ship with the intention of taking them away. When the men intervened and prevented this, they showed much resentment, one 'stamping with his foot pushed me [Banks] from him with a countenance full of disdain'.

The Aborigines tried several more times, furious at being frustrated, and then suddenly leaped into their canoe and paddled ashore. Here, in a closely synchronised movement, they grabbed armfuls of the tall, tinder-dry grass and thrust it into the fire heating the pitch for the ship. In an instant the encampment on shore was encircled with a 'vast fury' of flames, as Banks described this alarming incident. The tents were got down to the water just in time. A sow and a litter of piglets were more difficult and one was burnt to death.

Cook pursued the culprits along the shore, fearful that they might set fire to a drying seine net and many washed clothes lying in the sun. They disregarded his cries, and one Aborigine started another blaze before Cook aimed his musket and hit him with small shot as he ran off. He and Banks pursued the gang for about a mile inland until they met an old man carrying a spear lacking its point, which they took as a peace offering. The other Aborigines then ostentatiously piled their spears against a tree and sat down near Cook and Banks with every sign of friendliness.

Clearly, these people suffered from the same volatility which had marked the behaviour of the Polynesians. Communication was not easy, but the Aborigines' signs indicated that they wished to come back to the ship to show it to some newcomers, and that they would not fire the grass again. Cook distributed some musket balls among them, half as gifts, half as threats, and then with Banks at his side led them back to the *Endeavour*. Refusing an invitation to come on board, they seemed amiably contented to sit on the shore and watch pitch being applied to the ship. After two hours of this, they arose and sauntered off as if nothing had happened.

Further proof of how the Aborigines prized turtle meat was found in one carcass a boat's crew brought back. Sticking through both shoulders, the wound evidently long since healed, was a wooden barbed harpoon. Certainly, as Cook made clear to his readers, no canoe could have carried one .of these giant turtles, and he presumed that the Aborigines killed them when they came ashore to lay their eggs.

By the last days of July the carpenters had completed their work on the *Endeavour*, and the men were employed airing the sails, getting the coal and ballast on board, stowing the water casks, and much else. Cook determined to take away as many turtles and as much dried fish, shellfish and fodder for the livestock as could be found room for. Every day he sent Molyneux away in one of the boats to seek a passage through what he now named 'the insane labyrinth' of obstructions of every kind through which he must shortly navigate. He and Banks several times climbed as high as they could – once to over one thousand feet – in order to draw some sort of escape chart. But the more he looked through his glass, the more hopeless it seemed. Besides, day after day the wind blew gently but consistently from the south-east, pinning them into their anchorage.

By 20 July Cook was 'now ready to put to sea at the first opportunity'. But the following frustrating day was typical of so many:

Strong breezes at SE . . . In the p.m. sent a boat to haul the seine which returned with as much fish as came to 1¾ pound a man . . . As the wind would not permit us to sail I sent the boatswain with some hands ashore making rope and a petty officer with two men to gather greens for the ship's company . . .

By 4 August Cook and the entire ship's company were becoming exasperated. Cook declared that 'laying in port spends time to no purpose, consumes our provisions of which we are very short . . . and we have still a long passage to make to the East Indies through an unknown and perhaps dangerous sea'. In the afternoon in quiet weather he prepared to warp out the following morning if conditions allowed. As if God were at last on their side, at dawn they were able to warp out, and then by 7 a.m. a gentle breeze from the land allowed them to make sail, with the pinnace sounding ahead.

The wind backed to the south-east again, but Cook was going to anchor soon after noon anyway. He climbed to the masthead:

I did not think it safe to run in among the shoals until I had well viewed them at low water . . . that I might be better able to judge which way to steer, for I had not resolved whether I should beat back to the southward round all the shoals, or seek a passage out to the eastward, or to the northward, all of which appeared to be equally difficult and dangerous . . .

It was not until Cook landed on an island and discovered what he took to be the outermost reef of rocks because the sea broke so high against them that he decided what he must do. Although it was hazy, he also got the impression that there might be breaks in the reef.

The next day he sent the pinnace to seek one of these breaks and, if successful, to sound the entrance.

On the afternoon of 13 August, more than two months since they had been so close to disaster, the pinnace signalled the all clear, and for the ship to follow. Sounding all the way, Cook took the *Endeavour* slowly through the narrow passage between the fearsome rocks of the outer reef. For several minutes the sound and sight of the Pacific rollers beating against the reef were overwhelming. But for everyone, with nothing but open sea ahead of them and the leadsman finding no bottom with 150 fathoms of line, there was a deep sense of relief and renewed confidence in the commander who had brought them through so many dangers.

By the following day they were out of sight of land for the first time for many weeks. However, now Cook began to suffer from a new anxiety, 'being fearful of overshooting the passage, supposing there to be one, between this land and New Guinea', according to Charles de Brosses's chart. He therefore put over the helm and headed west. All too soon the land came into sight again, together with the white line of breakers on a reef stretching as far south and north as they could see. At the same time, the wind which had been blowing from ESE suddenly backed to EBN. Cook tried standing to the south.

It was an anxious night. There was no possibility of anchoring and, through the darkest hours, 'we found the ship was carried by the waves surprisingly fast'. So fast indeed that at 4 a.m. they could plainly hear the roaring of the surf, while at first light, 'the vast foaming breakers were too plainly to be seen not a mile from us'.

This distance from the reef diminished to less than fifty yards, and it now seemed inevitable that within minutes the *Endeavour* and all who sailed in her would be shattered on the rocks.

'At this critical juncture,' Banks recorded, 'at this, I must say, terrible moment, when all assistance seemed too little to save even our miserable lives, a small air of wind [from the land] sprang up, so small that at any other time in a calm we should not have observed it.'

The yawl and the longboat were both launched, and were soon joined by the pinnace which had been under repair, and the men began pulling for their lives. They were further supported by long sweeps pulling through the *Endeavour*'s gun ports aft. The faint breeze from the land lasted no more than ten minutes, but with the slight help of the oars relieved them from immediate danger. But there were many more hours of anxiety and exertion before a passage, barely wider than the ship, was discovered. As Banks described this merciful, almost miraculous escape, with the help of the tide, 'we were hurried in by a stream like a mill race'.

Cook anchored at once in a dead calm, observing the irony of being 'happy once more to encounter those shoals which but two days ago our utmost wishes were crowned by getting clear of'. At the same time he made the decision to keep the mainland close alongside, 'let the consequence be what it will', in order not to miss the hoped-for passage which would lead them to the East Indies, and the first outpost of civilisation at Dutch Batavia.

12

Paradise to Stinking Hell

THE INSANITY OF THE LABYRINTH lessened the farther north the *Endeavour* bore. It was not easy sailing and required constant vigilance, the yawl and the pinnace frequently sounding ahead. But by the afternoon of 20 August they had 'run out of New Holland'.

The end of Australia was like the southern tip of New Zealand, confused by islands. Shoals, sandy islands no more than spits, larger islands, all spoke of geographical untidiness and of the continuing need for caution; but it was no longer insanity.

On the following day their position became clearer. Preceded by the fully rigged longboat, Cook worked his ship between some islands and the northernmost mainland. He named the islands York Islands, and the cape off his larboard quarter Cape York, 'in honour of his Late Royal Highness the Duke of York'. This bleak, unpromising area of northern Australia became even more regal as Cook, now on a westerly heading, named a narrow channel and a large island ahead in honour of the Prince of Wales, the future Regent and King George IV.

At the opening of what was to be named Endeavour Strait, the passage which Cook was now confident would lead them through and on to the route to the Indies, he ordered a boat and landed on an island. No reader of his journal for this late August day in 1770 can escape the reflected sense of occasion. Cook knows that he has completed an historic piece of navigation and discovery, and he gives himself full credit without immodesty:

I may land no more upon this eastern coast of New Holland, and on the western side I can make no new discovery the honour of which belongs to the Dutch navigators. But the eastern coast from the latitude of 38 south to this place I am confident was never seen or visited by any European before us. Notwithstanding I had in the name of His Majesty taken possession of several places upon this coast, I now once more hoisted English colours and

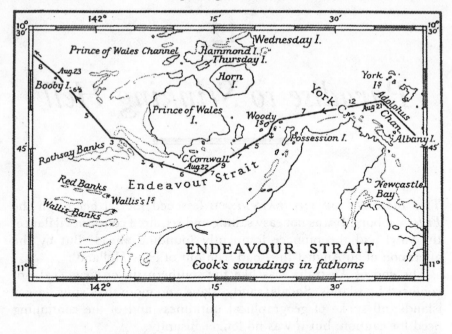

ENDEAVOUR STRAIT
Cook's soundings in fathoms

in the name of His Majesty King George the Third took possession of the whole eastern coast . . . by the name of New South Wales,* together with all the bays, harbours, rivers and islands situated upon the said coast. After this we fired three volleys of small arms, which were answered by the like number from the ship, followed by three cheers.

And the island upon which this ceremony was performed? With tiresome inevitability, Cook named it Possession Island.

The past three weeks had been so busy, or dangerous, or both, that the *Endeavour*'s company had thought little of home, but as soon as they were free from Endeavour Strait, the men began to 'sigh for roast beef', as Banks had earlier described homesickness. He gave it a new name now: nostalgia. 'We made sail and steered away from this land,' he wrote, 'to the no small satisfaction of I believe three-fourths of our company. The sick became well and the melancholy looked gay. [They] were now pretty far gone with the longing for home which the physicians have gone so far as to esteem a disease under the name of nostalgia.'

However, the run to Batavia took longer than anyone, least of all Cook, had expected. There were days of contrary winds, distractions

---

* The choice of this name, and precisely when Cook chose it, is wrapped in doubt
and scholarly speculation. Readers wishing to pursue the subject further may turn to
Beaglehole (ed.), *op. cit.*, vol. I, p. 388, or Wood, *op. cit.*, p. 444.

and, unusually for Cook, hesitancy and indecision. There was no need to follow the coastline of New Guinea and no good purpose was served in going ashore on this inhospitable island. But they made good sailing across what is now called the Arafura Sea: eight days from west New Guinea to the east coast of Timor. Banks had more to report than Cook during this passage, the bird and sea life both being rich. Tropic birds, man-o'-war birds and shearwaters were abundant, and on one day of calm Banks launched his boat and shot three dozen boobies and gannets. They made a welcome change to the diet, as did the two sharks, together weighing 126 pounds. 'I may venture to affirm, from the Captain to the swabber [ship's sweeper], dined heartily upon it.'

A great cloud bank ahead turned into the mountains of Timor, confirmed by their matching Dampier's description in his *Continuation of a Voyage to New Holland*. Cook attempted to ply along the shore, but the wind turned foul and the *Endeavour*'s 'croakers' (the inveterate pessimists to be found in every ship) expressed their ill-informed view that the westerly monsoon had caught them. But two days later, 'The wind came fair', reported Banks, adding caustically, 'and left our melancholy ones to search for some new occasion of sorrow.'

There had been the smoke of fires by day and the glow of flames at night all along the Timor coast, indicating that it was a populous island, although there were no signs of villages. This ever varying spectacle by night was exceeded when, at 10 p.m. on 15 September, 'a phenomenon appeared in the heavens in many ways resembling the Aurora Borealis [actually Aurora Australis and rare in this low latitude] . . . It consisted of a dull reddish light . . . through and out of this', Banks wrote, 'passed rays of a brighter coloured light tending directly upwards . . .' He watched it for two hours before falling asleep at midnight.

This strange spectacle was only the overture to the bizarre events which occurred on the island, which came into sight at dawn. Cook approached it cautiously. The closer they sailed to it, the more like a fragment of paradise it became, and a civilised paradise at that. Banks wrote of sloping hills and vales, innumerable palm trees, and near the beautiful sandy beaches, many houses, flocks of grazing sheep, a village close to a cove and two men on horseback, 'who seemed to ride for their amusement, looking often at the ship'. It was twenty-one months since they had sailed from Rio de Janeiro, the last evidence of Western civilisation upon which they had set their eyes. The fact that this island did not exist on any known chart added to its unreality and to the occasion.

Cook ordered the pinnace into the water and charged John Gore with the duty of making contact with these people, taking with him 'some trifles'. But they were above 'trifles', as the American was soon to discover. More horsemen appeared while Gore was being rowed ashore, one of whom wore 'complete European dress, blue coat, white waistcoat and lacquered hat', according to Banks, who was led to believe that 'there were Europeans among the islanders, by whom we should be received at least more politely than we were used to be by uncivilised indians'.

Later, when he was back on board, Gore told of the warm welcome they had enjoyed, being offered two dozen coconuts, and, more importantly, informed that at the port on the other side of the island, where they could anchor, 'sheep, hogs, fruits, fowl, etc.' would all be available. The American had conducted negotiations rather unsatisfactorily in sign language, and it was not until Cook had sailed the *Endeavour* round the headland and was approaching a town that the Dutch colours were hoisted, first on a hill and later on the shore.

Everything now became clear. This was the island of Savu. The Dutch tended to be secretive about their East Indies possessions, as had the Portuguese before them, and the Spanish throughout their empire as it expanded. None of the charts made by these imperial powers were to be relied upon, and cartographers were as likely to omit an island as to place it incorrectly on maps made available to others. On the night of 17 September Cook anchored a mile and a half from the shore. He was concerned about their reception the following day, recalling the suspicion and inhospitality they had suffered at Rio de Janeiro.

It turned out to be one of the strangest days of the entire voyage. John Gore was again assigned the task of representing Cook and making known to the appropriate authority their needs. He was received by a ragged guard of some thirty native soldiers armed with muskets and carrying the Dutch colours. Gore allowed himself to be led by this body of infantry, who marched 'without any order or regularity', to the island's rajah, a man of about thirty-five years and 'the fattest man we saw upon the whole island and the only one also upon whose body grew any quantity of hair, a circumstance very unusual among indians'.

Through a Portuguese interpreter, Gore explained that their ship was an English man o' war, that they had been at sea for a long time and had many sick on board, who would benefit from the fresh food of the island. (In fact, there was no one sick in the *Endeavour*; Tupia had suffered a dose of scurvy but was now as fit as any of the crew.)

The fat rajah, whose name was Madocho Lomi Djara, appeared eager to let them have whatever they wanted, but had to apply, he said, to the representative of the Dutch East India Company for authority. A message was despatched without delay to this notable, and was answered by the gentleman himself, one John Christopher Lange. It was now early afternoon and dinner-time on board the *Endeavour*. Gore suggested that the rajah and the administrator should return to the ship with him and dine with the officers and gentlemen.

It was a very convivial occasion. At first the rajah protested that so many white men would never sit down to eat with a black man. Vehement assurances were given, and in no time everyone was tucking in to fresh mutton from one of the last of their sheep, and the liquor circulated freely, diluting any of the rajah's inhibitions about asking for gifts. His first request was for an English sheep, like the one he was eating. It was the very last, but was fetched and handed over to the rajah's attendants. Next the Dutch representative asked for a spying glass (a small telescope) and this, too, was handed over, one can assume without much enthusiasm.

The last gift was also the most surprising. The rajah had taken a fancy to an English dog. Now Banks was known to be exceedingly attached to his greyhounds, but (presumably deep in his cups) he offered one of them to the fat rajah, and it was at once accepted.

The two guests now judged this to be an appropriate moment to describe how

the island abounded in buffalo, sheep, hogs and fowls, all of which should the next day be driven down to the beach and we might buy any quantity of them. This agreeable intelligence [Banks continued] put us all into high spirits and the liquor went about as much as either . . . could bear, who however expressed a desire of going away before they were quite drunk.

The *Endeavour*'s marines were on parade as the shore party prepared to disembark. The rajah, much impressed, indicated that he would like to see them exercise, and at once Sergeant Edgcumbe ordered the firing of three rounds. The rajah showed his appreciation of the speed and precision of the firing when he likened the cocking to a single strike with his stick on the ship's rail.

Banks and Solander accompanied the distinguished, but really rather drunk, company ashore, giving three cheers with the rest. This was answered by a salute of five guns from the ship. Banks and Solander, in the company of the rajah, Mr Lange and the attendants then walked through the town to what Banks took to be the royal palace. There, before returning, they were offered palm wine, which was very sweet and much to their taste.

On the following morning Cook led a large party ashore, including Spöring and Solander, who both understood Dutch, and young seaman John Dozey, who could speak Portuguese. Expecting to see the beach alive with stock, like market day in a British country town, Cook was not pleased to find it quite deserted. The English party walked boldly through the town, led by Banks, who soon discovered that what he had thought was the royal palace was in fact the house of assembly, or town hall. But the fat rajah was there, together with 'Mynherr' Lange, as Banks called him. The Dutchman at first made the excuse for the absence of livestock the 'very ill' conditions he had suffered all night, which was no great surprise to those who had been at the carousing. But when Cook tried to settle a price for the stock, Lange became evasive and indicated that this was a matter they must settle with the natives themselves.

Lange then told a cock-and-bull story about having received instructions from the Governor of Timor in Concordia that if the ship which had been sighted sailing along the coast of the island were to call in at Savu for supplies, she was to be given all that she required but allowed to remain for the minimum time to meet her needs. Cook called this a 'fiction'. Banks noted mildly that 'some of our gentlemen were of opinion that the whole of this letter was an imposition' – a deception.

It was now clear that the promises of the night before was all alcoholic big talk. Holding back his fury, Cook then asked the rajah through Lange if he could purchase for himself and his party a hog and some rice, and someone to cook their dinner as the day was fast advancing. 'Oh no!' replied the rajah; 'if you can eat victuals prepared by my subjects, which I can hardly suppose, I will do myself the honour of entertaining you.'

What else could Cook do but accept, hoping that this might lead to firmer and more harmonious relations the next day? At the same time he sent back to the ship for wine and liquors to accompany the promised meal.

About 5 o'clock [Banks recounted] dinner was ready, consisting of 36 palm baskets containing alternately rice and boiled pork, and three earthenware bowls of soup, or rather the broth in which the pork had been boiled. These were ranged on the ground and mats laid round them for us to sit on. We were now conducted by turns to a hole in the floor near which stood a man with a palm basket of water in his hand. Here we washed our hands and then ranged ourselves in order round the victuals waiting for the Rajah to sit down.

But the rajah hastened to explain that it was the custom of the country that the host never took meat with his guests, but that if they thought the food might be poisoned he would willingly do so. Cook explained that there were no suspicions about the food and that he wished only to follow the customs of Savu. After that they all settled down to eat – the pork and rice, both excellent, Banks remarked – including the rajah, who abstained only from the liquor, saying that it was improper for the host to get as drunk as his guests.

Before the end of this second spree Cook learned from a messenger that no buffalo or hogs, and only a few sheep, had been brought to the beach. Protests to 'Mynherr' Lange were met with the explanation that the owners wanted cash and had been offered only unwanted goods in exchange. It became clearer later that Lange was expecting a commission on cash purchases. Cook's patience and persistence at length paid off. After their pork dinner he, Banks and the rest of their party returned to the ship with nothing more than promises of buffalo the next morning, which Cook did not believe for a moment.

Their last day at Savu proved to be as eventful and ridiculous as all the others. When Cook's and Banks's party went ashore again, there was one man and one rather miserable-looking buffalo on the beach, for which five guineas was asked. Cook indignantly refused and offered three. This message was despatched to the rajah, who returned a dusty answer: five guineas or nothing. This was soon followed by the arrival of a large but dishevelled mob of infantry armed with muskets or lances. They were 'led' by a new figure, a white Portuguese who turned out to be 'Mynherr' Lange's assistant.

This Portuguese had come with a message and with a military force to back it up: there was to be no more trading and they must leave before the end of the day. Cook himself described what followed:

There happened to be an old Raja at this time upon the beach whose interest I had secured in the morning by presenting him with a spy glass. This man I now took by the hand and presented him with an old broad sword. This effectually secured him in our interest, for the moment he got it he began to flourish it over the old Portuguese.

The military force at once retreated, and a large number of natives who had gathered in the hope of trading descended upon the beach, driving buffalo, sheep, hogs and chicken and bringing great quantities of the island's syrup. Buffalo went for a musket each, but guineas also changed hands and trading continued uninterrupted and at a hectic pace until Cook had enough of everything he needed. The moment all this livestock had been got on board the *Endeavour*, he sensibly ordered anchors to be weighed and sail made without delay.

No TWO PARTS of the Dutch East Indies could contrast more strongly than the island of Savu and the city of Batavia. The events at the little gem of an island had an unreal quality about them, and as they sailed west, past the satellite Rai Jua and into the Indian Ocean, Savu, its eager, happy Malaysian people and their volatile authorities were already assuming a dreamlike memory.

The *Endeavour*, with decks crowded with livestock and their fodder – which ran seriously short on this leg of the voyage – made steady progress south but out of sight of Sumbawa, Bali and Java. Winds were mainly favourable from ENE or ESE, hurrying them home. Spirits were high and the health of the men good, as it should have been with their daily ration of fresh food, although more than half the hen eggs they had brought were bad.

In the last few days of August the *Endeavour* stood to the northward, Cook being anxious not to miss the narrow entrance to Sunda Strait which would lead them to Batavia. His charts, which for so long had been speculative or non-existent, were now as safe as for the English Channel. His role as discoverer had long since ceased, and his sole remaining task was to take his ship and her complement safely home, after making her fit for the voyage at the capital of the East Indies and the Dutch East India Company's headquarters.

The foundations of the great city of Batavia had been laid 150 years earlier by a Dutchman, Jan Pieterszoon Coen, an ambitious, unscrupulous and determined man who had first visited the Indies in 1607 and so improved the finances of the Dutch East India Company that he was appointed Governor-General in 1618. With remarkable speed and efficiency Coen drove out the English from their lightly protected possessions, and with his vastly superior sea power took over most of the Portuguese and Spanish colonies, too.

In 1619, less than a year after the beginning of his Governorship, Coen attacked and burnt the town of Djakarta and founded the city of Batavia on its site. When complete, it resembled as closely as possible the great cities of the Netherlands:

At Batavia a few hundred Dutchmen formed the aristocracy and endeavoured to recreate their life. Canals criss-crossed the town, as in Holland, and the houses were placed in close ranks along them. The citadel was built at the seashore, and inside were the residence of the Governor-General, the homes of workmen of the Council, and of those employed at the Arsenal. A large garrison, consisting of more than 1,200 men, paraded every day on a small square in front of the Governor-General's house.

Batavia became the trading capital of the East, and remained so at the time of the *Endeavour*'s visit in 1770. It also had excellent ship-repairing facilities and stores of all kinds.

Cook knew that he had enjoyed a favourable current for much of the passage from Savu, and took that into account in his dead-reckoning navigation. However, he underestimated its strength and slightly overshot Java Head and the entrance to the Sunda Strait. But soon shipping was sighted, the first since their departure from Brazil. Two Dutchmen were heading out to sea, and there was also a fly boat on guard duty.

Hicks was despatched in a boat to pick up any news. The Dutchmen were remarkably well informed. The first lieutenant learned that there was much disorder in London with demonstrations against the King and in favour of that colourful, powerful, reckless, political reprobate, John Wilkes. On the other side of the Atlantic, according to this intelligence, the American colonists had refused to pay taxes and substantial military forces were being sent to put down the first signs of a rebellion. Everyone on board the *Endeavour* was hungry for news (and in Batavia there were actually London newspapers).

After anchoring on 7 October 1770, Cook was concerned not only with the security of his ship, but also, in another sense, with the security of his voyage. The Dutch authorities would certainly ask him to fill in a comprehensive form in which he was required to describe his voyage, and did so, twice, but he merely informed them of the name of his ship, that it belonged to His Britannic Majesty King George III, and that they had come from England. At the same time he called in all private journals kept on the voyage and locked them away. He then made up a heavily sealed packet containing a copy of his journal and charts of the Pacific, New Zealand and of the east coast of New South Wales. Also included were a letter to Stephens, the Admiralty Secretary, and two letters to the Royal Society, one from him and the other from Green, with details of the transit of Venus observations.

In his letter Cook gave full credit to his 'officers and the whole crew [who] have gone through the fatigues and dangers of the whole voyage with that cheerfulness and alertness that will always do honour to British seamen'. He then added a boast that was not quite accurate (what about Forby Sutherland?) and that he was later to regret: 'I have the satisfaction to say that I have not lost one man by sickness during the whole voyage.'

Cook had not yet handed over this package to the commodore of a Dutch convoy sailing to Europe when it became known that they had come to a gravely unhealthy city. Even before they had landed they had seen evidence of this. As an official boat came alongside with an officer on board, 'both himself and his people', Banks noted, 'were almost as spectres, no good omen of the healthiness of the country we were arrived at. Our people, however, who might truly be called rosy and plump . . . jeered and flouted much at their brother seamen's white faces.'*

When the refit and repair of the *Endeavour* was at length put in hand, the experienced and skilful Dutch dockyardmen discovered that her condition was much worse than Cook had feared. The carpenters had done their best back at the labyrinth, but she had leaked steadily ever since, requiring the use of a pump day and night. Having examined the bottom of the *Endeavour* for himself, Cook reported:

The false keel was gone to within 20 feet of the sternpost, the main keel damaged in many places very considerably, a great quantity of sheathing was missing, several planks much damaged, especially under the main channel near the keel, where 2½ inch planks near 6 feet in length are within one eighth of an inch of being cut through. Here the worms had made their way quite into the timbers, so that it was a matter of surprise to everyone who saw her bottom how we had kept her above water. And yet in this condition we had sailed some hundreds of leagues in as dangerous a navigation as is in any part of the world, happy in being ignorant of the continual danger we were in.

On first learning from the Dutch authorities that their men must make the repairs, Cook had expressed indignation. But by the time the true horror of the damage was revealed, he knew that it would be impossible for them to carry out the work. This was not because they lacked the skills, but because the diseases of this terrible place were already taking their toll and there were only twenty men fit enough to work.

Various forms of dysentery and malaria were the prime killers in Batavia. Long ago the canals and once fresh rivers and streams of this part of Java had become silted up following an earthquake. The

* Deaths from disease at Batavia averaged around fifty thousand per annum at this time.

absence of drains when the waters of the town were free-flowing was of little importance, but the canals were now the breeding ground of multitudes of mosquitoes, and the stench of ordure hung over the town like a cloud.

Unhappily, and ironically, the first victim was the *Endeavour*'s surgeon, Bill Monkhouse, on 5 November. Bill Perry, his assistant, took charge and conscientiously did all he could for the increasing toll of victims. Banks early fell ill, as did his two surviving servants, Peter Briscoe and Jim Roberts. Banks was too ill to attend Monkhouse's funeral, but Solander managed to drag himself to the church, although feeling ill himself.

Immediately after landing, Banks had rented a house with several slave servants. But these Malaysians were lazy and useless and, naturally, knew no English. Banks and his fellow sufferers were visited daily by a local doctor, Jaggi, but their condition failed to improve and at one time Dr Solander's life was despaired of. Nor was their spirit enhanced by the news of Tupia and Tiata. When they first entered the town, the two Tahitians were beside themselves at all they saw, the shops and houses, the heavy horse traffic with carriages on the streets, the variety of clothes. But they were almost immediately struck down, probably with putrid dysentery. Their natural defences against disease were very frail, as Tupia had already shown, and their decline was swift and implacable.

Sydney Parkinson left a moving account of their last days:

When Tiata was seized with the fatal disorder, as if certain of his approaching dissolution, he frequently . . . said 'Tyau mate oee', or 'My friends, I am dying.' He took any medicines that were offered him; but Tupia who was ill at the same time and survived but a few days, refused everything of that kind, and gave himself up to grief, regretting in the highest degree that he had left his own country. When he heard of Taita's death he was quite inconsolable, crying out [his name] frequently . . .

Cook was taken ill at one stage and characteristically made light of it. He stayed at a hotel when not in the *Endeavour*, supervising the work on her. The sick crew were confined to a tent on one of the harbour's numerous islands, fending for themselves as best they could. Banks spares us no detail of his own and Dr Solander's sufferings. When the Swedish professor was close to death, Dr Jaggi applied mustard plasters to his legs. 'Weak as I was I sat by him till morn,' Banks claimed, 'when he changed very visibly for the better. I then slept a little and waking found him still better than I had any reason to hope.'

There was a serious relapse later, but by this time the two men had moved house. 'Dr Jaggi . . . insisted on the country air as necessary for our recovery,' claimed Banks, and money being no consideration, he rented a house well out of the town, beside a swift running river 'and well open to the sea breeze'. Cook sent his own servant and a seaman to look after the two men, Spöring joined them, and Banks fixed himself up with two Malay women and no fewer than eight Malay slaves.

While Banks, Solander and Spöring recovered in relative comfort, wanting for nothing except complete health, the rest of the *Endeavour*'s company, officers and men alike, fought their own malaria battles under canvas and in the dampness preceding the monsoon. John Reynolds, Green's servant, died. So did the Irishman, Tim Rearden, and John Woodworth and one other seaman. The only man to escape entirely from any disease at Batavia was the elderly sailmaker, John Ravenhill, the Yorkshireman who was 'generally more or less drunk every day'. There were few doubters in the ship that liquor and good health marched together, and these were now convinced.

The Dutch congratulated Cook on not losing half his men, the average death rate here. That might be so, but he still had fewer than twenty hands capable of working the *Endeavour* when her repairs were complete, and if he was ever going to get away from this 'stinking hellhole' he must recruit more men. This he did seemingly with little trouble, most being British, nineteen in all, and thankful to be able to leave for home.

By Christmas Day 1770, their third Christmas on this voyage, all stores were on board, and on the next day sail was hoisted with relief on what Cook now called 'my hospital ship'. There were forty men incapable of moving, and many more just able to look after themselves but quite incapable of standing watch. Heading down the Sunda Strait was as slow and tortuous a business as sailing up it – all changing currents, changing winds and sounding, and with a skeleton crew. After eleven days Cook anchored off Princes Island, where he had heard that he might get fresh fruit and vegetables for his sick, as well as fish and fowl. Almost all who were sick at Batavia were worse now, and hopes that fresh sea breezes would improve everyone's health proved horribly false.

As Cook had written on the day of their grounding in the labyrinth, 'here began all our troubles'. It was as if they had stowed in the hold, with their stores and ballast and coal, all the foulest germs of Batavia. As they headed out into the Indian Ocean again, the deaths from dysentery inflicted on malaria-weakened bodies were dreadful to witness. John Truslove, the admirable marines corporal, was the first to go. Then in tragic succession Spöring and Parkinson, whose numerous drawings of landscapes and people, canoes and animals, besides the hundreds of botanical drawings for Banks and Solander, had uniquely embellished the voyage.

When Charles Green died on 29 January, it seemed as if the dysentery was singling out those with the greatest talent; but when the aged John Ravenhill fell victim in spite of the 'protection' of liquor, then it appeared that there was to be no discrimination and any – or all – might die. On 31 January Cook wrote despairingly:

In the course of this 24 hours we have had four men died of the flux, viz John Thompson, ship's cook, Benjamin Jordan, carpenter's mate, James Nicholson and Archibald Wolfe, seamen. A melancholy proof of the calamitous situation we are at present in, having hardly well men enough to tend the sails and look after the sick. Many of the latter are so ill that we have not the least hope of their recovery.

This was no ordinary epidemic that sometimes swept through a ship. Could it derive from the water they had collected at Princes Island? Cook ordered lime to be added to the casks, and then cleaned the ship between decks, washing with vinegar. The rate of deaths did not diminish: John Bootie, the midshipman who had kept a spirited journal; gunner's servant Daniel Roberts; Jonathan Monkhouse, the late surgeon's brother; the boatswain John Gathrey; another of the marines, Daniel Preston; and John Satterly, carpenter 'a man much esteemed by me and every gentleman on board' – all died during the first days of February.

However, the health of several men improved, bringing new hope that the dysentery was losing its strength. Cook notes on 20 February: 'This morning the carpenter and his mate set about repairing the long boat, being the first day they have been able to work since we left Princes Island.' The *Endeavour* continued to sail with fresh and favourable winds across the Indian Ocean.

The coast of Africa loomed up out of the dusk on 4 March, unexpectedly and, later, alarmingly. 'In the evening', Cook wrote, 'some people thought they saw the appearance of land to the northward, but this appeared so improbable that . . . I was not acquainted with it until dark, when I ordered them to sound but found no ground with 80 fathoms, upon which we concluded that no land was near.'

Cook's dead-reckoning navigation was badly at fault again, certainly confused by unknown currents, and perhaps also by his continuous concern about the health of his men. First light on 5 March revealed an unattractive coast, much beaten by rollers, a mere two leagues ahead, and with a fresh wind from the south-east driving them on to it. Urgently, he wore the *Endeavour* and hauled her off to the eastward.*

They were back to the business of coasting, with winds as variable as anywhere off New Zealand or eastern Australia, but the Agulhas current helped them along consistently. Cape Agulhas, the most southerly point of the African continent, was sighted to the west on 11 March, was doubled the next day and they were off Cape Town on 14 March 1771. A gale prevented them from entering the roadstead for twenty-four hours, and instead they were obliged to lay fast. But the air smelt pure by contrast with that of Batavia, and for those, like Cook, who had never been here before, the spectacular skyline dominated by Table Mountain with Cape Town huddled at its base was one of the wonders of a sailor's world. As Cook commented later:

Such is the industry, economy and good management of the Dutch that not only the necessities but all the luxuries of life are raised here in as great abundance, and are sold as cheap if not cheaper than in any part of Europe ... The inhabitants of Cape Town are in general well bred and extremely civil and polite to all strangers; indeed it is in their interest so to do for the whole town may be considered as one great inn fitted up for the reception of all comers and goers. Upon the whole there is perhaps not a place in the known world that can equal this in affording refreshments of all kinds to shipping.

Even before they entered the bay they were able to count no fewer than sixteen ships at anchor – Dutch, Danish and French. An English East Indiaman saluted them with eleven guns as the *Endeavour* sailed in and anchored close to the wooden jetty. Cook had twenty-nine sick on board, some in a bad way, and it was his first business to get them ashore and into the hands of a physician. Even so, another died before he could be moved, making a total loss of thirty-four** since he had despatched from Batavia that boastful claim of not losing a man through sickness. For a man of Cook's sensitivity and diligence in the care of his men, this was a terrible blow, striking at the very heart of his pride in his profession.

* Their landfall was south of present-day Port St Johns in Cape Province.
** Five more died at Cape Town or on the way home.

13

'A Voyage Such as Had Never Been Made Before'

CAPE TOWN, THEY NOTED, WAS MUCH LIKE BATAVIA, with a gridiron layout of the streets and the same Flemish architecture – small standard houses with thatched roofs – but with only two canals, both pure enough to drink from, and a fine breezy and healthy climate. The people were clean, hospitable and courteous, and it was in their interest to be so as ship repair, hospitality and trade were almost their only occupations. All menial work was carried out by Malay slaves, the native Hottentots having been obliged to seek work inland, mainly on the numerous scattered Dutch farms.

Banks took a favourable view of the Governor of Cape Town, who had been in this post for twenty years. He also examined, as usual and closely, the Dutch women, with whom he also found no fault:

In general they are handsome with clear skins and high complexions, and when married (no reflection on my countrywomen) are the best housekeepers imaginable and great child-bearers. Had I been inclined for a wife I think this is the place of all others I have seen where I could have best suited myself.

Banks was able to give the most comprehensive description of the town, the adjacent area, its products and people, because he was among the first to land when the *Endeavour* had been cleared by the authorities and the sick taken ashore. He and Solander put up in a house, of which there were many to let, and he had no other responsibilities, except to look after Solander when he was struck down by some bowel complaint very similar to dysentery. The Swede was poorly for several days, but the two men were able to ride inland and botanise on two days before they left.

John Gore, with typical vigour, also came ashore and with the company of one sailor, climbed to the summit of Table Mountain (3,600 feet). He noted the mostly barren country, broken by farmsteads where the soil allowed, neatly laid out and producing vines, every sort of fruit and vegetable, as well as European cereal crops. He brought back plants for Banks and reported seeing wolves and lions – almost certainly brown hyenas and leopards.

His senior lieutenant, Zachary Hicks, was too ill to accompany Gore. In spite of his weakened condition he had survived both malaria and dysentery, but the consumption now had a fatal hold over his lungs and he knew that he had not much longer to live.

Cook had little time for viewing the country, or even socialising with the officers of other English ships anchored in the roadstead. However, there was brief contact with Captain Riddle of the East Indiaman *Admiral Pocock*, homeward bound from Bombay. Even before the *Endeavour* had dropped anchor Riddle sent over a boat commanded by one of his officers 'with a compliment of a basket of fruit', which was much appreciated by Cook. The *Admiral Pocock* sailed for England before the *Endeavour*, and Riddle gladly offered to take to the Admiralty several letters Cook had written to Stephens giving him the latest news.

In the month they were at Cape Town, besides supervising the overhaul of the rigging and repairing of the sails, Cook wrote an anguished account of the passage from Batavia and of the dreadful plague which had swept through his ship:

It is to be wished for the good of all seamen and mankind in general that some preventative could be found against this disease [dysentery] and put in practice in climes where it is common; for it is impossible to victual and water a ship in those climates but what some one article or another . . . must be the means of bringing on the flux . . .

In the early days of April 1771 the rigging had been overhauled and the ship painted. The eleven men still too sick to stand watch were brought on board on 11 April, and salutes of eleven guns were exchanged with the East Indiaman *Europa* just arrived from Bengal; while a Dutchman from Europe reported that Spain was on the brink of war with England.* Two days later, on 16 April, with no further confirmation of this news, Cook weighed and stood out of the bay, exchanging salutes with the *Europa* again, the castle and the Dutch commodore. Soon he was to order the exercising of

* The dispute was over possession of the Falkland Islands, but Spain had already agreed to cede the islands and the crisis was over.

'the great guns and small arms' in case they should be needed in earnest.

Cook's delight and relief at being on the last leg of his voyage was clouded by the death of Bob Molyneux, the *Endeavour*'s master, 'a young man of good parts but had unfortunately given himself up to extravagancy and intemperance which brought on disorders that put a period to his life': their second death from drink. He also continued to remain concerned about his first lieutenant and doubted that he would survive the passage home.

Cook had determined to put in at St Helena. With favourable winds, the ship sailed 441 miles in three days before 'crossing the line of our first meridian, viz that of Greenwich' on 29 April, 'having now circumnavigated the globe in a west direction'. On 1 May they sighted the island bearing west, and by noon had anchored in the roadstead. Cook counted no fewer than twelve English East Indiamen and their naval escort. This seemed to confirm that war had been declared, but a signal was received to reassure them that all was well.

The only one of the *Endeavour*'s company to show the least curiosity about St Helena was the indefatigable Banks. Everyone else, including, one suspects, Cook himself, had their minds only on their homeland and were consumed with impatience to get to sea again. Banks had just one day to go botanising and to climb to the highest point on this precipitous twelve-mile-long island, noting that this was where Nevil Maskelyne, the inspiration of their voyage, had set up his instruments to observe the transit of Venus in 1761, shortly before he became Astronomer Royal.

In spite of the brevity of their stay Banks treated the readers of his journal to a detailed account of the island and its products, at the same time censuring the inhabitants, first for not making use of carts, or even wheelbarrows, and second for their cruelty to their slaves, something he always felt strongly about.

Cook had decided to sail in company with the convoy and its man o' war. Therefore, at 6 a.m. on 4 May, when HMS *Portland* made the signal to unmoor, the *Endeavour* conformed with the twelve East Indiamen. This great company of ships made sail at noon and during the afternoon, with stately grace, slipped out of the roadstead. For a ship's company which had circumnavigated the world alone, and for much of the distance in unknown waters, it was an odd experience to be one of so many ships, all bigger than their converted cat, including the 50-gun 4th rate, their escort.

Cook also suspected that the *Endeavour* would fall behind this convoy 'as we sail much heavier than the fleet', and his ship was never built for speed anyway. Soon after they sighted the grim little island of Ascension, therefore, Cook made a signal inviting the *Portland*'s commander, Captain Elliot, on board. He explained that he wanted a letter and a box of officers' journals and other papers to reach the Admiralty as soon as possible. Elliot gladly agreed to take them and a few days later, while the entire convoy was becalmed, Banks was invited on board the man o' war and dined with the captain.

For a few more days during intermittent calms the *Endeavour* remained in touch with the convoy. This allowed Cook, who was deeply concerned about the health of Zachary Hicks, to call for a surgeon from one of the East Indiamen. But there was nothing that could be done for him, for, as Cook wrote, 'he is so far gone in a consumption that his life is despaired of'. A week later, on Sunday, 26 May, this admirable thirty-one-year-old officer died and was committed to the sea 'with the usual ceremonies'.

Cook then promoted the master's mate, Charles Clerke, to the rank of lieutenant. Everyone was pleased about this as Clerke had not only been singularly efficient throughout the voyage but had also remained cheerful during their most difficult times. Cook also took advantage of the occasion to promote Isaac Smith, who had been such a support, from midshipman to master's mate.

By now the entire convoy had outsailed them, and they were alone again on the Atlantic Ocean. Very little of note occurred over the following few weeks. Banks observed the bird life – 'Many shearwaters were seen about the ship' – but there was a tragic note in his entry for 4 July: 'My bitch Lady was found dead in my cabin lying upon a stool on which she generally slept, she had been remarkably well . . . in the night she shrieked out very loud so that we who slept in the great cabin heard her, but becoming quiet immediately, no one regarded it.' She was less than a week from home and the Lincolnshire countryside where she had grown up.

Cook dutifully entered the weather, the wind, their position, the mileage covered and any sail sighted, including what he took to be their old friends the East Indiamen briefly. On 19 June they sighted in succession several whaling schooners from America. He sent a boat to one of them for any news. Her master confirmed that there was not only peace in Europe, but that the disputes between England and her American colonies were at an end. 'To confirm this the Master said that the coat on his back was made in old England', a reference to the 1768–9 colonial boycott of imports in protest against the duties imposed by England on exports to America in June 1767.

Then, at last, at noon on 10 July, 'we saw land from the masthead bearing north which was judged to be Land's End'. The boy at the masthead with this glad news was keen-eyed Nick Young, who had first sighted New Zealand.

Up-Channel was their first coasting without the need to take bearings and make a running survey since they had left England in August 1768, two years and eleven months before. In clear summer weather they sailed past the familiar coastline of Cornwall, Devon and Dorset – the Lizard, Start Point, Portland Bill. At 6 a.m. on 12 July they were off the high white undulations of the Sussex Seven Sisters, Beachy Head looking as tall and final as Cape Horn.

Like a horse returning to stables after a long ride, the *Endeavour* sailed bravely, and it seemed eagerly: 197 miles in two days and nights. And yet her condition was deplorable. It was only a few days since she had split both topgallant sails, and Cook reported that 'in the morning the carpenter reported the main top mainmast to be sprung in the cap . . . our rigging and sails are now so bad that something or another is giving way every day'.

But the old bark held together, rounded Dungenness at two miles offshore, and anchored in the Downs off Deal at 3 p.m. on Saturday, 13 July. The afternoon was windy and cloudy. The pilot boat came alongside at once, and the pilot took charge of the ship while Banks, Solander and Cook, with light luggage, went ashore.

These three men, so different in age and temperament, who had been living together within the confines of the great cabin for so long, sharing the pleasures and excitements of their circumnavigation, as well as the sufferings and anxieties; and who had also shared sights never seen by Western man before, and latterly grieved together over the loss of friends and shipmates – what did they say to one another on the seven-hour post-chaise ride through Kent? There is no record, and we shall never know.

Nor were these three men, the steady sea captain, the ebullient botanist and his quiet and earnest Swedish friend, to know that they would never again enjoy the intimacy of the last 1,074 days and nights.

They said good-bye to one another at Piccadilly in the early hours of Sunday morning, Cook repairing at once to the Admiralty, a short walk distant, Banks and Solander to Banks's house in New Burlington Street.

For Cook it was an unsociable hour to head for the Mile End Road. On the following morning he would send a message to Elizabeth, informing her that he was safely home and would see her later in the day.

WHILE RUNNING UP-CHANNEL Cook had composed a letter to Stephens at the Admiralty:

Endeavour Bark, DOWNS
'The 13th of July 1771'

SIR, – It is with pleasure I have to request that you will be pleased to acquaint my Lords Commissioners of the Admiralty with the arrival of His Majesty's Bark under my command at this place where I shall leave her to wait for further orders, and in obedience to their Lordships' orders immediately and with this letter repair to their office, in order to lay before them a full account of the proceedings of the whole voyage.

I make no doubt but what you have received my letter and journal forwarded from Batavia in a Dutch ship in October last, likewise my letters of the 10th of May together with some of the officers' journals which I put on board His Majesty's Ship *Portland* . . .

Cook went on to trust that what had already been despatched 'will be found sufficient to convey a tolerable knowledge of the places they are intended to illustrate, and that the discoveries we have made tho' not great will apologise for the length of the voyage.'

The Admiralty did not detain Cook for long on that morning of 14 July. Stephens, into whose hands he passed his letter, released him after greeting him warmly, and probably by noon Cook was on his way, down the Strand and Fleet Street, past St Paul's Cathedral, through the city and on to the Mile End Road. The greeting, the embraces, the first exchange of words after three years' absence can only be imagined.

No doubt the two elder boys were at home, aged seven and eight, bursting with questions and probably forgetful of the sad news Elizabeth had for her husband. For their young brother Joseph had died nearly three years earlier at the age of three months when his father had only reached Madeira. Cook had just known him as a little wrinkled infant in his cot. But his beloved daughter Elizabeth, named after her mother, he had known for over a year and could remember her crawling about the floors of the house. She had died only recently, while the *Endeavour* had been beating her way north from the Cape. No matter that Cook himself had lost so many brothers and sisters, these two deaths were hard to bear.

There was some easing of the burden of grief in the amount of paperwork immediately facing Cook, even if much of it at first concerned the grief of death: Hicks's family needed writing to, as did Stanfield Parkinson, Sydney's brother. George Monkhouse had to be informed how his two sons had died, told how much their possessions had fetched – £229 17s 6½d – and asked where the money should be sent. 'My respects to all your family,' Cook concluded, 'and remain, dear Sir, Your most Obliged Honourable Servant, James Cook.' The circumstances of Green's death had to be recounted both to the Royal Society and to the astronomer's family. And so it went on: Forby Sutherland's family in the Orkneys, John Bootie's parents, the next of kin of the one-handed cook, John Thompson.

In the midst of the hurly-burly of preparing reports and the final version of his journal, checking through the *Endeavour*'s log, and making fine copies of his charts and views, Cook found time to write two long letters to John Walker, his old teacher, guide and employer, of Whitby. Cook had always recognised how much he owed this man, now very old and retired, and it was typically generous-spirited of him to continue to pay his respects sixteen years later.

The one man of Cook's company in the *Endeavour* who needed no letter was Joseph Banks. Banks, of all people, could look after himself; in fact, he was enjoying the time of his life. As Beaglehole has written, 'Banks did not need to bring back a lion or tiger or a Tupia; he was a lion himself.' The lionisation of Banks started modestly enough with a report in *Bingley's Journal* on Monday, 15 July:

On Saturday last an express arrived at the Admiralty with the agreeable news of the arrival at the Downs of the *Endeavour*, Captain Cook, from the East Indies. This ship sailed in August 1768 with Mr Banks, Dr Solander, Mr Green, and other ingenious Gentlemen on board, for the South Seas, to observe the Transit of Venus; they have since made a voyage round the world, and touched at every coast and island, where it was possible to get on shore to collect every species of plants and other rare productions in nature . . .

At least, in this first press report, Cook gets a mention as the captain of the *Endeavour*. Later, thanks to Banks's unashamed publicity-seeking, giants of science and the arts sought his company and Cook's role was increasingly forgotten. The *Westminster Gazette* told of 'The honour of [Banks] frequently waiting on his Majesty at Richmond.' Summoned to Oxford to receive an honorary doctorate of civil law, he was described as 'the immortal Banks'.

Linnaeus himself addressed a letter . . . whose tenor was that the entire cohort of botanists, vehemently and with a single voice, called out Banks's praises. Banks, who had surely seen more than any other botanist who had lived before him, was the glory not only of England but of the whole world – he should be the botanists' oracle, and they should raise a monument to him more lasting than all the pyramids . . .

Often, Cook's name was not mentioned in reports; or if it was, he is seen in a subsidiary capacity, almost as the ship's master rather than the captain. Cook did have an audience with the King, and of course the Admiralty remained aloof from this near hysteria, as did Cook himself, though he might have raised an eyebrow at the report in the *Gazetter and New Daily Advertiser* (26 August 1771): 'Mr Banks is to have two ships from government to pursue his discoveries in the South Seas, and will sail upon his second voyage next March.'

By contrast, Cook read with pleasure the Admiralty minutes for 1 August 1771:

... Resolved that [Lieutenant Cook] be acquainted the Board extremely well approve of the whole of his proceedings, and have great satisfaction in the account he gives of the good behaviour of his officers and men, and of the cheerfulness and alertness which they went through the fatigues and dangers of the Voyage ...

Cook was equally gratified with the more personal note from Stephens, sent to him at the Mile End Road on the following day, which also acknowledged 'your several letters dated the 23rd October 1770 at Batavia, 10th May last at sea, and 12th of last month in the Downs'.

As for the poor old *Endeavour*, battered by a hundred gales, cursed by Banks for slow sailing, blessed by those who understood her qualities in heavy seas and for her ability to claw off a lee shore, almost broken apart by Great Barrier Reef coral, within a week of her anchoring in the Downs the Admiralty informed the Navy Board:

Endeavour Bark to be docked at Woolwich as soon as may be, resheathed, and fitted in all respects proper for carrying a supply of provisions and stores to Falkland Islands, reporting when she will be ready to receive men, and the number of men and guns it may be proper to establish upon her.

The *Endeavour* made two voyages to the Falklands, on the second in 1774 bringing home the small garrison stationed there, but leaving the stores for the Spaniards to whom Britain had agreed to hand over the islands.*

Her naval service over, the ship was sold in 1775 for £645, now reverting to her old role as a collier. Kitson tells us that some time at the turn of the century a Mr Gibbs of Newport, Rhode Island, while taking a walk with the British Consul, pointed out the remains of a wooden ship – a bark once called the *Endeavour*. She had apparently

---

* In 1832–3 the British reoccupied the islands at the expense of Argentina, to whom Spain had passed sovereignty.

made her last voyage under French colours, had been chased by an English man o' war, but had safely delivered her cargo of oil to Mr Gibbs's firm in Newport.

Later, when attempting to put to sea, the *Endeavour* (no doubt renamed) ran aground and was considered not worth repairing. She slowly fell to pieces in the harbour. It appears that the credentials of the old ship were considered satisfactory, for a box was carved out of her timbers and presented to J. Fenimore Cooper, the American author, together with letters from the English Consul, authenticating as far as possible the vessel from which the wood had been taken.

IMMEDIATELY UPON HIS RETURN, Cook drew up his recommendations for promotion:

Cook to Admiralty Secretary. The under mentioned persons late belonging to His Majesty's Bark the Endeavour, are humbly recommended to my Lords Commissioners of the Admiralty as worthy of promotion (Viz)

1. Mr Richd Pickersgill, Master – deserving of a Lieut^s Commission
2. Mr Richd Orton Clerk, formerly Purser of the ⎧ wishes to have some
Barbados Sloop & Ship Arundel ⎮ place in the Custom-
3. Mr Fran^s Wilkinson Master's Mate, was with Capt ⎬ house or any other
Wallis in the Dolphin ⎩ public office
4. Mr Jno Edgcumbe Sergt of Marines, a good Soldier very much of a gentleman & well deserving of promotion in the Marine Service
5. Richd Hutchins Boatswain's Mate, well deserving of a Boatswain's Warrant – would be glad to go in the Endeavour in case Mr Evans present Boatswain is removed.
6 & 7. Mr Isaac Smith & Mr Isaac Manly, both too young for preferment, yet their behaviour merits the best recommendation. The former was of great use to me in assisting to make Surveys, Plans, Drawings &c in which he is very expert.

What then of Cook's own promotion? There can be no doubt that he was due for it, nor that Philip Stephens would ensure that he received his just deserts. Banks reappears at this point – early August 1771 – to take time off from his dizzy round of visits parading his plants and Parkinson's drawings to illuminate his accounts of his voyage. His old friend Lord Sandwich had just been appointed, for the third time, First Lord of the Admiralty, greatly to Banks's pleasure and convenience. For the *Gazetteer and New Daily Advertiser* had been correct in its announcement: Banks was indeed planning a second voyage, a voyage on a grander scale, with many more of his cronies. He also needed Cook as a trusty navigator and captain, of course in a naval role, and secondary to his own. It would be Banks's voyage. But what if Cook had other ideas, or was sidetracked into some other command? Cook needed to be secured and this could best be done through Sandwich, who was brought into the plan early and persuaded to promote Cook to the rank of captain.

As soon as Sandwich had given this undertaking, which was not difficult as it was already in hand, Banks wrote to Cook, in order to ensure that he, Banks, got the credit. 'Your very obliging letter was the first messenger that conveyed to me Lord Sandwich's intentions,' wrote Cook in grateful reply on Sunday, 11 August. He was sitting in Will's coffee house, Charing Cross, at noon, perhaps to escape from the boys' uproar in his tiny Mile End Road house. 'Promotion unsolicited to a man of my station in life must convey a satisfaction to the mind that is better conceived than described.'

Cook then makes clear that earlier on that Sunday he had attended on Sandwich at the Admiralty, and that for the first time, officially, he had been told of the proposed new voyage, with himself to lead it. He did not add that its prime purpose was to settle, once and for all, the speculative existence of the Great Southern Continent. If he discovered it, he was to take possession in the name of King and country; it was as simple as that.

So, within a month of his return after almost three years away, Cook was committed to the leadership of another long voyage. Elizabeth had always understood the separations she must suffer in marrying a sailor, but she had hoped to have him at home for a little longer.

In the event, it was much longer before Cook got away on his next voyage, mainly due to the extraordinary behaviour of Joseph Banks. The delay allowed Cook to make the long journey to north Yorkshire in December to visit his father and the daughter with whom he was still living at Redcar, as well as John Walker and his old friends at Whitby. He took Elizabeth with him, in spite of her being pregnant again, but not the boys. They both knew that there were risks involved, but Elizabeth was as anxious to meet her father-in-law for the first time as he was to see her before he died.* The stagecoach to York, taking three days, was reasonably comfortable on well-maintained roads, but after that, through Thirsk, Northallerton and Stockton, the journey became rougher and Cook had to arrange for Elizabeth to have frequent rests along the way. Redcar was a pretty little fishing port about the size of Staithes. For Elizabeth, who had never travelled

---

* James Cook Senior was seventy-six and outlived his son, dying at the age of eighty-four on 1 April 1779.

far from London, the sight of the Cleveland hills and stark moors were as new and spectacular as the sea crashing in on the Yorkshire shoreline.

As for the meeting between father and son, brother and sister and brother-in-law; between wife and father-in-law and wife and sister-in-law, we can presume – safely, I think – that it was excited and loving with the talk continuing far into the night. Perhaps we can also assume that Cook, ever solicitous, ensured that Elizabeth was early to bed after her long and strenuous journey.

For the same reason Cook did not take Elizabeth to Whitby to stay with Walker and visit old friends from his apprentice days, 'Mrs Cook being but a bad traveller' and the road so rough. He therefore took a hack and rode along the clifftops, past Staithes, and down the road to the seaport where he had learned his trade. It was December and the smoke from Whitby's chimneys reminded him of coming into port from London in the *Three Brothers* on winter evenings long ago.

Here in Whitby, which he had once regarded as his home town, his fame was unqualified by any reference to Joseph Banks except perhaps as some grandee passenger. But there was no excessive hero-worshipping either, just warm affection and pride in the man who had lived among these people as a boy and had learned to sail and navigate with such success that he had taken one of Whitby's boats clear round the world. For his part, Cook quickly sought out Fishburn, the designer and builder of the *Endeavour*, and congratulated him on the qualities of the bark in which he had spent three years. Cook also greatly pleased the shipbuilder by telling him that, just before leaving London, he had selected two more ships from Fishburn's Whitby yard for his next voyage on which he hoped to embark in March 1772. They were the 462-ton *Marquis of Granby* and the 340-ton *Marquis of Rockingham*, now renamed *Resolution* and *Adventure*. Jugs of ale would certainly have appeared and the new voyage toasted.

As for the Walker household, 'no one received him with more cordiality than good old Mary Prowd who had distinguished him with her special regard when an apprentice boy . . . She had been delighted to hear of his adventures and overjoyed at the thought of once more seeing him.' The Walkers had instructed the old woman to address him formally and remember that he was now a captain in the Royal Navy. But 'forgetting all her lessons, she stretched out both her arms to welcome him, and exclaimed in her own native phraseology, "Oh honey James, how glad I's to see thee!"'

The new year was celebrated while Cook was in Whitby and doubtless more mugs of ale were raised to celebrate both the year

1772, the success of the voyage, and the health of Elizabeth Cook and her unborn child. Cook left the Walkers the following day and rode quickly back north to Redcar to rejoin Elizabeth and his father. On 4 January the Cooks were on their way south, pausing for a rest of two days in York, and greeting the boys and uniting the family in the second week of January.

Cook was anxious to be away as soon as possible, and he at once visited his two ships which were in dockyard hands fitting out for the voyage. The *Resolution*, his own ship, was at Deptford and would be out of her drydock in about three weeks; while the *Adventure* at Woolwich was less advanced, and there was still much else to do: officers to select, stores to be ordered, and, above all, plans and route to be agreed with the Admiralty – that is to say Sandwich as First Lord and Palliser as Comptroller, or head of the Navy Board, who had been appointed while Cook was absent in the Pacific.

The purposes of this new enterprise varied as widely as those responsible for it, by contrast with the clear definition of the *Endeavour* voyage. The only thing the authorities all had in common – the King, Sandwich, the Prime Minister Lord North, Banks and Cook himself – was that Cook's first voyage must be followed by a second voyage as soon as possible.

Since the conquest of Canada and Newfoundland, securing the greater part of North America for the British crown, imperial ambitions had expanded, and the southern hemisphere and its largely unexplored territory offered the best prospects. The regaining of the Falkland Islands was more than a token step. In British hands they provided a valuable staging-post for voyagers to the East and the Indian Ocean and west to the Pacific.

Cook believed that there had already been two Spanish ships at Tahiti. The fact that he later discovered that they were French, that Bougainville had falsely claimed to be first at the island and had also claimed it as a French possession, added further urgency to British planning.

Then there was *Terra Australis Incognita*, the Great Southern Continent. Yes, almost incredible as it may seem, the preoccupation with this mythical land mass had not died with Cook's return. Responsible people believed it was there – somewhere – because it had to be somewhere. Quiros had recounted his sighting of it and, much more recently and reliably, Wallis, too. A more blatant fantasist was Dalrymple, who could scarcely restrain his fury at Cook's failure to venture farther south than the 40th parallel after his circumnavigation of New Zealand. Dalrymple could even place this continent. In 1769, while Cook was himself far away, he published a chart of the South Atlantic and South Pacific, which featured not only the French explorer, Lozier Bouvet's Cape Circumcision* but also, even more boldly, a great southern land mass and an enormous bay descending below the 60th parallel, which he named the Gulf of St Sebastian. 'Very doubtful,' commented Cook sardonically when he was first shown this map on his return. It transpired that it was based on the fanciful world map of Abraham Ortelius of 1587, before even the charting of Cape Horn by the Dutch in 1616.

More responsible authorities than Dalrymple, while recognising the man's fantasies, saw no reason why there should not be a southern continent west of Cape Horn and east, say, of New Zealand; or in the South Atlantic east to New Holland. Banks was among these believers, forgetting his earlier disillusionment south of New Zealand. Cook, while holding to his view that there was no such land mass, had paradoxically to agree 'that it must be here [west of Cape Horn in a high latitude] or nowhere'.

Learning again from the lessons and discoveries of the first voyage, Cook determined to operate this exploration of the southernmost South Pacific with two fixed, reliable bases. One was to be Queen Charlotte Sound in New Zealand, the other Matavai Bay in King George's Land – Tahiti. At both these places he could be confident of finding provisions, wood and water. Giving his reason for embarking on this search when he was so widely known as being a sceptic, he wrote:

I think it would be a great pity that this thing which at times has been the object of many ages and nations should not now be wholly cleared up, which might very easily be done in one voyage without either much trouble or danger or fear for it.

After proving his doubts – as he fully expected – Cook intended then to search the vast wastes of the South Pacific for further discoveries, this part of the voyage promising greater personal satisfaction. This, then, would be a voyage of vast ocean sweeps, conditioned inevitably by prevailing winds and currents, about which he knew a great deal more than before he had embarked on his first voyage.

After his troubles at Rio de Janeiro, and the disasters at Batavia, Cook this time intended to circle the globe in an easterly direction,

---

* On 1 January 1739, deep in the high latitudes of the South Atlantic, Bouvet sighted (or alleged that he had sighted) snow-covered land, the nearest point of which he named Cape Circumcision, as it was the feast day of that name.

'touching and refreshing at the Cape of Good Hope, from thence proceed to the southward of New Holland for Queen Charlotte Sound'. Later, and who knew how much later, he intended to double the Horn from the west, search for Cape Circumcision, however mythical he believed it to be, and then head for Cape Town again before returning home, thus completing 'a voyage such as had never been made before'.

14

'Disgracing the Country'

BETWEEN SUPERVISING THE FITTING OUT of his two ships, Cook drew up for Sandwich a memorandum of intent, which was precise, concise and geared to the seasons. Shortly before the ships sailed in July, this was followed by secret instructions drawn up by the Admiralty Commissioners, with Sandwich's name heading the signatures. This was, in the way of such documents, unnecessarily wordy – 1,600 words in all – and not always precise. It was structured around the long conversations that Cook and Palliser in particular had held during the intervening period, and were submitted as a formality and a record: Cook knew it all, and a great deal more besides. His relationship with the hierarchy of the Admiralty was very different from 1768. He was not only a captain instead of a junior lieutenant, but his record also demanded respect, and throughout the preparations for departure he was able to use his authority and cut many corners.

The reason for the delay in departure of this new expedition lay in the hands of one man, the Malvolio of the *Endeavour*, the big-headed botanist, Joseph Banks. As soon as the word was spread abroad that there was to be a second Pacific voyage, it was assumed by the public that Banks would be sailing on it; further, that it would be 'Mr Banks's voyage', just like the first. To do him justice, his friend Lord Sandwich had early asked him if he would care to sail with it and had received a very positive reply. This was in September 1771, and since that month, while Cook worked every day on the charts, drawings and journal of the *Endeavour* voyage and prepared for the next (taking three weeks' leave to visit Yorkshire, it is true), Banks was doing a grand tour of the great houses of the land and the salons of London. With every passing day, with every expression of admiration and wonder he received, his conceit grew, until he was able with no difficulty whatever to persuade himself that indeed it was his voyage. The King, who had added his voice to the accolades, thought so too.

Letters came pouring in from the Continent from men begging to be granted a berth on Banks's voyage. Old Linnaeus himself, regretting that he could not travel to England to see Banks and his wonders of botany from all over the world, had to make do with a letter. It concluded: '*Vale vir sine pare*' or 'Farewell oh unequalled man'.

Long before March 1772, Banks had assembled a team, starting of course with steady Dr Solander. There were fifteen in all, excluding servants, and included Dr James Lind, the Scottish physician, and John Zoffany, the famous painter; there were draughtsmen and secretaries as before, and a pair of horn players for entertainment and relaxation. Their equipment and luggage grew in proportion with their number. Everything that was missed last time in the way of comforts and instruments was now included. The Royal Society, assisting at every turn, added further in the way of instruments.

It must be said in his defence that Banks was not all bravado and conceit, and even some of that can be excused by the nature of his upbringing when there was no one to stem the natural flow of his exuberance turning to egocentricity. He was still not yet thirty years old, and three of those years had been spent far from the civilising influence of society. Also in his favour was the genuineness of his enthusiasm for his chosen subjects – botany, geology, ornithology, mammalogy, and so on. He could now fairly be described as a serious authority on botany.

Banks was not much interested in exploration and the discovery of new lands except for what they offered in widening his knowledge and the collection of samples. As before, he was keen to be present if they did discover the Great Southern Continent for the satisfaction of being there, and, as he put it, 'O how Glorious would it be to set my heel upon the Pole! and turn myself round 360 degrees in a second!' There is something engaging about this childish exhibitionism, but it could also be very tiresome, and worse than that when he first inspected 'his' new ship and pronounced himself disappointed. The *Resolution* might be larger than the *Endeavour*, but it was not large enough. He had in mind something at least as spacious as a frigate – surely the Admiralty could spare one? – or an East Indiaman. But another cat-built collier – so confined below decks, so slow to sail – no, that would not do at all.

After a perfunctory inspection he went to Palliser and gave him his opinion of the ship. There was not enough room to accommodate and provide working space for his entourage. The ship must be modified or replaced by a larger one. Palliser, courteously and in a roundabout way, effectively said that was not possible. The *Resolution* had been selected because, according to Cook, 'she was the ship of my choice and as I thought the fittest for the service she was going upon of any I had ever seen'. Banks immediately took the question to higher authority, to the First Lord himself, his friend Lord Sandwich.

Sandwich was told in no uncertain terms that unless the *Resolution* was extended so that Banks could carry out his work properly, he would cancel his voyage. Banks knew that he was presenting his friend with a predicament. A great many people, from the King and members of the Royal Society, to the man-in-the-street, who regarded this voyage as Banks's own, would view the Admiralty critically for not providing the nation's great hero with the ship he needed. John Montagu, the 4th Earl of Sandwich, could brush aside the personal odium he might attract, but he cared very much for the Royal Navy and its reputation with the public. Without further ado, he ordered the Board to authorise the required modifications.

Cook accepted this decision with as good a grace as he could muster while doubting that his ship would be manageable with this additional top hamper. For what the dockyard had been ordered to carry out was the raising of the waist of his ship and the building of an entirely new deck, complete with a raised poop to accommodate Cook himself, whose cabin as well as the great cabin were also taken over for Banks's party. Any hope of a March sailing was now ruled out, along with the carefully calculated itinerary.

An army of carpenters and shipwrights set to work, hampered intermittently by Banks arriving with large numbers of his friends and admirers. On one evening Banks put on a great party for his grandest friends. All this was additional to the hordes of the merely curious. 'Scarce a day passed', Cook noted mournfully and with a touch of irony, 'when [the *Resolution*] was not crowded with strangers, who came on board for no other purpose but to see the ship in which Mr Banks was to sail round the world.'

Two months after she had been due to sail, the *Resolution* was ordered to the Downs to test her sailing qualities. She did not complete the voyage. The pilot gave up at the Nore for fear that she would capsize. She was, according to the senior naval officer on board, 'an exceeding dangerous and unsafe ship'. Banks received a letter from his old friend from the *Endeavour* voyage, Charles Clerke, which contained this defiant but fearful sentence: 'By God, I'll go to sea in a grog-tub, if required, or in the *Resolution* as soon as you please, but must say I think her by far the most unsafe ship I ever saw or heard of.'

To Cook's relief, the Board acted promptly and decisively. Without reference to Banks, the *Resolution* was ordered to Sheerness, where an even greater army of carpenters and shipwrights – 200 in all – began demolishing the extra deck and raised poop. As Beaglehole put it, 'Accommodation was to be made for the passengers such as would fit in the ship, not such as would fit the ship to the passengers. In addition the guns were to be reduced in weight and the masts shortened.'

John Elliott in his *Memoirs* gives the best brief account of what followed:

Mr Banks was requested to go to Sheerness and take a view of the accommodations, as they now stood, to try if he could go out in her, for in no other state could she go to sea, and go she must . . . When he saw the ship, and the alterations that were made, he swore and stamped upon the wharf, like a madman; and instantly ordered his servants, and all his things out of the ship . . . upon the whole, it has always been thought that it was a most fortunate circumstance for the purpose of the voyage that Mr Banks did not go . . . for a more proud, haughty man could not well be, and all his plans seemed directed to shew his own greatness, which would have accorded ill with the discipline of a man of war . . .

Elliott's view does not seem to have been general. Indignant letters were written to the press:

From what I can see, Mr Banks, Dr Solander, Dr Lind and Mr Zoffany are likely to be excluded from a voyage which, from their sharing it, did honour to the nation; and in all probability, the noblest expedition ever fitted out will dwindle to nothing, and disgrace this country.

Many protesting letter writers were most outraged by the manner in which 'servants of the crown', i.e. the Royal Navy, had deliberately flouted the known wishes of the King. One letter in the June issue of *Gentleman's Magazine* ran:

As the expedition with a view to new discoveries, which Mr Banks, Dr Solander and Mr Zoffany were to embark in, is now, after raising the expectations of the literati throughout Europe to the highest pitch, abruptly laid aside . . . is a memorable instance how little it is in the power of Majesty to perform, when the servants of the Crown are determined to oppose the Sovereign's will.

Despite his flouncing out of the Sheerness dockyard with his servants and luggage, Banks had not yet given up hope of persuading Sandwich to reverse his decision. In a letter some two thousand words long, unctuous, self-justifying and arrogant, he finally 'petitioned your lordship' for HMS *Launceston*, a 44-gun ship-of-the-line:

Was your Lordship to think proper to let us have her for our intended expedition I would gladly embark on board a ship in which safety and accommodation both which must be consulted in a voyage of this kind are more nearly united than in any other kind of ship . . .

Sandwich replied three days later, on 2 June, coldly and decisively, concerned chiefly with Banks's implied threat to make public his accusations, and telling him that if he did, an answer would be necessary, 'for it is a heavy charge against the Board to suppose that they mean to send a number of men to sea in an unhealthy ship . . . and that her crew will be in danger of losing their lives if they go to sea in her'. Banks at last recognised, to his fury, that his was a lost cause. After failing to receive any co-operation from the East India Company, he simply chartered a ship, complete with officers and men, and set sail for Iceland with all his team and piles of luggage and instruments, to continue his studies there. He also took along as a guest John Gore, who had become his friend. The American, after three circumnavigations with Byron, Wallis and Cook, evidently preferred a voyage of less than two or three years' duration.

With the passing of time, Banks's friendship with Sandwich was repaired, and Cook was forgiven, too. But not Palliser, whom Banks regarded as the leading culprit in the 'plot' to exclude him from a second voyage to the Pacific. As for Miss Harriet Blosset, his fiancée, she never saw him after his return, though Banks assuaged his conscience by 'making arrangements' for her: 'The marriage is not to take place and she is to have £5,000.'

WHILE ALL THIS DRAMA was unfolding, the *Adventure* was lying idle at Plymouth, fully refitted, her officers and men ready to sail.

Tobias Furneaux owed his position as commander of Cook's second sloop to his wide experience and to his conduct when both Wallis and his first lieutenant fell ill for much of the Pacific crossing of the *Dolphin*. He showed himself as highly responsible and, although there was one serious fracas with the Tahitians, he later cemented a friendship with the natives by tact and restraint. His personality did not match the power and colour of Cook's, and he was a touch weak on discipline, but he was a good man to sail with and much liked by those who did. He was a Devonian from Stoke Damerel and was thirty-seven years old when he was appointed.

Furneaux's first lieutenant was Joseph Shank, of whom little is known except that he was a slave to gout and had to be discharged at Cape Town. Not much more is known of Arthur Kempe, the *Adventure*'s second lieutenant, except that he became an admiral nearly fifty years later. As he had served at the siege of Quebec in 1758, he was evidently a strong survivor, although his date of birth is unrecorded. There were also a dozen marines, the usual rough lot, commanded by Lieutenant James Scott, described as 'a man of unbalanced mind, suspicious and quarrelsome' and 'a great stickler for *Honour*', according to the ship's astronomer, William Bayly, who in turn was about the only man on board the *Adventure* who did not get on with the captain.

Little is know about the *Adventure*'s people. There was one black among them, Furneaux's personal servant, who was named after him, James Tobias Swilley. There were also several West Country relations of Furneaux serving under him, including the master's mate, John Rowe.

JAMES COOK WAS NO LONGER a young man – he was forty-three as he prepared for yet another long voyage – and, although his tough constitution kept him physically fit, the stress of command over so many months was beginning to take its toll. Even when ashore he worked long hours sifting the reports and findings, checking the log and journal, the charts and drawings of the three years he had spent at sea. Elizabeth Cook remains a shadowy figure, but we know that the marriage was a close one, and it is hardly conceivable that she failed to notice that his patience was more vulnerable than it had been when he was in his thirties.

In addition, the Banks affair, running on for weeks, was an almost intolerable added burden. Cook blamed himself for not protesting more vehemently at the modification to his ship. He knew Palliser would have been on his side if he had fought the Board, who had had the decision imposed on it by Sandwich. In his heart he had known from the beginning that adding a new, weighty deck must make the *Resolution*, previously a perfect sloop, unseaworthy. And now he had lost two precious months and the goodwill of many people by failing to confront Sandwich with the almost certain reality.

A more normal but still taxing task before Cook sailed was the selection of his officers, and also some of the lower deck whom he especially wanted, the rest being chosen for him.*

The absence of the colourful Banks, the less colourful Dr Solander, the cheerful and intelligent Sydney Parkinson, and the other supernumeraries was compensated by the diversity and interest of the officers and some of the men. Some had greatness ahead of them, others had already enjoyed an adventurous past – eleven of them, plus one of the marines, had been on the *Endeavour*'s last voyage. To pick out

---

* There was always a high desertion rate before sailing on a long voyage because of the sailors' fear of the desertion of their women in their absence. Fifty-eight deserted from the *Resolution*, more than half the complement, before she sailed. They were readily replaced.

a few: of the two senior lieutenants, Robert Cooper and Charles Clerke, the latter is much the more vivid though both were fine officers. Perhaps it is only because his journal is this time lucid and revealing, with original observations and matured wit, that Clerke shines more brightly than before. When Cook was in sombre mood or preoccupied with difficult decisions, Clerke was ready with his wisdom as well as his wit.

Two youngsters, well-born, good-looking, intelligent and articulate, giving early evidence of successful careers, were George Vancouver, aged fifteen, from King's Lynn, the future surveyor of the north-west coast of North America (hence that large island's name); and twenty-one-year-old James 'Jem' Burney, lively, eccentric, observant and a great man to have on a long voyage. He came from a privileged, talented background. His father was the distinguished musicologist, Dr Charles Burney, and his sister Fanny was the novelist and diarist, though this lively young woman had not yet published at this time. Both Vancouver and Burney signed on as ABS.

Another talented AB was Alex Hood, aged fourteen, a cousin of Admirals Lord Hood and Lord Bridport. He was to be promoted captain at twenty-one and died when in command of HMS *Mars*, 74, in a furious action with a French ship-of-the-line in 1798.

The *Resolution*'s master was Joseph Gilbert, who was about the same age as Cook and, therefore, one of the oldest men in the ship. He was a considerable surveyor, known to Cook as a fellow surveyor of Newfoundland, and recommendable to him for that reason. He was to be a boon and a blessing to his captain. Elizabeth Cook's nephew sailed with him again. Isaac Smith, now eighteen, was quite a veteran, and 'clever and steady'.

Although the first purpose of this voyage was discovery and surveying, the Royal Society agreed with the Board of Admiralty and the Board of Longitude that astronomers, with all their instruments, must have an essential function. It was Dr Nevil Maskelyne, still the Astronomer Royal, who chose the two men, William Wales for the *Resolution*, and William Bayly for the *Adventure*. Cook had the better man.

Wales had first made his mark with his contributions to (however improbable it may sound) the *Ladies' Diary*, which was largely made up of mathematical problems 'of an advanced Nature'. Astronomy and mathematics were his twin fortes, and when the 1769 transit of Venus arrangements were being made by the Royal Society in association with the Board of Admiralty, Wales was chosen as the astronomer to make the observations at Prince of Wales Island in Hudson's Bay. So

Cook and his astronomer had in common both Canada and transit of Venus experience.

Wales was the cleverest and one of the most amiable men in the *Resolution*, getting on well with the ship's artist, William Hodges, and for more obvious reasons with Cook himself. It has been said that Wales's experiences on this voyage were the inspiration for Coleridge's *The Rime of the Ancient Mariner*. They were certainly of critical importance in his own treatise, *The Method of Finding the Longitude by Timekeepers*, published in 1794.

William Bayly did not possess the style or brilliance of his fellow astronomer, and he was not to enjoy the same warm relationship with his captain as Wales did. He was a self-taught mathematician and astronomer, had worked at the Royal Observatory and, like Wales and Green, had been selected as observer of the 1769 transit, his base being North Cape.

One of the reasons why the Astronomer Royal was so insistent that two capable astronomers should be included in this voyage was that Cook was taking with him a new instrument for calculating longitude. All his earlier innumerable calculations had been made by lunar observation. He had refined this method almost to a fine art, as their accuracy proves. However, this was an inconvenient and tiresome method of calculating longitude, for the obvious reason that the moon was not always available for observation.

Since 1714 the Government had put aside a prize, varying from £10,000 to £20,000 according to degree of accuracy, for the winner who invented a clock which could be taken to sea in order that the time at Greenwich could be set against the local time at the ship's position. That was all that was needed, but it took almost the entire adult working life of one clockmaker to achieve success and claim the top prize.

The man was John Harrison, another Yorkshireman and an undoubted genius. He was twenty-one when the Board of Longitude made its offer. Within one year Harrison had designed and built (largely of wood) a clock that was sufficiently promising for the Board to encourage him to continue his efforts. An ex-hydrographer to the Royal Navy described the next serious effort thus:

Harrison's first marine clock was a massive affair controlled by two large balances instead of a pendulum, connected together by wires so that their respective motions were opposed, thus overcoming the effect of the ship's motion upon them. There were many other innovations including a new form of escapement, two mainsprings, a device to ensure its speed was maintained when being wound, and compensation for the varying effects of hot and cold weather . . .

Although it was cumbersome and weighed some seventy pounds, the Admiralty gave it a brief trial and awarded Harrison £500 as an encouragement. Now with his son as assistant, Harrison broke through with his fourth chronometer, a masterpiece of ingenuity, at five inches in diameter little larger than the fob watch of the future. On-board ship it lay flat in a wooden case. This 'watch-machine' was tested twice to the West Indies and was proved to be accurate to a tenth of a second a day. It was a replica of this machine made by Larcum Kendall that Cook carried with him, although he was also requested to continue his lunar observations as before, checking one means against the other. From then on, Cook never went to sea without this priceless instrument, giving Greenwich Mean Time wherever he went, a refinement to be greatly valued.

To offset the joys and advantages of this Harrison-invented 'watch-machine', Cook was also obliged to take to sea in Banks's place a tiresome German botanist-philosopher-church minister, Johann Reinhold Förster. Förster, who was a year younger than Cook, had suffered a chequered career. He first studied theology and became a minister near Danzig. Here he married a cousin, who produced a son, Georg, in 1754. This boy seems to have been highly intelligent and mercifully lacking the trying aspects of his father's character. Johann either made enemies or aroused exasperation by his pedantry, self-righteousness, vanity, habitual acrimony and downright rudeness. It is a puzzle to know how he lasted the voyage. Many times he came close to being thrown overboard. He was once felled by a blow, Cook had to turn him out of his cabin, and Charlie Clerke once threatened him with arrest. When affronted, which was pretty well every day, he threatened his 'victimiser' with a report to the King when he returned. After a while the men began teasing him mercilessly and then, weary of that sport, ignored him and refused to rise to his provocations.

To add to this German's demerits was improvidence. There was little or no evidence of this on a long voyage, but it was the reason why he and his son were of the *Resolution*'s company. He had lost his position as a minister near Danzig, sought teaching posts, failed, lived for a time on various inheritances and then sought his fortune in England. The teaching job he obtained in Lancashire lasted no more than a year – row following row, one suspects – and a second teaching job hardly longer.

It has to be conceded that Förster never entirely lost his spirit. Now, with his son at his side, he began writing and publishing highly derivative pamphlets on a wide range of subjects, among them botany and mineralogy, which attracted the attention of the Royal

Society. Georg, meanwhile, took up the profitable task of translating Bougainville's narrative of his famous voyage.

By his persistence in cultivating the powerful and influential in London's scientific circles, Johann Förster became known to members of the Royal Society, and even contrived to become a member. It is significant that his supporters included Banks, Solander and an extremely well-connected judge, the Hon. Daines Barrington. Among his friends was the ubiquitous Sandwich, which was helpful when Barrington conceived the notion that, with the withdrawal of Banks from the expedition and the need for a scientific element, Förster should be invited to go in his place, with Georg as artist and general factotum. As for remuneration, Parliament had already voted a sum of £4,000 for the scientific factor in the voyage. Förster was asked whether he would care to take up this position, and if this sum would be sufficient, and one imagines that there was a quick agreement. Considering that Wales was on £400 a year, this was amazingly generous, but Förster was complaining of its inadequacy even before he sailed.

Beside Banks and his party, the goat would also be missing on the voyage. This double-circumnavigator, who had never once failed to provide milk for the officers, had been declared superannuated. In conversation with Dr Johnson before their withdrawal from the voyage, Banks and Solander mentioned the unparalleled record of this much-loved goat. Banks intended to present her with a collar, and begged from the good doctor a motto to carve upon it. The following day Johnson, belatedly inspired, wrote:

To JOSEPH BANKS Esq.

Perpetua ambitâ bis terrâ preamia lactis
Haec habet altrici Capra secunda Jovis
Sir,
   I return thanks to you and to Dr Solander for the pleasure which I received in yesterday's conversation. I could not recollect a motto for your Goat, but have given her one. You, Sir, may perhaps have an epic poem from some happier pen than, Sir,

Your most humble servant,
SAM JOHNSON

This couplet roughly translated reads:

In fame scarce second to the nurse of Jove [Jupiter],
    This goat, who twice the world had traversed round,
Deserving both her master's care and love,
    Ease and perpetual pasture now has found.

There was poignant irony in that last line. The goat, with her engraved silver collar, grazed in Cook's garden in the Mile End Road and then died, perhaps of shock at this new soft life, just four weeks after Dr Johnson's letter was written.

WITH THE FÖRSTERS as additional passengers, the carpenters had to busy themselves tearing down and re-erecting the cabins to accommodate them. But this was a trivial business and did not again postpone departure. Meanwhile, victualling and stowage had been completed, supervised very closely by Cook, who had a special interest in it and was generally regarded as the only man in the *Resolution* who understood the order of stowage. 'Captain Cook never explained his scheme of stowage to any of us. We were all very desirous of knowing, for it must have been upon a new plan entirely,' wrote Clerke to Banks on 31 May 1772. The total number on board was 118, and the rations for two years appear to have been generous. The list included 60,000 pounds of ship's biscuits,* 7,637 four-pound pieces of salt-beef, and twice that number of two-pound pieces of salt pork, 19 tons of beer, 642 gallons of wine, 1,400 gallons of spirits, 1,900 pounds of suet and 3,102 pounds of raisins. To these must be added the antiscorbutics to offset the effects of the scurvy-inducing protein: 20,000 pounds of sauerkraut, salted cabbage and portable broth (cakes of meat essence that could be boiled with wheat), and 30 gallons of carrot marmalade, a recent German innovation.

The basic daily ration per man was a pound of biscuits, 'as much small beer as he can drink or a pint of wine, or half a pint of brandy, rum or arrack' ('an ardent liquor obtained by the fermentation of toddy, rice and sugar'), plus, on Monday for example, half a pound of butter, ten ounces of Cheshire cheese, and as much boiled oatmeal or wheat as he could eat. Then, the next day: two four-pound pieces of beef or one four-pound piece of beef, three pounds of flour and one pound raisins or half a pound of suet.

The 'secret instructions', read again before departure, have a distinctly chilly effect on the reader. There are phrases like 'prosecuting your discoveries as near to the South Pole as possible' and 'keeping in as high a latitude as you can'. There is plenty of evidence that this is to be a hazardous voyage, with orders to Cook to remove himself and his crew to the *Adventure* 'if any action should happen to the *Resolution* in the course of the voyage so as to disable her from proceeding any farther'.

---

* Flour well kneaded, with the least possible quantity of water, into flat cakes and slowly baked. It was heavier by one-third than the grain from which it was made.

On 21 June 1772, a Sunday and the longest day of the year, Cook embraced Elizabeth, said good-bye to all his family, including the new infant, and embarked in the *Resolution* at Sheerness with William Wales. They bucked the usual contrary winds down-Channel, meeting *en route* the Admiralty yacht *Augusta*. On board were Palliser and Sandwich, who had been inspecting dockyards in the west country. Asked how the ship had behaved since she had left the Thames, Cook reported that, 'I was now well able to give them so much in her favour that I had not one fault to allege against her.' He added gratefully: 'It is owing to the perseverance of these two persons* that the expedition is in so much forwardness. Had they given way to the general clamour and not adhered to their own better judgement the voyage in all probability would have been laid aside . . .'

* Cook is generous to Sandwich, who in yielding to Banks's wishes had held up their departure for three months.

15

'Such a Long Passage at Sea'

COOK'S MOST IMPORTANT DUTY in Plymouth Sound before leaving
was to set the watches, as they were called. Besides his own Kendall
instrument, with which he was now familiar, he had been instructed
to take with him three watches made by another watchmaker, John
Arnold, which were relatively untested and, in the event, proved
unreliable. Two of these Arnolds were to be carried by Furneaux,
the other installed in the *Resolution* with the Kendall. All were
taken ashore on Drake's Island by Cook and the two astronomers,
where 'Mr Kendall's watch when put in motion was seven-tenths of
a second fast of mean time [per day] and its rate of going when tried
at Greenwich was five-eighths of a second per day slow of mean time',
while the Arnolds were far less accurate.

Soon after dawn on 13 July 1772 in cloudy summer weather, with
a favourable wind, the *Resolution* and *Adventure* sailed out of the
Sound into the Channel and stood south-west. Dick Pickersgill wrote
'Farewell Old England' in large letters in his journal; and many of
the men in the two sloops echoed this sentiment in their hearts. Only
Cook knew where they were heading, but they all knew that they were
likely to be away for a long time.

As for Cook himself, because he appeared so resolute, so much the
archetypal mariner, tall and craggy, erect and keen-eyed, it might have
been difficult for his officers to associate their captain with measures of
emotion or regret at leaving his wife and children, or even of having to
steel himself for the daunting prospect of another two years at least of
command. Only in a letter he wrote later to his old friend and master,
John Walker at Whitby, is there any evidence of his feelings:

Having nothing new to communicate I should hardly have troubled you
with a letter was it not customary for men to take leave of their friends
before they go out of the world, for I can hardly think myself in it so long
as I am deprived from having any connections with the civilized part of it,

and this will soon be my case for two years at least. When I think of the inhospitable parts I am going to, I think the voyage dangerous. I however enter upon it with great cheerfulness, providence has been very kind to me on many occasions, and I trust in the continuation of the divine protection; I have two good ships well provided and well manned . . .

It was a mainly uneventful and speedy passage to Madeira. They sighted the coast of Spain on 20 July, and three days later boarded a French fishing boat which was in serious need of water. Cook supplied it and, at the same time, bought (for £5) 100 bottles of Frontenac wine, which sounds like a good exchange. On another day, three Spanish ships-of-the-line ordered them to heave to by sending a couple of shots across the *Adventure*'s bows. At first they feared the sort of trouble they had experienced at Rio de Janeiro on the previous voyage, but in the event the Dons proved to be merely curious and wished them all *bon voyage* when Cook answered their enquiry about his destination: 'Madeira.'

Before they had even reached Funchal Roads, Madeira, the two ships and their crews had begun to shake down. Cook was more pleased than ever with the *Resolution* and reported to the Admiralty on 1 August:

I have now the pleasure to acquaint you that the *Resolution* answers in every respect as well, nay even better than we could expect. She steers, works, sails well, and is remarkably stiff and seems to promise to be a dry and very easy ship in the sea. In our passage from Plymouth we were once under our courses but it was not wind that obliged the *Resolution* to take in her topsails, though it blowed hard, but because the *Adventure* could not carry hers. In point of sailing the two sloops are well matched; what difference there is is in favour of the *Resolution*.

The brief stay at Madeira was satisfactory in all respects: the astronomers and the Försters had some nights in accommodation ashore; and the Germans, father and son, went botanising, just as Banks and Solander had on the last voyage, though they could have found nothing new.

Funchal even provided Cook and his officers with a hearty laugh. They learned that three months earlier, the period of delay of their arrival due to Banks's fuss and bother, a 'gentleman' of the name of Burnett had arrived at the island who claimed that 'he' was waiting to join Banks's party as a botanist, but had been unable to board the ship in England. Burnett, it seems, spent much of 'his' stay botanising in order to support his claim. Shortly before the *Resolution*'s arrival, 'he' (now widely recognised as a woman) learnt of Banks's failure to sail and immediately embarked on the first ship sailing for Europe. Cook was highly amused that Banks had thought that he could have deceived him into carrying his mistress round the world for his own convenience and comfort when 'every part of Mr Burnett's behaviour and every action tended to prove that he was a woman,' Cook claimed, adding, 'I have not met with a person that entertains a doubt of a contrary nature.' It can perhaps also be recognised as the botanist's final act of maritime buffoonery.

SECOND TO THE LESSON of having two ships rather than one, Cook had learned the value of keeping his men healthy. Although he had lost a third of his men on the last voyage, there was nothing he could have done about dysentery and malaria. However, no one had died of scurvy, the scourge of the age. It was not uncommon for Dutch East Indiamen to lose half their men from scurvy on the double journey to the East Indies, and Spanish, Portuguese, French and English sailors on long voyages were still suffering fearful casualties. In the *Endeavour* the first signs were invariably snuffed out by lavish consumption of antiscorbutics and great concern for cleanliness.

Almost as soon as they were at sea, the men who had not sailed with Cook before became aware of the healthy regimen that was to be imposed on them for the length of the voyage. At a time when personal cleanliness of the crew was not a high priority for most commanders, the men found that they were made to change and wash their clothes with irritating frequency, and any failure was harshly dealt with. It also appeared that their captain was obsessional about diet. The eighteenth-century sailor was the ultimate traditionalist, and any injustice concerning food, of quantity or quality, caused the sort of outrage a bank customer serves out to his manager over faulty figures to his disadvantage.

Fresh fruit, vegetables, meat and fish were nearly always welcome, but many of the antiscorbutics, like sauerkraut, were loathed. Cook was unmoved by the tastes of his men. He simply imposed these foods on them under the threat of punishment. After leaving Madeira, loaded with fresh water, 'having taken on board a large supply of wine, fruit and other necessities' along with fresh beef and 1,000 bunches of onions, 'a custom I observed last voyage and had reason to think that [his men] received great benefit therefrom', he called at two of the Cape Verde islands, scarcely more than a week later, for more fresh fruit and water in order to avoid rationing.

No ship afloat was cleaner than the *Resolution*. Again, sailors fresh to Cook's captaincy were astonished at how much time they were occupied in cleaning, especially below decks. Cook's journal notes over and over again: 'In the a.m. cleaned and smoked the sloop betwixt decks', or 'got the cables and every other thing up from betwixt decks in order to clear and air the sloop'. When a number of men brought monkeys on board as pets, and their droppings became offensive, Cook ordered them all overboard. Förster was outraged. Wales commented calmly: 'The Captain paid more attention to the health of his people than to the lives of a few monkies.' Every day there were charcoal fires, bedding to be aired, and the well and bilges to be swilled with salt water.

Clerke was deeply engaged in brewing beer:

The essence of beer having left off fermenting, put the remains which was nine casks down in the hold after having brewed 11 puncheons which proved a very salutary and I think pleasant drink [he wrote]. Many of the people disliked it vastly – preferred water to it – but I believe it was more caprice than any absolute distaste for it. I've seen many whims of this kind among seamen.

As the *Resolution* sailed into Table Bay on 30 October, well within her schedule, Clerke was able to note: 'Our people all in perfect health and spirits, owing I believe in a great measure to the strict attentions of Captain Cook to their cleanliness and every other article that respects their welfare.' By contrast, he wrote a few days later: 'Anchored here a Dutch East India ship bound from Middleburgh. She's been 4 months upon her passage . . . has buried 150 men with the scurvy and sent about 60 to the hospital here immediately upon her arrival.'

The *Adventure* had avoided the scurvy but had suffered other casualties, mysterious ones, too. In succession, two of Furneaux's midshipmen had died. Their captain accounted for this double mishap by their 'bathing and making too free with the water in the heat of the day'. Or was the cause related to the undoubted fact that Tobias Furneaux was not as diligent as Cook in supervising the health of his crew? His first lieutenant was very unwell, too; he was bad enough to beg to be sent home, and he was no scrimshanker. Lieutenant Arthur Kempe was promoted first lieutenant, and Jem Burney promoted and sent into the *Adventure*: a sorry loss to the *Resolution*.

'By the healthy condition of the crews of both sloops at our arrival', Cook noted, 'I thought to have made my stay here very short.' But several important items among their requirements before venturing south were not immediately available and they were delayed for more than three weeks. As always, Cook kept his men busy on minor repairs and in caulking and painting both ships so that 'in every respect [they] were] put into as good a condition as when they left England'. The

Försters spent every day botanising with a zeal equal to Banks's. They met a Swede, Andreas Sparrman, who, like Solander, had studied under Linnaeus. Recognising his usefulness, Förster begged Cook to allow him to join the expedition. Against his better judgment, he agreed. In the event, this enterprising and energetic Swede was to prove more cheerful and better company than his compatriot.

Hodges employed himself with an oil painting of Table Bay, Cape Town and Table Mountain. The astronomers 'got all their instruments on shore in order to make astronomical observations for ascertaining the going of the watches'. As always at a great port, the talk ashore was mostly of the comings and goings of ships of many nationalities. The French, it appeared, were particularly busy in exploration, and Cook and his officers listened with interest to stories and rumours about their activities.

Clerke learned from the Dutch that 'there had lately been a French ship in the bay, who had reported that, that ship with another, had been fitted out at Mauritius and sailed thence upon a voyage of discovery'.* The two ships had sailed due south in the waters where the *Resolution* and *Adventure* were shortly to be heading, when at the latitude of 48° they discovered land, 'which they had coasted eastward 60 leagues' and found a bay in which they intended to anchor. Boats had been sent ahead to sound for the best ground for anchoring, the account continued, but while they were occupied on this duty, a fierce gale had sprung up, driving the ships off the coast, leaving the boats to make the best shift they could for themselves.

Clerke was outraged by this tale:

I think it's totally improbable that any set of beings should be so inhumanly unfeeling as not to make the best of their way upon the coast again, as soon as the weather would permit, to look after the people and not leave the poor fellows to perish in wretchedness and want upon a barren land.

And yet, 'the good people here seem to give the most implicit confidence to this story'.

Cook evidently heard this story, too, but with a few variations (he reported the coasting distance as forty miles), and appeared less concerned about the morality of the stranding and more interested

* The leader of this expedition was Yves-Joseph de Kerguelen-Trémarec, French navigator and nobleman, charged by the King of France to discover the Great Southern Continent. He discovered and named after himself a group of desolate islands which he thought might be outlying islands of *Terra Australis Incognita* in February 1772. But on a second voyage two years later, when he rediscovered Kerguelen, he was convinced that they were well isolated (as they are) and that the continent did not exist.

in the discovery of land in this comparatively low latitude. Had these Frenchmen really discovered the Great Southern Continent? The mere suggestion added an edge of urgency to their affairs.

Cook ordered anchors to be weighed on the afternoon of 22 November 1772, exchanged salutes of fifteen guns with the Cape Town garrison, and headed due south for Bouvet's Cape Circumcision. The craggy, rock headland was surmounted by an ice cap, and ice and glaciers fell away on both sides. The fog came and went, it was bitterly cold, and the mountainous ice, sleet and snow storms added to the sense of unreality. Bouvet had been convinced that this was a continental land mass and coasted it for 400 leagues without sighting more rock or evidence of land rather than pack ice. His pilot judged that Cape Circumcision was no more than the northern tip of a small island.*

With the warm, sunny Cape of Good Hope scarcely out of sight, the two ships struck sub-Antartic weather, with gales and high seas. Cook ordered fearnought jackets and trousers to be issued. Water got into the sail room and the weather prohibited the making of observations. Before the end of the month Cook was reporting: 'Very hard gales with rain and hail, lying-to under a mizzen stay-sail most part of these 24 hours, the sea running very high.' Clerke commented on 'very disagreeable weather' in shaky writing as proof.

In the last days of November and early December they began to sight 'ice islands'. On 12 December, in bitter cold, Clerke reported: 'Passed an ice island I believe as high as the body of St Paul's church [Cathedral].' In turn they suffered every climatic extreme. On 16 December Clerke noted mournfully:

The fog so very thick we can scarcely see the length of the quarterdeck . . . these 24 hours we've abounded rather too bountifully in fogs and ice islands . . . either one or the other we can very well cope with, but both together is rather too much.

Cook ordered Furneaux over to the *Resolution* to discuss plans if they should become separated, which seemed inevitable if the weather failed to improve. Wales and Förster out in the jolly boat with the ship's master to test the water for current and temperatures were lost for an alarming two hours. It seemed impossible that conditions could

---

* He was right. It is five miles long and three miles wide, the loneliest spot on earth, not less than one thousand miles distant from the nearest land in any direction. Sealers and whalers rediscovered the island in the early nineteenth century. In 1825 some sealers managed to get ashore.

grow worse, but they did, significantly. They became embayed by ice fields and, at the same time, the ice on the rigging increased so much in weight that the sloops became difficult to handle. The only possible comfort for Cook was that conditions would have probably been even worse if they had not been held up at the Cape. Mid-summer was approaching in these waters even if the term seemed ridiculously inappropriate. But they managed to catch a few albatrosses on hooks and lines, which made good eating, as before. On the other hand, nearly all the stock they had brought from Cape Town – pigs, sheep, chickens – had died from the cold. 'Served fresh mutton to the people,' reported Dick Pickersgill on, appropriately, a Sunday, for the roast joint.

But always it was the icebergs which impressed, with a strong measure of fear, the men in both ships. Few of them had seen such phenomena before, and they were indeed an awesome sight.

We was obliged to proceed with great caution on account of the ice islands, six of which we passed this day [Cook noted on 12 December], some of them near two miles in circuit and 60 feet high, and yet the sea broke quite over them, such was the force and the weight of the waves which broke against them, which for a few moments is pleasing to the eye, but when one reflects on the danger this occasions, the mind is filled with horror, for was a ship to get against the weather side of one of these islands when the sea runs high she would be dashed to pieces in a moment.

Whales rolled and gambolled about the sloops, contrasting in size with the little Rockhopper penguins with twin yellow head combs standing singly or in groups on the icebergs watching the sloops go by, bemused and miserable in their summer moult.

On 13 December the *Resolution* was in latitude 54°, Bouvet's latitude when he had sighted Cape Circumcision, but they had been driven 118 leagues to the east. They could never recover that distance now, but, more important, they had to persevere on this southerly course. Yet time after time the pack ice defeated them.

The second week of January 1773 brought them a respite from the devilish weather. 'Very gentle breezes of wind with tolerable clear and serene weather,' Cook wrote in relief on 15 January. 'We have now had five tolerable good days succeeding one another.' During this lull both the *Resolution* and *Adventure* were able to lower boats and conduct an experiment Cook had longed to carry out for some time. Armed with ice axes and ropes, the men began attacking loose ice which surrounded all the bergs, breaking it up when necessary, and dragging chunks into the boats in baskets or loops of rope.

To the astonishment of many of the men, the ice yielded excellent sweet water. 'As everybody was employed it afforded a very humorous sight thus to see people busied, some hacking away at a large piece of ice, others drawing it up out of the sea in baskets,' wrote Irishman John Marra, gunner's mate, 'and I believe is the first instance of drawing fresh water out of the ocean in hand baskets.'*

It was a laborious business, however, for once on the sloops' deck the chunks of ice had to be chopped into pieces that could be melted down in the ovens. But in forty-eight hours they had casked more fresh water than they had stowed away at Cape Town. Cook had been rationing the water; now, thankfully, he was able to order the people to wash all their clothes.

Operations were concluded at the end of the second day. 'At half past 6 o'clock, hoisted in the boat and made sail with our *invaluable* cargo,' noted astronomer Wales. Cheered by this exercise and warmer weather, Cook succeeded in finding a way through the pack ice, with a great deal of difficulty, and on 17 January, 'at about 14 past 11 o'clock, we crossed the Antarctic Circle for at noon we were by observation four miles and a half south of it and are undoubtedly the first and only ship that ever crossed that line,' Cook wrote jubilantly, while forgetting the *Adventure* still safely with him.

But the next day, 18 January, marked the end of their southerly heading. From the masthead he counted thirty-eight 'islands of ice' and, in two hours,

the number had increased so fast upon us that at 34 past 6, being then in the latitude 67° 15's, the ice was so thick and close that we could proceed no further . . . I could see nothing to the southward but ice, in the whole extent from east to wsw without the least appearance of any partition.

It was almost as if the ice, which had dominated the scene for so long and in such variations of form, had merely been teasing them up to now. But this was serious, this was the end.** They might have been in a canal boat facing a closed lock gate. All the two sloops could do was to tack and stand away. The following day they saw only four icebergs.

Cook now determined to search the area reported by the French

---

* Marra kept a short journal, which was not handed in as required at the end of this voyage and was sold to Francis Newbery (who had, ironically, supplied the *Resolution*'s stock of Dr James's Fever Powders and had premises in St Paul's Churchyard). Newbery published it in 1776, followed by a Dublin edition and translations the following year in French and German. Cook had engaged Marra at Batavia on his previous voyage.
** They were just seventy-five miles from the continent of Antarctica.

expedition twelve months before as a coastline many hundreds of leagues long. Clerke recorded the negative result of this:

We've been for these 6 or 7 days past cruising for the land the Frenchman gave intelligence of at the Cape of Good Hope . . . if my friend Monsieur found any land, he's been confoundedly out in the latitudes and longitudes of it for we've searched the spot he represented it in and its environs too pretty narrowly and the devil an inch of land is there . . .

Clerke further observed sardonically that, instead of finding the Frenchman's continent, 'we've made [instead] rather a disagreeable discovery – which is – that our friends the French were only amusing the good folks at the Cape with a little of the marvellous'.

The two sloops recommenced their eastward run, sailing well south of Tasman's course in 1642. They were for the time being beyond the reach of the 'ice mountains' yet confident that they were not far distant from both pack ice and bergs, which on some days were distantly observed to the south.

On 7 February the weather was suddenly so fair and clear that Cook ordered all bedding to be aired and the *Adventure* to station herself four miles distant on the *Resolution*'s starboard quarter to increase their joint range of vision. But the following morning visibility was sharply reduced and, once again, with its fatiguing frequency, the fog closed in. When last seen the *Adventure* had closed to a distance of one-and-a-half miles. At 8 a.m. the two sloops lost sight of one another, the fog coming down between them like a grey canvas curtain, impenetrable and bringing with its dampness and chill a sense of unreality as if they were cut off not only from each other but also from the world beyond their own small stage.

At 9 fired a gun [Clerke noted] and continued it every hour . . . the fog coming on then much thicker than before. At noon tacked ship and fired three guns as a signal to our consort but have not heard a single gun returned from the first . . . What method they've taken I'm at a loss to guess . . . but fear they hear no more of our guns than we of theirs.

The next day, 'the weather became tolerably clear when we every one made the very best use of our eyes . . . but to our great mortification we found [the *Adventure*] was not within our horizons'.

At one time Förster was convinced that he heard an answering cannon shot. He was alone in this belief, but Cook hove to for an hour without response.

Poor Mr Förster was dreadfully scared when he realised that the two ships had really parted company; he [writes] that none of the crew 'ever looked around the ocean without expressing concern on seeing our ship alone on this vast and unexplored expanse'.

Cook and his officers, however, had long recognised the likelihood of this separation and had made proper provision, which included returning close to where they had last seen one another, remaining three days and nights, and then proceeding to their rendezvous in Queen Charlotte Sound, New Zealand.

On the morning of 10 February, in latitude 50° s and longitude 64° 53′ E, in hazy weather with intermittent rain and high seas from the west, the *Resolution* bore away to the south-east, the number of penguins increasing the expectations of some of the officers of finding land. A week later, two events occurred which again confirmed in the men's minds the strange nature of this lonely Antarctic world.

On 18 February,* 'between 12 and 3,' wrote Clerke, 'the Aurora Australis cast a fine light at different times throughout the atmosphere . . . it sometimes broke out in spiral rays in a circular form, then its light was very strong and its appearance very beautiful'. Dick Pickersgill found it a fine sight, too: 'superior to the Aurora Borealis, for the colours are finer and the flashes more quick and beautiful'.

Towards the end of February in the low 60s latitude, ice became a problem and a danger again. In 'very thick hazy weather with sleet and snow together with a very strong gale and a high sea from the east,' Cook reported on the 24th, '. . . and surrounded on every side with huge pieces of ice equally dangerous as so many rocks, it was natural for us to wish for daylight'.

Yet when daylight came, Cook – not inclined to over-dramatise – 'was so far from lessening the danger . . . it served to increase our apprehensions thereof by exhibiting to our view those mountains of ice which in the night would have passed unseen.'

The appearance, and even the behaviour, of these icebergs was singular. 'As we were passing one this morning,' Clerke recorded, 'it fell all to pieces – 'twas about four times as big as the ship.' While Wales wrote:

About 19 hrs a very large island of ice burst in an instant into three large, and many small pieces, just as we came abreast of it; it made no report, or at least so little that we could not hear it for the noise of the sea & the whistling of the wind in the rigging.

Later, he added:

About 22 hrs we passed by one of the most curious islands of ice I ever saw:

---

* Cook dates it 17 February, but other accounts put it on the 18th.

its form was that of an old square castle, one end of which had fallen into ruins, and it had a hole quite through it whose roof so exactly resembled the Gothic arch of an old postern gateway that I believe it would have puzzled an architect to have built it truer.

Another great iceberg was surrounded by so many fragments of ice that, in fine weather, Cook ordered the boats launched, equipped as before with baskets and ice axes, in order to augment their water supplies. Just as they were about to begin this operation the whole 'ice mountain' suddenly and silently turned turtle, creating waves which nearly swamped the boats and set the *Resolution* rocking.

Förster remained terrified by these sights and experiences, describing 'the whole voyage . . . as a series of hardships such as had never before been experienced by mortal man'. His son stood up better to the ordeal.

Cook and his officers, and many of the crew, too, while recognising the dangers, were also struck

by the very curious and romantic views many of these [ice] islands exhibit which are greatly heightened by the foaming and dashing of the waves against them . . . The whole exhibits a view which can only be described by the pencil of an able painter and at once fills the mind with admiration and horror.

Cook continues with uncustomary lyricism: 'The first is occasioned by the beautifulness of the picture and the latter by the danger attending it . . .'

With unwavering determination to keep as far south as the safety of the ship and the wellbeing of his men determined, Cook continued his easterly heading at around the 60° latitude line. On 24 February, at the time of the adventures with the icebergs, the *Resolution* was at 61° 21′ s. On the last day of February, in fine weather and with all sail set, they had eased a little north and were at 59° 58′ s. But the cold was excessive and a number of the men were suffering from chilblains. Cook noted sorrowfully: 'We have a breeding sow on board which . . . farrowed nine pigs, every one of which was killed by the cold before 4 o'clock in the afternoon notwithstanding all the care we could take of them.'

Still, throughout these sub-Antarctic days, Cook nursed his men's health as the men had nursed – albeit unsuccessfully – their piglets. Antiscorbutics were issued, and consumed, as regularly as ever. On 6 March he personally examined his men for cleanliness, cutting the grog ration of those not up to standard. On the same day he issued every seaman with needles, thread and buttons, 'Captain Cook having observed many of the people in rather a tattered condition'. By the middle of March, when they were in about the same longitude as Van Diemen's Land, Cook made a sudden and important decision, again in favour of the welfare of his crew. He determined now to put into Dusky Bay, South Island, New Zealand. The image of that extensive, protected sound, the great mountains towering above, had remained strong in his memory. He remembered how the *Endeavour* had been swept past it in the night, to his regret. That had been in March 1770. Now, three years later, he hoped for better fortune. If Furneaux and the *Adventure* had already arrived at their rendezvous in Queen Charlotte Sound, then a delay of a few days would·be of no account. At 5 a.m. on 17 March, to the relief of all on board, the *Resolution*'s helm was put over and for the first time for too long they were heading north-east into warmer latitudes. Later that day Cook wrote:

If the reader of this journal desires to know my reason for taking [this] resolution I desire he will only consider that after cruising four months in these high latitudes it must be natural for me to wish to enjoy some short repose in a harbour where I can procure some refreshments for my people of which they begin to stand in need. To this point too great attention could not be paid as the voyage is but in its infancy.

Cook had no need to give an explanation. He had judged the condition and mood of his men with his usual accuracy. Even Clerke was writing (23 March): 'We now begin to long for a sight of the land.' And five days later he wrote triumphantly: 'We've now arrived at a port with a ship's crew in the best order that I believe was heard of after such a long passage at sea . . .'

Sublime navigation had brought the *Resolution* from Cape Town along the ice edge of Antarctica without once sighting land, and only intermittent sightings of sun and moon, for 122 days, 11,000 miles, to a bay on the other side of the world which he had only briefly glimpsed at dusk three years earlier. It was 23 March 1773.

16

Queen Charlotte Sound Rendezvous

NO SHIP'S COMPANY MORE DESERVED the benefits and abundance of this beautiful and spectacular Dusky Bay. On leaving it six weeks later, Clerke was to write: 'I cannot in gratitude take my final leave without doing some justice to its many good qualities . . .' Wales wrote of its beautiful appearance, 'but our pleasures were not all merely ideal: a boat which was sent to fish soon returned with as much fine fish as the whole ship's company could eat'. Cook himself was captivated by it. Besides its beauty and convenience, 'there is no port in New Zealand I have been in that affords the necessary refreshments in such plenty as Dusky Bay'.

The Swede Sparrman waxed lyrical about the 'beautiful archipelago' of Dusky Bay:

Little waterfalls and brooks, peeping forth here and there from the mountains towards the sunlight, crystal clear and shining silver, could hardly fail to make a most lovely effect . . . Enormous mast-trees raised their cedar-like tops proudly and majestically high above the other tall trees in the valleys; the flight of sea birds and pelicans along the shores, and various chirpings and pleasant songs of the land-birds in the nearby dells, enlivened the whole scene. What a heavenly contrast to storms, ice, and the occasional scream of a penguin in a boundless Antarctic sea!

Sparrman added speculatively, 'No one can tell how many fertile farms might be brought into cultivation by an extensive settlement from Europe . . .'

Beaglehole, himself a New Zealander, described Dusky Bay years later as

one of the most remote and wildly magnificent spots in New Zealand. The great sheets of water, screened within its entrance from the ocean by an irregular line of islands, and extending into a number of long arms and a vast number of smaller indentations, lies over a bottom anciently gouged in the land by stupendous glaciers, so that its shores tend to stand up immediately from the sea.

Dissatisfied with his first anchorage, Cook sent steady Dick Pickersgill in search of a better. Goodness knows, there was no shortage. The entire Royal Navy could have found safe anchorage, but Pickersgill's little creek, later named after him, might have been tailor-made for the *Resolution*. Here she was moored head and stern to the trees which grew to the water's edge. One great tree had at some time been blown almost horizontal, the top reaching the sloop's gunwale, thus providing a natural gangway.

'Wood for fuel was here so convenient that our yards were locked in the branches of the trees,' Cook recorded, 'while about one hundred yards from our stern was a fine stream of fresh water.' Not only were there fish in tremendous abundance, but also wild fowl for the gun and seals for their blubber (for lighting and fuel) and flesh, pronounced as good if not better than the roast beef of old England, 'so that', Cook summarised, 'we expected to enjoy with ease what in our situation might be called the luxuries of life'.

Another feature in great abundance in Dusky Bay was rain. Sparrman complained of one consequence of excessive rain, water spiders, and large bumps resulting from their bite 'so that the entire face and hands of some were swollen up as if by smallpox'. On their first morning in the creek, several officers took a small boat to reconnoitre the neighbourhood. They had not gone far before they spotted a party of Maoris on the shore. The rain was pelting down and, with their muskets useless, they chose caution and returned to the *Resolution* to consult Cook.

Almost immediately some canoes made an appearance about a mile away, but disappeared when the rain intensified. After Cook's earlier experiences with the warlike Maoris, he determined on a cautious approach in his friendly overtures. In the afternoon when a canoe with eight Maoris approached the ship, he would have found poor Tupia a godsend. Clerke probably had the best knowledge of the Polynesian language but his efforts to encourage them to come nearer failed, and the Maoris just sat staring at the sloop from a musket-shot's distance for half an hour before paddling away. Later,

The Captain and some of the officers went in search of the Indians. They returned but have seen none of them. I believe they had retired into the woods upon the approach of one pinnace and large cutter full of men ... They found a canoe, some huts and many fish strewed about the ground and hung on boughs of trees, quite fresh. The Captain left by the canoe some medals, axes, beads, etc. – trinkets we know they are fond of.

Cook also caught the smell of the Maoris' fires somewhere in the dense forest, which added to his own feeling of intrusiveness into the lives of these people who must have lived here for centuries.

There was no further sign of the Maoris over the next few days, and Cook speculated that, like the Tahitians, they had just moved camp. Certainly, a second visit to the canoe and hut revealed that the trifling gifts had not been touched. Meanwhile, expecting to be in Dusky Bay for several weeks, he had the men ashore clearing sites by the stream for tents in which the waterers, sailmakers, coopers and others could take shelter when the rain was at its hardest. William Wales also wanted to erect an observatory. By the time the blacksmith had set up his forge, and the shoreline about the *Resolution* became a hive of industry, the Maoris – had they returned – must have judged that these intruders intended to stay for ever.

It was not until 7 April that Cook renewed contact with the locals. He and Dick Pickersgill, Charlie Clerke and several of the midshipmen went out when the weather permitted to explore and chart as much of the bay as they could, at the same time shooting wild fowl and killing an occasional seal to add variety to their mainly fish diet. On one of these expeditions they took with them a large, black dog someone had brought from Cape Town. Unfortunately, at the first musket shot, the dog raced into the forest and could not be persuaded to emerge. He remained free for two weeks before returning, presumably from hunger. But it appears that he was not a much-loved pet, and these normally sentimental sailors put him into the roasting pot two months later. The Försters, who had their own pet dog, were outraged at this heartlessness.

On another morning Cook with Hodges, who had already completed several oil paintings of the bay, the two Försters and a party of seamen took out the pinnace to explore the north side of the bay. They found a cove so rich in duck that Cook shot fourteen and named the place Duck Cove. There were several beautiful small cascades whose water, Cook reckoned, could be hosed into any ship so steep was the shoreline. Perhaps more importantly, they at last renewed contact with the local Maoris.

They were a man and two women, standing on a rock, and the man called out. They were all holding spears and, when Cook ordered the pinnace to close the rock, the three held their ground. Johann Förster described what followed:

Captain Cook went to the head of the boat, called to him in a friendly manner, and threw him his own and some other handkerchiefs, which he would not pick up. The Captain then taking some sheets of white paper in his hand, landed on the rock unharmed, and held the paper out to the native. The man now trembled very visibly, and having exhibited strong marks of fear in his countenance, took the paper: upon which Captain Cook, coming up to him, took hold of his hand, and embraced him, touching the man's nose with his own, which is their mode of salutation.

Encouraged by this display of decisiveness the Försters and several of the seamen joined Cook on the rock, 'and we spent about half an hour in chit-chat, which was little understood on either side, in which the younger of the two women bore by far the greatest share'. Cook continued: 'We presented them with fish and wild fowl which we had in our boat, which the young woman afterwards took up one by one and threw them into the boat again.'

An odd relationship developed between this Maori family and the men of the *Resolution*. The family consisted of the man, his two wives, his daughter ('one jolly wench of a daughter,' Clerke called her), a boy of about fourteen and three younger children, one still at the breast. Several of what Cook called 'the sportsmen' made advances to the girl, but with 'indifferent success'.

The following day the Maoris indicated that they wished to show Cook and his officers their habitation, 'which was but a little within the skirt of the woods and were two low wretched huts made of the bark of a tree'. The father presented Cook with a piece of cloth and, at the same time, indicated how much he would value a boat cloak such as the captain was wearing. On returning to his sloop Cook ordered one of these great cloaks, which could be wrapped several times round the body, to be made at once, in red baize.

Cook made the presentation of the cloak the following day, the Maoris all prepared for them as if they wished to make a solemn ceremony of the occasion. 'They were all dressed, men, women and children, in their best clothing, with their hair combed, oiled and tied upon the crown of their heads and ornamented with white feathers.' Cook then presented the father with the cloak, with which he was highly pleased.

Two days later, at 10 a.m., the family was seen approaching the *Resolution* in their canoe. Cook went out in a boat to greet them, but at first was unable to persuade them to come alongside. So he climbed into their canoe to confirm his trust. At length they landed on the shore nearby, near enough for conversation of a sort, Cook noting that they spoke Polynesian with a harsh grating accent compared with the Maoris of Queen Charlotte Sound.

Another week passed before Cook had a visit from the family.

Before they came on board I showed them the sheep and goats which they viewed for a moment with a kind of stupid insensibility. After this [continued Cook] I conducted them to the brow, but before the chief set his foot upon it to come into the ship he took a small branch in his hand with which he struck the ship's side two or three times, repeating at the same time a speech or prayer, which when done he threw the branch into the main chains and came on board followed by the girl.

Cook then led them down to the cabin where breakfast had been laid, but they would taste nothing. Instead, father and daughter wandered about the cabin, looking at everything with surprise, 'but it was not possible to fix their attention to any one thing [for as long as] a single moment'. This absence of concentration strongly contrasted with the lustier bloods and blades among the officers. Cook chose to ignore their behaviour – or at least omit to record it – but Clerke's sly innuendos leave no doubt:

The gallantry of our people in general made them very anxious to pay some compliment to the young lady, as 'twas the first female we had seen for many months, but the young gypsy did not seem at all inclined to repay them in the kind Indian women in general trade in and indeed the kind that's most welcomed I believe by all men after so long an absence from the sex.

Instead, more prosaically, Maori clothes were exchanged for what they most appreciated, axes and large nails.

By the end of the first week in May Cook decided that it was time to resume their voyage, now for the first time in southern hemisphere waters he had sailed before. They had ample water, plenty of smoked fish, enough beer brewed from the leaves and branches of trees to cancel the grog ration for some time, and fresh fowl and seal meat to last them a week in this cool climate. The carpenters had the ship in good order and the sailmakers had long since completed their repairs.

The *Resolution* was eased out of Pickersgill Cove and, at 9 a.m. on 11 May, 'We got under sail with a light breeze at SE' and headed up a long narrow passage which separates the mainland from the great mountainous island to which Cook gave his sloop's name. There was not a man on board who was not relieved to be at sea again. They were thoroughly rested and restored by the unlimited food – Clerke was not the only one to be complaining about straining buttons. The wet combined with the increasing cold made a northern passage attractive in prospect, and they knew that the paradise of Tahiti lay ahead after Queen Charlotte Sound, and there were plenty of men to cite the delights of the South Pacific.

Cook spent nine days working his sloop up the west coast of South Island. This time they had little trouble with the weather until they had almost reached their destination. They were sailing fast with a favourable wind, and almost ready to fire signal guns for the *Adventure*, when a dead calm fell over the ship, the sky turned black and water spouts suddenly began darting about them – huge and threatening columns of whirling water. There was no way to evade them. One passed within fifty yards of them, tauntingly, and then raced away unevenly to the north-east.

It was difficult not to interpret this shocking phenomenon as an ill omen of the fate of their consort. But, to everyone's relief, when the sea returned to normal and the wind blew as before, they distinctly heard the sound of the *Adventure*'s signal guns and observed the flashes when they were abreast of Cape Jackson. Furneaux had found Ship Cove some six weeks earlier.

The wind had dropped and Cook ordered the boats to assist the *Resolution* into the anchorage. At the same time a boat put off from the *Adventure* and headed for them. It was not Furneaux himself but Lieutenant Arthur Kempe. Cook greeted him warmly and was given a summary of the events his other sloop had experienced since their parting. Kempe also brought with him a token gift of local fish and salad for Cook's supper. After thanking him, Cook said that he would anchor shortly and then bring his ship alongside the *Adventure* the following morning.

THERE IS NO RECORD of the meeting and conversation between the two captains the following morning after Cook had the *Resolution* moored close alongside the *Adventure*. But we can be sure that Cook, after being piped on board Furneaux's sloop, descended to his cabin and the two men sat down side by side with the ship's log between them. This log showed that Furneaux had followed the order to remain in the area where they had become separated for three days and then, at noon on 11 February, 'bore away for the rendezvous in New Zealand'. With the season so far advanced, Furneaux had felt no further need to return to the high latitudes which had proved so troublesome and, without a second ship, even more dangerous. Cook thoroughly approved of this decision and listened eagerly to Furneaux's account of sighting land on 9 March. The *Adventure* was badly short of water.

Cook recognised that Furneaux had followed Tasman's route along the south coast of Van Diemen's Land and had put into the same bay used by Tasman for wooding and watering. Tasman called it Storm Bay. Furneaux, inappropriately, named it after his ship. Adventure Bay is the ideal sailing ship's haven, a deep, regular semi-circle, with a sandy beach, an excellent pure stream at the east end and dense woodland coming down close to the beach. It is unchanged today except that Bruni Island, on which the bay is situated, is connected to the mainland of Tasmania by a short bridge; and, alas, the little Tasman Aborigines have long since been wiped out.

Furneaux's log showed that the *Adventure* had left this bay, well wooded and watered, after four days, and that they had then coasted up the east coast of Van Diemen's Land with the intention of confirming or otherwise that this land was part of New Holland, or an island. It was clear from the log that Furneaux had searched only perfunctorily for a strait north of Van Diemen's Land, much discouraged by the shoal water that extended far from the islands off the north-east coast. He indicated to Cook that he was confident that there was no strait, only a deep bay, just as Cook himself had concluded back in 1770. It is highly unlikely that he mentioned that one of his officers* was firmly of a different opinion.

The voyage across the Tasman Sea, in the wake of the Dutch navigator's *Heemskerk* and *Zeehaen*, was swift and uneventful, and on 3 March they had sighted Cape Farewell. Cook was pleased to hear that the posts he had erected, with the name of his ship and the date carved upon them, were still in position; and moved by the news that the few Maoris still living near Ship Cove had asked after Tupia, 'but could not be made sensible of his death'.

However, Cook was by no means totally pleased with Furneaux and his officers. They could not be blamed for the separation of the two sloops, but it became increasingly clear that discipline was not as tight as it should have been on a long and arduous voyage of this nature. The crew again were 'much inflicted with the scurvy', and the first thing they had to do on arrival was to set up tents for the sick on Motuara Island. The *Adventure* had as generous a supply of

---

* Bayly, the astronomer, wrote of finding 'the mouth of a strait which separates New Holland from Van Diemen's Land'.

antiscorbutics as Cook's ship, and it can only have been slackness in implementing the formula as prescribed by Cook that had led to this trouble. In the *Resolution* the petty officers, like hospital nurses, ensured that the medicine – not all of it very palatable – was taken, at the risk of a flogging for those who did not conform.

Bayly, who had just discovered to his fury that his cask of porter in the fore hold and a quarter cask of Madeira belonging to another officer had been entirely consumed, recounted an incident in the *Adventure* on 16 February which was not isolated, it was later made clear:

This afternoon Mr Scott [the lieutenant commanding the Royal Marines] [was] turned out of our mess. He behaved in an insolent manner to the Captain so that the Captain took him by the shoulders and put him out of the great cabin and shut the door after him. He was of an unhappy temper, always quarrelling with the Captain and officers, he being a great stickler for *Honour*, that if you spoke the least word in a joke his Scotch blood would be up.

A few weeks later there was a more serious affray involving the ship's officers, in which Bayly was the victim:

After I was in bed, Mr Kempe the 1st Lieutenant, & Mr Burney 2nd Lieutenant, Mr Andrews the Surgeon, & Mr Hawksey Midshipman all came to my door and asked me to give them brandy which I refused to do, thinking they already had had enough, it being between 12 o'clock and 1 o'clock at night, and begged them to go to bed. But they procured a hammer and chisel and began ripping the hinges off my door.

This was too much for Bayly, who opened the door, seized Burney and thrust him down on to the arms-chest. The others then set about Bayly, beating him about the head while the surgeon threatened to strike him with the hammer. Furneaux then made a belated appearance and put an end to it. There is no mention of this incident in Furneaux's journal, nor in the ship's log; nor is there any mention of retribution.

Another midshipman was the victim of some form of dementia. The *Adventure*, having already lost two midshipmen early in the voyage under doubtful circumstances, nearly lost a third. On 3 March late at night George Moorey, who had been promoted midshipman from AB to replace one of these earlier casualties, suddenly left his post on the forecastle and ran aft 'in violent agitation crying out he would never see his father again'. He was clearly going to plunge into the sea, but was seized on the quarterdeck and pacified by some members of the watch. It seemed that this very sober midshipman was suddenly joined in his pacing of the forecastle by the ghost of his father, who was dressed as when Moorey had last seen him. This terrified him out of his wits and led him to believe that his father had died and that he would never see him again.

All that Cook had learned about the *Adventure*'s voyage so far led him to judge that Furneaux and his men should not be allowed to linger around Queen Charlotte Sound any longer. It took less than a single day for Cook to recognise that Furneaux and his company were preparing for a winter of ease in Queen Charlotte Sound, something that Cook had no intention of permitting. It was with some surprise, then, that Furneaux learned from what one suspects was a rather stony-faced Cook that he planned to leave within a few days and that the two sloops would sail together again.

Cook explained his plans verbally to the lieutenant, then followed it with a written account for the record. They were to proceed to the east between latitudes of 41° and 46° s until the longitude of 140° or 135° w. This would be a sweep that would cover the ocean south of the Society Islands, which he had only partly covered in the *Endeavour*, and would take him farther to the south and to the east of his previous sweep. They would then turn north and west for Tahiti, bisecting a large area of the Pacific previously unexplored. Here they were to wood and water and refresh themselves at this known haven before returning to New Zealand.

It may be thought by some an extraordinary step in me to proceed on discoveries as far south as 46° in the very depth of winter for it must be owned that this is a season by no means favourable for discoveries [Cook wrote]. It nevertheless appeared to me necessary that something must be done in it . . . Besides if I should discover any land in my route to the east I shall be ready to begin with the summer to explore it; setting aside all these considerations I have little to fear, having two good ships well provided and [now] healthy crews.

Förster, when he heard, called this a dangerous and unnecessary expedition, as Cook was 'far from expecting to discover new lands, and greatly doubted the existence of a southern continent'. Every voyage in these seas in winter could be called dangerous, but he was right in judging that Cook doubted that they would find anything larger than islands. This of course had been his belief for years, but he had his orders, and no one would have been more delighted if this belief had been proved false.

Cook ensured that for the few days before they sailed all the men of both sloops were kept busy. Most of the work was of an agricultural nature, collecting bundles of celery and scurvy grass, clearing and digging up the ground on Mouara Island and planting wheat, peas 'and other pulse', carrots, parsnips and strawberries. Cook had brought from Cape Town a number of sheep and rams, but this had been a disappointing exercise as without proper fodder they had succumbed to a form of scurvy, and only a single sheep and ram survived to Ship Cove. When put ashore here to graze, they died almost at once, probably from a poisonous grass, Cook surmised. However, goats, a boar and a sow, also put ashore, appeared quite happy and looked likely to survive and breed.

Cook's final journal entry before quitting Ship Cove takes on a high moral tone, which tells us something of the man:

The women of this country I always looked upon to be more chaste than the generality of Indian Women. Whatever favours a few of them might have granted to the crew of the *Endeavour* it was generally done in a private manner and without the [Maori] men seeming to interest themselves in it. But now we find the men are the chief promoters of this vice, and for a spike nail . . . will oblige their wives and daughters to prostitute themselves whether they will or no, and that not with the privacy decency seems to require, such are the consequences of a commerce with Europeans . . . We debauch their morals already too prone to vice and we introduce among them wants and perhaps diseases which they never before knew and which serves only to disturb that happy tranquillity they and their forefathers have enjoyed.

Cook concludes with the unanswerable challenge: 'If anyone denies the truth of this assertion let him tell me what the natives of the whole extent of America have gained by the commerce they have had with Europeans.'

Quoting Cook, Sparrman is equally censorious:

Captain Cook states that on his first visit in the *Endeavour* he had reason to consider the New Zealand women more chaste than those in the other South Sea islands, and that whatever favours a few of them might have granted to the people in the ship, it was generally done in a private manner, and the [Maori] men did not seem to interest themselves much in it, but that on the second visit the [Maori] men were the chief promoters of a shameful traffic. Undoubtedly the most surprising point about all this is there should have been some members of a civilised nation who were not revolted by the embraces of cannibal women, which one would have thought disgusting enough without the painting, smearing, filth, and vermin.

For the second time, and with none of the accompanying dangers of the first, Cook put to sea from Queen Charlotte Sound to ply through the strait carrying his name. And this time he was not alone. It was 7 a.m. on Monday, 7 June 1773. For a time the two ships dipped down south of the 45° parallel, just below the latitude of the southern tip of New Zealand. The weather varied from foul to very foul, with strong gales, haze and torrential rain, but it was not fearnought weather, and there were no icebergs nor ice in the rigging. While old Förster grumbled and grumbled, no one listened or suffered themselves – relatively, that is, within the normal range of discomfort in a wet and crowded ship in heavy running seas, 16,000 miles from home.

Most of the events over the following taxing weeks stemmed from the weather: 'A great irregular swell', 'at 4 p.m. carried away the fore topgallant yard in the slings', 'Close reefed the topsails, at 7 a.m. out all reefs', are typical references in Cook's journal. Wales noted an odd and potentially dangerous event ten days out of Cook Strait:

A very hollow sea caused the ship to labour much and a sudden jerk of the tiller carried the man at the wheel clear over it. Luckily the officer of the watch caught it, replaced him, & put a man on the lee side to assist him. They had been there scarce ten minutes before another jerk carried the man on the weather side over again. The tiller stayed not a moment a-weather, but returned with such velocity as brought the man on the lee side over to windward.

Again the lieutenant caught it, and it was lucky he did as the unfortunate fellow had got his leg jammed between a spoke of the wheel and the standard supporting it, 'so that if the helm had had time to return it [the leg] must have been broke to pieces'.

In conditions like these the wonder is that any of the livestock and pets on board, of which there were many including the Försters' dog, survived. A goat did fall overboard on 9 July. They put about at once, lowered a boat and rescued the animal, but she died soon after. In other cases the population of some animals actually increased, as Clerke noted:

This morning [2 August] a bitch littered on board when a young New Zealand whelp fell to and had devoured the best part of one of the pups (very characteristically) before he was detected – and then 'twas with many hard thumps that he was prevailed upon to spare the rest.

After about six weeks at sea the fresh antiscorbutics from New Zealand, the wild celery and scurvy grass had become exhausted, but Cook continued to implement the healthy diet, with plenty of malt and sauerkraut. He was also just as severe about personal cleanliness, the airing of blankets and the frequent airing of the ship, Decks were scrubbed with vinegar and salt water, and smoked with 'fire balls'.

Tobias Furneaux apparently found it impossible to apply this same strict regimen. The consequences were inevitable. After little more than six weeks at sea scurvy had again got a strong grip on the *Adventure*'s company Clerke noted the miserable news on 29 July, by chance a fine, warm, calm day when they were sailing – but scarcely moving – just south-west of Pitcairn Island:

Hoisted out the boat and sent her on board the *Adventure*. She soon after returned and brought on board Lt Kempe, the Captain being indisposed [gout in foot]. Mr Kempe gave us the very disagreeable intelligence of that ship's being very sickly – having now upwards of 20 men down with the scurvy – and having buried their cook who fell a martyr to that confounded disorder a few days ago.

Cook was furious and exasperated. Would his subordinate captain never learn? He had spoken to him severely at Ship Cove, where his men were 'eating few or no vegetables . . . partly for want of knowing the right sorts and partly because it was a new diet which alone was sufficient for seamen to reject it'. With justified firmness, Cook laid it down: 'To introduce any new article of food among seamen, let it be ever so much for their good, requires both the examples and authority of a Commander', neither of which, it seemed, Furneaux possessed.

Cook wrote a letter instructing him to brew beer of the inspissated juice of wort, essence of spruce and tea plants, to increase the allowance of sauerkraut, to boil cabbage in their peas, to serve wine instead of spirit and to cut down on the salt beef. Every item in this list was guaranteed to be unpopular with almost all of the *Adventure*'s men; but Furneaux, gout or no gout, knew that he must follow these instructions or it would be an end to his naval career when he got home. Little more than a week later, himself evidently over the worst of his gout, Furneaux took a boat to the *Resolution* and 'gave the agreeable intelligence that his people were much better and all rather upon the recovery'. This surely proved how simple it was to bring about a cure.

Cook had been heading N½E since 17 July, bisecting the area of the Pacific between his course towards Tahiti and south from that island in the *Endeavour*. He was confident that he would find nothing except a small island or two, but those were his instructions and nothing could be proved without sweeping the South Pacific in this way. By early August they were among the Tuamotus and heading west towards Tahiti, a little north of their old course in the *Endeavour*. 'This sea abounds in these paltry little islands . . .', wrote Clerke with some authority, this being his third passage among them. 'They are very low and render the navigation here in the night dangerous for there are coral reefs about them which would with great difficulty be [seen] by night unless exceedingly well illuminated by the moon.'

For this reason Cook frequently ordered his sloops to lay to at night or 'run under an easy sail'. But at last they were in the trade winds now, and on 9 August they logged 126 miles in spite of losing four hours of the night before the moon appeared. Cook had another reason to hurry: scurvy had again broken out seriously in the *Adventure*, and on shore at Tahiti he could supervise the patients' recovery.

So urgent did he consider the need to provide fresh fruit and vegetables to these victims that he decided to anchor first in Vaitepiha Bay on the east coast of the island, which he had discovered on his tour of Tahiti before sailing away in the *Endeavour*. Unfortunately, due to a miscalculation of the officer of the watch while Cook slept, they found themselves driving towards the reef. The *Resolution* struck several times, and every means was tried to drag her clear by the boats of both sloops. Was the nightmare of 'the insane labyrinth' of the Great Barrier Reef to be repeated?

While this crisis was occupying the attention of all crew members, the Tahitians swarmed on board both sloops in their hundreds, hell-bent on trading and seizing anything upon which they could lay their hands. They were back in Tahiti all right, noted the old veterans, as they got the sloop clear and then through a gap in the reef to a safe anchorage.

'Rather too warm,' noted Clerke succinctly.

17

Horrors of Grass Cove

JUST AS JOHN GORE, CHARLES CLERKE AND OTHERS of the *Dolphin* had found Tahiti different on landing from the *Endeavour*, so the island had suffered more changes since 1769. The cause, however, was the same: the curse of civil war. Cook learned that

Toutaha, King of the greater Kingdom of Otahiete, was killed in a battle which happened between the two kingdoms ... and that Otoo was now the reigning Prince. Tiboura and several more of our principal friends about Matavai fell in the same battle and likewise a great number of the common people.

Hog breeding was one of the victims of the war, and Cook's hopes of acquiring a large number when they landed were dashed at Vaitepiha. But two characteristics of the Tahitians had not changed at all: their thieving and their terror of firearms. On the first day after anchoring, with the *Resolution* suffering a mass invasion of Tahitians and Cook wishing to show goodwill, he invited a chief and his entourage into the great cabin. Soon they were all pilfering everything that could be moved, handing out books, instruments and much else through the quarter gallery to collaborators in canoes alongside.

Many complaints of the like kind were made to me against those on deck [Cook reported], which induced me to turn them all out of the ship. My cabin guest made good haste to be gone. I was so exasperated at his behaviour that after he had got a good distance from the ship I fired two musket balls over his head which made him quit his canoe and take to the water.

This was followed by the firing of a 4-pounder, which cleared the beach. But after a few hours they returned, 'well reconciled as if nothing had happened'.

The *Adventure*'s scurvy-stricken men were able to walk after a few days of fresh fruit and roots, so Cook decided to quit this unpromising place and move to the more familiar Matavai Bay. With the two sloops anchored where the *Endeavour* had been four years earlier, with the astronomers setting up their observatory on Point Venus, surrounded by tents and guarded by Royal Marines, the local Tahitians could view the scene as a repeat of what had occurred before.

But there were many new faces, and many missing faces, at Matavai. One of the first on board the *Resolution* was a chief called Maritata and his wife and entourage. He promised to take Cook to meet Prince Otoo in Oparre the next morning, 26 August. Furneaux accompanied Cook with Maritata and his wife. Otoo was sitting on the ground when they found him, surrounded by his family and a number of his subjects, all stark naked, to Cook a new form of obeisance. However, it was a thoroughly friendly meeting, Cook offering the Prince the usual rather superior presents he reserved for these occasions – axes, mirrors, as well as beads and medals. Otoo in return offered a large quantity of local cloth, which Cook refused, explaining that his were gifts for *tiyo*, for friendship, not for trading.

Lieutenant John Edgcumbe, the officer commanding Cook's marines, greeted the party on their return and saw them off to their respective ships. Maritata and his wife, however, remained at the encampment with the Royal Marines. Edgcumbe, a sound and sensible officer, was somewhat puzzled by this situation until, one imagines to his embarrassment, the wife showed her intentions all too clearly:

This lady [the officer later recounted] wanted neither youth nor beauty, nor was she wanting in using those charms which nature had given her to the most advantage. She bestowed her caresses on me with the utmost profusion, and before I could get clear of her I was obliged to satisfy all her demands, after which both she and her husband went away and I was never troubled with either the one or the other afterwards . . .

Just where this seduction took place, whether in private or public, was not made clear by the gallant officer.

Cook's relations with Prince Otoo and his wife were more orthodox, but for the first few days they were intense, with much mutual hospitality and present exchanging. At first Cook had some difficulty in persuading the Prince to come on board the *Resolution*, the reason being that he was *mataou poupoue* – or afraid of the guns. In fact, Cook wrote that 'all his actions showed him to be a timorous Prince'. At one of their meetings Furneaux presented

Otoo with a male and female goat, which were accepted gratefully; but Cook's own handsome present of a large broadsword was viewed with terror, especially when it was buckled upon Otoo. After a short time he asked permission to have it removed and taken out of his sight. Although he was unquestionably the Prince, it seems unlikely that he could have taken an active part in the recent war.

This social life was rudely interrupted by an affray on the evening of 30 August. Cook was alerted to it by the sound of shouting from the shore in the opposite direction to Point Venus. He at once called for a boat with marines to investigate, and ordered Furneaux to do the same. The *Resolution*'s boat returned with a marine from the *Adventure* and four of Cook's own people. They were all ordered in irons for the night and lashed the next morning, twelve for the seamen and eighteen for the marine. The charge, according to Clerke, was absenting themselves from duty and quarrelling 'with the natives', the second a very serious charge in Cook's reckoning. It appeared that 'they were making too free with the women', and it can safely be presumed they were also drunk.

Cook was not surprised to find the shore deserted in the morning. Nor could Prince Otoo be found at Oparre, which was not surprising either. But Cook had decided to sail the following day and was determined to find him, both to apologise for the unforgiveable behaviour of his men and to wish him good-bye. He at length found the Prince and his entourage 'many miles removed from his abode'. Otoo did complain about the fighting and attempted rape, but was mollified by the presents Cook had brought just for this purpose. In exchange, Cook received some fine big hogs, and there was much embracing and many mutual expressions of goodwill.

Shortly after this episode, which shocked him deeply, Cook inserted into his journal an interesting piece of social observation, which certainly came as a surprise to his contemporary readers:

Great injustice has been done to the women of Otaheite and the Society Isles by those who have represented them without exception as ready to grant the last favour to any man who will come up to their price. But this is by no means the case; the favour of married women and also the unmarried of the better sort, are as difficult to obtain here as in any other country whatever. Neither can the charge be understood indiscriminately of the unmarried of the lower class . . . That there are prostitutes here as well as in other countries is very true, perhaps more in proportion, and such were those who came on board the ship to our people . . . By seeing these mix indiscriminately with those of a different turn, even of the first rank, one is at first inclined to think they are all disposed the same way and that the only difference is in their price. But the truth is, the women who become prostitutes do not seem in their opinion to have committed a crime of so deep a die as to exclude her from the esteem and society of the community in general . . .

From this little essay, it appears that Lieutenant Edgcumbe's experience was unusual.

With a favourable wind on 1 September, Cook prepared for sea. Almost at the last moment 'a young man whose name was Poreo came to me and desired I would take him with me,' Cook noted. Remembering how useful Tupia had been on the earlier voyage, 'I consented, thinking he might be of service. Many more would have gone if I would have taken them.' Typically, Clerke touched on this incident more romantically:

A young Otahitean whose name was Poreo, having a curiosity to know a little more of the world than he would experience on Otaheite, came on board and desired to be admitted as a volunteer. He met with a cordial reception and very cheerfully set out upon his travels, though, notwithstanding his spirit and resolution, when he saw the dear isle sinking in the horizon, he could not refrain the tribute of a few tears. [Clerke added] Poor Poreo's are not the only tears I've seen roused upon leaving this good isle by some hundreds, though I've been in a condition myself at the time not to see a great way.

It had been Cook's original intention to sail directly for New Zealand and prepare for his new sweep in the sub-Antarctic to the east. This, he was confident, would finally settle the matter of *Terra Australis Incognita* and thus fulfil his instructions. But Matavai Bay had produced little in the way of supplies for the long leg back to Queen Charlotte Sound and he determined to seek them elsewhere. He therefore headed first for Huahine, with its fine harbour on the west coast. Here Chief Ori, whom Cook remembered affectionately from his last visit, fell upon his shoulders, weeping copiously when he recognised his old friend 'Tute'. The warmth of the welcome was reflected in the volume and the range of the provisions that were made available. 'Great plenty of hogs coming from all quarters,' wrote Clerke with satisfaction. 'People at no allowance, they abound most plentifully in pork, yams, plantains, etc.'

On one of the days here, in perfect weather, the two astronomers 'walked quite across the island . . . Our path lay along one of the pleasantest valleys that I ever saw. It is a perfect orchard from one end to the other, interspersed with the houses of the inhabitants . . .'

Like everyone else, Wales and Bayly were 'nowhere offered the least incivility'. But even in this paradise, where no one seemed wanting for anything, thieving was rife. The astronomers had their pockets picked, and poor Sparrman, botanising alone, was stripped of all his clothes but his trousers, and was much abused and somewhat hurt. 'When, finally, red with anger and out of breath, I reached the market I saw many of my friends turn pale at the sight of me.' Sparrman continued, 'I gave them to understand that my adventure must be regarded as an abominable insult albeit feeling no pain from the injuries I had sustained.'

A chief got most of the clothes back for the Swede, and he was invited ashore to witness the punishment meted out to the thieves. He was disinclined and, anyway, Cook was anxious to leave.

Meanwhile, over at the *Adventure*, Furneaux had been pestered for days by a young priest (as he called himself) named Omai. He, too, wanted to see 'Britannia'. Furneaux, who recognised unusual intelligence and charm in the young fellow, agreed to accommodate him. Conversely, Cook lost his Poreo when the Tahitian lost his heart to a young girl of the island. His place was taken by a young man called Odiddy by the *Resolution*'s men.

At this island and later at Raiatea Cook and Furneaux acquired almost an embarrassment of riches in the form of hogs and sows, hens and cocks, some dogs, and yams and breadfruit in great quantities. When the time came to set sail from Raiatea, the decks were alive with beasts and poultry, and for weeks the ships' provisions were not touched.

Many of the Society Islands veterans were sorry to be leaving. They had formed a real affection for the people and their beautiful homeland. Clerke expressed his feelings:

I must own that 'tis with some reluctance I bid adieu to these happy isles where I've spent many very happy days, both in the years '69 and '73. In the first place (for we must give this consideration the preference after a long sea voyage) you live upon, and abound in, the very best of pork and the sweetest and most salutary of vegetables. In the next place, the women in general are very handsome and very kind, and the men civil and to the last degree benevolent, so that I'm sure whenever we get among them we may with very great safety say we've got into a very good neighbourhood. In short, in my opinion, they are as pleasant and happy spots as this world contains.

The *Resolution* and *Adventure* finally sailed from the Society Islands on 18 September, but still Cook did not head directly for New Zealand. The lure of discovery *en route* was irresistible and he headed west rather than south-west, in order to check on some of the islands of the Tonga group first sighted by Tasman on his great 1642 voyage. Five days later, at 10 a.m., 'Saw land from the mast head, and at noon from the deck, extending from SBW to SWBS, hauled up in order to discover it plainer.' This land had been noted by neither Tasman nor Quiros, and it was scarcely worth noting anyway: two or three islets connected by reefs, 'low and clothed with wood', mostly coconuts. Cook named them Hervey after his friend, the great Admiral Augustus Hervey, who had fought with Admirals Edward Hawke, George Rodney and Augustus Keppel, becoming a Lord of the Admiralty in 1771. Perhaps he deserved better.

Cook brought to at night for fear of missing the Tongan Islands, which he had reason to believe were now close at hand. On 1 October he sighted a much bigger island to the south-west, Tasman's Middleburg, and the next day Amsterdam (Eua and Tongatapu today). He was now deep among the Tongan Islands, more than one hundred of them spread about the ocean like scattered grain, but varying in size from atolls all but washed over by the sea, to substantial islands like Middleburg. Every day there were sightings to record and name, and Cook could have stayed a month and only half completed his charts.

A good anchorage was noted at Middleburg, which was soon seen to be heavily populated. In a few minutes hundreds of natives of both sexes were swarming over the two sloops, eager for trading. Cook, by now with an experienced eye, picked out the chief among them, offered lavish gifts and suggested that he should accompany him ashore.

'We were welcomed by acclamations from an immense crowd of men and women,' Cook recounted, 'not one of whom had so much as a stick in their hands. They crowded so thick about the boats with cloth, matting [etc.] to exchange for nails that it was some time before we could get room to land.'

The chief cleared the way and led them through the crowds to his nearby house. How many times was Cook to go through this ritual on his Pacific voyages! He was not incurious about the people, their manners and practices, and he endured the formalities with as much patience as he could summon. He had not only been charged with 'cultivating a friendship with the natives', but it was also highly important that he did so for the sake of good trading and the means of supplementing his supplies of food and water. But Cook was also aware of the price of stress and time they demanded, each occasion adding an ounce or more to the weight of command.

Cook's party, including Furneaux and the Försters, and the chief's entourage, all sat down on the matting. Then a bowl of liquor made (Cook was to learn) from the pepper root was passed round, bananas and coconuts offered, and three young women sang a song or two, which they did with a very good grace, according to Cook: 'Their songs were musical and harmonious, in no way harsh or disagreeable.' Cook ordered the pipers from his ship, whom he often brought ashore on these occasions, to play the bagpipes. It was a curious setting for a lament by the MacCrimmons.

Both this island and Amsterdam, to which the two sloops sailed after two days, were maintained in a high state of cultivation, and in all respects these Friendly Islands (as they became known) appeared more advanced than the Society Islands, though visitors were just as subject to thieving as anywhere else in the South Pacific. A one-man expedition by astronomer Wales exemplified all three aspects of these islands.

Always keen to explore, he took a boat ashore, but could not reach land without wading. This he did, sat down to put on his shoes and lost them to nimble fingers. So there he was, helpless with bare feet, surrounded by coral like razors. Luckily, Cook and a chief were within earshot, and the chief had the stolen shoes returned quickly.

Nevertheless, Wales felt completely safe walking about Amsterdam and recorded his findings:

The island seems to be in the highest state of cultivation, there being scarce a foot of land which is not enclosed and planted, except the public roads [footpaths], one of which runs between every plantation ... At several intersections there are square areas of perhaps 50 or 100 yards left unenclosed and planted round with large spreading trees. Towards the upper end there is raised a small mount whose top is enclosed with a sort of low parapet of square, flat, hewn stones, set on edge in the ground. The mount is ascended in the front by a flight of steps of the same stone. At the top of the mount within the parapet is covered with gravel ... and in the midst is a building which I took the liberty to enter.

Inside, Wales found a small wooden image, while, mysteriously, beside it there was a heap of small, black pebbles in oval form, topped by a pile of brown gravel, all kept 'very neat and clear of weeds'.

Wales could only conclude that these people were very different from those of the Society Islands, much more industrious and organised, and with a different religion.

I returned on board in the evening [he tells us], after making a considerable circuit of the island, without meeting with the least insult or incivility from any of the natives, after that which happened at my landing, although I met with many hundreds on the roads I travelled and that frequently in large bodies . . .

In a very much more detailed account of the Friendly Islands they visited, Cook confirms some of the details of his astronomer's findings: the nose flutes, which were more elaborate than those of Tahiti; the drums to accompany them, which were made from hollowed logs; and, above all in Cook's estimate, their canoes, which were far superior to the Tahitian kind, especially their catamarans, which were beautifully made: they were sewn so that caulking could be dispensed with, had platforms with little cabins on top, and were double-ended, too, and therefore reversible.

It was time to be away, back to Queen Charlotte Sound, or they might miss the season in their second Antarctic sweep. In two weeks North Island was in sight, the silhouette of mountains now familiar. It was almost like coming home, including the weather, which around Cook Strait was as foul as it could be. For a time they were under bare poles, the seas as mountainous as the gale was furious.

The conditions tested them all to the utmost, and for the second time they lost the *Adventure*. Cook hoped to find her in Ship Cove when they at last struggled into the Sound, but there was no sign of Furneaux's sloop, and after the last few days of wild weather, they all feared for her safety.

Two weeks after their arrival Clerke expressed all their anxieties when he wrote: 'We're all much surprised at this long absence of our fellow travellers.' There were fears that the *Adventure* had succumbed to the fury of the gales off Cape Palliser, or worse still had found shelter only to succumb to the savagery of the Maoris. These fears were redoubled after Dick Pickersgill's experience a week later, on 24 November:

The 3rd Lieutenant went onshore in a little cove [Clerke recounted] about a mile distant from the ship, where there was a party of the natives, of whom, among other curiosities, Mr Pickersgill bought a man's head, apparently very lately severed from the body, with which they had just been regaling themselves. The heart and entrails they saw then lying quite fresh upon the ground. Soon after the head was brought on board some Indians of another party came, as they frequently did, to the vessel upon a friendly visit. They eyed the head very wistfully and as I was standing by it begged me to give it to them. I questioned what they wanted of it. They answered to eat. I then asked one of them if he would eat a piece there directly, to which he very readily and cheerfully assented. I then cut a piece off, carried it to the fire by his desire, gave it a little broil upon the gridiron and delivered it to him. He caught it in rapture, devoured it most ravenously, and licked his fingers half a score times over after it.

Cook had been absent from his ship during this surprising occurrence. He came on board in time to observe Clerke cut and dress another 'steak' for 'my friend', which the Maori consumed on the quarterdeck watched by Cook and almost the entire ship's company.

Cook took a pragmatic view of Maori cannibalism:

This custom of eating their enemies slain in battle (for I firmly believe they eat the flesh of no others) has undoubtedly been handed down to them from the earliest times, and we know that it is not an easy matter to break a nation of its ancient customs let them be ever so inhuman and savage, especially if that nation is void of all religious principles, as I believe the New Zealanders in general are ...

It is impossible to dispute Cook's argument, nor his belief that when they became more united, they would have fewer enemies 'and become more civilized'. What seems odd about the episode is that the moral disciplinarian was prepared to condone this brutish spectacle on the quarter-deck of his ship.

TOBIAS FURNEAUX WAS as concerned for the safety of the *Resolution* as Cook was for the *Adventure*. October can be a wicked month in New Zealand waters, as Cook had earlier discovered, and the gales of late October and early November were particularly vicious. It was during the night of 29–30 October that the sloops became separated. Furneaux was about three miles astern of the *Resolution* when he last saw her, and in the morning there was nothing to be seen except grey spume-lashed rollers. Unlike Cook, Furneaux was unable to beat up to Queen Charlotte Sound. Instead, he lay off the south-east coast of North Island.

On the 4th November [he wrote] we again got in shore near Cape Palliser and was visited by a number of the natives in their canoes with a great quantity of crayfish, which we bought off them for nails and Otaheite cloth. The next day it blew hard from WNW, which again blew us off the coast and obliged us to bring to for two days, during which time it blew one continual gale of wind with very heavy squalls of sleet. By this time our decks were very leaky, the people's beds and bedding wet ... and we began to despair of ever getting into Charlotte's Sound or joining the *Resolution*.

At length they succeeded in getting into Tolago Bay and anchored thankfully. Here they found water, for which they had a great need, and fresh fish from Maoris who were disposed to be friendly. But it was not until the early days of December that Furneaux was able to fight his way to Queen Charlotte Sound. There was no sign of the *Resolution*. Had the sloop come and gone, or had she perished in the mountainous seas of the past weeks? But when Furneaux anchored in Ship Cove and went ashore, he learned with relief that his consort had come, remained three weeks and left on her Antarctic exploration.

On going ashore we saw the place where [Cook] had erected tents, and on an old stump of a tree [Furneaux recounted] found the following words cut out LOOK UNDERNEATH where we dug and soon found a bottle corked and waxed down with a letter in it from Captain Cook.

Cook, it seemed, had left a week earlier, 'intending spending a few days in the entrance to the Strait to look for us'.

As Captain Cook had not the least hope of meeting with Captain Furneaux [ran the second half of this letter] he will not take upon him to name any place for a rendezvous. He however thinks of returning to Easter Island about the latter end of next March. It is probable that he may go to Otaheite or one of the Society Islands, but this will depend much on circumstances that nothing of any degree of certainty can be determined upon.

JAMES COOK

So Furneaux was now left with a free hand: no rendezvous and no instructions. The freedom offered to this commander was heady. For, above all, he and his officers and men were anxious to go home, and soon. 'We immediately set about getting the ship ready for sea as fast as possible,' he wrote with some relish, adding that the Maoris were very helpful. 'The inhabitants ... supplied us with fish and other things of their own manufacture, which we bought of them for nails and appeared very friendly.'

As early as 17 December Furneaux wrote of 'having refitted the ship, completed our water and wood and got everything ready for sea, we sent our large cutter with Mr Rowe, midshipman, and the boat's crew to gather wild greens for the ship's company, with orders to return that evening as I intended to sail the next morning'. It appeared that the *Adventure*'s captain had at last learned the lesson on the importance of antiscorbutics. As Furneaux intended to sail via the Horn, halfway round the world to Cape Town, possibly without even anchoring in the Bay of Good Success, this was as well if he hoped to escape scurvy on the scale he had previously suffered.

Furneaux and his officers were worried when the cutter failed to return that evening, and 'under great uneasiness' when the party did not turn up the following morning. Jem Burney was at once ordered to take the launch, together with a strong party of marines, to search up the Sound. 'I examined every cove, on the larboard hand, as we went along,' Burney wrote later. By dinner-time they had reached and were examining a deep bay in which there was a large number of Maoris, some of them 'appearing to be frightened'. Burney tried to reassure them by offering gifts, then one of them advanced carrying a bundle of spears. But 'when I looked very earnestly at him, he put them on the ground and walked away with seeming unconcern'.

By this time Burney was becoming very concerned and was beginning to suspect the worst. At the next settlement:

We went ashore and searched a canoe, where we found one of the rullock ports of the cutter, and some shoes, one of which was known to belong to Mr Woodhouse one of our midshipmen. One of the people at the same time brought me a piece of meat, which he took to be some of the salt meat belonging to the cutter's crew. On examining this and smelling it I found it was fresh. Mr Fannin [the master] who was with me, supposed it was dog's flesh, and I was of the same opinion; for I still doubted their being cannibals. But we were soon convinced by most horrid and undeniable proof.

A great many baskets [about twenty] lying on the beach tied up, we cut them open. Some were full of roasted flesh and some of fern root, which serves them for bread. On farther search, we found more shoes, and a hand, which we immediately knew to have belonged to Thomas Hill, one of our fore-castle men, it being marked T. H. with an Otaheite tattow-instrument. I went with some of the people a little way up the woods, but saw nothing else. Coming down again, there was a round spot covered with fresh earth, about four feet diameter, where something had been buried. Having no spade we began to dig with a cutlass; and in the meantime I launched the canoe with intent to destroy her; but seeing a great smoke ascending over the nearest hill, I got all the people into the boat and made what haste I could to be with them before sunset.

On opening the next bay, which was Grass Cove, we saw four canoes, one single and three double ones, and a great many people on the beach, who, on our approach, retreated to a small hill within a ship's length of the water side, where they stood talking to us. A large fire was on the top of the high land, beyond the woods, from whence all the way down the hill, the place was thronged like a fair. As we came in, I ordered a musquetoon to be fired at one of the canoes, suspecting they might be full of men lying down in the bottom; for they were all afloat, but nobody was seen in them. The savages on the little hill still kept hallooing and making signs for us to land. However, as soon as we got close in, we all fired. The first volley did not seem to affect them much; but on the second they began to scramble away as fast as they could, some of them howling. We continued firing as long as we could see the glimpse of any of them through the bushes. Amongst the Indians were two very stout men, who never offered to move till they found themselves forsaken by their companions; and then they marched away with great composure and deliberation; their pride not suffering them to run. One of them, however, got a fall, and either lay there or crawled off on all fours. The other got clear, without any apparent hurt. I then landed with the marines, and Mr Fannin stayed to guard the boat.

On the beach were two bundles of celery, which had been gathered for loading the cutter. A broken oar was stuck upright in the ground, to which the natives had tied their canoes; a proof that the attack had been made here. I then searched all along at the back of the beach to see if the cutter was there. We found no boat, but instead of her such a shocking scene of carnage and barbarity as can never be mentioned or thought of but with horror; for the heads, hearts and lungs of several of our people were seen lying on the beach, and, at a little distance, the dogs gnawing their intrails.

In a fever of disgust and fury, Burney's men set about destroying the canoes, while above them from the forest there came the sound of many voices raised in argument. Burney assumed that it was about delivering an attack before all the canoes were destroyed. Darkness was falling, it began to rain, and in the last volley of musket fire, four of the pieces misfired. Burney recognised that by remaining there, 'we could expect to reap no other advantage than the poor satisfaction of killing some more of the savages'. So they hauled off and headed back to the ship.

Behind them, an immense fire had been lit high up in the hills, and from the same direction came the cries of many thousands of voices. Burney recalled that he had sailed up here with his captain several times and had seen no signs of inhabited settlements and no Maoris. Where had they all come from? And why had they come? Although he was to return here several years later, he would never know the answer, nor why poor Midshipman Rowe and his men had been set upon with such savagery.

The shock to Furneaux, a friend and relative of the admirable Rowe, and to the other officers and men was profound. Many sought immediate vengeance, with a massive bombardment of the settlement and the destruction of every canoe in the Sound. Furneaux recognised that nothing would be gained by such action. They had best be gone, as soon as possible, while mourning the loss of eleven good men, which would also make the manning of the *Adventure* more difficult on their long passage home.

18

From Icebergs to Tropical Heat

CAPTAIN COOK EMBARKED ON his new Antarctic search for the Great Southern Continent at 4 a.m. on 25 November 1773. The *Resolution* was well found and well provisioned for the long and arduous voyage that lay ahead. During their time at Ship Cove the men had been amply supplied with fish and fresh vegetables, including some of the fruit and vegetables from the garden they had set up the last time they had been there. In addition, Cook ensured that plenty of celery and scurvy grass were included in their diet. There was not a sick man on board, and even Förster *père* could find little to grumble about.

For a day or two Cook, more as a formality than with any hope of success, searched coves on both sides of the Strait for the *Adventure*, firing half-hour guns.

On our quitting the coast [he wrote] and consequently all hopes of being joined by our consort, I had the satisfaction to find that not a man was dejected or thought the dangers we had yet to go through were in the least increased by being alone, but as cheerfully proceeded to the south or wherever I thought proper to lead them as if she or even more ships had been in our company.

Although it was Cook who had originally pressed for a second ship, there can be no doubt that Furneaux and the *Adventure* had so far been more of a liability than a support, and he was glad to be relieved of his second-in-command.

Even though it was mid-summer in New Zealand, the temperature dropped with remarkable speed as the *Resolution* headed south from South Island, from 62° on 27 November to 46° on 2 December, and to 32° on 12 December. This was partly caused by the favourable winds, which led to the ship logging over 150 miles on several days. They were soon among showers of hail and sleet. On 12 December Clerke reported: 'Saw an island of ice – the first this southern expedition.'

This preoccupation with the weather was broken by a piquant discovery by Cook, who wrote in his journal simply, 'At half-past 8 p.m. Antipodes to London.' Wales enlarged on this and wrote:

Passed directly opposite to London [longitude 180°] & drank to our friends on that side of the globe. The good people of that City may *now* rest perfectly satisfied that they have no antipodes besides penguins and petrels, unless seals can be counted as such.

As Christmas drew near, Clerke wrote of 21 December:

Very cold. The sleet as it falls freezes to the rigging which, in the first place, makes it exceedingly disagreeable handling and, in the next, makes it so thick with ice that 'tis with difficulty we render the ropes through the blocks.

According to Clerke, on Christmas Day they were 'fairly beset by these devilish ice isles'. But nothing, it seemed, could deter the people from traditional drunkenness on this day. Johann Förster, who had an abiding terror of icebergs, noted censoriously:

The sailors feasted on a double portion of pudding, regaling themselves with the brandy of their allowance, which they had saved for this occasion some months beforehand, being solicitous to get very drunk, though they are commonly solicitous about nothing else.

The clear weather lasted some forty-eight hours, then the wind got up, the temperature dropped even lower, and visibility became scarcely the length of the ship due to snowstorms or fog, or both. 'Icicles frequently hung to the noses of the men more than an inch long,' wrote gunner Jack Marra, 'the men cased in frozen snow, as if clad in armour, where the running rigging has been so enlarged by frozen sleet as hardly to be grasped by the largest hand . . .'

Cook might be constipated and low in spirit, the *Resolution* might be in daily danger of being smashed against a 200-foot-high iceberg as she nudged just north and just south of the Antarctic Circle, but the responsibilities of command had to be attended to, day and night. On the second day of the new year (1774), Cook learned of an affray on the lower deck. The guilty party was the troublesome midshipman, Charles Loggie. He came from a respectable naval family, but, after an accident as a boy, had had to be trepanned. 'Consequently', according to John Elliot, 'when he got liquor he was a mad man', and the drinking had recently become serious. In a drunken riot Loggie had drawn a knife and cut two other midshipmen. Cook had him flogged, a rare action to take against a 'young gentleman'.

A few days later, on 7 January and the following day, with the weather permitting, Cook gave his full attention to their longitude. Wales, Gilbert, Clerke and Cook himself 'observed several distances of the sun and moon'. The figures varied from 133° to Cook's own 133° 37'. Kendall's watch recorded 133° 34' W. 'Our error can never be great', wrote Cook in satisfaction, 'so long as we have as good a guide as Mr Kendall's watch.'

After several days on a NE heading, which persuaded the men that the worst might be over and that they would soon be enjoying lower latitudes and warmer weather, Cook suddenly put the *Resolution* on a southerly heading again on 11 January. 'All our hopes were blasted in a minute,' Elliot noted. 'Captain Cook ordered the ship to steer due south, to our utter astonishment, and had the effect for the moment, of causing a buzz in the ship.'

Elliot thought that Cook's closeness about his intentions made him 'the fittest man in the world for such a voyage'. Johann Förster perversely took the opposite view. 'Nothing could be more dejecting than the entire ignorance of our future destination.'

The *Resolution* crossed the Antarctic Circle for the third time on 26 January. Almost immediately, as if this line were a signal, Cook 'saw an appearance of land to the east and south-east'. Wales, not given to fantasising, wrote of 'a remarkably strong appearance of land'. Then, later, Clerke the realist noted: 'The haze covered our supposed land. We're confoundedly afraid it's nothing more than mere supposition.' By the following morning, 'We were convinced to our sorrow that our land was nothing more than a deception of the sight.'

The last weekend of January 1774 was an occasion that none on board the *Resolution* would ever forget. During these two days they penetrated farther south than any man before, or since for that matter, at sea and in this part of the Antarctic. On the Saturday they reached 71° 10' S.* It was 'clear pleasant weather', according to Cook. 'Air not cold.' A little after 4 a.m. (there was no night):

We perceived the clouds over the horizon to the south to be of an unusual snow white brightness which we knew announced our approach to field ice. Soon after it was seen from the topmast head and at 8 a.m. we were close to the edge of it. It extended east and west far beyond the reach of our sight. [Cook continued this memorable passage:] In the situation we were in just

---

* James Weddell (1787–1834) penetrated to 74° 15' s in the sea named after him during his expedition of 1822–4. James Clark Ross (1800–62), with the specially strengthened *Erebus* and *Terror*, forced his way through the pack ice to 78° 9' on his 1839–43 expedition, in the sea named after him. Both these penetrations were far to the east and west of Cook's longitude.

the southern half of our horizon was illuminated by the rays of light which were reflected from the ice to a considerable height. Ninety-seven ice hills were distinctly seen within the field, besides those on the outside, and many of them were very large and looked like a ridge of mountains rising one above the other till they were lost in the clouds . . . I will not say it was impossible anywhere to get farther to the south, but the attempting it would have been a dangerous and rash exercise, and what I believe no man in my situation would have thought of.

It was indeed my opinion as well as the opinion of most on board, that this ice extended quite to the Pole or perhaps joins to some land to which it had been fixed from the creation . . . As we drew near this ice some penguins were heard but none seen and but few other birds or any other thing that could induce us to think any land was near . . .

I who had ambitions not only to go farther* than anyone had done before, but as far as it was possible for man to go, was not sorry at meeting with this interruption as it in some measure relieved us, at least shortened the dangers and hardships inseparable with the navigation of the southern polar regions . . .

Since Cook could not penetrate 'one inch farther to the south', he tacked and stood back to the north. He considered himself 'now well satisfied no Continent was to be found in this ocean but what must lie so far to the south as to be wholly inaccessible for ice'. The season was already too far advanced to double the Horn and make a final search in the South Atlantic. He intended, therefore, to look for Easter Island, 'the situation of which is so variously laid down that I have little hopes of finding it'.

En route, Cook

was now taken ill of the bilious colic, and so violent as to confine me to my bed, so that the management of the ship was left to Mr Cooper, my first officer, who conducted her very much to my satisfaction.

Marra wrote: 'This day the Captain was taken ill, to the grief of all the ship's company.' He could have added the word 'anxiety' to this entry. Cook was so positively and incontrovertibly the men's leader, and captain, who had led them through so many dangers, and for so long, that there was not an officer, petty officer or man of the *Resolution* who did not regard him as a father-figure.

Cook soon recovered and later found Easter Island, the most

---

* 'Vancouver used to say that he [Cook] had been nearer the South Pole than any other man, for when the immortal Cook in latitude 72° was stopped in his progress by impenetrable mountains of ice, he went to the very end of the bowsprit and, waving his hat, exclaimed "*Ne Plus Ultra*".' (*The Naval Chronicle*, vol.1, 1799, p.125.)

isolated island in the world, without difficulty. The first and most singular impression Easter Island offers is the 'stupendous stone statues erected in different places along the coast'. Jacob Roggeveen, the island's discoverer in 1722, had noted these – it was impossible to be blind to them – but had been as unsure as Cook was now of their purpose, though he supposed them to be burial places 'for certain tribes or families'. Another theory was, and is, that they were carved from the solid rock, dragged to randomly selected sites along the coast, and erected in groups, in order to instil fear in would-be invaders,* the island being incapable of sustaining a large population.

The inhabitants, by contrast with the impression given by the statues, were mild and friendly, anxious to trade but possessing few surplus provisions. Water was scarce, too, so Cook determined to be on his way after a few days.

Odiddy justified himself here as translator, proving beyond doubt that the people were Polynesian.** Cook sailed from Easter Island and shaped course NW for the Marquesas on 17 March.

They were back at Matavai Bay, Tahiti, on 21 April, where they were warmly greeted and supplied with hogs and other provisions. Several weeks later, at Raiatea, Cook left behind a weeping (and very drunk) Odiddy, before heading not directly back to New Zealand again, but to Tonga in the Friendly Islands.

By the last days of June the *Resolution* was deep in the Tongan archipelago, among islands which Tasman had charted, but only superficially; there was a year's work for Cook here if he had had the time. He was still north, by about one degree, of his old course through this widely scattered group. On 27 June he anchored off the island Tasman had named Rotterdam, and the natives called Annamocka, or Nomuka.

Charles Clerke wrote particularly warmly about these islands. He counted as many as seventeen from the masthead, well-made canoes paddling peacefully from one to the other as if their inhabitants were visiting relations or exchanging gifts. 'They appear in a happy state of mutual confidence and peace with each other,' he commented. But he had to admit that these paragons of virtue 'were very industrious in the pilfering scheme', and over only two days they made off with – but were prevailed upon to return – several muskets amongst other booty.

* This writer, arriving at Easter Island by sea and at early dawn, can attest to the discouragement to landing the fierce visages and giant size of these statues engender.
** Easter Island is the eastern corner of the Polynesian Pacific triangle, Hawaii to the north and New Zealand in the west. How these vast distances were navigated by canoe is another, and fascinating, story.

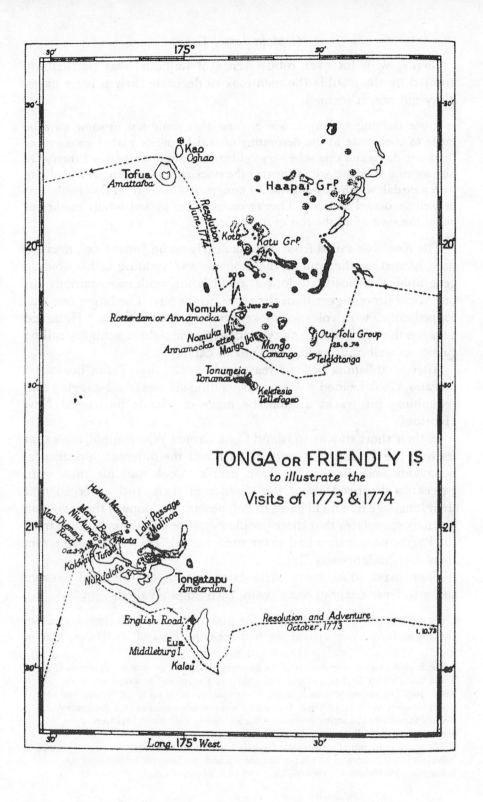

Kao
Oghao

Tofua
Amattafoa

Resolution
June 1774

Haapai Gr?

20'   20'

Kotu
Kotu Gr?

June 27-29

Nomuka
Rotterdam or Annamocka

Otu Tolu Group
25.6.74

Nomuka Iki
Annamocka etree   Mango Iki

Mango
Camango
Telekitonga

Tonumeia
Tonamai

30'   30'

Kelefesia
Tellefageo

TONGA or **FRIENDLY IS**
to illustrate the
Visits of 1773 & 1774

Hakau Mamoo

Maria Bay
Niu Aunofo
Atata

Lahi Passage
Malinoa

Van Diemen's
Road
oas?

Kolovai Tufaki

Nukualofa

21°   21°

Tongatapu
Amsterdam I.

Resolution and Adventure
October, 1773
1. 10.73

English Road

Eua
Middleburg I.
Kalau

30'   30'

Clerke, with his ever robust sense of humour, was particularly amused by the trouble the men took to decorate their private parts. They did not, it seemed,

care one farthing for any article of dress that could not in some form be made to contribute to the decorating of that favourite part. I gave one of them one day a stocking – he very deliberately put it on there – I then gave him a string of beads, with it he tied the stocking up – I then presented him with a medal, which he immediately hung to it – in short let that noble part be well decorated and fine. They're perfectly happy and totally indifferent about the state of all the rest of the body.

The *Resolution* sailed from Nomuka early on 29 June. Cook decided now, almost on the spur of the moment and yielding to his abiding geographical curiosity, to look at two islands, both mountainous but one many times bigger than the other, to the NW. The larger one was topped either with volcano smoke or cloud. It was Tofua.* He sailed between them, his mariner's eye caught by the sight of a mighty sailing canoe, as well built as all the Tongan canoes.

After establishing beyond reasonable doubt that Tofua boasted a volcano, Cook headed NW again, spending six weeks zig-zagging and redoubling his tracks among the maze of islands he named New Hebrides.

In their short stay at an island Cook named Whitsuntide, after that festival, the *Resolution*'s company all noted the different appearance, behaviour and manner of these people. Cook and his men were agreeably surprised about the absence of theft, and observed that their language had no likeness to Polynesian. But none of the surviving journals speculates that these people might be of a different race from the Pacific people they had so far encountered. They had, in fact, met their first Melanesians.**

There were to be more Melanesian islands on this final passage south to New Zealand once again. Sparrman recalled:

On 5th August . . . we discovered the island of Tana, with its volcano. On the night before our arrival we had seen the glow of its flames, and in

---

* The *Resolution* was in the position of the *Bounty* on the day of the mutiny. It was to Tofua that Fletcher Christian intended to paddle on a rough raft as a deserter on 28 April 1789. The natives of these Friendly Islands had not lived up to their name, and he would certainly not have survived. Instead, he was prevailed upon to lead the mutiny. Tofua's volcano was as active as ever, the flames making a dramatic backdrop to the violent events that followed.

** The group of islands of west-central Oceania bounded by Micronesia in the north and Polynesia in the south and east. They include Fiji and the Bismarck archipelago, the Solomons, New Hebrides, New Caledonia and parts of New Guinea.

the morning, as we drew nearer, we could hear a thunderous roar from the bowels of the earth. This roar was sometimes accompanied by heavy explosions, besides which clouds of flames were thrown high into the air, while columns of fiery smoke reared up towards the sky.

The temperament of the people of Tana seemed to reflect this turbulence. While Clerke mildly reported that the natives 'did not insult us 'tis true, but they did by no means seem reconciled to the liberty we took in landing upon their coast', Cook thought that 'everything conspired to make us believe they intended to attack us as soon as we were on shore'.

In Cook's determination to wood and water here, and if possible to trade for provisions, there was a good deal of threatening behaviour on both sides, including musket fire and on several occasions the use of cannon grapeshot over the heads of the people. On the last of fourteen days here one of the marines, provoked beyond his endurance, fired his musket, loaded with ball shot, at a threatening native, killing him instantly. Cook witnessed this incident and became white with fury. The marine was flung into irons and ordered to be flogged. Cook's officers pleaded for the man and the punishment was remitted, though not gladly.

On one afternoon (10 September) as they were anchored off the east side of New Caledonia, Clerke made an unusual observation:

I saw a man on shore as white as Europeans in general are, with light coloured hair, nothing inclining to the woolly order . . . It had a most singular and striking appearance to see a white fellow naked running about among these dark coloured gentry. It really appeared to me highly unnatural and disgusting.

Just a month later, far south of New Caledonia and Melanesia, they chanced upon an isolated little island. In spite of the heavy surf, Cook made a landing, found no inhabitants but, most prominently, giant spruce pines. The island had a New Zealand feel, and New Zealand birds. He named it Norfolk, 'in honour of that noble family', and took possession for King George in the traditional manner.

To approach New Zealand in stormy spring weather had become almost traditional for Cook, and he awaited the first storm's onset imperturbably:

Midnight heavy squalls with rain. Thunder and lightning . . . split the jib to pieces . . . Daybreak [17 October] saw Mount Egmont covered with everlasting snow . . . Steered SSE for Queen Charlotte Sound.

By the following morning the *Resolution* was at anchor in Ship

Cove. Cook at once went ashore and searched for his bottle. It had gone; there were other signs that the *Adventure* had been there, but no message. This was typical of the unimaginative Furneaux. Cook guessed that his number two had gone straight home.

19

'The Most Horrible Coast in the World'*

THERE WAS AN EDGINESS ABOUT THE MAORIS of Queen Charlotte Sound which Cook and Clerke found puzzling. There was no one about for the first few days; no sign of fires, no canoes. It was as if there had been a mighty exodus, and there was speculation that a plague or war had led survivors to flee the area.

It was not until the morning of 24 October that two canoes were spotted coming down the Sound. But the moment the Maoris saw the *Resolution* and her men on shore, they turned about and rapidly disappeared. This was very unusual behaviour. Cook at once ordered out a boat and, with the Försters, progressed along the shore, from time to time shooting birds. The musket shots were answered by the calls of many voices from the forest, yet only two men were briefly seen, both armed.

'But the moment we landed,' Cook recounted, 'they knew us again, joy took place of fear, they hurried out of the woods, embraced us over and over and skipped about like madmen, but I observed that they would not suffer some women who made their appearance to come near us.'

As the days passed and relations with the local Maoris returned to the same friendly basis as before, and great quantities of fish were traded for the usual nails, medals and mirrors, Cook's officers and gentlemen picked up strange and alarming stories, which were denied later, or contradicted or repeated. The one that Cook heard over and over again but in different forms was that a ship 'had been lately lost in the Straits, that some of the people had got on shore, and that

---

* This refers to Bristol Isiand, South Sandwich Islands, on the 58° parallel, south-east of Cape Horn.

the natives stole their clothes &c for which several were shot: but afterwards when they could fire no longer the natives got the better and killed them with their patapatoos and ate them'. At the same time it was repeatedly emphasised that this was at another place and with other people; it was not them, not the local Maoris.

This and similar stories renewed Cook's worries about Furneaux and the *Adventure*, and perhaps had accounted for the nervous, even guilty, behaviour of the Charlotte Sound Maoris when they first arrived. His anxieties were further reinforced when a party of Maoris from far up the Sound appeared, spreading undefined rumours of recent killings. They were also keen to trade, bringing greenstone and girls for a price. Cook gave them no sort of a welcome, but some of his men did, for, as he had to concede, these were 'two articles which seldom came to a bad market'.

Within a few days of their arrival the shoreline of Ship Cove assumed the familiar aspect of industry, with the forge operating round the clock and the observatory as and when conditions allowed Wales to make his observations. The sailmakers, carpenters and caulkers in particular scarcely had time to trade for greenstone or the comely Maori girls. There was a tremendous amount to do, and Cook was in a hurry. The *Resolution* was in a worse state than he had anticipated. Their supplies of pitch and tar, and varnish of pine, had long since been exhausted, and makeshift substitutes, gunners' chalk and fat from the galley, well mixed, were used for pitch. Most of the sails were in poor order and Cook resorted to using some of the canvas from the ship's boats.

All this industry, and continuing worry about Furneaux, did not stunt Cook's urge to explore and chart locally. Although this was his third time here, he had never taken a boat high up the Sound. Could there be another entrance? What was there at the head? On the morning of 5 November, therefore, he took the pinnace and, accompanied by the Försters, set out in fine weather. Five leagues west they intercepted a canoe and 'made the necessary enquiries'. Cook had a considerable Polynesian vocabulary by now and was adept at sign language. He was told that soon the Sound would end, but there was indeed another passage to the sea.

They found the inlet without difficulty and followed it on the south-east side of the Sound. There was a large settlement of Maoris, who were extremely friendly and anxious for them to come ashore. Now on a ENE heading, Cook followed the passage* until they could clearly see Cook Strait ahead of them, the inlet now being a mile wide.

* This is today used by the ferry service from Wellington to Picton.

It was 4 p.m. and Cook wanted to be back with his ship before dark, so they did not linger, signalling to the friendly people as they passed on a strong flood tide, before turning on to a heading for the *Resolution*.

It sometimes happened that there was talk of desertions shortly before sailing, and this occurred once again here in Ship Cove. One of the would-be deserters was John Keplin (not listed in the muster roll, so when did he join the *Resolution*?), who boasted so loudly about his intentions that word soon reached Cook and a dozen lashes were meted out. The other was John Marra, drunk again and hell-bent on some girl. Cook was reported to have declared that he would let him go, such a nuisance had he become, if he did not know that he would very promptly have been dealt with and eaten up. Instead, he received a dozen lashes, too.

Before they set sail Wales, from his observatory ashore and with Kendall's watch at hand, redesignated their longitude. Cook had previously been 40' too far east, with the result that his charts would now have to be redrawn. For a man who was conscientious and proud of his surveying skills, he experienced, quite unnecessarily, much chagrin when he was given this news by his astronomer friend.

Shortly before leaving Queen Charlotte Sound for the fourth time, Cook summarised his views on the Maoris of this part of South Island:

I have before made some remarks on the evils attending these people for want of a union among themselves, and the more I am acquainted with them the more I find it to be so. Notwithstanding they are *Cannibals*, they are naturally of a good disposition and have not a little share of humanity.

Cook's plan was to sail down to 50°–60° S, then head east to cross the Pacific on a heading between these latitudes, double the Horn, explore again the southern South Atlantic, before making for the Cape of Good Hope and then home. Keeping these plans to himself as usual – and, as usual, to the Försters' fury – Cook weighed early on 10 November. His ship was as repaired and secured as far as local resources allowed; his men were also in good heart and good health, thanks to New Zealand's fresh fruit and vegetables, fresh fish, fowl and meat.

The thermometer fell in reverse ratio to the latitude, an experience to the men of the *Resolution* as familiar as the donning of fearnoughts and hood-like Magdalen caps and the renewed popularity of the area about the ship's stove. At the 55th parallel the ship's bow swung east on 23 November and there was relief among the people. They had had enough of freezing fogs and icebergs. This was a latitude they could tolerate. Their sloop now bowled along at a speed which would have pleased even Joseph Banks, at that time hobnobbing with King George and discussing Kew Gardens with him. In four days in late November they logged for each twenty-four hours between 140 and 183 miles. Of the last of these figures, on Sunday, 27 November, Clerke commented: 'We've had a fine steady gale and following sea these 24 hours, and run the greatest distance we've ever reached in this ship.'

In little over five weeks the *Resolution* spanned the South Pacific from New Zealand to Chile, and on this same Sunday Cook felt able to write:

I now gave up all hope of finding any more land in this ocean and came to a resolution to steer directly for the west entrance of the Straits of Magellan, with a view of coasting the out, or south, side of Tierra del Fuego, round Cape Horn to Strait le Maire . . .

There is a hint of weariness in what follows: 'I have now done with the SOUTHERN PACIFIC OCEAN, and flatter myself that no one will think that I have left it unexplored, or that more could have been done in one voyage towards obtaining that end than has been done in this.'

Cook must have read the account by Francis Fletcher, Francis Drake's chaplain, of the *Golden Hind*'s suffering along this coast in 1578, when that earlier navigator had been driven far south and had briefly sighted Cape Horn:

The winds were such as if the bowels of the earth had set all at liberty, or as if all the clouds under heaven had been called together to lay their force upon that one place. The seas . . . were rolled up from the depths, even from the base of the rocks, as if they had been a scroll of parchment . . . The impossibility of anchoring or spreading any sail, the most mad seas, the lee shores, the dangerous rocks, the contrary and most intolerable winds . . . all offered us such small likelihood of escaping destruction, that if the special providence of God himself had not supported us, we could never have endured this woeful state . . .

Even the official Chilean Government chart, corrected to 1964, warns, 'Owing to the incomplete nature of the surveys, this chart should be used with caution.' But 'Cook luck' governed the weather and he endured none of the sufferings of Drake even if, as he wrote, 'It is the most desolate and barren country I ever saw.' Reasonably enough, he called the first cape he passed Desolation. From a mariner's view this was indeed a terrible lee shore of vertical rocks and jagged reefs rising in anarchic formations to saw-tooth summits, some naked, others snow-washed, broken only here and there by patches of forest, all of evergreen Antarctic beech.

At noon on 20 December, with the festival of Christmas and

wooding and watering in mind, Cook decided to seek shelter and rest for his men for a few days. Ahead was a giant rock formation on the tip of an island (Waterman today) which reminded Cook of the twin towers of York Minster, and so he named them, then doubled into a narrow passage. Running along it under a fair breeze, the wind suddenly dropped, leaving the ship helpless as, to Cook's discomfort, there was no bottom for anchoring, even at 170 fathoms.

Two boats were hoisted out to tow. Cook described this awkward moment:

They would have availed but little if a breeze of wind had not, about 8 o'clock, sprung up at sw, which put it in my power either to stand out to sea, or up the inlet. Prudence seemed to point out the former, but the desire of finding a good port and learning something of the country got the better of every other consideration and I resolved to stand in. But as night was approaching our safety depended on getting to an anchor.

This brief journal quote confirms so much we have learned of the man: his curiosity, his audacity, his concern for his men's wellbeing. As so often before, he recognises the risks and finds that they are acceptable. And once again good fortune favours him: a small cove appears on his larboard bow, like a hospitable guiding light in the dusk. The sounding boat finds a bottom of sand and broken shells at thirty fathoms. He anchors.

In calm and pleasant weather the following morning, Cook took two boats and searched for a better anchorage. He soon found another cove 'with a small stony beach, a small valley covered with wood and a small streamlet of fresh water so that here was everything we could expect to find in such a place, or rather more for we shot three geese'.

Charlie Clerke was charged with bringing the *Resolution* round to this new anchorage, and did so with his usual diligence and efficiency. Like everyone else, Clerke was enchanted with the place and the mild weather, more especially because of the reputation and fearful coastline which can so deceive the visitor. Clerke began his summary of Cook Cove and Christmas Harbour (names retained today): 'These have been eight such days as I never had the least idea of spending in Tierra del Fuego – the weather fine, ship safe, and abundance of good provision . . .'

On Christmas Eve two shooting parties went out and shot five or six dozen geese, which were prepared for dinner the next day. Only one wretched event took the edge off the pleasure of the season. The marine private, Bill Wedgeborough, disappeared overboard after visiting the heads around midnight and was never seen again. He was a notorious drunk and was very much 'in liquor'.

From the first visits ashore there had been signs of local inhabitants, and due precautions had been taken to secure the observatory and tents ashore. Then, as if they were guests at a party, four canoe-loads of Fuegians turned up on Christmas evening. 'They behaved very civilly', Clerke reported, 'and were received with the utmost cordiality so that a friendly correspondence was soon established between us.' He added in his summary:

The appearance of the inhabitants bespeaks your pity. They are a diminutive race, walk exceeding ill, being almost crippled from the perpetual attitude of sitting upon their heels, and though it was now mid-summer they were continually shaking and shivering as though half killed with the cold.

Considering that they wore nothing but a sealskin over their shoulders, this was hardly surprising, although they did daub themselves with seal oil as some sort of additional, and malodorous, protection.

Cook weighed and stood out to sea at dawn on 28 December. He would have preferred to remain longer and explore this bay* more thoroughly. It was of a similar size and configuration to Dusky Bay, and only 10° higher in latitude at 55°s, but even harsher in its aspect. However, he had other work to do: the exploration to high latitudes in the South Atlantic again, which could only be done advantageously in the summer months.

All that day, the *Resolution* coasted on a SE heading off this wildly fractured coastline, with the mountains inland – again like New Zealand – snow-capped and seemingly inaccessible to man. They passed inside the Islas Ildefonso, little more than massive rocks projecting menacingly from the sea like Diego Ramírez, and first seen by Admiral Jacob Hermite's Dutch fleet in 1624. By sunset, in spite of mist which had prevailed all day, they could just make out the dagger-like tip of False Cape Horn, quite unlike the real thing.

This was no coastline to take liberties with, even if the weather was almost unnaturally calm. 'At 10 o'clock shortened sail and spent the night making short boards [tack frequently] under the topsails.' It was light enough at 3 a.m. to make sail again, crossing the wide entrance of the Nassau Passage to the Hermite Group, of which Horn Island marks the southernmost tip.

Cook and his master, Joseph Gilbert, assisted as usual by Isaac Smith, together drew up a chart of the 'South Coast of Tierra del

---

* Had he done so, Cook must certainly have discovered the narrow inlet now named Brazo del Suroests, which would have led him into the Beagle Channel and a more peaceful route to the Straits of le Maire and the Atlantic, bypassing Cape Horn.

Fuego and Staten Land', but it is a disappointing piece of work and added little or nothing to earlier charts, not even recognising that the famous cape was the southern tip of an island of its own. This is partly accounted for by Cook's reluctance to linger, and partly by the misty conditions.

It had, however, been an interesting experience to approach the Horn from the opposite direction to the 1769 approach: a mirror image of what they had seen before. Nor could he resist a note of triumph in his entry: 'At half past 7 we passed the famous Cape and entered the *Southern Atlantick Ocean.*' Pausing neither to confirm nor to add to his earlier surveys, Cook hove to only to hoist colours and fire two guns in case the *Adventure* was in the Bay of Good Success, and to send Dick Pickersgill ashore to search for evidence of their fellow sloop having been there. Furneaux's fate was, clearly, still on Cook's mind, no doubt a daily preoccupation, another burden to add to his weight of responsibilities.

Pickersgill found nothing but friendly, if smelly, Fuegians. He stuck a note to a tree, written by Cook, giving the particulars of their visit. It was equally malodorous out in the strait owing to the great number of whales frolicking about. 'They are blowing on every point of the compass,' noted Charlie Clerke, 'and frequently taint the whole atmosphere about us with the utmost disagreeable effluvia that can be conceived . . .' There was to be one more halt before the *Resolution* headed for the Antarctic again, at a small island just off the east coast of Staten Island. Cook had seen on it an 'abundance of seals and birds. This was a temptation too great for people in our situation to withstand, to whom fresh provisions of any kind was acceptable.'

The last day of 1774 was a day of bloody slaughter. Southern sea lions and fur seals were in great abundance, screaming deafeningly as the men went about their slaughter, clubbing the smaller beasts and shooting the big males. There were as many penguins as they wanted, fish of many choice varieties, and shags and ducks. The larger and less palatable sea lions were cut up for their blubber on shore, which was brought on board in puncheons for lighting and heating fuel. Most of the other prey was brought to the *Resolution* piled high in boats and dealt with on deck. By the middle of the following day, the sloop took on the aspect of an abattoir, with gulls and skuas wheeling and screaming overhead, diving to enjoy the feast of a lifetime.

Cook weighed on the evening of 3 January 1775 and headed SE. His intention was to explore, down to the 60th parallel, that vast area of ocean west of his earlier route south from Cape Town just two years earlier on this same voyage. He regarded all this as an area rich in mythology, and there was nothing that gave him greater satisfaction than exploding myths and at the same time establishing the truth. Alexander Dalrymple's *South Atlantic Chart* of 1769 laid down a great land mass between 40° and 55° W, E and SE of Cape Horn. The coastline was shown in the detail Dalrymple always provided, and this New Southern Continent included a deep thrust towards Antarctica, named the Gulf of St Sebastian.

Dalrymple had read assiduously the accounts of earlier voyagers and geographers, like the Frenchmen Ducloz Guyot and Jean-Baptiste Bouguignon d'Anville; the London merchant, born in France, Antoine de la Roche; and more recently Bouvet and others. Then with much creative imagination and seeming authority, Dalrymple drew up his charts and published them for a gullible public. Cook had no time for Dalrymple, not because he denigrated him so persistently but because his work was bogus.

Johann Förster, it is scarcely necessary to add, thought the world of Dalrymple, and of all his works, including this particular and recent chart of his, 'which bears indisputable testimony of the laudable enthusiasm with which that gentleman has prosecuted his enquiries on this subject'.

Thanks to favourable and very strong westerlies, already by 6 January the *Resolution* was in the latitude and longitude 'assigned for the SW point of the Gulf of St Sebastian', Cook recorded, 'but as we saw neither land nor any signs of any, I was more doubtful of its existence'. He therefore hauled away to the north in search of other reported sightings of land.

A week later, after steering ENE, the ship was close to the position laid down so firmly by Dalrymple as the north-east point of his great gulf. Again there was nothing, but on the following day, after the clearance of fog, land or a great snow-capped iceberg was sighted. Over the following days, through a delaying storm with much snow and sleet, opinions veered as wildly as the weather. 'For my part,' Clerke noted, 'I believe it really is land.' But almost at once he qualified his conviction: 'All the land we've yet seen has a most dreary appearance.' On the following day, he wrote: 'Hoisted out the cutter, in which the Captain and the botanical gentry went ashore to take possession of this new country (southern continent I hope).' But later he said: 'They give a wretched account of the country.'

Cook was in dramatic vein as he wrote of this 'savage', 'horrible' land:

The wild rocks raised their lofty summits till they were lost in the clouds and the valleys laid buried in everlasting snow. Not a tree or shrub was to be seen, no not even big enough to make a toothpick. I landed in three different places and took possession of the country in his Majesty's name under a discharge of small arms . . .*

Clerke's hopes that this was the Great Southern Continent were soon dashed:

I did flatter myself from the distant soundings and the high hills about it we had got hold of the southern continent, but alas these pleasing dreams are reduced to a small isle, and that a very poor one, too. As to its appearance in general I think it exceeds in wretchedness both Tierra del Fuego and Staten Land, which places till I saw this I thought might vie with any of the works of providence . . .

The Försters were equally disappointed, because they 'found here only three plants, the one is a coarse strong bladed grass [tussock grass], which grows in tufts, wild burnet, and a plant-like moss which grows on the rocks'. There was no sign of human life, no bent little people stinking of seal oil like the Fuegians, though they were no farther south than Cape Horn; indeed, they were in no higher latitude south than Cook's Yorkshire in the northern hemisphere, and yet in high summer there was perpetual snow, ice and glaciers.

Of his proof that this was no more than an island, and not the elusive Southern Continent, Cook commented pungently: 'I must confess the disappointment I now met with did not affect me much, for to judge of the bulk by the sample it would not be worth the discovery. This land I called the *Isle of Georgia* in honour of His Majesty.' According to Johann Förster, it was at his prompting that Cook made this choice of name. Perhaps he hoped that some of the honour might rub off on his son Georg.

Clerke, by contrast, was given only a scattering of rocks south-east of Georgia, although he had earlier had coves, capes and islands named after him. The Queen was given a cape – Cape Charlotte – on the lower east coast of this godforsaken island.

After this Cook penetrated farther south, found nothing but fogs and ice, and suddenly and understandably confessed to his journal, 'I was now tired of these high southern latitudes where nothing was to be found but ice and thick fogs'; he then headed east. Even though the *Resolution* eased north, there was nothing but icebergs, including one monster, the biggest they had seen on the voyage, Cook reckoned.

* South Georgia remains a British possession today, though claimed by Argentina.

Then, on the last day of January, they chanced upon the most southerly land they had recorded. He named it, suitably, Thule.*

Working NNE, later on the same day they sighted 'a towering pillar of rock' pointing vertically 900 feet out of the sea, and beyond it another curious construction of nature, an island a mere five miles long but with peaks of 3,000 to 4,000 feet, the summits rising above the cloud concealing their waists. Cook did not care for it at all, nor for the swell which at one time threatened to cast them upon 'the most horrible coast in the world'.

During the first three days of February 1775 Cook worked the *Resolution* north through blizzards and fogs, catching glimpses of land but unable to distinguish individual islands. For this reason he named Bristol and the next island thirty miles farther north, Montagu, as capes. It was not only the low visibility that confused, but it was also possible to mistake mountains and coasts, when white from snow (and sometimes from bird-droppings), for the abundant icebergs. The last land Cook saw with any certainty he described: 'They are of no great extent, but have a considerable height and were covered with snow; a small rock was seen between them . . .' It was the afternoon of 2 February, Candlemas Day,** and so they were marked on Cook's chart.

Monday, 6 February, was an important, even epochal, day on this great voyage. Nothing much happened, they saw little and were in no danger. Cook named the islands he had charted Sandwich Land, because he had no means of telling whether 'they were a group of islands or else a point of the Continent'.

Clerke agreed with his captain. On the day Candlemas faded astern in the mist, he wrote:

These are the last bearings we had of this coast – we saw it in several places so have reason to suppose it one continuous land . . . the continued haze and fogs we've been troubled with has rendered abortive all our endeavours to come at any certainty concerning it, only its situation on the globe . . . We can by no means positively say whether it is a continued land or isles.

Cook explained his belief that what we know today as the South Sandwich Islands could have been 'a point of the continent' by adding, 'I firmly believe that there is a tract of land near the Pole, which is the source of most of the ice which is spread over this vast Southern Ocean.' His conclusion which followed effectively put an end to the

---

* *Ultima thule*, the end of the world (Virgil).
** The feast of the purification of the Virgin Mary at that time; the day when Roman Catholic churches consecrate all the candles they will need for a year.

centuries of speculation, myth-making and even map-making which had amused, vexed, puzzled and infuriated geographers since classical Greek times when the world was known to be round, and renewed in the fifteenth and sixteenth centuries with the voyages of Vasco da Gama and Ferdinand Magellan, who confirmed the earliest belief.

Cook continued his thesis:

The greatest part of this Southern Continent (supposing there is one) must lie within the Polar Circle where the sea is so pestered with ice that the land is thereby inaccessible. The risk one runs in exploring a coast in these unknown and icy seas, is so very great, that I can be bold to say that no man will ever venture [by sea] farther than I have done, and that the lands which may lie to the south will never be explored. Thick fogs, snowstorms, intense cold and every other thing that can render navigation dangerous one has to encounter, and these difficulties are greatly heightened by the inexpressibly horrid aspect of the country, a country doomed by nature never once to feel the warmth of the sun's rays, but to lie for ever buried under everlasting snow and ice.

The natural harbours which may be on the coast are in a manner wholly filled up with frozen snow of a vast thickness, but if any should so far be open to admit a ship . . . she runs a risk of being there for ever.

After such an explanation as this the reader must not expect to find me much farther to the south. It is, however, not for want of inclination but other reasons.

These reasons, Cook went on to explain, were the risk of losing all the knowledge, all the charts, built up during this long voyage if the *Resolution* and her company were to be lost now. These same reasons impelled Cook to head east and then, some three weeks later, north, for Cape Town.

Thirty months had passed since they had left home waters, and there was much jubilation among the crew as they left behind the last icebergs and day by day the temperature rose. Tom Perry AB, a forty-year-old Londoner, who fancied himself as a versifier, composed what he called *The Antarctic Muse*, which catches some of the spirit of the men and of that time in the voyage:

I

It is now my brave boys we are clear of the Ice
And keep a good heart if you'll take my advice;
We are out of the cold my brave boys do not fear,
For the Cape of Good Hope with good hearts we do steer.

2

Thank God we have ranged the Globe all around,
And we likewise have the South Continent found;

But it being too late in the year as they say,
We could stay there no longer the Land to Survey.

3

So we leave it alone, for we give a good reason,
For the next Ship that comes, to survey in right season;
The great fields of Ice amongst them we were bothered,
We were forced to alter our course to the Northward.

4

So we have done our utmost as any men born,
To discover a land so far South of Cape Horn,
So now my brave Boys we no longer will stay,
For we leave it alone for the next Ship to survey.

5

It was when we got into the cold Frosty air,
We were obliged our Mittens and Magdalen Caps to wear,
We are out of the cold my brave boys and perhaps
We will pull off our Mittens and Magdalen Caps.

6

We are hearty and well and of good constitution,
And have ranged the Globe round in the brave Resolution,
Brave Capt. Cook he was our Commander,
Has conducted the Ship from all eminent danger.

7

We were all hearty seamen no cold did we fear,
And we have from all sickness entirely kept clear
Thanks be to the Captain he has proved so good
Amongst all the Islands to give us fresh food.

8

And when to old England my brave boys we arrive
We will tip off a Bottle to make us alive;
We will toast Captain Cook with a loud song all round,
Because that he has the South Continent found.

9

Blessed be to his wife and his Family too,
God prosper them all and well for to do,
Blessed be unto them as long as they shall live,
And that is the wish to them I do give.*

While Perry was composing his poem, his captain was summarising,

* See Appendix 2 on page 372.

neither modestly nor immodestly, his record of what they had accomplished:

I had now made the circuit of the Southern Ocean in a high latitude and traversed it in such manner as to leave not the least room for the possibility of there being a continent, unless near the pole and out of reach of navigation. By twice visiting the Pacific tropical sea, I had not only settled the situation of some old discoveries but made there many new ones, and left, I conceive, very little more to be done even in that part. Thus I flatter myself that the intention of the voyage has in every respect been fully answered, the Southern Hemisphere sufficiently explored and a final end to the searching after a Southern Continent . . .

The voyage to the Cape was uneventful, and at dawn on 16 March they sighted two sails to the NW, one of them showing Dutch colours. It was like meeting friends after too many months in the wilderness. On the same day, as further proof that they were returning to civilisation, Cook called in any log books or journals compiled on the voyage by officers and petty officers, while the men's chests were searched for any records (Marra succeeding in concealing his journal).* Before darkness fell, land was sighted ENE, about eighteen miles distant.

The next day, finding the Dutch East Indiaman close by, Cook sent a boat to her. The captain was hospitable and offered the *Resolution*'s men fresh provisions when he learned how long they had been without them. Several English sailors on board had news of the *Adventure*. She had, it seems, 'arrived at the Cape of Good Hope twelve months ago and that one of her boat's crew had been murdered and eaten by the people of New Zealand'. Cook was horrified but not entirely surprised to hear this news. The stories of some sort of disaster associated with a ship were too persistent to have been founded entirely on imagination. The Charlotte Sound Maoris knew that the crime would at some time be uncovered, and as a precaution against vengeance had set the scene of the massacre on the north side of Cook Strait.

He also suspected that some folly committed by Furneaux had led to the attack, and wrote:

I shall make no reflection on this melancholy affair until I hear more about it. I must, however, observe in favour of the New Zealanders that I have always found them of a brave, noble, open and benevolent disposition, but they are a people who will never put up with an insult if they have an opportunity to resent it.

---

* Strict rules of confidentiality applied in ships of most navies on long voyages of discovery. Governments were anxious not to disclose details of lands that they might wish to colonise. See page 160 with reference to the Spanish occupation of Savu.

The look-out sighted Table Mountain at noon on 21 March, and soon the reality of Hodges's painting of the town and its environs was presented to the ship's company again. None of the romance and pleasure it offered after this long circumnavigation escaped James Cook; but ever practical, ever curious, he and Wales checked their longitude as shown by Kendall's watch and the well-established reality of the town's longitude. The watch was accurate within 18', or less than a third of a degree.

20

'A Communication between the Atlantic and Pacific Oceans'

AGAIN, THE ROADS AND HARBOUR OF CAPE TOWN were thick with shipping, giving this modest Dutch outpost a metropolitan air. Dutch, French and English ships predominated, some outward bound, others returning to Europe. Captain Newte of an English East India Company ship, headed home from China, was asked to carry to the Admiralty in London a copy of Cook's journal to date, together with charts and drawings, all the work of Cook, his sailing master and young Isaac Smith.

Meanwhile Cook sent one of his officers to conduct the usual courtesies with the colony's Governor, Baron Joachim van Plettenberg. All requests for provisions, and permission to set up tents ashore for work on the ship and the observatory, were gladly granted. On the officer's return to the *Resolution* Cook ordered a salute of thirteen guns, which was at once answered by the fort.

An examination of his sloop revealed to Cook, as usual, its sorry condition. The hull and decking were not too bad, but the rigging, except the standing rigging, would all have to be replaced. On this subject Cook commented:

That our rigging, sails, &c should be worn out will not be wondered at when it is known that during this circumnavigation of the globe, that is since we left this place to our return to it again, we have sailed no less than 20,000 leagues [approx. 60,000 sea miles], a distance I will be bold to say was never sailed by any ship in the same space of time before.

Here at Cape Town Cook was to learn more about Furneaux's

experiences since the two sloops became separated for the second time. Before embarking for home, Furneaux described in some detail the circumstances of the loss of ten men and his relation and midshipman, Rowe. 'This, together with a great part of his bread being damaged, was the reason he could not follow me in the route I had proposed to take,' Cook reported, ever discreet in the comments in his journal which would be studied by Philip Stephens and the Board. In fact, the *Adventure* had made a swift passage from New Zealand to south of Cape Horn, either a little above or a little below the 60th parallel, and then with a brief diversion to look for Cape Circumcision, headed straight for Cape Town, arriving a year ago. No attempt had been made to supplement the sloop's rations, and by the time this immense non-stop voyage was completed his men were weak and emaciated, scarcely able to handle their ship. Furneaux had reached home, Cook learned later, on 12 July the previous year.

Apart from the work on the *Resolution*, Cook offered his officers and men a relaxed regime at Cape Town. The officers and gentlemen lived ashore as guests of a resident, and forebear of many distinguished South Africans, Christoffel Brand, 'well known to the English by his obliging readiness to serve them', according to Cook. The men were given generous shore leave, 'for pleasure, or refreshment, and it was no uncommon thing,' John Elliott recalled, 'in our rides in the country, to see three of the sailors on a horse, in full sail, and well-filled with grog. At other times I have seen them lying asleep by the roadside, and the horses standing over them.' Elliott thought this behaviour quite justified 'when it is considered how long they had been confined, and I will here do them the justice to say that no men could behave better, under every circumstance, than they did [on this voyage]'.

Elliott and all the other people of the *Resolution* were equally admiring of their captain, who had brought them through so many dangers. Andreas Sparrman was more inclined to give credit to the Almighty for his safe return to Cape Town:

It was only possible to accomplish this most hazardous of all voyages round the world . . . through the help of an all-wise Providence and its wonderful guiding grace . . . There were countless perils from storms, uncharted rocks, the danger of running aground, cliffs, floating ice-masses and bergs; from the poisoned arrows and other evils of savages, sometimes by direct conflict with them, or through the treacherous and faithless protestations of friendship from such people.

One is left with a less favourable impression of this Swedish botanist than of Banks's Dr Solander, and that relations with Cook were not always happy. Certainly Cook's judgment on the Maoris in particular was a great deal more generous than this Swede's, whose accommodation on board had been agreed to by Cook only reluctantly. Sparrman remained in the company of the Försters until the *Resolution* sailed, when he returned to his botanising in the Cape area.

For Cook, the high point of their time in Cape Town was a meeting with the French explorer and navigator, Crozet. Cook had heard much, all of it favourable, of Julien Crozet, who was in Table Bay this time as captain of a French East Indiaman. Cook invited the Frenchman and his officers on board for dinner. It was an evening of discoveries. The Frenchman had heard much of Cook's first voyage and was a great admirer. We can imagine that this admirable French navigator now listened with avid attention to Cook's account of his Antarctic and tropical island sweeps just concluded.

For his part, Crozet had brought with him and now unfolded a great chart showing the track of the expedition on which, as second-in-command to Marion du Fresne, he had discovered islands south-east of the Cape of Good Hope. They had then sailed to New Zealand not long after Cook's own first discovery, where they had anchored in the Bay of Islands. Here, Crozet told the diners, his commander and a number of his men had been killed by the local Maoris – and no doubt put in the pot.

Crozet himself, as surviving senior officer, then led the expedition north to the Philippines, and back to his base in Mauritius. Cook had also heard of Kerguelen. The aristocrat Yves-Joseph de Kerguelen-Trémarec in his voyage in search of the Southern Continent in 1771 had left the Cape on a SE heading and discovered a group of stark, mountainous islands on the 49th parallel which both the *Adventure* and, independently, the *Resolution* had come close to rediscovering on this voyage. His route, too, was marked on Crozet's chart, which included the islands named after this Frenchman not far distant from the Kerguelen group.

Most interesting of all to Cook, however, was the tracing of the course of Jean-François-Marie de Surville. This told Cook and Clerke for the first time that the Frenchman had been off Doubtless Bay, North Island, New Zealand, a few days after the *Endeavour* had been there, and that they had missed one another by only a few miles off North Cape. But, as Crozet no doubt recounted to Cook, Captain Surville was soon after drowned off Callao.

The discoveries of that evening in the great cabin of the *Resolution* were much more welcome than those of another day when Cook's attention was drawn to three massive volumes, recently arrived from London. It was *An Account of the Voyages undertaken . . . for making Discoveries in the Southern Hemisphere*. It had recently been published and written by the clever journalist John Hawkesworth. The work had been sponsored by Hawkesworth's friend Banks, and Dr Charles Burney, and supported by Sandwich.

Hawkesworth had been given the journals of Byron, Wallis, Carteret and Cook, to adapt as he wished and retell in the first person throughout. The first massive volume was concerned with the first three navigators, the second and third volumes with the *Endeavour*'s voyage. Cook was not in the least mollified by this imbalance when he began to read the title page, which said: 'Drawn up from the Journals which were kept by the several Commanders and from the Papers of JOSEPH BANKS ESQ. by JOHN HAWKESWORTH L.L.D.' The dedication was to THE KING.

The long introduction was marked by its sycophantic praise of Banks. The journal of Captain Cook, it seemed, was received from the Admiralty, and Captain Cook 'was so obliging as to put it into my hands, with permission to take out of it whatever I thought would improve or embellish the Narrative . . . This was an offer I gladly and thankfully accepted.'

Not only that, but Hawkesworth claimed to have read his manuscript to Cook at the Admiralty, and that he, Cook, had taken it away and had suggested some emendations, which had been made in the final text. In fact, the text was full of nautical howlers, and full, too, of Joseph Banks either directly acknowledged, or worse, and more frequently, unacknowledged. The numerous engravings were also credited to Banks, to whom 'the Public is indebted for the designs of the engravings, which illustrate and adorn the account of this voyage'. Poor Sydney Parkinson and Alexander Buchan did not receive even a mention, but then they were both dead.

Cook was mortified and furious. Who had given this journalist permission to misuse his journal? Surely not Stephens? Sandwich? He was more likely to be the culprit. He would find out when he arrived home.*

---

* At home he also saw the long review in *The Annual Register* for 1773. The reviewer could not understand why Hawkesworth had used the subterfuge of the first person. He was critical of other aspects of the three volumes, especially Hawkesworth's claim that in total these voyagers made far greater discoveries 'than those of all the navigators in the world collectively'. 'The real merit of these voyages', the reviewer continued, 'was too solid to make it at all necessary to transgress the bounds of truth.' The bounds of truth were not of much interest to Dr John Hawkesworth.

The damaging consequences of Hawkesworth's meddling with Cook's journal became clear at St Helena. Cook had left Cape Town on 27 April, in company with an English East Indiaman, the *Dutton*. There was a new Governor of the island, with a name engraved on Cook's memory: Skottowe, the son, no less, of Thomas Skottowe of Great Ayton, who had paid for Cook's schooling, among many generous kindnesses. Both John Skottowe and his spirited wife welcomed Cook with special warmth, but there was a teasing quality in his reception which at first puzzled him. The first evidence was the presence of an unnaturally large collection of carts and barrows outside the Governor's house in which he had been invited to stay. Over the following days, when Cook and the Försters and several officers were dined by the best people – who lived extremely comfortable lives on the island – it became increasingly evident that Cook was regarded as having been critical of aspects of the life of the islanders when last here on his first voyage. Eventually, he was reminded of what he had written in his journal recently edited by the learned Dr Hawkesworth, which had reached the island some time previously and been read with great curiosity.

Cook now read the passage and realised at once that these were Banks's critical observations about the treatment of the island's slaves, and the curious lack of wheeled traffic, not even wheelbarrows. Cook explained the situation with some embarrassment, heightened by the evident inaccuracy of both of Banks's criticisms. The islanders took the episode in good heart and lavished further hospitality on Cook, his officers and the gentlemen.

In return, Cook recorded warm praise on all aspects of St Helena life, only suggesting that they might grow more vegetables for passing mariners. On a more personal level, while at this island he made a packet of charts for the Admiralty, observing of them that they were 'very accurate charts of all the discoveries we have made, executed by a young man who has been bred to the sea under my care and who has been a very great assistance to me in this way, both in this and my former voyage'. The young man was, of course, Isaac Smith. These papers were consigned to the care of the captain of the *Dutton*, which was likely to reach England before the *Resolution*.

After spending six days at St Helena, Cook weighed and sailed on 21 May. He paused briefly at Ascension for turtle, known to be numerous at this time of the year, and then considered whether or not to satisfy a curiosity about an island he had for long wished to locate and fix its position. This was Fernando de Noronha, believed to be about 185 miles north-east of the tip of Brazil's bulge into the South Atlantic.

To be a successful navigator and explorer demands a well-developed spirit of opportunism, as shown by Cook's musings on the last day of May:

The truth is I was unwilling to prolong the passage in searching for what I was not sure to find, nor was I willing to give up every object which might tend to the improvement of navigation and geography for the sake of getting home a week or a fortnight sooner. It is but seldom that opportunities of this kind offer and when they do they are but too often neglected.

So here they were, in the centre of the South Atlantic, *en route* to England. After the immense distances the *Resolution* had already covered, what was a diversion to Brazil, a mere 1,500 miles? With favourable winds they sighted the island on 9 June. It appeared 'in detached and peaked hills, the largest of which looked like a church tower or steeple. After standing very near [some] rocks, we hoisted our colours and then bore up round the north end of the isle.' To Cook's astonishment, they sighted a number of forts, which displayed Portuguese colours and fired guns. Cook answered with a single gun. This was clearly a well-protected outpost of Portugal's empire. Several of the *Resolution*'s officers, as well as Wales and Cook, had taken readings, with confirmation from the watch. The mean result was 3° 53′ s and 32° 34′ w. Cook's curiosity satisfied, the *Resolution* bore away north for the Azores with favourable winds.

'After leaving these islands,' runs the final entry in Cook's journal, 'I made the best of my way for England. On Saturday the 29th [July 1775] we made the land near Plymouth and the next morning anchored at Spithead. Having been absent from England three years and eighteen days, in which time I lost but four men and one only of them by sickness.' He could have added that Marine Wedgeborough certainly drowned through drunkenness, and two fatal falls, of ABS Simon Monk and Henry Smock, might well have been through drink. Nor could Cook or anyone have done anything to cure Marine Taylor's tuberculosis, from which he died at Tahiti. But the important thing about this final entry in Cook's journal is that it is concerned first with the wellbeing of his men, something on which he prided himself, even above his skill as a navigator.

The opening words of Cook's final despatch bear out the closeness of the relationship he always succeeded in establishing with his men: 'The behaviour of my officers and crew during the whole course of the voyage merits from me the highest recommendation . . .'

The news of Cook's arrival at Portsmouth reached London rapidly, the message being thoughtfully passed on to Elizabeth Cook at the Mile End Road. After attending to the formalities at the naval dockyard, Cook took a post-chaise up the Portsmouth Road, in company with the Försters, astronomer Wales (clutching his clock), artist Hodges and seaman Dick Grindall, who had married just one hour before the *Resolution* had sailed and, Cook considered, warranted the highest priority. As before, he went straight to the Admiralty, where he was greeted by Stephens and members of the Board who had been alerted. Cook's communications and charts had arrived at the Admiralty from Cape Town a month earlier, and those from St Helena ten or twelve days before.

This could have been no more than a preliminary discussion. Here was a man who had recently confirmed one of the great negative discoveries in history – the final, incontrovertible proof that the Great Southern Continent did not exist – and, as a considerable postscript, had marked his chart with dozens of newly discovered islands, while at the same time correcting the position and even the shape of dozens more. These were not subjects that could be dealt with in an afternoon. Besides, Cook was impatient to greet his family, and their Lordships appreciated this natural need.

Dr Solander, who had also been informed of the safe return of the *Resolution*, had hastened to the Admiralty, too, and waited for Cook to emerge from the Board Room. The botanist then greeted him and found Cook in fine health, even better than when he had sailed all those months ago.

Then, for Cook, it was a cab to the Mile End Road.

LACKING ANY OFFICIAL BULLETIN from the Admiralty, the newspapers fabricated their own stories. To report that after three years' search Cook had failed to find the Great Southern Continent was hardly newsworthy, so the *Morning Post*, 11 August, wrote:

We hear from good authority that Captain Cook, who lately arrived in the river from the South Sea in His Majesty's Ship *Endeavour* [*sic*] has discovered an island of vast extent and well wooded in the Great Pacific Ocean, between Juan Fernandez and the continent of China. The island, it is said, is inhabited by a race of people as singular in their manners as they are whimsical in their appearance.

Another newspaper reported Cook's account of discovering a more modest-sized island of 160 by 140 miles, with a delightful climate, 'soil of the most luxuriant fertility and natives of a mild and civilised disposition'.

After the Hawkesworth experience, Cook had become cynical about the printed word and neither confirmed nor denied these and other fancy stories. In any case, he was much too busy to trouble with this sort of rubbish. One of his tasks was to recommend promotions and appointments for his officers and men. Among them was Lieutenant Cooper to be commander of the sloop *Hawke*, Charles Clerke to be commander of another sloop, HMS *Favourite*, and Isaac Smith, promoted to lieutenant and appointed to HMS *Weazle*, a thirty-year-old sloop. Cook himself was promoted post-captain, his commission being personally handed to him by the King during an audience on 9 August. In exchange, Cook presented George III with a number of maps and charts, which went into the Palace's private museum.

During these early days after his return, Cook saw much of Palliser and the other Lords of the Admiralty, and, as soon as he had returned from visiting dockyards, Lord Sandwich himself, who greeted Cook with much warmth. He saw Banks several times, too, and relations between the two men were cordial and no reference was made to the disagreement of three-and-a-half years earlier. To John Walker in Whitby he wrote a long and affectionate letter giving him a resumé of the entire voyage, and ending, 'Mrs Cook joins me in best respects to you and all your family, and believe me to be, with great esteem, yours most sincerely'.

As for Dr Hawkesworth, Cook had worried intermittently all the way from the Cape how he was going to deal with this charlatan. It was with some relief, therefore, that he learned soon after his return that Hawkesworth had died, when the *Resolution* had been moored in Ship Cove, on 17 November 1773. After being paid the enormous sum of £6,000 for his 'work', from the time of its publication in June 1773 it had been subjected to almost uniformly hostile reviews, of which the *Annual Register*'s notice was mild by comparison, and public denigration. This was too much for Hawkesworth. He had hoped to be taken seriously, to acquire some pride and rid himself of his reputation as a mere hack. His health went into a serious and swift decline.*

Of Elizabeth and James's two surviving boys, who had been on the

---

* James Boswell, the famous diarist, remarked indignantly to Cook of the late Hawkesworth: 'Why, Sir, Hawkesworth has used your narrative as a London tavern-keeper does wine. He has brewed it.'

muster roll of the *Resolution* and 'served' in her as far as Cape Town and there 'discharged', in reality James, now twelve years old, had been entered in the Portsmouth Naval Academy, and Nathaniel was due to follow his elder brother there the following year. Elizabeth had given birth to five children and now there was only one son left at the Mile End Road, besides Frances Wardale, her faithful, steady companion. But, within a week or two of her husband's return, Elizabeth Cook knew that she was pregnant again.

Domestic and career considerations became related when Cook applied to Stephens for a vacancy which had occurred among the quota of four captains at the Royal Hospital at Greenwich. This hospital for pensioned-off or disabled seamen had been set up in 1705. The captains' appointments were sinecures, with few duties and usually granted as a reward for distinguished service. However, by no means did Cook regard himself as ready to be pensioned off, and he was expecting to be offered a new commission.

The Lords Commissioners replied immediately and positively through Stephens. This meant comfortable quarters for his family, £230 *per annum*, plus ls 2d table money *per diem*, and free fire and light. In the long letter to Walker at Whitby, reporting on the performance of the *Resolution*, Cook made this rather rueful observation:

The *Resolution* was found to answer on all occasions even beyond my expectation and is so little injured by the voyage that she will soon be sent out again. But I shall not command her. My fate drives me from one extreme to another. A few months ago the whole southern hemisphere was hardly big enough for me, and now I am going to be confined within the limits of Greenwich Hospital, which are far too small for an active mind like mine.

Clearly, Cook had his tongue in his cheek when he wrote those words. He was confident that he would be re-employed in some capacity, and in the meantime there were a number of matters to clear up in connection with his recent voyage. The most tiresome concerned the Försters. Johann Förster was preordained to being a nuisance throughout his life, as he had demonstrated before joining the *Resolution*'s company. Banks had been a nuisance, too, from time to time, but he had been good company throughout the first voyage and had been little trouble as a passenger. The same could not be said of the elder Förster; and now that he was back in London, he was making ridiculous demands – demands for extra money, and about publishing his journal.

Throughout August Cook was beset by complaints that the £4,000

Förster had been given was inadequate to cover his expenses. Kitson described the situation:

It seems that Förster had not been judicious in his purchases of curiosities from the natives of the different islands at which they had touched; in fact Mr Wales says this was very soon noticed by the sailors, and it became a common occurrence for one of the crew to buy something for a mere trifle, and then re-sell it to Mr Förster at a very considerable advance. He also engaged Mr Sparrman . . . at a considerable expense, to do the work he himself undertook to do.

Furthermore, Förster now claimed that Sandwich had given him a verbal undertaking that he was to be given the exclusive rights to the history of the voyage, which he and his son were already writing – 'and to be provided with permanent employment for the remainder of his life'.

Sandwich denied vehemently that he had given any such undertaking. But shady bores are persistent people, and after some weeks Sandwich agreed that Förster could add to Cook's account of the voyage a special section on the scientific findings. This led to so much verbal and written scrapping that Sandwich eventually laid it down that Förster was prohibited from writing and publishing anything. Förster got round this prohibition by writing his book under his son's name, using a draft of Cook's own journal which he had earlier acquired, spattering it with maritime howlers, fabricating incidents to discredit Cook – like the 'bombardment' of Madeira – and attacking individuals, especially poor Wales, of whom he had always been inordinately jealous.

All that needs to be added to this sorry tale is that Förster achieved publication six weeks before Cook's own journal was in the booksellers' hands. But Cook was by then far away and never saw it.

A much more agreeable business was Cook's election to the Royal Society, his nomination being supported by no fewer than twenty-six of the great in the land in the fields of the sciences. In the month of Cook's election, he contributed a paper on the health of seamen to the Society's *Philosophical transactions*. No subject could be more appropriate, for, as surely as he had opened up the Pacific and confirmed that the Great Southern Continent did not exist, of even greater substance than this was that he had proved for all time that with strict cleanliness and adherence to an antiscorbutic diet, men could remain at sea for long periods without suffering the fearful and deadly ailment of scurvy.

Cook claimed no credit for devising the diet which prevented scurvy; and others had experimented successfully with antiscorbutics before him. But his voyages were of such duration and distance, and of such world-wide fame, that it was now only a matter of time before every maritime nation followed his example. How many seamen's lives were saved as a result is incalculable. But the achievement was one of seafaring's great landmarks.

THERE IS NO RECORD of Cook meeting Furneaux after he returned home. He knew that his number two had been in England for a year, and he was later given the opportunity to read Furneaux's journal and the *Adventure*'s log. But he felt no urgent desire in the first days of August, when there was so much to do and so many people to meet, to talk to the officer who had proved something of a disappointment, chiefly because of his lack of imagination and curiosity, and the slack discipline exercised in the *Adventure*, which had led to so many outbreaks of scurvy. The likelihood of a chance meeting between the two officers was eliminated within ten days of Cook's return by Furneaux's appointment as captain of the frigate *Syren*, which was destined for the American colonial revolt. (This had broken out in April, when Cook had been in Table Bay.)

If Furneaux was absent preparing his ship for war service, his bequest to the nation, Omai, was still very much in evidence. While Cook had been ranging south through the New Hebrides, with a year's voyaging still ahead of him, Omai was being lionised by English Society. Joseph Banks especially took a proprietorial interest in the young man, having him dressed in the fashionable suits of the day, instructing him in the correct handling of a stick, in bowing stylishly and in strolling down London's West End streets as a young Polynesian boulevardier.

There was competition among the hosts and hostesses of the country's great houses for having Omai as a guest, when his amiable manners were greatly admired. On first meeting George III he remarked cheerfully, 'How do, King Tosh.' His Majesty was amused rather than indignant. Later, Banks took him to the House of Lords to listen to the King making his speech from the throne. Jem Burney, who had taught Omai the rudiments of English on the voyage back from the Society Islands, and who had learned Tahitian himself, spent much time with him. Once established in London, the Burneys had Omai to dinner. Coming downstairs, Fanny found Omai seated on the great chair, and my brother [Jem] next to him, and talking Otaheite as fast as possible ... Jem introduced me, and told him I was another sister. He rose and made a very fine bow, and then seated himself again ... He had on a suit of Manchester velvet, lined with white sateen, a *bag*, lace ruffles, and a very handsome sword which the King had given to him. He is tall and very well made, much darker than I expected to see him, but has a pleasing countenance.

Banks and Sandwich made themselves chiefly responsible for Omai and, by the time Cook returned, were wearying of the self-imposed task. Omai, predictably, became spoilt and touchy, but the fashionable intelligentsia continued to lavish praise and attention upon this 'noble savage'. Sir Joshua Reynolds and other portraitists painted him, and James Boswell reported that Dr Johnson

had been in company with Omai, a native of one of the South Sea Islands ... He was struck by the elegance of his behaviour, and accounted for it thus: 'Sir, he had passed his time ... only in the best company; so that all he had acquired of our manners was genteel. As a proof of this, Sir, Lord Mulgrave and he dined one day at Streatham; they sat with their backs to the light fronting me, so that I could not see distinctly; and there was so little of the savage in Omai, that I was afraid to speak to either, lest I should mistake one for the other.'

Even before the return of the *Resolution*, plans were being discussed for a further Pacific expedition. The ambitions of the British establishment – the Government, the Admiralty, the Royal Society and King George himself – had been further widened and sharpened by Cook's two voyages, and the arrival of Cook's first despatches and letters from Cape Town ahead of his return enlarged on what information Furneaux had brought back on his foreshortened voyage a year earlier.

British curiosity and ambitions now pointed towards the North rather than the South Pacific. They were not new and they were specific. Nor were they influenced by the revolution in the colonies of North America. It was, no less, the discovery and exploitation of a north-west passage between Canada and the pole, linking the Atlantic and Pacific Oceans. A short route to the trade and riches of the East avoiding the two capes, Horn and Good Hope, would be of priceless value, so valuable that a prize of £20,000, to be shared among the ship's company, was offered.

Off and on for almost three hundred years efforts had been made by Russian, French, Spanish, English and Dutch explorers, many expeditions ending in tragedy. The first phase of North-West Passage exploration was initiated indirectly by the Ottoman Turks with their capture of Constantinople and the expansion of their empire, effectively severing the ancient overland caravan routes. These had for centuries brought the riches of the East, and especially the spices of Cathay, to the European markets. John Cabot from England, though a Venetian, attempted to reach the Orient by sailing west from Bristol, with Henry VII's authority. He discovered Newfoundland, landed on it, took possession in the name of the King, and even convinced him when he returned that he had found Cathay. That was in 1497. Thirty-eight years later the French navigator, Jacques Cartier, convinced himself that the St Lawrence River led to the North Pacific.

When Spain and Portugal effectively drew a line down the South Atlantic and assigned exclusive use to Spain of the ocean west of it, and to Portugal east of it, the Dutch, French and English found themselves excluded from the route to the Orient round both the Cape of Good Hope and Cape Horn, when these routes were discovered and exploited. The Treaty of Tordesillas of 1494 confirmed this duopoly. Although it was flouted many times by privateers like Dampier and Drake, and Dutchmen like Schouten and le Maire, the treaty brought about a renewed need to discover a north-west passage. English explorers like Martin Frobisher, Charles F. Hall, John Davis and Henry Hudson were all associated with these gallant efforts. The Dutch even attempted an eastern passage to the Pacific north of Russia.

The North-West Passage gradually became as deeply entrenched an obsession as *Terra Australis Incognita* in the south, attracting a mythology equally imaginative. An Irishman, Arthur Dobbs, convinced himself that Irish trade would be much increased by the use of a passage which led from the north-west corner of Hudson's Bay into open ocean. It was the Pacific because of the numbers of Pacific whales to be seen there. Then there was Juan de Fuca, who like Vitus Bering, a Dane working for the Russians, found it convenient to operate from the Pacific and work east. De Fuca was despatched by the Viceroy of Mexico, north up the coast of California, to search for the Strait of Anian, the legendary passage through North America to the Atlantic. In 1592, it was said, de Fuca discovered a broad inlet into which the gallant explorer sailed, discovering a people clad in beasts' skins and a land 'rich of gold, silver, pearl, and other things.' Beyond, indeed, lay the Atlantic, so he turned round and came home to report to the Viceroy. Just as there had to be a great southern continent, ran this tenacious legend, so did there have to be a passage linking the two great oceans.

It was not long after Cook's return that the Admiralty, probably in the person of Philip Stephens, divulged to him the plans being formed to despatch a two-ship expedition to search for a northern passage from the east, from the Pacific to the Atlantic. The plan was undeveloped, highly confidential, and the return of Omai to his homeland was to be the cover for the voyage. From the beginning of these first conversations Cook was excluded as a candidate for the command of the expedition. It was accepted by all parties, and by Cook himself, that his responsibilities were to be of a purely advisory character. He had, after all, spent almost six of the past seven years at sea, burdened with the unremitting demands, day and night, of a commander. He was in need of a long rest from the decisions upon which depended the wellbeing, and often the lives, of his ship's company. He was also tired, and Elizabeth Cook needed and deserved his company for a while.

It was impossible for Cook to hear of the new plans without experiencing a tingle of excitement, a re-arousal of the curiosity which had driven him on his discoveries for all these past years. He had, after all, ranged the South Pacific from east to west, from 10° s to 71° s. Several of his officers may have recorded more circumnavigations, but no one in the world had seen more of this ocean's seventy million square miles, had sighted and recorded more islands, and experienced this ocean's moods and manners more intensely. And now, he learned, some other commander was to enter the North Pacific, there to make more and perhaps greater discoveries, even force a passage through Arctic seas and sail home triumphantly, the £20,000 reward an additional bonus.

None of this could be excluded from his mind during the meetings at the Admiralty. He would take the eastern route to the Pacific rather than the western route, he advised the Board. He knew them both, with their advantages and disadvantages. He had been fortunate at the Horn on both voyages, but the better route was east from the Cape of Good Hope, after wooding, watering and refreshing at Cape Town.

Cook advised a few days at Adventure Bay, Van Diemen's Land, so warmly recommended by Captain Furneaux, and also at Ship Cove in New Zealand, before proceeding north-east to Tahiti, where Omai would be left at the island of his choice. From the Society Islands he would allow two months to reach the coast of New Albion, and a further two summer months for working north in search of a promising outlet of a passage, or passing through the Bering Strait. Here he would rely on the Harris Map of Bering's first voyage, and the recent Stählin map.* From here, north of Alaska, all was speculation.

As for the ship, there could be none better than the *Resolution* sloop, suitably checked and refitted; and if not, the *Adventure*, known to be a fine sailer, better than the *Resolution* in some respects, or a cat of similar specification.

Through the early winter of 1775–6, Cook worked for long hours on his journal. Writing did not come easily to him, as the number of drafts bore witness, but within his own limitations he was a perfectionist. But the prospect of this new expedition was unlikely ever to be far from his thoughts. It was certainly on his mind early in the New Year, on 9 January, as he made his way to another Admiralty meeting, this time for dinner, the only guest, he had been told, of Palliser, Stephens and Sandwich – Comptroller, Secretary and First Lord. Earlier in his career, certainly before the first voyage, he would have felt both honoured and agitated at such an invitation. But now he took his position as a senior post-captain and adviser on all matters relating to exploration for granted, while of course conforming to all the formalities and procedures of service life. Cook knew these men well, Palliser for twenty years.

Over dinner it became clear that the selection of the officers for this new expedition was to be the main subject for the evening. The natural choice was Clerke, close friend of Cook, whose skill and reliability were cast iron. The four men discussed Clerke with deep intensity. Did he have the gravitas? Well . . . Did he have the confidence of the men? Certainly. He was well known, was he not, for his womanising and yarning with the men over a bottle? Would his new status bring with it the necessary dignity and detachment this wider responsibility demanded? What about Lieutenants John Gore or Richard Pickersgill?

The wine had been passing round the table for some time, but it was not this, nor the flattery of Sandwich in particular, that led to Cook's uncharacteristically sudden decision. He stood up at the table, looking at the three men in turn as if toasting them, and then, after this dramatic pause, announced in a firm voice, 'I will myself undertake the direction of this enterprise if I am so commanded.'

---

* Jacob von Stählin, *An Account of the New Northern Archipelago, Late Discovered by the Russians* . . . published in German in 1774 and translated and published in English the same year. The volume included a 'very accurate little map of the new discovered Northern Archipelago . . . drawn from the original accounts'.

It was said later that a cheer rang out from the three most senior and important men in the Royal Navy, and that glasses were charged again, and a real and heartfelt toast to Cook's health proposed.

21

A Stalled Departure

COOK WROTE TO JOHN WALKER AT WHITBY on 14 February 1776:

Dear Sir,

I should have answered your last favour sooner, but waited to know whether I should go to Greenwich Hospital, or the South Sea. The latter is now fixed upon; I expect to be ready to sail about the latter end of April with my old ship the *Resolution* and the *Discovery*, the ship lately purchased ... I know not what your opinion may be on this step I have taken. It is certain I have quitted an easy retirement, for an active, and perhaps dangerous voyage. My present disposition is more favourable to the latter than the former, and I embark on as fair a prospect as I can wish. If I am fortunate enough to get safe home, there's no doubt but it will be greatly to my advantage ... My best respects to all your family ...

Your most sincere friend and humble servant,

Jams. Cook

So at Whitby the news was out: their James was off again. And no doubt at Redcar, too. No letter survives, but Cook would certainly have written to his father, even if the pressure of time did not allow a visit. If he had got away in the latter part of April as he had hoped, the pressure of time would have been even more intense. But, as before, he was being optimistic. Like great building constructions, the preparation for an extended voyage always took longer than expected. The Admiralty had instructed Cook, 'You are hereby required and directed to use the utmost despatch in getting [the *Resolution*] ready for the sea', but the delays in victualling, in sheathing the *Resolution* and getting her ready for sea at Deptford set back the date for departure time and again. One of the causes was the Admiralty's own additional and belated instructions, like this, dated a month after Cook's volunteering:

Admiralty to Navy Board. On additional stores. Both ships to be fitted with a camp forge and copper oven, and have coppers fitted with Irving's [water distilling] apparatus and Lieut Orsbridge's machine for rendering stinking water sweet. Frames of two decked vessels, of about 20 and 17 tons, to be packed in cases for exploring or surveying or any emergency.

Deptford was not only proving dilatory, with many excuses for delays, but its workmanship was also suffering, as it inevitably did, through lack of supervision. Navy yards were notoriously corrupt and slack. Like recalcitrant children, the men there needed constant supervision. Cook knew this and had in the past watched over every detail, the soundness of every mast and yard, the quality of the caulking. Nothing used to get past him. His tall, straight-backed figure was familiar to everyone at Deptford, and feared by the scrimshankers. This time he was rarely seen. He was working on his journal, at loggerheads with the Försters, studying what charts there were of the North Pacific and that gulf, only recently discovered to be a gap, between eastern Siberia and western Alaska, Asia and America. Above all, he was engaged in the lengthy business of selecting his commissioned officers and petty officers.

Another time-consuming business which kept Cook from Deptford was sitting for his portrait, first to Sir Nathaniel Dance RA, a leading painter of that time. This was in May 1776, a month after he had hoped to be away. Joshua Reynolds painted him, too, as did William Hodges, who had had plenty of time to study Cook's features on the most recent voyage. Dance's is the best known, and generally thought to be the best likeness.

Did Cook feel that it was his duty to sit for portraits, a time-consuming business with any artist? Surely it was not vaingloriousness? These speculations lead to others. In his letter to Walker, the reference to the imminent voyage being 'perhaps dangerous' and his safe return being 'fortunate' are to be found elsewhere, too, and are not characteristic of the commander of the first two voyages. Did he have some kind of portent that this time he would not return and that his portrait should be painted for maritime posterity? Did he have doubts about his health and physical capacity to survive the rigours of command in both the tropics and the Arctic? Were any doubts about his own fitness and resilience subconsciously reflected in his neglect of the condition of his ship? It is all conundrum made no more solvable by the strange events of the following three years.

MOST OF THE PEOPLE had been selected by the end of February. After that, as usual, there were many desertions and replacements, unusually many because of the four months-long delay before the *Resolution* and *Discovery* were ready for sea. As for the officers, one man Cook had determined upon from the moment he had offered his own service was Charlie Clerke to command the *Discovery*. Whatever faint doubts he had aired at that dinner about Clerke's capacity to lead the expedition, they certainly did not apply to his old friend as second-in-command. As he had told Sandwich and his other hosts, Clerke was cheerful, able, sound, undeviatingly courageous, and loved and admired by his fellow officers and the people equally. We have seen enough of this thirty-two-year-old man to know him already: the bright-eyed, fair-complexioned sailor from Weathersfield Hall, Braintree, Essex. Although sixteen years younger than Cook, he had seen more fighting service. As a young man in action, stationed in the mizzen top, the mast had been shot from under him. He had been the only survivor. 'Clerke is a right good officer,' one of his fellows had written of him in the Pacific. 'At drinking and whoring he is as good as the best of them.'

Clerke had sobered up somewhat since that comment had been made. But in 1776 his belief that life was to be lived to the full was as strong as ever, and the happier he made others, the better he felt. Cook thought that, of all his officers, he knew Clerke best.

As first lieutenant of the *Resolution*, Cook was thankful to have John Gore back again. Gore had enjoyed his expedition with Banks to Iceland in the brig *Sir Lawrence*, but the prospect of sailing to the South Seas again with Cook was irresistible. His red hair had thinned since Cook had last seen him four years earlier, but his close-set pale eyes were as keen as ever, and he looked at least as fit as before. At forty-six, a year younger than Cook, he was the second oldest in the ship. Gore had none of Clerke's natural *joie de vivre*, but Cook enjoyed his company and, more seriously, liked this New York-born sailor for his reliability, cheerfulness in adversity, and skill in all branches of marine work, except surveying for which he had neither interest nor aptitude. A lee shore was something to avoid, in his reckoning, not to chart.

Since Cook had last known John Gore, the lieutenant seemed to have got himself a woman. She was either called Nancy or was Gore's nancy, as sailors often referred to their fancy nancy. There is also a reference in the Banks papers to his agreeing to look after his 'young one' in the event of Gore's death.

Between them the two ships could muster in all seven Americans, none of whom, it seemed, had any urgent wish to return to the colonies and fight for their liberty. William Ewin from Pennsylvania, aged thirty-three, had been a boatswain's mate on the last voyage and was to be boatswain in the *Resolution* on this voyage; while Ben Whitton, also an elderly thirty-seven, was a carpenter's mate from Boston.

For second lieutenant Cook appointed James King, on the recommendation of Palliser and the astronomer Thomas Hornsby. Young King had met Hornsby at Oxford and learned much from him, enough to qualify for looking after the ship's watch and thus obviating the need for a professional astronomer. Although only twenty-six, King was the best educated, best read and most intellectual officer in the *Resolution* and *Discovery*. 'King was a gentle, fastidious, hypochondriacal and kindly man who might be regarded as effeminate by the ruder members of the *Resolution*'s company – of which there were many – but who was to be a great solace and close companion to Cook during the difficult months ahead.'

This admirable officer had entered the Navy at the age of twelve and, like Cook, had served in Newfoundland under Palliser – there is no record of a meeting – and in the Mediterranean, being promoted lieutenant at twenty-one. Three years later, using family influence, he left the service temporarily to study science in Paris, and then at Oxford, where he came under the influence of Hornsby. King's brother Walker King, worked in journalism with Edmund Burke, the Whig politician and philosopher, and author of *Vindication of Natural Society* at the age of twenty-seven. The two brothers' unusual charm and intellectual talent led to connections in politics, the sciences and the arts, which took them from a humble parsonage in Lancashire to high levels of accomplishment, Walker King to the Bishopric of Rochester.

Cook's third lieutenant was a strongly contrasting figure, whose selection by Cook, normally a good judge of men, remains one of the mysteries of the preparatory work for this voyage. John Williamson was one of those uneven characters who can make life at sea on a long voyage so tiresome and exhausting. His temper could be frightful and without apparent cause, and it is doubtful that his presence enhanced any occasion throughout the four years on board the *Resolution* or the *Discovery*, to which ship he was discharged at one point. The people, as usual, rumbled Williamson within hours of putting to sea, and loathed and despised him throughout the voyage.

Another 'awkward fellow' selected by Cook as his sailing master was William Bligh, although Cook is less blameworthy for this second misjudgment. Cook was attracted to Bligh by his reputation as a talented navigator, surveyor and cartographer. His unevenness and hasty temper, his intolerance and impatience, were not to be discerned at a single meeting, and Cook had the strong recommendation of no less a figure than Sandwich. Bligh was twenty-two when he was given this appointment. Although his background was not as humble as Cook's, he was a great deal more conscious of being underprivileged. While Cook never grew a seedling of a chip on his shoulder, in Bligh's case they were numerous and flourished for all his life.

Like Cook at Staithes, Bligh had lived during the most susceptible period of his young life in a seaport. His father was a customs officer at Plymouth, a city as historically concerned with the sea and the coming and going of ships as Whitby. William, an only son, was as well educated as Francis Bligh could afford, and by the time the boy was fifteen he could write a good hand and had become accomplished in mathematics and the sciences. He had also determined to become a sailor, a career of which his father approved.

Like Cook again, William Bligh had entered the service from the lower deck. His father possessed no patron, and only 'sons of noblemen and gentlemen' could enter the Royal Navy through the Naval Academy at Portsmouth. At sixteen he was an able seaman, and served in the West Indies and in home waters. His keen ambitiousness led him to specialise successfully in navigation, hydrography and cartography and, at twenty-one, he earned his certificate as a midshipman. When the colonial rebellion broke out, he looked forward to action and to proving himself further. Instead, fate led him to Cook and a prime appointment as this famous navigator's sailing master. Like many others on board the *Resolution* in 1776, the immense voyage was to shape the rest of his life.

William Anderson, surgeon's mate on the last voyage, was to sail again, this time in the promoted capacity of surgeon. Cook was pleased about this. Anderson had proved to be good company and able. He was now four years older in medical experience as well as knowledge of natural history and ethnology, in which he was a competent amateur. He was liked and respected by the entire ship's company. His first mate, David Samwell, was popular, too, especially on the lower deck where this Welshman made them laugh and amused them with his anecdotes and poems. Like many a Welsh parson's son, he was wholeheartedly irreverent, and spoke much and wrote much about 'the dear girls'. He kept a journal reflecting the lighter side of life in the *Resolution*. Samwell idolised Cook: 'His great qualities I admired beyond anything – I gloried in him . . .'

Only the admiration of James Trevenen for Cook matched Samwell's. Trevenen, a midshipman from Cornwall in his late teens, had been recommended by Wallis, and once wrote to his mother of 'the sublime and soaring genius' of Cook. But for some unclear reason, this young man could not get on with John Gore. He also liked Bligh, under whom he worked a great deal, and Bligh seems to have been kind to him, as he was to all deserving youngsters.

Cook was less fortunate in his marines lieutenant than before. Molesworth Phillips, an Irishman of only twenty-one, had originally joined the Navy but had switched to the Royal Marines, perhaps in the belief that life would not be as hard, which was a reasonable assumption. He was bone idle, slack and amiable. He was also a 'fine made, tall, stout, active, a manly looking young fellow'. He must also have had some Irish charm to him, for he had already attracted the favourable attention of Banks, who had recommended the change of service. Jem Burney's sister, Susan, was also attracted to him. They later married, but he 'did not treat her well', according to Beaglehole.

Fortunately for the marines' discipline, they had Samuel Gibson, now a Pacific veteran. Though he had attempted desertion on the first voyage, and had been something of a trial, he must have later earned Cook's approval for he became a corporal on the second voyage, and now a sergeant. Cook also valued him for his knowledge of the Polynesian languages and dialects.

Then, as one of the two corporals, there was John Ledyard, aged twenty-four, from Groton, Connecticut. He was a tall, good-looking adventurer with an attractive disposition. He had earlier trained as a missionary with the Red Indians, grown impatient with the discipline and shipped as a sailor. He eventually ended up at Plymouth, penniless, walked to London, where he heard of Cook's imminent voyage, and persuaded him to take him on as a marine.

By contrast with the first voyage, the *Resolution* this time numbered only two supernumeraries, though between them they boasted much talent and unsurpassed eccentricity. John Webber was a twenty-four-year-old landscape painter of singular talent. He was the son of a Swiss painter who had migrated to England and settled in London. Watching his son's talent grow, he sent him to Berne, and later to Paris, to be trained. When he returned to London at the age of twenty-four, he had few friends and certainly no patron. But never had there been such a time for quick recognition, and Webber benefited from this in no uncertain way. Someone persuaded the young man to admit his work to the Royal Academy. This he did, and one of the first to admire it was Solander. The Swede knew that Cook was off again to the Pacific and that no artist had so far been selected.

At breakneck speed, Webber and his work were seen and admired by the Royal Society, the Admiralty Board and Cook himself. He received his appointment on 24 June and joined the *Resolution* at Plymouth on 5 July, just seven days before she sailed. He was still only twenty-five. No one appears to have recorded how he responded to the idea of sailing in a converted collier to the other side of the world instead of setting up his studio in London. Nor is there any record of how this young artist got on with his fellow supernumerary, Omai.

Omai matched Banks in the quantity and range of his luggage. He was not discouraged from piling up his possessions to show to his kinsmen. It drew public attention to him and added to the veracity of the deception that the prime purpose of the expedition was to return him to his homeland. First, there was his furniture, his bed, table and chairs for his new house, together with crockery and kitchenware; port wine to serve to his guests at the end of dinner, just as they had at Badminton and other great houses of England. Naturally, there must be music to accompany the port, so there was a hand organ, and to amuse his guests later there was a jack-in-the-box in the form of a cylindrical case containing a sprung serpent which leapt out with the removal of the lid. An immense Bible with coloured engravings was included for late-night reading and to keep alive his newly acquired religion. A large globe would enable him to retrace his travels, for his own satisfaction and for the education of his friends.

To protect himself and his possessions from attack by jealous neighbours, he took with him a coat of mail as well as a complete suit of medieval armour, and a number of muskets, ball shot and gunpowder. Cook jibbed only at the armoury, but the Board overruled him. Sandwich had witnessed the Polynesian's enthusiasm with the musket.

On the whole, Cook took a tolerant view of Omai, in spite of his disapproval of Furneaux's bringing him to England. It was none of his business, he accepted, to stem the flow of ridiculous wonder and praise he aroused wherever he went, the Rousseauesque 'noble savage' view taken by King George down to the cheering crowds on the streets of London. Cook regarded him as a spoilt, precocious, rather tiresome Polynesian, and knew it would be a great relief to have him rehoused on Huahine, his home island.

Among the *Resolution*'s people, the usual rough, fearless, sentimental, unscrupulous lot to be found in almost any of HM ships, two stand out. George Gilbert was only eighteen, a midshipman and son of Joseph Gilbert, Cook's sailing master on the second voyage. He was as good company as his father, was another ardent admirer of Cook and kept a perceptive journal. The second is William Watman, aged forty-four, regarded as the old man of the lower deck, and also 'beloved by his fellows, for his good and benevolent disposition'. He was another Cook admirer from the second voyage, and Cook reciprocated his respect and affection. When Cook acquired his governorship of Greenwich Hospital, he found a billet for Watman, too, but when the sailor heard that Cook was going to sea again after all, he prevailed upon Cook to take him.

The *Discovery*, the smallest of all Cook's ships, and with a complement of only seventy officers and men, was also quite as well endowed with a rich range of talent. Certainly, it promised to be a better managed ship than the *Adventure*. Clerke as captain was supported by officers of the quality of Jem Burney,* and as lively a bunch of midshipmen as could be found anywhere. One of these highly talented young men was Vancouver of the last voyage; another was Edward Riou, who was to become one of the finest frigate captains of his day, distinguishing himself but losing his life at Copenhagen fighting with Nelson.

Adding further lustre to the cultural content of the *Discovery*'s men was William Ellis, surgeon's mate, who had been educated at Cambridge, was a friend of Banks and a fine draughtsman. His bird paintings were to complement the work of John Webber. The Board of Longitude insisted that Bayly should sail again, and he had his berth in Clerke's ship, together with a gardener from Kew, David Nelson, included at the request of Banks. Banks was privy to the secret destination of the expedition and was particularly anxious to acquire specimens of plants from America's western seaboard, and perhaps Siberia, too.

In the two ships there was a fine international mix of Welsh, Scots, English, Americans and a German, one Heinrich Zimmerman, a nomad who could turn his hand to anything. David Samwell later summed up the quality of the mariners on this third voyage: 'We are perhaps somewhat partial to one another, for it is an article of faith with every one of us that there never was such a collection of fine lads, take us for all in all, got together as there was in the *Resolution* and *Discovery*.'

Cook's instructions for this third voyage are even wordier than before, full of platitudes about cultivating a friendship with the natives, collecting samples of metals, stones, plants and fruit, and taking possession of any uninhabited places in the name of His

---

* It happened that young Burney had to sail the *Discovery* from the Thames to Plymouth, to the delight of Fanny and the rest of the family.

Majesty. 'If any accident should happen to the *Resolution* in the course of the voyage', runs one profound passage, 'so as to disable her from proceeding any farther, you are, in such case, to remove yourself and her crew into the *Discovery* . . .'

On his third great voyage, the Lords Commissioners still found it necessary to instruct their commander to 'cause the sloops to be supplied with as much provisions and water as you can conveniently stow' at harbours of refreshment *en route*, like Cape Town and Queen Charlotte Sound. But there were one or two points of interest. Although enjoined not to spend too much time, this being of the essence, Cook was to search southward of the Cape of Good Hope for the islands the French discoverers had reported and claimed for France, 'in the latitude of 48° South and about the meridian of Mauritius'.

Only the Spaniards themselves knew how far north up the west coast of North America they had claimed and colonised. Little was known of the coastline north of present-day California, but the west coast of Canada was named New Albion on English maps while not yet formally claimed for the crown. Cook was therefore instructed to be circumspect and 'not to touch upon any part of the Spanish dominions on the western continent of America, unless driven thither by some unavoidable accident, in which case you are to stay no longer there than shall be absolutely necessary'.

Furthermore, and as proof of Admiralty ignorance of what he would find farther north, should 'you find any subjects of any European Prince or State upon any part of the coast you may think proper to visit you are not to disturb them or give them any just cause of offence, but on the contrary to treat them with civility & friendship'.

After wooding and watering and procuring refreshments on the coast of New Albion, the two sloops were to probe farther north to the latitude of 65°, or higher if ice allowed, aiming to arrive 'in the month of June next'.

Cook would now have reached the culminating point of the voyage, and he was 'carefully to search for, and to explore, such rivers or inlets as may appear to be of a considerable extent and pointing towards Hudson's or Baffin's Bays'. If he had no success, he was to retire for the winter months to the Russian port of St Peter and St Paul in Kamchatka, 'or wherever else you shall judge more proper', and in the spring to try again 'in further search of a North-East or North-West passage, from the Pacific Ocean into the Atlantic Ocean, or the North Sea'.

No mention is made in these instructions of another expedition working from the east at the same time as Cook's from the west. Some sensationalist seam in the thinking of the Board of Admiralty imagined the ships meeting halfway against an Arctic backdrop of blizzards and icebergs. Dick Pickersgill was to command this expedition. Cook had been denied the services of his old friend on this new voyage, but without any explanation. Pickersgill had proved himself a cheerful and reliable officer time and again on the first two voyages.

It is scarcely possible to believe that Cook was not informed by Palliser or Stephens of this second and simultaneous voyage of discovery for the North-West Passage, but there is no written record. Nor does it seem that Cook was informed of Pickersgill being appointed its commander.*

IN ORDER TO REACH the Barents Strait in June 1777, it was desirable that Cook's predicted departure date in April 1776 should be adhered to. Instead, two months later the *Resolution* was still in the Thames estuary, having taken on at Long Reach 'our artillery, powder, shot and other stores'. On 8 June Sandwich, Palliser and other members of the Board, as well as 'other Noblemen and Gentlemen', came on board for dinner, being received with a salute of seventeen guns and three cheers from the men, who manned the yards in honour of the guests.

Sandwich greeted Cook warmly and asked him if he was satisfied with his ship and its equipment. 'I answered him that whatever might be the event of our endeavours,' said Cook, 'our equipment was every way adequate to the voyage: at which his Lordship was pleased to express his satisfaction.' They then ate Westmorland ham, pigeon pie, chicken, turbot, trout, lobster and strawberries.

What these grandees would have said if they had seen the dockside on the Monday following this dinner can only be speculated. It had suddenly taken on the appearance of a farmyard. George III, who had recently honoured Cook with an audience, had asked him if he would take a number of animals from his own farms 'with a view of stocking Otaheite and the neighbouring islands with these useful animals'. 'Farmer George' had conceived an ambition of creating a near replica of the British countryside at Tahiti and its neighbouring islands. The drawings he had seen showed the primitive nature of farming in

---

* The expedition was a shambles from the beginning. Pickersgill's ship, the armed brig *Lyon*, was unsuitable for the task, the maps were useless, the men were not provided with suitable clothing, and Pickersgill was soon defeated by ice and icebergs, and drink. He was not the only officer of his time to drink himself out of the Royal Navy.

Polynesia: no tilled fields, no hedgerows or ditches, no apparent equipment, and above all no livestock. This monarch felt that it was his duty to ensure that his newest subjects should benefit from latest English farming practice, which would provide them with a wider and more varied diet of healthy meat and vegetables, while their landscape would be transformed from a hugger-mugger confusion of strange trees and undergrowth to a more agreeable pastoral scene. Doubtless the King had been told that these Otaheitians had few occupations beyond picking wild vegetables and fruit, and occasionally going fishing. As a consequence of their lack of occupation they were frequently engaged in bloody civil wars. The demands of husbandry would put a stop to all that, the King judged.

Cook's maritime menagerie waiting forlornly on the dockside at Long Reach consisted of sheep, rabbits, a mare, a stallion, a large number of sows and several hogs, two cows with their calves and a bull to increase the herd. The *chef-d'œuvre* was a magnificent peacock and peahen from King George's friend and Lord of the Admiralty, the Earl of Bessborough, Viscount Duncannon, Baron Ponsonby of Sysonby.

Sailors were accustomed to living among animals and were sentimentally attached to them, the officers having goats for their milk, the men their pet dogs and cats, as well as hens for eggs, all of which were additional to the King's farm animals. But the space required for the King's animals, their pens or cages, their fodder and water in a 562-ton ex-collier, resulted in extreme discomfort on a voyage to the other side of the world.

During his last weeks in London, Cook and Elizabeth dined widely with the great families in the city, especially among those whose interests were in the arts and science. There was dinner with Sir John Pringle, President of the Royal Society. Elizabeth arrived on Cook's arm. She was eight months pregnant but still enjoyed the social round. James Boswell was there, too, and later commented: 'It was curious to see Cook, a grave steady man, and his wife, a decent plump English-woman, and think that he was preparing to sail round the world.'

Cook also dined at the House of Commons as the guest of the Speaker, an unscrupulous lawyer called Sir Fletcher Norton, also known as 'Sir Bull-face Double Fee'.

A few weeks later, shortly before he sailed, Elizabeth gave birth to another boy. They named him Hugh in honour of Cook's early commander and patron, Sir Hugh Palliser, to whom he owed so much.

Quotations from Cook's own letters during these last days in London, and later at Plymouth, fill out the picture of him as he deals with the final obligations of a conscientious man. He had given a paper to the Royal Society on the methods he had used, especially diet, to preserve the health of his men. On 10 July he writes to Banks: 'Sir John Pringle writes me that the Council of the Royal Society have decreed me the Prize Medal of this year [Sir Godfrey Copley's annual gold medal]. I am obliged to you and my other good friends for this unmerited Honour.'

The following day, 11 July, he writes on board his ship to the Rev. Dr Richard Kaye, another Fellow of the Royal Society, and evidently a rather vain man who had asked for his name to be given to some feature on the western American coast. But he was also chaplain to the King, and Cook replied:

I cannot leave England without answering your very obliging favour ... and thanking you for the kind tender of your service to Mrs Cook in my absence. I shall most certainly make an acknowledgement in the way you wish, if it please God to spare me till I reach the place for discoveries ...

Cook's concern with the welfare of Elizabeth and his family during his absence, or in the event of his failure to return, is again shown in a final letter to Sandwich:

I cannot leave England without taking some method to thank your Lordship for the many favours conferred upon me, and in particular for the very liberal allowance made to Mrs Cook during my absence. This, by enabling my family to live at ease and removing from them every fear of indigency, has set my heart at rest and filled it with gratitude to my noble benefactor. If a faithful discharge of that duty which your Lordship has entrusted to my care be any return, it shall be my first and principal object.

Cook's last letter to his father does not appear to have survived, but to his old friend and his father's one-time neighbour at Great Ayton, Commodore Wilson, Cook wrote on 22 June:

I am at last upon the very point of setting out to join the *Resolution* at the Nore, and proceed on my voyage, the destiny of which you have pretty well conjectured. If I am not so fortunate as to make my passage home by the North Pole, I hope at least to determine whether it is practicable or not. From what we yet know, the attempt must be hazardous, and must be made with great caution.

June 1776 was a beautiful month. Cook spent much of it at Mile End polishing his journal before the printers came to collect it. Hugh Cook, one month old, spent much of his time with his mother in the garden. Both the older boys were at Portsmouth Naval Academy under instruction. Then, early on the morning of 24 June, Sandwich's carriage arrived at the door with Omai its solitary passenger; thankfully, his luggage had earlier been stowed in the *Resolution*. We can only imagine Omai's deep bow to Elizabeth; perhaps he even kissed her hand, and gave her a touch on the cheek and compliments to Hugh in her arms. The carriage sped away and turned into Sydney Street to the river, where a boat awaited them. 'Omai left London with a mixture of regret and joy,' Cook was to write later.

At Chatham they were met by Captain Charles Proby, an old sea-dog with much fighting behind him, who was the Commissioner of the Navy Board at this important base. They dined together, and Proby ordered his yacht to carry them down to the Nore. Cook was greeted by his officers, and the men stood to attention as he was piped on board. The next day, 25 June, Cook weighed and made sail at noon, reaching the Downs at 8 a.m. the following day. Two boats had been completed for them at Deal, and these were brought on board. A large crowd had collected along the shore, less to view the famous ship and her famous captain than to catch a glimpse of the famous Polynesian. But Omai, never usually one to be shy of an audience, failed to appear on deck. He was no doubt seasick.

An uneventful voyage with favourable winds brought the *Resolution* into Plymouth Sound on 30 June. There were, as always, last-minute tasks, like taking on fresh water, provisions, port wine, rum and brandy, and receiving on board the Royal Marines. These were more numerous than before with Lieutenant Molesworth Phillips leading a sergeant, two corporals, a drummer and fifteen privates. It seemed that the Board was taking precautions against possible trouble on the North American west coast.

The existing trouble on the American east coast was signalled by the arrival in the Sound, sheltering from foul weather, of no fewer than sixty-two transports containing an entire division of mercenary Hessian troops with horse bound for the revolutionary war. They were escorted by three warships.

It could not but occur to us as a singular and affecting circumstance [ran the entry in Cook's published journal] that at the very instant of our departure upon a voyage, the object of which was to benefit Europe by making fresh discoveries in North America, there should be the unhappy necessity of employing others of his Majesty's ships, and of conveying numerous bodies of land forces, to secure the obedience of those parts of that continent which had been discovered and settled by our countrymen in the last century.*

---

* However appropriate, these words were actually introduced into Cook's journal of the third voyage by the editor, Dr John Douglas.

The *Discovery* was also safely in Plymouth Sound, anchored a short distance from the *Resolution*'s anchorage. Burney had had a satisfactory voyage from the Thames estuary and had already asserted his authority by having a man lashed for 'absenting himself from the ship and selling his clothes'. But there was still no sign of Clerke. Cook fretted. He wanted to be away. Then, as he wrote on 8 July, 'Received by express my instructions for the voyage and an order to proceed to the Cape of Good Hope with the *Resolution*, and to leave an order for Clerke to follow as soon as he joined his ship, he being at this time in London.'

COOK MUST SURELY HAVE KNOWN the reason why Clerke was still in London and unable to take up the command he so much cherished. For Lieutenant Charles Clerke was in prison. His improvident elder brother, Sir John Clerke RN, had sailed off to the West Indies, leaving behind debts for which Charles had stood surety. He was on board his ship at Deptford when the King's Bench officers arrested him and took him away to the King's Bench prison in St George's Fields. Every effort was made to have him released – by the Navy in the person of Lord Sandwich himself, by the House of Commons in the person of the Speaker – all to no avail.

Clerke was in this foul-smelling, unhealthy place of confinement for several weeks. 'There's a fatality attends my every undertaking,' he wrote in despair to Banks, who was as unsuccessful as everyone else in having him released. At the same time, he added determinedly, 'I'm resolved to decamp without beat of drum, and if I can outsail the Israelites, get to sea and make every return in my power.'

It was not until the end of July that he bribed or climbed his way out of the prison and hastened down to Plymouth. 'Follow me to the Cape of Good Hope without loss of time,' Cook had instructed him. Jem Burney greeted him thankfully and warmly. The *Discovery* was ready to sail. 'Huzza my boys, heave away,' Clerke is reported to have called out, 'I shall get hold of him [Cook] I fear not.' He was in a state of euphoria at his escape and at the prospect of another long sea voyage with all the discoveries they would make under the command of his beloved James Cook.

Clerke had rid himself of his brother's debts, but, alas, had acquired something worse in their place – the fatal seeds of tuberculosis.

COOK HAD FINALLY GOT AWAY on 12 July. The winds were not favourable and he had to ply down-Channel. It was a case of the old saying about Plymouth weather:

A Stalled Departure

The west wind always brings wet weather
The east wind wet and cold together;
The south wind surely brings us rain,
The north wind blows it back again.

But Lieutenant King noted optimistically: 'It was on this day four years ago that Captain Cook sailed in this ship from Plymouth on the expedition in search of a southern continent. The singularity of the circumstance makes us look upon it as an omen of a like prosperous voyage.'

Lieutenant Williamson sounded an ominous and gloomier note: 'The rain pouring into the officers' cabins through the ship's sides to the destruction of everything therein: a barbarous neglect of the officers in Deptford yard . . .'

In London, Gibbon's *Decline and Fall* . . . had just been published.

22

Delays and More Delays

THE POOR CONDITION OF THE *Resolution* and the burden of King
George's farm animals both made themselves evident from the very
outset of this voyage. The forward sail room and store rooms became
soaked by leaking water with the first rough weather; and rougher
weather in the Bay of Biscay caused damage to the hay and corn for
the livestock, which made necessary a halt at Tenerife. They therefore
anchored in the roads of St Cruz on 1 August.

They enjoyed three relaxing days there, which allowed Anderson
to compile a catalogue of the chief features and sights of the island.
He noted, amongst much else, that the trade of brandy for North
American grain had all but ceased as a result of the revolutionary
war. Therefore, Cook was able to buy the spirit at a most favourable
rate, though it was, he found later, of poor quality.

They were at sea again on 4 August and continued south until the
evening of 10 August, when

> about nine at night saw the island of Bonavista about half a mile to the
> westward, when we hauled our wind and stood SEBE. Between 10 and 11
> [continued Anderson] we bore away steering first SE, and in a few minutes
> after S. A little after I was looking over the starboard quarter at the land
> as it still appeared very near, when I thought something like breakers
> appeared . . .

No one had been a greater admirer of Cook's navigational skill
and experience than Anderson. But what had led his captain to
allow his ship to get into such a hazardous situation? Moreover,
it was Cook's watch and he was on deck at the time. By chance,
he walked over to stand beside the surgeon just as Anderson was
about to shout a warning. Cook recognised the acute danger at once
and gave appropriately urgent orders. He described the alarming
incident:

> On Saturday 10 [August] at 9 o'clock in the evening we saw the island of

Bonavista bearing south distant little more than a league, though at this time we thought ourselves much further off, but this proved a mistake; for after hauling to the eastward till 12 o'clock to clear the sunken rocks that lie about a league from the SE point of the island, we found ourselves at that time close upon them, and did but just weather the breakers. Our situation for a few minutes was very alarming . . .

There was nothing but open sea for many days after this incident, and there were no more crises. But there came instead increasing evidence of Deptford neglect of the poor old *Resolution*. It was not only the sea that entered the ship through decking and the hull; days of heavy rain took their toll, too. Cook cursed and grumbled, complaining that he had particularly 'represented to the yard officers' the importance of securing the sail rooms, 'but it did not appear to me that anything had been done that could answer that end'. On previous voyages, including his numerous passages to North America, he would have checked not only the sail rooms but all obviously vulnerable parts of the ship, including the upper works and masts and yards before passing the vessel as seaworthy.

As soon as the weather allowed, the caulkers were set to work on the decks and undertake internal repairs. At the same time, what sails that had survived their soaking, and the men's clothes, were aired. Below decks was similarly aired with fires and smoke.

Of 1 September Anderson wrote: 'The afternoon was spent in the old ridiculous ceremony of ducking those who had not crossed the equator before.' The surgeon continued grumpily: 'This is one of those absurd customs which craft and inconsiderate levity has imposed on mankind and which every sensible person who has it in his power ought to suppress instead of encouraging.'* Bligh was even more condemnatory: 'We had the vile practice of ducking put in execution to afford some fun.' Bligh did not believe in fun.

The familiar configuration of Table Mountain and its neighbours appeared on the horizon on 17 October, and on the following day the *Resolution* for the third time anchored in the bay. Formalities were exchanged with van Plettenberg and the other officials. King George's tiresome stock was painstakingly sent ashore to graze and take exercise. Unfortunately, some local scoundrels set dogs among the sheep in their pen, and all but half a dozen were scattered, four of them being savaged.

To offset the misery of this mishap, the *Discovery* sailed into Table

---

* Bayly of the *Discovery* noted that Clerke, characteristically, gave the people a double allowance of grog to enable them to be merry and not to have any ducking.

Bay triumphantly on 1 November, Clerke having made a swifter passage by ten days than Cook. He was in the highest spirits, and his men climbed the rigging and gave three cheers for the *Resolution*'s men. He wasted no time in ordering six half-hogsheads of brandy and three puncheons (around 100 gallons) of wine.

From 18 October until 1 December the officers and men of the *Resolution* enjoyed what was in effect an early summer holiday at the Cape, living off fresh beef every day with all the fruit and vegetables this rich and beautiful colony could provide. It was spring weather and no one seemed to be in any hurry. Only the carpenters and caulkers had full-time occupation, and Cook never seemed to drive them much, inspecting the ship every day but occupying himself, like his officers, in social life ashore and going on horseback expeditions inland and to settlements like Stellenbosch, centre of the Cape wine trade.

Anderson describes one of these trips, when, on the return journey, they called by invitation on the owner of a farm:

This gentleman entertained us with the greatest hospitality . . . He received us with music and a band also played while we dined . . . He showed us his wine cellars, his orchards and vineyards, all of which I must own in what manner these industrious people could raise such plenty in a spot where I believe no other European nation would have attempted to settle . . .

Clerke and his officers and men lived the same relaxed life for their month at the Cape. There were plenty of compliant women in the busy port of Cape Town, and the men had the forward pay they had been given in Plymouth before they sailed.

Far from being relieved at the loss of almost all his sheep, Cook replaced them with Cape sheep, which were inferior, and in an excess of zeal for his monarch's farming cause, he 'added two young bulls, two heifers, two young stone horses, two mares, two rams, several ewes and goats and some rabbits and poultry, all of them intended for New Zealand, Otaheite and the neighbouring islands'. How all this livestock was to stand up to the sub-Antarctic climate facing them had yet to be seen. Moreover, although it is nowhere quantified, the fodder for all this livestock must have been prodigious in order to keep them alive until they reached Van Diemen's Land or New Zealand after the deviation to search for the French-discovered islands.

When the sloops put to sea out of Table Bay on 1 December, it was the first time they had sailed in company. There was not a man in the *Resolution* or *Discovery* who was not comforted and reassured by the sight of another sail, a steady reinforcement in the battle with the elements.

Anderson and Burney, Clerke and Cook himself, and many others who had been on the last voyage, recalled the sense of deprival, the sudden feeling of loneliness, caused by the two separations.

In the subsidiary task of finding the French-discovered islands Cook was greatly assisted by the chart Crozet had copied for him at the Cape when he had last been there. Cook never minded being a second discoverer, but on this occasion he had little need to make corrections to the islands' position. Captain Marion had stated an accurate position for the island to which he gave his name, and Cook checked it at 46° 53′ s, 37° 46′ E. Perhaps the visibility when Marion was here prohibited his sighting another smaller island to the north. Cook and Clerke sailed between them, Cook naming the more northerly island Prince Edward.* Cook failed to discover

with the assistance of our best glasses either tree or shrub on either of them. They seemed to have a rocky and bold shore and excepting the SE parts . . . a surface composed of barren mountains which rise to a considerable height, and whose summits and sides were covered with snow [it was mid-summer].

Ignoring the Crozet Islands, Cook now took his ships on a heading for Kerguelen, which was thought to be on the higher latitude of 49°s. M. de Kerguelen in 1772, like so many navigators before him, had been in search of the Great Southern Continent, but when he proved that it was an island, albeit a quite large one, claimed it as a possible base *en route* to future French dominions. The British Government, equally expansionist and competitive, had an equal need for bases for future trade. Cook recognised this, and for the need to make his own assessment of its suitability. Some of his officers did not appreciate this. They were more concerned with reaching the Pacific as soon as possible. Lieutenant King was amongst them. He, and others, had become concerned at the loss of time, and were fearful of missing the season when they sailed north to fulfil the first purpose of the voyage.

It was dreadfully foggy. Clerke and Cook, anxious not to become separated, fired signal guns every hour, 'sometimes oftener'. King recorded:

We look upon our present situation as very critical. We may, by standing on, should [Kerguelen] be small, miss it . . . In order to keep in a parallel, the Captain has since morning hauled on a wind. Although there is great

* George III's fourth son, later Duke of Kent, later still (1819) the father of the future Queen Victoria.

hazard in sailing in so thick a fog, yet to lie by till it clears would be losing more time I suppose than can possibly be spared. We . . . conceive that the smallest delay would hazard the loss of a season, and even wish the search for this land which has already, and may still longer, detain us . . .

The approach to Kerguelen, sometimes zig-zagging, was dangerous, and all the officers realised it. There were numerous outlying islands, each one a hazard looming out of fog and rain. There was scarcely time to plot and name them, but a high round rock was named Bligh's Cap, because that was what it resembled. 'There ran a prodigious sea that broke on all the shores in a frightful surf . . . We did but just weather it,' Cook agonised.

They saw the high mountains of Kerguelen first, the summits looming intermittently above the swirling fog. As they approached the coast with extreme caution, Cook recognised that this was at least the equal of the South Sandwich islands of the last voyage in its stark, rocky, treeless condition. It was, he and Williamson noted, productive of moss, patches of scurvy grass and great sweeps of saxifrage, the only brightness against a background of grey rock, white freshets, snow and ice.

Bligh went ahead in a boat and sounded an inlet. He signalled that they had a safe anchorage. It was 25 December and Cook called it Christmas Harbour, the whole dreadful island Desolation. There was no wood here, not enough for a toothpick, but plenty of water, an embarrassment of it, pouring from the rocky ravines and from the sky. They could almost have left the casks open on deck and they might have half-filled them. Instead, every boat was launched, piled high with casks. Besides filling them, the men knocked the tame little rockhopper penguins on the head, part for sport, part for dinner, at which they were found to be acceptable if carefully cooked. There was a seal slaughter, too, for lamp oil from the blubber. It might be Christmas Day but there was no fresh roast beef for the men, only a double ration of rum or brandy, according to taste, and roast penguin.

Surely no man had ever been here. Why would they come? Yet, one of the sailors wandering about on shore with nothing better to do brought back to Cook an empty bottle which he had found hanging to a rock on the north side of the harbour. It was sealed with wax, and inside was a sheet of parchment. Cook read:

Delays and More Delays

Cook flattened out the parchment and decisively wrote out in his neat hand on the reverse side

'I put it again into the bottle together with a silver 2 penny piece of 1772, covered the mouth of the bottle with a leaden cap,' he wrote, 'and the next morning placed it in a pile of stones erected for the purpose on a little eminence on the north shore of the harbour.' He then hoisted the British flag.

Desolation Island was not as cold as its latitude suggested, but the livestock did not flourish there, though never short of fodder. Perhaps the beasts were seized with dejection. Certainly, it was not much of a life on board the *Resolution* compared with one of King George's farms, or the rolling veldt of the Cape. Many of the goats and three of the heifers died here.

After a few days, the two sloops pulled out of Christmas Harbour, but Cook had not done with this island yet. With no sign of haste, he continued along the full extent of the north side of the island, charting and naming features, while Bligh drew the coastline and made his own chart. Both were brilliant and could be used today in the unlikely event that anyone would wish to sail these waters. As for Cook's names, it seems in retrospect scarcely flattering to those who appear on charts of such an appalling coastline: Cumberland Bay, Point Pringle, Howe's Foreland, Port Palliser, Cape Sandwich, Point Charlotte, Royal Sound, Prince of Wales Foreland and Cape George, every one a sub-Antarctic nightmare.

Another week had passed, and they were already more than a month behind their timetable. They sailed on the last day of 1776, Gore noting thankfully, 'Took our leave of this cold, blustering, wet country of islands, bays and harbours.' Cook had determined to sail directly to Queen Charlotte Sound, arriving, he hoped, with much of the summer still remaining.

THE TWO SLOOPS made good sailing for the first week of this long leg to New Zealand, which was to be the rendezvous if, like the *Adventure* before, the *Discovery* became separated in the fogs of the southern Indian Ocean. But Clerke was no Furneaux, and they remained close together, bowling along on the trade winds. Then on 19 January an early morning squall struck hard, carrying away the *Resolution*'s fore topmast and topgallant mast. Deptford again! How Cook cursed as they fought for a whole day to clear the wreck of rigging, sail and broken masts, and secure a spare topmast.

Whether it was this incident that caused Cook to change his plan, or his old curiosity, we do not know, but, making as an excuse the need for wood, water and (urgently) fodder, he altered course more to the NE, heading for Tasman's and Furneaux's Adventure Bay in Van Diemen's Land.

Adventure Bay has changed neither in name nor appearance over the two hundred and more years since Cook sighted Tasman Head on Bruni Island, the gateway to this bay a few miles to the north. The bay is an almost perfect semi-circle of sandy beach fringed by dense forest, and broken here and there by freshets running down from the hills. Furneaux had been right to report on it so favourably. It was paradise by contrast with the hell of Desolation Island.

Cook and Clerke went through the usual procedure of sending parties ashore, well guarded by marines, to search for the products they most needed. No inhabitants were to be seen, only the smoke of their fires inland. Understanding that they would be here for some days, Bayly set up his tent observatory. Anderson and Nelson went botanising.

William Bligh, as always, busied himself charting and drawing this bay, the adjacent Storm Bay and the fractured coastline of the Tasman peninsula. He took no part in, nor even witnessed, the odd goings-on along the shore of Adventure Bay. The Aborigines soon made an appearance, in twittering, nervous groups. They were smaller and darker than their counterparts in New Holland, stark naked, only the women with babies having a kangaroo skin over their shoulders to cradle their infants. These same women submitted to the closest examination by the men without any sign of self-consciousness. But when one or two of the *Discovery*'s men made indiscreet advances, in spite of the women's unwashed, lice-covered, painted bodies, an elder of the tribe appeared very shocked and despatched them back into the forest.

On this same beach outing Omai had the time of his life. First he indicated that an Aborigine should throw his pointed stick at a target some twenty yards distant. Samwell tells us that he threw it 'in the same manner that the rabble in England throw at cocks'. Omai at once seized the opportunity of showing off, something to which he was strongly addicted, raised his musket and fired. The natives fled like starlings into the forest, their hands over their ears. Later in the day Omai shared with Samwell a fancy for a particular Aborigine, a hyperactive hunchback who celebrated the arrival of the two ships by leaping about with joy and excitement like some circus clown. Omai wanted to give him a gift and chose some cloth. There then followed the bizarre ceremony of a Westernised Polynesian decorating a Melanesian Negritoid with a length of white English cloth, cut Tahitian style, on a Van Diemen's Land beach. Omai failed to appreciate the irony and just thought it very funny.

Most of the men were passive and dull, however. Anderson recorded that they just 'played with their penises, as a child would with any bauble or a man twirl about the key of his watch while conversing with you'. Then, without any preliminaries, they would suddenly lie down and fall fast asleep on the sand in the burning midday sun. Nor did these amiable people seem to take any interest in a group of four marines, noted for their heavy drinking, who purloined all the bottles of spirits intended for the entire landing party. They made themselves paralytically drunk and later were thrown unceremoniously into a boat and winched back on board the *Discovery*. (They each received twelve lashes from the boatswain's mate the following day.)

However, the most surprising occurrence at Adventure Bay was not the behaviour of Omai, or the passivity of the Aborigines unless their women were molested, or their refusal to eat nothing but crustaceans when the sea was so rich in fine fish, but the sudden appearance on the beach of Cook himself. He visited Bayly's observatory, which was not yet fully set up, and pronounced: 'I have altered my mind. I intend to sail for New Zealand as soon as possible.' He required the astronomer to dismantle his observatory and bring his instruments on board.

No *sensible* reason appeared to account for this sudden change of plan. The carpenters had managed to fell one or two trees, but the grass-cutters had not succeeded in getting more than a nominal amount of fodder, which, only a day or two earlier, had been so urgently required for their livestock. At least the number of the animals was reduced by two when, at the last moment, Cook sent a sow and a pig ashore and presented them to the Aborigines. 'The instant they saw them,' according to Cook, 'they seized them by the ears like a dog and were for carrying them off immediately, with no other view as we could conceive but to kill them.' It was a final incident that was typical of the insane proceedings at Bruni Island.

COOK DEPARTED FROM ADVENTURE BAY firm in his conviction that it was 'the southern point of New Holland'. Before this time he had been doubtful about present-day Tasmania being part of present-day Australia. He had accepted Furneaux's contention that there was no strait separating Van Diemen's Land from New Holland, but he had also criticised him for not proving that to be the case. Now the *Resolution* was only a few days' sailing from what we now know as the Bass Strait. It could have been another Cook Strait if he had taken two or three days to coast north and then another day or two on a westerly course. The discovery would have made a neat parallel with his earlier revelation that North and South New Zealand were two separate islands. But he was suddenly imbued with this new sense of urgency. As so often when Cook was in a hurry, the elements worked on his side. After a mere eleven days' sailing, they sighted Rocks Point, so named on the first voyage, and less than fifty miles south from Cape Farewell, South Island.

The Maoris of Queen Charlotte Sound showed the same signs of nervousness exhibited during Cook's last visit there. It was at first plain that they regarded the arrival of the two ships as the prelude to a war of revenge. Cook was equally cautious, instructing that no boat should work outside Ship Cove without armed escort, especially – after Furneaux's experience – grass-cutting parties. The Cove itself rapidly assumed the appearance of a white man's settlement, if not permanent then not that of an overnight encampment. Bayly set up his observatory, the blacksmiths their forge and the carpenters their workshop. Many of the men preferred to sleep on shore and this was allowed so long as security was adequate. An elaborate refit of both sloops was put in hand, damaged masts and yards replaced.

One day Cook led an expedition of five boats, including two launches, far up the Sound. Clerke was among the officers, and of course Omai, darting about restlessly, chattering to anyone who would listen, though it was difficult to understand his Polynesian English. The ostensible purpose was to collect grass, and this was soon dealt with, both launches being filled in a short time. On the way back to the ships Cook led the boats into infamous Grass Cove. Here they were met by a minor chief Cook knew well and had called Pedro. He and another man were fully armed and showing 'manifest signs of fear'. Cook and Omai placated the men, offering presents, and soon relations between Cook and Pedro were restored to their old basis.

Cook then instructed Omai to question Pedro about the massacre. Cook later recorded:

They told us that while [Furneaux's] people were at victuals with several of the natives about them, some of the latter stole or snatched some bread and fish, for which they were beaten. This being resented, a quarrel ensued, in which two of the natives were shot dead by the only two muskets that were fired, for before they had time to discharge a third or reload those that were fired, they were all seized and knocked on the head.

Cook was confident that this was the correct version of events, and it was confirmed by another account later. He does not add the near certainty that Rowe and his men were under the influence of drink at the time, which would have led to short tempers, but there is no doubt that a boat party out for the day would have taken liquor with them for refreshment.

On 23 February, some two weeks after the sloops' arrival in the Sound, Cook made preparations to leave on the last leg of their voyage to Tahiti. Local chiefs and their people, who had formed a surrounding settlement in Ship Cove, once their fears had been banished, came on board for farewells. Two Maori boys had prevailed upon Cook to take them with him, and several of the chiefs also persuaded Cook to leave behind some of his stock. 'Two chiefs begged me for some goats and hogs,' Cook recorded. 'I accordingly gave to [one of them] two goats male and female, the latter with kid, and [to the second chief] two pigs a boar and a sow.' According to Midshipman Bill Charlton of the *Resolution*, Cook earlier had 'likewise set two couple of rabbits on shore', unknown to the natives. The consequences of this innocent enough action were beyond calculation.

COOK AND CLERKE BOTH KNEW that their expedition had 'lost its season', that is to say they could never reach the Arctic Circle and begin their probe for the North-West Passage in the summer of this year of 1777. It had been an unrealistic target even before they left England. Cook had long since recognised this, and it would account for the relaxed examination of Kerguelen and the deviation to Adventure Bay, but it would not account for the sudden attempts to speed their voyage. It is possible that the two commanders discussed this problem. Clerke may have confided in Burney or Bayly, Cook in King or Gore. But the lack of any serious concern in any of their journals, least of all Cook's, is puzzling.

If Cook still harboured any lingering hopes of reaching New Albion this coming summer, they must have been extinguished over the few weeks after leaving Queen Charlotte Sound on 25 February. For a captain who had been so consistently fortunate with his winds, it came as a shock to suffer day after day, with obstinate consistency, unfavourable winds, or breezes that scarcely gave the sloops any way. 'The wind continued invariably fixed at ESE seldom varying above two points on either one side or the other,' reported Cook on 17 March. 'It also blew very faint, so that it was the 27th before we crossed the Tropic . . .' 'These nasty light breezes', wrote Clerke in the *Discovery*, 'render this passage exceedingly tedious.'

This continued frustration brushed off on the men, who were as anxious to reach Tahiti as Cook himself. There were thefts of food, and the culprits could not be found. Cook lost his temper and cut the meat ration by half. The men refused any, Cook talked of mutinous proceedings. For a commander who had always cared so carefully for his men, this was strange behaviour.

The new course from New Zealand led to the discovery of new islands, Mangai and Atiu, both typical coral islands, the pounding of the reefs giving warning and sounding like distant thunder. Neither was productive of the water and fodder they now urgently needed after two months at sea. The scattered little Palmerston Islands yielded coconuts, scurvy grass and palm saplings, which were relished by the cattle.

The shortage of water worried Cook most. The *Resolution* had twenty-seven tons on board at New Zealand. Now (21 April) they were reduced to seven-and-a-half tons, the consumption by the cattle being prodigious. The men were rationed to two quarts daily. The distilling apparatus proved inefficient and the only way they could supplement their supplies was by spreading awnings during heavy rain. They caught three to four tons by this means in a week. The two sloops were now heading on an opposite course from the Society Islands, and the word soon got around that they were returning to the Tongan (or Friendly) Islands, where they knew that they could get all the water they needed and fresh provisions, too. Soon they were back at Nomuka, and on 1 May Clerke was writing with immense satisfaction: 'This day, having purchased among the canoes as much fresh pork, breadfruit, yams and plantains as would serve the people for the present, I stopped every species of their sea provisions, except the grog . . .' Cook was especially relieved that the men could now be ordered to wash their clothes.

They spent two-and-a-half months among these islands, a whole month from 10 June to 10 July at Tongatapu alone. Anderson and King spent much of the time ashore, studying equally the manners of the people and the plant life; Bligh was out in a boat every day, drawing and surveying. But wherever they went they were followed by thieving by the natives, like some plague. Cook was increasingly exasperated, and increasingly resorted to savage punishments, having the guilty flogged, in one case with five dozen lashes. Young Midshipman George Gilbert was not the only one to be shocked by their captain's savagery. He wrote:

This [thieving], which is very prevalent here, Captain Cook punished in a manner rather unbecoming of a European, viz by cutting off their ears, firing at them with small shot, or ball, as they were swimming or paddling to the shore; and suffering the people as he rowed after them to beat them with the oars, and stick the boat hook into them . . .

Clerke, who suffered equally in the *Discovery*, devised a simpler, less cruel and more effective punishment. He shaved half their heads, half their face and beard, and then slung them overboard to swim ashore and be mocked by their fellows.

It was a turbulent relationship, and puzzling to the Tongans. One day there would be a public lashing, the victim secured to a tree, the next the marines and their band, dressed in their regimentals, carried out evolutions and gave a concert for the locals' benefit. The Tongans were not much impressed. Nor was Bligh – 'a most ludicrous performance', he called it. A firework display was a little more successful. Then, after some particularly savage beatings of Tongans, Cook persuaded all the local chiefs to assemble, when he presented one with an English bull and cow, another with a Cape ram and two ewes, and a third with a horse and mare. Omai was then instructed to inform these chiefs that, 'there were no such animals within many months sail of them, that they had been brought at vast trouble and expense, and therefore they were not to kill any till they became very numerous, and, lastly, they and their children were to remember that they had them from the men of Britain'. This presentation in turn led to the theft of a kid and two turkey-cocks. Cook was outraged, rounded up the chiefs and held them hostage against the return of everything stolen since they had arrived.

WHAT WAS THIS EXPEDITION doing here, it might well be asked, and Clerke was not the only puzzled officer. What were they doing among these islands, which they had visited before anyway? They had all the fodder, food and water they needed. Rather than lay themselves open to more or less continuous thieving, leading in turn to violence and cruelty, why was not Cook heading for the Society Islands, thus relieving themselves of the burden of all King George's livestock?

Or, instead of remaining for one month at an island they already knew intimately, why was not Cook exploring and charting the other Friendly Islands? What had happened to that burning curiosity, that determination to record accurately more islands on the great wastes of the Pacific? There was no limit to these questions, and no answers to any of them – except from Cook himself, who would never be asked, even by his old friend Charlie Clerke.

At Tongatapu there was frequent talk about an island called Fidgee. All the Tongans knew about Fidgee.

The dogs at Tonga had been brought from Fidgee. The natives spoke in awe of the island. They were very fierce people always at war, possessed great weapons, great canoes, ate their captives, were famed warriors. Sometimes Tongans went to Fidgee to learn fighting prowess. Clerke even saw one of their canoes and the men who had sailed it from Fidgee, 'the masters of this part of the world'. He noted their curious ears from which the gristle had been cut out so that the loose flesh hung about their shoulders.

Cook also knew about this great island (today we spell it Fiji). He knew that it was only three days' sailing distant, according to the Tongans. Bligh could have found it, charted and drawn it, and returned all in three weeks. He was not given the opportunity.* Instead, on 17 July 1777, the *Resolution* and *Discovery* left the Friendly Islands on a southerly heading, Cook intending to approach Tahiti from the south, which he had previously found the best course. Also as before, Cook found it necessary to land on the south-east coast at Vaitepiha Bay, so short of fodder and water were they after their four-week-long voyage.

As always, the canoes were around them before they had dropped anchor. Among them was that of Omai's sister, loaded with provisions for her brother. There was a tearful reunion followed by Omai's presentation of a large number of red feathers which he had earlier accumulated in the Friendly Islands. These Tahitians not only wanted trade, but they also had news. Omai, now dressed half as a London boulevardier and half in Polynesian costume, listened to his compatriots and translated rapidly. Spaniards had been here, they informed Omai, with two ships. They had built a fort, erected a cross and claimed possession of the island for the King of Spain. They had

---

* He was, in the event, to do so twelve years later in the launch of the *Bounty*, into which he was cast by Fletcher Christian and his fellow mutineers.

left behind two priests from Lima, Omai translated, and had presented the islanders with cattle. The priests lived in a house but hardly ever emerged, and had gone home when another ship called.

Cook took this news as a personal affront. Although he had not been the first European at Tahiti, he now regarded the island proprietorially, himself as a plenipotentiary from the court of King George. Here at Tahiti he was a patriarchal figure with the power of life and death, an intimate of the great chiefs of the island. The chiefs at Vaitepiha, welcoming Cook with all the honours that he considered his due, expressed their disdain for the Spanish visit, and the Spaniards themselves. The Spaniards had boasted that Spain had conquered 'Bretanee', had 'erased the rascally breed from the face of the earth'. But here was 'King Toote' with two fine ships, living proof of continuing British power and prosperity.

Cook went ashore and discovered that the cattle was one tethered bull and the fort a frail, wooden structure already falling apart. He examined the cross they had erected, engraved with the words 'CHRISTUS VINCIT CAROLUS IMPERAT 1774'. He had it removed and replaced with another, carved by one of his carpenters: 'GEORGIUS TERTIUS REX ANNIS 1767, 1769, 1773, 1774 & 1777'.

23

Farewell Omai

COOK REMAINED AT THE SOCIETY ISLANDS for so long that it occurred to some of his officers that the prime purpose of the voyage had been forgotten. Meanwhile, the secondary purpose, the resettlement of Omai, took up much of their time, and almost to the end of their stay provided a non-stop tragi-comedy with Omai in the dual role of those earlier islanders, Trinculo and Caliban.

On first arrival in Matavai Bay Omai acknowledged no one but his brother-in-law and a minor chieftain of his earlier acquaintance. For their part, these two Tahitians failed to respond with any warmth to these overtures until Omai took them down to his cabin and disclosed the secrets of his immense luggage. Omai then revealed his drawerful of red feathers. As soon as word got about of this treasure, Omai became the centre of attention at Matavai Bay.

We get a glimpse of Omai during these first days at Tahiti from Samwell:

Omai prepared an elegant dinner ashore according to his own country fashion to which he invited Captain Cook and Clerke and the officers of both ships . . . While we stayed at Matavai he gave two or three of these dinners at which [King] Otoo and other chiefs were guests as well as our gentlemen. However, in general Omai did not pay that attention to Otoo and the rest of the royal family which it would have been in his interest to have done, but chose rather to associate with the blackguards of the island of which his brother-in-law was one of the chief. Among these he squandered most of his red feathers and other articles. Notwithstanding the admonitions he had to the contrary, he employed much of his time in acting the part of merry Andrew [buffoon], parading about in ludicrous masks and different dresses to the great admiration of the rabble.

The next day he might take the part of an English gentleman riding in London in all the correct dress. Cook and Clerke frequently rode along the black sandy beach at Matavai Bay, which greatly impressed

the locals, but when Omai joined and attempted to emulate them on
the third surviving horse, he would slide off frequently and have to be
helped back into the saddle, to the great amusement of the spectators.
(In spite of frequent instruction in England, he never did become
a rider.)

It so happened that soon after Cook's arrival, there were threats of
renewed war with the people of Eimeo, or Moorea, the spectacular
satellite island a few miles to the west of Tahiti. This coincided with
news that the Spaniards were back on the other side of the island.
On hearing this, Cook put his two sloops on a war footing, which
required the reinstatement of 4-pounder cannons from the holds.
Williamson was despatched on a reconnaissance trip in the cutter,
but found nothing. The imminent Polynesian hostilities also came to
nothing.

Meanwhile, Omai had put himself on a war footing, too. He had
acquired, probably by barter for red feathers, a war canoe of his
own. He named it, suitably enough, the *Royal George*, donned his full
medieval armour and had himself paddled out into Matavai Bay. Like
King Tosh at Spithead, he seemed about to review his fleet. Cook and
Clerke did not know whether to laugh or cry. 'Everyone had a full view
of him,' Cook recalled, 'but it did not draw their attention as might
be expected.'

The earlier threat of attack by Eimeo drew Cook's attention to that
island. In all the weeks since 1769 that he had been in Matavai Bay, he
had never visited the island with its saw-tooth silhouette. He had once
sent a cutter to reconnoitre the island, and the report it brought back
was of an unbroken reef and no anchorages. He now decided to see for
himself. He did not care to leave Omai amongst his own people until
he had been settled in, either at Tahiti or Huahine, so he despatched
him ahead as a member of a reconnaissance party to seek a suitable
anchorage. He travelled, of course, in the *Royal George* wearing his full
finery, a more modestly attired English officer at his side.

This party, on Tahitian advice, discovered that there we are two
similar inlets on the north coast of Moorea, each cutting deeply into
the near-4,000-foot volcanic peaks, both suitable anchorages and
more sheltered than any harbour on Tahiti. Cook chose the one
called Opunohu (the other is confusingly called Cook's Bay today).
Here was a paradise beyond compare. Eimeo stunned even the most
travelled, the most blasé of the officers and men of the two sloops.
Clear streams and a river poured into the bay, the slopes were a
mass of flowers and flowering shrubs, fruit of every description was
for the picking and the waters teemed with fish.

The sloops anchored and were hauled, close to, and secured by hawsers to flowering hibiscus trees. Although there were numerous and willing girls at Eimeo, the happiness of Cook's men was made complete by the arrival of their women from Tahiti. There had been much grief at Matavai Bay amongst the women who had formed special attachments to the men, some of them living on board for a month or more, contrary to Cook's usual prohibition. They had guessed, correctly as it turned out, that their men would not be coming back and there had been tearful farewells, but when they saw the *Resolution* and *Discovery* heading for Eimeo, they piled into canoes and headed for this satellite island.

For several days relations with the people of Eimeo remained friendly, and trading, mainly hogs for red feathers, was carried on satisfactorily. Anderson and Nelson went botanising, Webber painted the mountains. There was much love-making, not always in private. The King of the island turned up, whom Cook received solemnly and treated generously. Omai as translator was never more valuable. Then on the evening of the third day a messenger from the King asked if His Majesty could be given two goats, to which he had taken a special fancy. Cook refused the request, but sent the messenger away with other generous gifts.

Within twenty-four hours two goats in turn were stolen while grazing ashore. When told of this theft, Cook fell into a rage the like of which none of his officers had witnessed before. It was a frightening sight. Two canoes were seized and the local people were told that they would be burnt if the goats were not instantly returned. All trading at once ceased and the people fled into the hills. A cutter was despatched to the east, and returned, thankfully, with one of the goats. Cook was not in the least appeased. Of the following morning, 9 October, Samwell wrote:

The other goat not being restored and the chiefs of the island evidently the abetters if not the perpetrators of this theft, Captain Cook came to a resolution of punishing them severely for their treachery in order to put a stop at once to any further robberies . . .

Cook now embarked upon a punitive expedition as if going to full-scale war with the islanders. It consisted of a double-pronged attack. Williamson was despatched with three boats to the west, the crews armed with muskets, pistols and hangers, while Cook himself marched overland at the head of the ships' marines, Omai as translator at his side, and several of the 'young gentlemen', to make a rendez-vous with the sea party.

The terrain was very rough, the gradients steep, the heat at mid-day scarcely tolerable. Only glimpses were seen of the natives, flitting between the trees, always running away from this terrifying and unprecedented sight. Omai favoured shooting them and there was some difficulty in preventing him from doing so. Once a chief emerged and Cook told him that if the goat was not returned by a certain time, he would start burning houses and canoes.

When they reached the coast, where the settlements were all deserted, they took a brief rest and then set about their destruction. Smoke and flames were rising high in the sky from homes and canoes when Williamson arrived with his boats and reported with satisfaction that he had already destroyed twenty houses and numerous canoes. They all returned late in the evening in the boats, without the goat.

Cook's journal entry for the following day reads:

Early in the morning of the 10th I despatched one of Omai's men to [the King] to tell him if he did not send the goat I would not leave him a canoe on the island and that I would continue destroying till it came. And that the messenger might see I was in earnest, I sent the carpenters to break up three or four canoes that lay ashore at the head of the harbour . . . I afterward went to the next harbour, broke up three or four more and burnt as many and then returned on board about seven in the evening . . .

Later that same evening the wretched goat turned up. Cook claimed that it came from the area where he had been the day before. Samwell believed that the men who brought it in a canoe found it at Tahiti, the culprits coming from that island. The truth will never be known.

Nor will it ever be known what compulsion had seized Cook that he should have behaved in this astonishingly cruel and destructive manner. It was so out of character that we can only conclude that he had suffered some form of mental seizure. In his journal entry he writes only of this 'rather unfortunate affair . . . which could not be more regretted on the part of the natives than it was on mine'.

Thomas Edgar, the master of the *Discovery*, judged that the losses 'these poor people' suffered would affect them for years to come. In one incident alone eighteen large canoes with 100 or 120 paddles were destroyed, each one representing many months of work. Young Midshipman George Gilbert reported that neither tears nor entreaties of the natives could move Cook. He 'seemed to be very rigid in the performance of his order which everyone executed with the greatest reluctance, except Omai who was very officious in this business and wanted to fire upon the natives . . . all about such a trifle as a small goat.' He expressed the feelings of many officers and men when he wrote: 'I can't well account for Captain Cook's proceedings on this occasion, as they were so very different from his conduct in like cases on his former voyages.'

Only Samwell, who was something of a toady, expressed his full approval; while Clerke, who was feeling too ill to take any part in the proceedings, thought the people of Eimeo had brought it on themselves. But he had not seen the smoke and flames rising as high as the mountains from so many points that it was almost as if the island was the victim of a renewed volcano.

Loaded with some lengths of timber some far-sighted carpenters had saved from the canoe fires, with Omai's future home in mind, the *Resolution* and *Discovery* sailed out of their beautiful and once happy harbour, led by the *Royal George*, Canoe Captain Omai, as Edgar described him. They all knew that this was the last time he would be sailing with them and he made much of the occasion. In the event, it was nearly his last ever voyage. Jem Burney wrote that 'at 3 in the morning Omai fired a musket, which we imagined was intended as a signal for land: we learnt afterwards that his canoe had nearly overset in a squall by bad steerage and that his firing was meant to signify his distress'.

They sighted Huahine on the morning of 12 October. It was a short voyage but not a happy one. Aside from the near drowning of Omai and his men in the night, a fever had seized many of the *Resolution*'s men. Judging by descriptions at the time, it might have been yellow jaundice, and the superstitious could be forgiven for imagining that it was Polynesian revenge for all the unhappiness and destruction they had wrought at Eimeo.

Cook regarded sickness on board his ships almost as a sin, and as a reflection on his personal reputation. But he suffered from it in a mild form, too. Anderson and his two Welsh mates, Samwell and Robert Davies, did what they could for the worst of the sick, but this was mainly a matter of applying cold towels to fevered brows.

Besides this germ, there were other sicknesses to contend with in both ships. Charlie Clerke, pale, emaciated and coughing blood, needed no diagnosis from Anderson. He had tuberculosis. So had Anderson, who knew it, too, and that his was more advanced than Clerke's. The Scottish carpenter's mate, Alex McIntosh, had also been ill for some time, as was 'old man' Watman. Cook regretted not sending him home from Cape Town. And Quartermaster Tom Roberts was ill with dropsy.

Later, at Huahine, Anderson and Clerke discussed their mutual sickness. Anderson, the authority, made the point that the cold of the higher latitudes of the north would certainly exacerbate their tuberculosis, their *phthisis pulmonum.* Anderson had diagnosed his fatal disease at Tenerife and had noted the damaging effect of the cold at Kerguelen. In the benign climate of the Society Islands they might live for some time, even perhaps be cured, though that was unlikely. Arctic air would kill them both within months. They decided to ask Cook to leave them behind.

There is one last sorrowful footnote to the Eimeo affair. A stowaway was discovered below decks in the *Resolution,* and the native was holding a stolen object. Cook reverted to the state of anger which had consumed him for two days at the island. Lieutenant King was within earshot when he ordered the man to be taken to the barber to be shaved and have both his ears cut off.

After the barber had finished with his head [wrote King], 'he began to execute the other part of his orders, and would in a short time have completed it. Luckily for the fellow's ears, an officer [King himself] was looking on and stopped the barber . . . and the fellow escaped with the lobe of one ear cut away, and was then made to swim to the shore . . .

As soon as they landed Cook put in hand arrangements to settle in Omai. The young chief of the island favoured granting Omai as much land as he wanted, but Cook sensibly insisted on only a small plot at the water's edge with room for a vegetable garden behind the site of his house. And he insisted on paying for it with some fine axes. The carpenters of both ships rigged up a house in no time, using a minimum of nails in anticipation of their being stolen. Planks from the destroyed canoes allowed for an attic floor. This Omai used as a store for his armour suit, his toy soldiers, his sprung serpent, organ and other precious possessions. Working in shifts, sailors dug over the garden and then planted it with pineapples, vines, melons and numerous seeds. Cook himself planted a shaddock tree.

The house had a front door with lock and key, and above it one of the carpenters carved GEORGE TERTIUS REX 2nd NOVEMBRIUS 1777. Cook and some of his officers were several times invited for dinner, served up by the two Maori boys who were to act as personal servants to Omai, although they had wished to be taken to England. The surviving animals, a mare and stallion and some pigs and goats, were contained in a paddock.

Omai regarded his establishment as a miniature of the fine English estates he had so frequently visited in the past, and for many years to come this corner of Huahine was known locally as Baritani. Cook had done what he had been instructed to do, but he had little hope that the house and the garden would last long. Jealousy and the foolishness of its owner, he feared, would bring about the downfall of the house of Omai.*

On the same afternoon when the carpenters secured Omai's door plate, the two sloops sailed slowly out to sea from their anchorage. On board the *Resolution* was Omai, in his finest clothes and putting on a brave face, shaking in turn the hands of the officers and his other friends. 'He sustained himself with manly resolution till he came to me,' Cook reported. Then he threw his arms round the neck of the man to whom he owed so much and burst into tears. King led him away gently to the head of the gangway and down to the waiting boat. King retold later that the Tahitian wept all the way to the *Royal George*, where he joined his crew and the two Maori boys, who were almost equally distressed. The light was falling over the island when Cook looked back for the last time and saw Omai standing at the prow of his canoe, arms held high, like some carved figurehead.

No one, least of all Cook's own officers, understood why they now visited Raiatea. They knew the island well, had surveyed it, knew most of the chiefs, and certainly wanted for neither provisions, wood nor water. The ships were in good order, the men prepared for the long journey ahead of them. Nothing was gained by this visit, and any affection the islanders may have retained from the earlier visit was dissipated through the usual thieving and the unusually cruel punishments meted out to the guilty, and to Cook's own people judged guilty of neglect.

To the increasing astonishment of his officers, Cook announced that they would next call at Bora-Bora. The reason for this further delay was to hunt for an anchor which Bougainville had reported he had lost in the harbour. They had no need of an anchor, but Cook reckoned that they had great need of its iron in order to fashion axes for trading with the natives of New Albion. The anchor was indeed recovered, or part of it, and what was left made few axes. It was at this island, too, that the girls, by now all with steady paramours, were at last put ashore, amid much lamentation.

By this time, 8 December 1777, the expedition's timetable was in complete disarray. The Admiralty instructions called for them to have sailed from the Society Islands not later than the previous February 1777. They had lost one summer season in the Arctic. Now there was a real risk of losing another.

---

* Omai later gained short-lived prestige by turning the tide of battle with his muskets against an invasion from Raiatea, but was carried away by a fever shortly after. The Maori boys died soon after that, of loneliness and broken hearts.

Clerke and Anderson had decided after all to remain with their respective ships, but it was now clear to their fellow officers that they did not have very long to live. For Cook, the loss of these two old friends would indeed be serious.

THE INTERMITTENT BURSTS of urgency in the past were not renewed on this leg of the voyage north-east across the northern Pacific. A few days before Christmas, many tropic birds, boobies and men-o'-war birds were seen, all betokening land. Just after daybreak on 24 December, low land was sighted ahead. By noon it was only four miles distant, and with the aid of his glass Cook identified 'a few coconut trees . . . in two or three places, but in general the land had a very barren appearance'.

With turtle in mind for Christmas, Cook ordered his two sloops to anchor off a raging reef. He sent off a boat to reconnoitre. The petty officer in charge found no break in the reef. Cook was not satisfied, and the following morning, after naming the atoll Christmas Island, he sent off Bligh on a further reconnaissance. If anyone could find a way in, his sailing master would. Bligh soon returned having found a channel on the north side, though it was unlikely to be navigable by the sloops.

When they sailed to this entrance and anchored outside it, the channel proved to be scarcely navigable even by the boats. Midshipman James Trevenen was put in command of the small cutter and later recounted his experience:

The service was rather a perilous one, as we had to pull into the lagoon over a very high sea (which, however, never broke) through a narrow passage with which we were little acquainted, and where we could see the bottom the whole way; had any sunken rocks projected higher than the rest, we had been destroyed, but luckily we never encountered any. On every side of us swam sharks innumerable, and so voracious that they bit our oars and rudder, and I actually stuck my hanger into the back of one while he had the rudder in his teeth . . .

After relaxed days of turtling and fishing, Cook decided to remain even longer at this atoll in view of an imminent eclipse of the sun. He therefore went ashore on 30 December with micrometers and telescopes to set up an observatory. Clerke sounds a poignant note on this event:

Here happens an eclipse of the sun this forenoon, which Captain Cook, Mr Bailey &c are gone on shore to observe. I should be very happy to assist at it, but am sorry to have occasion to observe that my health is such as to render me totally incapable.

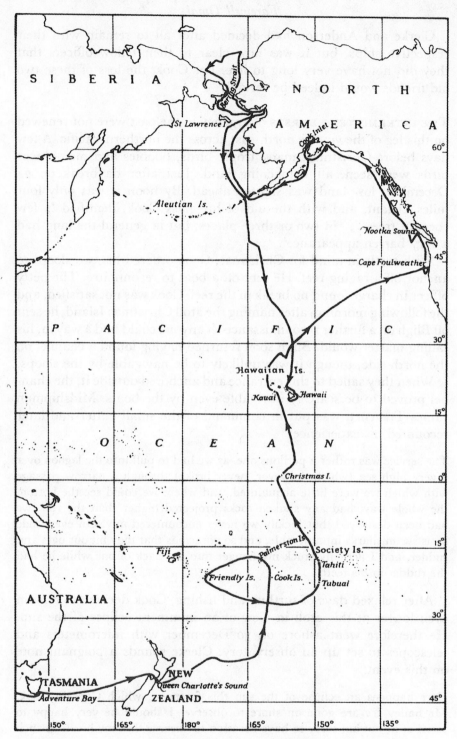

Cook's Last Voyage in the Pacific

As if time was still of no consequence, Cook remained at Christmas Island until 2 January 1778. He left behind a sealed bottle claiming the atoll for Britain and giving the names of his ships. (It remains a British colony to this day.) He took away in all 300 turtles, weighing on average ninety-five pounds each, 'all of the green kind and perhaps as good as any in the world'.

What they had not acquired at Christmas Island was water, and within a few days Clerke, in better health now, rationed his men to two quarts a day. He even felt able to dine with Cook during an extended calm. But mostly the winds were favourable, and at dawn on 18 January the look-out, Midshipman James Ward, cried 'Land!'

It could not be New Albion, which, according to his sketchy charts, Cook did not expect to reach for several weeks yet. Scarcely before Cook had noted that it had 'the appearance of being high land', the look-out called that he could see another island farther to the east. By identifying first Oahu, and then Kauai, this twenty-year-old midshipman could claim to be the first European to set eyes on the Hawaiian islands; while a few minutes later, John Gore became the first American to do so.

Cook knew that he was on the verge of one of his greatest discoveries. William Bligh, studying through his glass the undulating configuration of these islands, which he was to survey for the first time, along with the others in the archipelago, succumbed to the magic of discovery. He now understood how this had seized his captain and led him to volunteer for this third voyage to the Pacific.

A third, much smaller island, Niihau, bore NW. Cook headed for Kauai. Progress had been slow in light winds, but in the afternoon, 'We had now a fine breeze at EBN and I stood for the east end of the island.'

At dawn the following day, the sun was rising over Oahu, etching the volcanic mountains rising to an estimated 4,000 feet. Kauai was still directly ahead to the north, a spectacular sight with the rich, green coastline rising to the peaks of Mount Kawaikini, over 5,000 feet high. They were making for a headland where the south coast turned north-east at Makahuena. Soon they could identify the crowds of natives on this headland and other sightseeing points along the coast.

There were many canoes, too, breaking through the raging surf and heading towards the two sloops. Every officer and man of the *Resolution* and *Discovery* was on deck, wondering about the nature of these people, just as these Hawaiians showed caution and curiosity in about equal measure. The canoes held off for a while like shy animals surprised in a clearing. The sailors waved and called out to coax them nearer, and when one approached closer than the others, Cook held out temptingly a piece of red cloth, which he threw into the canoe as it came alongside. This was followed by a small bag of nails at the end of a rope. This action appeared to reassure the others, and as an equal gesture of friendship, they hurled handfuls of concealed stones, their ammunition, into the sea and came alongside.

There was only one language of the Pacific that the sailors had learned, most to the extent of a few words, others like Jem Burney with fluency. Burney was the first to call down to the men in the nearest canoe: 'What is the name of your island?' To his astonishment he was immediately told. The sailors then tried out words they had used frequently in New Zealand, the Society Islands and Easter Island, such as sweet potatoes, breadfruit, hogs and even different sorts of fish.

There was little wonder among these Hawaiians that these visitors spoke their language. They had never heard any other language but their own. For them there was wonder enough in the arrival of these strangers at all, the wonder of their great ships arriving without notice or warning, the wonder of their gifts of nails and axes, red feathers and red cloth.*

When at last some of these Hawaiians could be persuaded to come on board, the officers noted their amazement at all that they saw compared to the indifference shown by other Polynesians, and especially by the Fuegian tribes. 'I never saw Indians so much astonished at entering a ship before,' Cook related. 'Their eyes were continually flying from object to object, the wildness of their looks and actions fully expressed their surprise and astonishment.'

King later took some of them down to the gunroom and noted the same amazed response. Also 'in their behaviour they were very fearful of giving offence, asking if they should sit down, or spit on the decks, and in all their conduct seemed to regard us as superior beings'.

Now that it was established that these people were indeed Polynesians, Cook awaited fatalistically for the inevitable thieving. It occurred at once, a butcher's cleaver being the first to go. Clerke had a disturbing experience in his cabin which was crowded with Hawaiians, one of whom seized a window support to take away.

* They understood and highly prized iron. Though no ship had ever called at any of the Hawaiian islands before this day, it was subsequently established that timbers from shipwrecks had been washed up on these shores. The trading route between Spanish America and Manila followed a northerly curve, with favourable tides and winds, which avoided the Hawaiian islands.

Instead, it caused the window to slam shut. This led to a panic exodus through the other windows, with all the glass being broken as they dived into the sea.

Several journal keepers attempted to put down in words their first impression of these people. Most agreed that their skin was darker than the Tahitians', closer to that of the Maoris. Clerke, in spite of his weakness, was characteristically more concerned with the appearance and manner of the women than the men:

The women, who are rather masculine and by no means to be compared with the Otaheite damsels, have an ugly fashion of cutting their hair short behind, almost as close as though it was shaved, and letting it grow long in front, which gives them a strange savage appearance. [They wear] a little piece of cloth about the middle, which falls down like a short petticoat.

The Welsh womaniser, Samwell, summed them up: 'They seem to have no more sense of modesty than the Otaheitian women, and in general they were as fine girls as any we had seen in the South Sea islands.'

On the other hand, the aesthete-philosopher Lieutenant King was concerned with the women's ceremonial dress and decoration: 'They wear feather ruffs round their necks, made of red, yellow and black feathers, separately and variously combined, besides bracelets made of thin plates of turtle shell strung together, the large teeth of boars, and some of fluted shape; also shell necklaces . . .'

Turning to the men, King told that they wore nothing but a loin cloth, while Edgar described them as 'not tall, but of strong, muscular make, and there was great variety in the shape of their visages'.

Williamson was put in charge of a shore party to reconnoitre for an anchorage. The lieutenant was a disastrous choice. Even before the boat's prow had touched the beach, it was surrounded by excited, jubilant Hawaiians, half hospitable, half covetous of any iron to be seen. Williamson, not the most courageous of men, lost his head and opened fire with ball at one of the nearest men. He later wrote without shame that 'he was a tall, handsome man about 40 years of age and seemed to be a chief', adding that the ball 'entering under his right pap, he instantly dropped down dead in the water'. Edgar, among those most outraged, described how the victim's body was lifted from the water and dragged away amidst much lamentation. Ship's corporal Bill Griffin described the incident as 'a cowardly, dastardly action'.

Back on board, Williamson chose not to mention the shooting to

Cook. Of course the captain heard about it, but, strangely, only after leaving these islands, when he fell into one of his terrible rages.

The two sloops now ranged west along the coast, searching for a good anchorage and eventually finding one off a settlement called Waimea.

As soon as the ships were anchored I went ashore with three boats [Cook wrote] to look for water and test the disposition of the inhabitants, several hundred of whom were assembled on a sandy beach before the village. The very instant I leaped ashore, they all fell flat on their faces, and remained in that humble posture till I made signs to rise.

Both the disposition of the inhabitants and the water were excellent, and under the favourable eye of the locals (and with their assistance) the casks were soon being filled at a pond of sweet water and rolled down to the boats. The trade was excellent. Clerke, in one of his better states of health, supervised the trading. He found it 'the cheapest market I ever saw . . . A moderate size nail will supply my ship's company very plentifully with excellent pork for the day.'

Feeling safe among these people, Cook, Anderson and Webber took a walk up a valley, 'conducted by one of the natives and attended by a tolerable train'. The island compared in beauty with Eimeo if not so dramatic. The agriculture was well-ordered, with tidy fields of tara among other crops. Cook gratified these Hawaiians by handing out nails with some ceremony.

The more they saw of Kauai the more they recognised how much it had in common with Tahiti, even to the design of the *maraes*, the treatment of the dead and other religious activities. But the weather broke the following night, with driving rain and a fierce wind that made their anchorage unsafe. With difficulty, they moved the sloops farther out. They had acquired between them nine tons of water at Waimea. Cook wanted more, and in spite of the rising seas, King and Williamson led three boats ashore for more water. They managed to get off with two more tons, but it was a hazardous business.

The weather became very vexatious and variable for several days, but at the same time that Cook was going through one of his phases of impatience to continue the voyage, he determined to acquire more water at the neighbouring island of Niihau to the west, where they had been driven by high winds. Here he sent Bligh ashore to search, and unusually for him he failed to find any and had great trouble with the surf and high seas.

Later, still not satisfied, Cook sent John Gore with three boats, and he had better success. But he could not get off again because of rising seas in the evening. A night ashore for his men was just what Cook most wanted to avoid. He had issued strict instructions that there was to be no intercourse with the women of these islands. Too many of his men had suffered gonorrhoea at the Society Islands, and he was anxious not to spread it to these innocent, new-found islands.

When the weather moderated, Cook himself went ashore at Niihau, finding it as pleasant an island as Kauai. He took with him 'a ram goat and two ewes, a boar and sow pig of the English breed, the seeds of melons, pumpkins and onions'. He was received with the same ceremonial abasement as at Kauai, and when it was time to go, both Hawaiians and the guests were satisfied with the visit and the trade it had led to. Only Cook himself was dissatisfied with the proceedings among the Hawaiian islands. The fever of anxiety about their timetable had intensified. 'After spending more time about these islands [five weeks] than was necessary to have answered all our purposes, we were obliged to leave them before we had completed our water . . .'

24

'Very Nice Pilotage'

CLERKE AND ANDERSON KNEW that they were sailing north to their graves. They were both philosophical about it, determined to continue their responsible work as commander and surgeon. We hear less of Anderson, but Clerke retained his perkiness through all the variables of his condition. On 21 February he writes:

We have been so long inhabitants of the torrid zone that we are all shaking with cold here with the temperature at 60. I depend on the assistance of a few good north-westers to give us a hearty rattling and bring us to our natural feelings a little, or Lord knows how we shall make ourselves acquainted with the frozen secrets of the Arctic.

But would they ever reach the Arctic, at least in this coming season, in order to explore its secrets? Cook was again fretting and having doubts. The farther north they sailed, the worse the weather became and the slower their progress. At last, after five weeks and on 5 March, John Gore observed stars on the water, 'a great number of little sparks which exhibited a fairy light and swam about very briskly'. Gore, the veteran American, had shown his prescience before, and at dawn on the following day, 6 March, 'the long looked for coast of New Albion [North America] was seen extending from NE to SE', observed Cook. At noon he put their position at 44° 33′ N 235° 20′ E. Later, he was able to report:

The land appeared to be of a moderate height, diversified with hill and valley and almost everywhere covered with wood. There was nothing remarkable about it, except one hill, whose elevated summit was flat. It bore from us east at noon.

They had found the North American west coast approximately halfway between present-day Vancouver and San Francisco, more precisely at the nearest coast to present-day Eugene, West Oregon, the mountain inland being St Mary's Peak (4,100 feet).

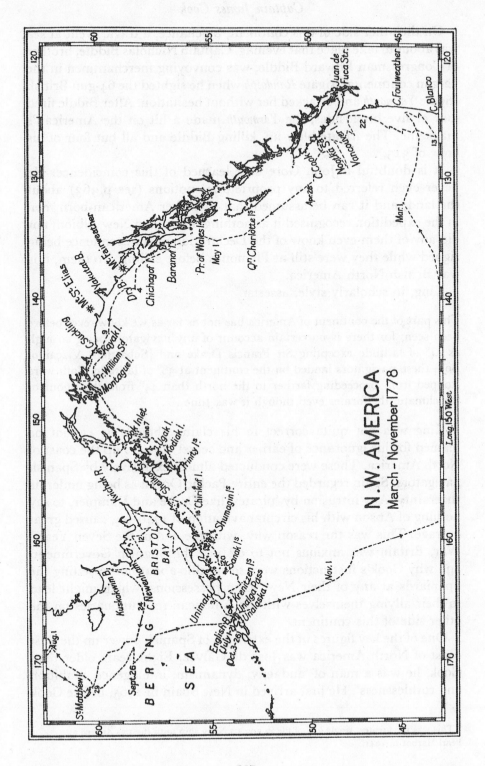

On the other side of this continent, by chance, a tragic event at sea was about to take place that evening. Captain Nicholas Biddle, brother of Congressman Edward Biddle, was convoying merchantmen in the 32-gun continental frigate *Randolph* when he sighted the 64-gun British frigate *Yarmouth* and attacked her without hesitation. After Biddle fired four or five broadsides, the *Yarmouth* made a hit on the American's magazine. The frigate blew up, killing Biddle and all but four of his crew of 315.*

It is doubtful if John Gore ever learned of this coincidence. He never even referred to any proprietorial notions (see p.363) about the land, and it can be assumed that the other American-born men in the expedition recognised it as nothing other than New Albion; nor did any of them even know of the Declaration of Independence being signed while they were still at Plymouth before sailing. To them, this was British North America.

King, in scholarly style, asserts:

This part of the continent of America has not as far as we know, ever before been seen; for there is no certain account of any navigators being so high as 44° of latitude excepting Sir Francis Drake and [Sebastian] Vizcaino. Both these navigators landed on the continent at 38° of latitude. Both were stopped from proceeding farther to the north than 44° from the rigour of the climate, the former even though it was June . . .

King was not quite correct in his claim, though he cannot be blamed for his ignorance of earlier and secret voyages up the coast of North America. These were conducted almost exclusively by Spanish navigators. Spain regarded the entire Pacific Ocean as being under its suzerainty. Any intrusion by 'pirates' like Drake and Dampier, to say nothing of Anson with his circumnavigation of 1740–44, caused great outrage. This was the reason why, with the end of the Seven Years' War, Britain was anxious not to disturb the Spanish Government, and why Cook's instructions were so specific about not upsetting the Spaniards at any of their New Spain possessions, which might lead to their allying themselves with the American revolutionaries on the other side of this continent.

One of the key figures in the extension of Spanish power up the west coast of North America was José de Gálvez. Eight years older than Cook, he was a man of 'audacity, dynamism, intelligence, ambition and ruthlessness'. He first arrived in New Spain in 1765, before Cook

---

* This was the greatest single loss of life in any US Navy ship until the USS *Arizona* at Pearl Harbor in 1941.

had embarked on his first voyage, charged by King Carlos III to report on and reform the administration and profitability of this colony.

Gálvez was especially concerned with the coastline north of Mexico, which was all called California. This was known to be unoccupied by anyone but local tribes, but was vulnerable to incursion, especially by the British, Dutch and Russians. The explorations of Vitus Bering were widely known, and with the British victory in Canada in 1763, there was a dual threat both overland and by sea from the British. Another concern was the European search for a north-east passage, which, if successful, would lead to an explosion of European trade in the North Pacific.

Gálvez's first step was to establish a base at Monterey, the harbour which had been discovered by Vizcaino, to whom Lieutenant King had referred in his journal entry. Vizcaino's voyage had taken place as early as 1602–3, but for 150 years it had remained unexploited, and San Diego was still the most northerly Spanish base on the west coast.

The Monterey operation proved successful, albeit at great cost. But the fear of Russian occupation farther north galvanised a new Viceroy, Antonio María de Bucareli, to press ahead and establish a new base at San Francisco, the harbour of which had recently been discovered. Bucareli, now determined to go even farther north, commissioned an experienced pilot called Juan Pérez to sail as far as the 60th parallel.

Pérez set out in January 1774, at a time when Cook was penetrating into the 60° s in the Antarctic. The voyage was a singular accomplishment, and Pérez reached about 55° N, the present Canadian–Alaskan boundary. But, unlike Cook in the south, he was crippled by scurvy amongst his men and he failed to take formal possession of the coastline as instructed. But he did succeed in identifying certain landmarks, including Nootka Sound, Vancouver Island, soon to be used as a base by Cook.

In the following year, 1775, when Cook returned home with a scurvy-free crew, another expedition commanded by Juan Bodega y Quadra pushed even farther north against great handicaps, especially scurvy, to 58° 30′, near present-day Juneau, Alaska. This gallantly led expedition sighted the mouth of the Columbia River and claimed the whole of the coastline in the name of Spain. Pérez served on this expedition, too, as a pilot, but became one of the numerous victims of scurvy and never returned home. It was again this sickness that prevented the charting of this coast, which would have supported Spain's tenuous claim. But no one, least of all Cook himself, could deny the enterprise and courage of these Spanish navigators, even if he could, and did, deny the Spanish claims.*

As IF TO DISCOURAGE further exploration by Cook's expedition, the weather became extremely hostile, so bad that the nearest point that could be made out through driving rain Cook named Cape Foulweather, and the two sloops were forced south. Whenever visibility permitted, 'each extreme of the land seemed to shoot out into a point', Cook wrote. He named all these points according to his custom, and whether or not under the influence of Spanish proximity, this firm Protestant officer named them after saints. There was Cape Perpetua on 7 March, after the African martyr who died on that day in 203 AD; and Cape Gregory on 12 March, the Feast Day of St Gregory, after whom the Gregorian Chant is named.

Cape Blanco, so named by Aguilar in 1603, a light-coloured cliff, proved the limit of their unintended drive to the south. Bayly described their condition:

Our situation was very disagreeable all the morning, we being within 5 or 6 leagues at most offshore, with a gale of wind and a great sea right on it as could blow, and had it increased it would have brought us under our courses, we must inevitably have gone on shore, and, it is highly probable, all perished.

Clerke's report was typically less gloom-laden, but he was not happy about their situation.

There have been 24 hours of heavy, dull, disagreeable weather. These western gales and the unsettled state of the weather, are a confounded nipper upon us; we can do nothing we would wish to do, but are reduced to the old remedy, patience . . .

However, by 22 March they had fought their way a substantial distance north, naming a prominent headland Cape Flattery. 'It is in the very latitude we were now in where geographers have placed the pretended *Strait of Juan de Fuca*, but we saw nothing like it, nor is there the least probability that ever any such thing existed,' Cook writes assertively. He also recorded 'a small opening in the land'

* I am indebted to Professor David J. Weber and his recent book, *The Spanish Frontier in North America*, for much of the information in the above paragraphs.

towards dusk, but darkness closed about it, and the sloops were thrust out to sea.*

It was almost a week before Cook could make a landfall again. At once (29 March) he sighted the entrance to two adjacent inlets. Both sloops were now desperately short of water, and there were repairs to be made that could be carried out only in harbour. He worked the *Resolution* towards the first of the two inlets, hoping to anchor within it before nightfall. Then the wind dropped to a calm which lasted so long that he gave orders for boats to tow them in. At once, and as if by magic, a breeze got up and gently nudged them into a vast bay, studded with islands, by a generosity of streams, and almost overwhelmed by high, snow-topped mountains. It was a near replica of Dusky Sound, South Island, New Zealand.

The evening air of St George's Sound,** as Cook named it, was richly scented with pine, and its freshness was matched by the purity of the water, as they discovered later.

The sky was full of birds, and the first sound after the anchor chains were silent was of whooping natives in massive canoes, bigger than anything they had seen in Polynesia, crowding about them, the paddlers in a great state of excitement and celebration.

Like a well-trained chorus without need for a signal, the canoeists all stood up when they were close alongside and began shouting at the tops of their voices. They were just shouting, it seemed, for the purpose of making a noise. All the sailors except for one or two sick were on deck to witness this sight and sound. King, the most vivid writer of the two crews, recorded:

We were surrounded by 30 or 40 [canoes]. It will require the assistance of one's imagination to have an adequate idea of the wild, savage appearance and actions of these first visitors, as it is difficult to describe the effect of gestures and motions. Their dark, copper-coloured bodies were so covered over with filth as to make it a doubt what was really the proper colour; their faces were daubed with red and black paint and grease, in no regular manner, but as their fancies led them; their hair was clotted also with dirt, and to make themselves either fine or frightful, many put on their hair

* This was no 'pretended' strait; it was, and is, Juan de Fuca's strait, which could have looked like 'a small opening' from the *Resolution*'s position in uncertain light. Cook made no attempt to explore it further owing to the weather conditions and onset of darkness. He was also in a hurry. This was a parallel to his failure to establish that Tasmania was an island earlier on this voyage. It has been suggested that de Fuca sailed up his strait for the length of Vancouver Island, found open sea at the other end, believed it to be the Atlantic and returned back down the strait,
** Note 'Saint', not 'King'; it was renamed Nootka Sound by the Admiralty later.

the down of young birds, or plaited it in seaweed or thin strips of bark dyed red . . .

St George's Sound provided vivid memories for all the visitors, and memories which would last all their lives, which were not long for Anderson and Clerke. For Anderson, it was the birds that gave him most pleasure. They varied from tiny humming-birds to giant albatrosses, geese, mallards, gulls, shags, bald eagles and red-breasted mergansers. Jem Burney loved the songs of the birds and contrived to make sense of the 'songs' of the Indians. Bligh and Edgar were out in their boats exploring the numerous creeks, islands and inlets.

Clerke, coughing heavily, went ashore several times with Cook to examine the settlements. Williamson was persuaded not to open fire on some pilfering natives. For most of the men, it was work that filled their waking hours, with a few breaks for trading: a single nail for the finest sea otter furs. The caulkers caulked; the carpenters found yet more evidence of criminal neglect by the men of Deptford, but were thankful to have unlimited and excellent timber at hand. Midshipman James Trevenen sheds a brief beam of light on this stage of the voyage when he and other midshipmen went out with their captain 'to take a view of the Sound':

. . . we rowed [Cook] not less than thirty miles during the day. We were fond of such excursions, although the labour of them was very great; as not only was this kind of duty more agreeable than the humdrum routine on board the ships, but as it gave us an opportunity of seeing different peoples and countries; and also another very principal consideration, we were sure of having plenty to eat and drink . . . Captain Cook also on these occasions would sometimes relax from his almost constant severity of disposition and condescended now and then to converse familiarly with us. But it was only for a time; as soon as on board the ship he became again a despot.

The two sloops weighed and cast off moorings on 26 April. The chief of the local tribe came on board the *Resolution* with a magnificent beaver-skin cloak for Cook, who reciprocated with a broad sword with a brass hilt. They were escorted out of the sound by many canoes, every paddler singing at the top of his voice a song of lamentation and fare-well. There was no lamenting on the part of the men of the *Resolution* and *Discovery*, however. They had mostly enjoyed their stay in New Albion – and some of the less fastidious among them had traded for the girls, giving them a good scrub down first – but their minds were set on the Arctic now, and the hope and expectation of finding a passage into the Atlantic: and so home to their share of the £20,000 reward.

By 1 May they were in 55° 20′ N and 500 miles nearer the Arctic

Circle, but it had been a rough passage and the *Resolution* had sprung a leak which would have to be dealt with. Fortunately the 60s were more pleasant than the 50s, 'the air so perfectly serene, the sea so perfectly smooth, and the weather altogether so perfectly pleasant,' Clerke commented. He was feeling better, too, unlike Anderson, who sat huddled in his cabin, shaking and unable to write.

On 12 May and on a westerly heading, they put into a promising sound, which Cook named Prince William after the King's third son, later King William IV. Here the *Resolution* was repaired. Gore named the entrance on his own chart – a rather rudimentary piece of cartography – Cape Hold-with-Hope. In his optimistic way, he felt certain that this would lead them through into the Arctic. Bligh pooh-poohed the idea and took the utmost pleasure in proving the American wrong. While the carpenters were busy, he took a boat and penetrated far enough to show it was only a large inlet. There was contact with the natives, the Eskimos* coming on board in numbers, either so loaded with furs for trade, looking like an invasion of bears and seals, or in an aggressive stance.

They weighed on 17 May, depressed that Bligh had been right in predicting a south-westerly trend of the rugged coastline. They followed it, at a discreet distance, fearful of being driven on shore by ever varying and near-gale winds. The prospect was taking on the guise of the south during one of Cook's penetrations into the uttermost Antarctic on his last voyage: mist turning to fog, drizzle to downpours, winds from all quarters and at all strengths, glimpses of mountains of indeterminate height, snow-capped summits here, snow down to the shore there.

It was a nightmare of confusion; they were days from their deadline of June, and this tip of the American continent was forcing them south again. Then suddenly, out of nowhere, there appeared a great open gulf, much wider than the last. There was an island in the centre of the opening. With this renewed encouragement, Gore named it Hope's Return. Officers and men were seized with optimism and excitement. King judged that this was the way into the Arctic. Clerke thought it 'a fine spacious opening', but warned that if it led nowhere, 'it might have a most unhappy effect upon this season's operations'.

Only William Bligh was emphatically against penetration. 'Here we have a great river, sir. No more,' he told his captain. Cook, now more emphatically than ever not the Cook of the previous voyages, remained

---

* They were identified by their facial characteristics and clothing, and the construction of their canoes, by sailors who had seen them in north-eastern Canada on earlier voyages.

uncertain, then compromised by ordering his two sloops to steer north on a reconnaissance into it. But even that was frustrated by contrary winds – and the days passed. They noted some hopeless-looking islands. Cook, in accordance with his state of mind, called them Barren Islands. Gore's name for them, also appropriately, was Entry Isles. But soon Gore began to have doubts: 'To the northward is a gulf, river or strait – the latter I hope.' But then, as if predestined, the skies cleared, and they could see nothing but open water ahead. Eskimos on shore pointed north as if to encourage them to persevere. Gore, all doubts dissolved, celebrated the expectation of seeing her soon and named a headland Nancy's Foreland, 'a fair foreland for a favourite female acquaintance'. The water was weighed and found to be as saline as the sea. But, a few days later, Clerke, out in a boat, 'made a discovery I was sorry to make, for I think it a very cogent argument against this being a strait betwixt two seas'. His more careful saline test close to the surface revealed the water to be pure and fresh.

Cook, to make sure, sent off two boats, one commanded by King, the other by Bligh. They found two inlets, north and east. Bligh took the north inlet (past present-day Anchorage) and found an end but no river, just many rivers and streams on both sides, tumbling down the mountainside. He was no doubt thinking, 'Of course, I was right!' King found much the same scene, and Cook named Bligh's Turnagain River. It was no river. It should have been Frustration Creek. They had been in this sound for sixteen days, every one wasted. And the wind which had opposed their progress up the inlet now turned to the south, and another week passed before they were back where Cook had decided to deviate up what is today called Cook Inlet.

Next came the fog again, as bad as any Cook had experienced in the Antarctic. Both sloops fired guns, sounded rattles and the men even shouted. They clung together in blind embrace. Momentary clearances revealed odd sights, once a tiny kayak, the bewildered paddler sheering off in terror; once a great volcano spewing smoke into a leaden sky; and once, on 18 June, the sky cleared altogether, allowing Cook to get a sighting. They were at 55° 18′ N, he reckoned, and still they were being forced south. They were following the warning finger which points down into the Pacific, the Alaska Peninsula, which in turn fractures into the Aleutian Islands.

Cook was behaving oddly again, almost as if he were at the end of his tether. One day he would be ultra cautious, passing by the Unimak passage, ten miles wide, which would have taken them out of the Pacific and into the Bering Sea, because he – and he alone – saw land beyond. Then on another day, 26 June, he horrified his own officers, and Bligh in particular, by sailing fast with the wind in fog which reduced visibility – according to the master – to no more than one hundred yards.

A sharp-eared look-out saved them. 'Breakers!' he shouted. Cook called for the lead. '28 fathoms.' '25 fathoms.' Cook ordered, 'Heave to!', and repeated it to the *Discovery*. When the fog cleared, they found themselves a few hundred yards from the breakers ahead, with more lethal rocks on both sides. They were sixty seconds from utmost disaster.

Clerke was heard to remark dryly, 'Very nice pilotage, considering our perfect ignorance of our situation and the total darkness which prevented our attaining any kind of knowledge of it.' Cook himself commented that providence 'had conducted us through between these rocks where I would not have ventured on a clear day, and to such an anchoring place that I could not have chosen a better'. Cook named the island beyond the breakers Providence. It was, in fact, Unalaska. A party which went ashore found amiable, tobacco-smoking Eskimos. It seemed that the Russians had provided the addictive leaf to ensure no lapse in fur trading. Samwell, ever the lusty opportunist, conceived the idea of trading tobacco for the women, whom he found 'very comely'.

At least they were through the Aleutians, but surely they had missed their season. They were running out of July as they coasted up Alaska towards the Bering Strait. It was now clear to all who saw him that Anderson would never see the Arctic in or out of season. Samwell did what he could to comfort his master, but he could do no more. The surgeon died in the afternoon of 3 August.

Everyone in the *Resolution* would miss him. 'He was a sensible young man,' wrote Cook, 'an agreeable companion, well skilled in his profession.' As soon as Clerke heard the next morning, he wrote a moving tribute which included these words: 'The death of this gentleman is a most unfortunate stroke to our expedition altogether; his distinguished abilities as a surgeon, and unbounded humanity, rendered him a most respectable member of our little society.' On a more prosaic level, Clerke lost his surgeon, John Law, who tranferred to the *Resolution* and Samwell was promoted surgeon and changed ships, too.

A few days later, on 9 August, the expedition reached the western limit of North America. Cook named it after the heir to the British throne, and the headland has retained the name Prince of Wales to this day. Low forest ashore soon rose to high peaks. Cook anchored but did not go ashore, where there was evidence of a settlement, and some of his people claimed that they saw figures among the trees. He wanted to fix his position with special care. He made it 65° 46′ N, 191° 45′ E.*

Cook ordered anchors weighed with the intention of heading north into the Arctic, but at once a great gale got up, driving them westwards at such a pace that in twelve hours they were swept from the American continent to within sight of Asia.

Cook went ashore in what he named St Lawrence Bay with his officers and a heavy escort of marines. There were many natives to greet them, fine, tall men armed with spears and bows and dressed from head to feet in furs. The women and children retreated. The men assumed an aggressive mode. Alone and revealing that he was unarmed, Cook walked towards them with the fearlessness he had shown on so many occasions like this. They backed away at first but lowered their spears and bows, and Cook succeeded in getting in amongst them, distributing beads and trinkets and, remembering his last hosts, tobacco.

These people were Mongoloid Chykchi, a friendly extrovert people, cheerful and honest in trading, fur hunters to the man. Suddenly, stacking their weapons, they began dancing to the beat of a drum which appeared from nowhere. Cook's men joined in, and on this beach, on this extremity of Asia, there was laughter and friendship as if in spontaneous celebration.

If this was one of the happiest calls, it was also one of the briefest. Cook wanted to be away. It was 11 August, long past their deadline, but still perhaps not too late.** The omens were good, as the weather was crystal clear, the temperature in the upper 30s. Neatly poised in the middle of the Bering Strait, they could see equal distances of coastline of Asia and America. How moved Anderson would have been at this moment, with just the right comment! But King was always a good second best:

We are in high spirits [he wrote], in seeing the land to the northward of these extremities [Cape Prince of Wales and East Cape] trend away so far to the north-east, and the other north-west, which bespeaks an open sea to the northward free of land and, we hope, of ice . . . All our sanguine hopes begin to revive, and we already begin to compute our situation from known parts of Baffin's Bay.

* Considering the hazy conditions, this was a pretty accurate calculation. Cape Prince of Wales is 65° 37′ N, 191° 54′ E.
** In fact, he could not have chosen a better time, June being much too early.

The Arctic, they all decided, was little different from the Antarctic, the weather as variable, the fogs as impenetrable and confusing, the rainstorms as ferocious. The difference – the improvement – was that now they had a coastline to follow, on the days they could see it. It was desolate low land and, puzzlingly, quite free of snow.

On 15 August the sun came out and it was relatively warm. The latitude, Cook and Bligh agreed, was 68° 18′ N. A swarm of little red phalaropes, weary from losing their way in the fog, settled thankfully on board, where many died. Two days later Cook got another observation: 70° 33′ N. Both sun and moon shone on them simultaneously but intermittently. Shortly before noon, 'we perceived a brightness in the northern horizon like that reflected from ice, commonly called the blink'. In anticipation, Cook named the cape nearby Icy Cape. Shortly after, in the early afternoon, the ice came into view through a chill mist. It stretched from horizon to horizon for as far as they could see, some twelve feet high, 'as compact as a wall', said Cook. At 70° 44′ N, less than half a degree from their latitude south where they had been halted finally by the ice in the Antarctic, they could penetrate no farther.

25

The Great Island

DURING THE NIGHT OF 18–19 AUGUST Cook and his men became increasingly aware of two strange and inharmonious sounds, a booming like a haphazardly struck heavy drum, and a deep croaking sound which scarcely altered in volume or pitch. Daylight revealed that the two sounds came from icefloes nudging one another on the lift and the fall of the sea, and from the throats of countless walruses perched upon the floes, packed so tightly in some cases as to overlap one another.

Cook, ever the opportunist when it came to fresh food, ordered out boats and armed crews. The massacre that followed was a messy and strenuous business, but soon the decks of both sloops were awash with blood from the 1,500-pound corpses. These were hung for twenty-four hours to drain off their oil, skinned, towed astern for another twelve hours, boiled for four hours, and finally cut into steaks and fried.

The result was judged disgusting by most. Many of the men simply could not keep the meat down. Trevenen likened it to train oil. Gilbert called it 'disgustful'. Petitions were drawn up requesting a return to salt rations. Cook fell into one of his rages, summoned the watches and called them 'damn'd mutinous scoundrels who will not face novelty'. Those who refused the 'steaks' were put on to ship's biscuit and nothing else. After a few days, the men began to collapse at their work. Cook was nearer to suffering a mutiny than at any time in his career as commander. He was as furious at lifting the ban on all food except ship's biscuit as he had been at imposing it.

The *Resolution*'s officers were puzzled and alarmed. Their apprehension increased when Cook told them that they were going to attempt a passage west, north of Siberia. Had their great and beloved captain, their navigator, lost his reason? When last seen the pack ice was advancing south – fifteen miles in ten hours, they had noted. Their season was June, and now it was almost September. When questioned, Cook merely replied, 'Those are my instructions.'

On 29 August they sighted the north Siberian coast through the mist. It was utterly featureless, a sort of non-land, not even snow-covered. But to the north, the pack ice, equally featureless, was also in sight and implacably advancing. Only then did Cook recognise how suicidal it would be to continue to head west. Again he called together all his men and addressed them:

You will know that the service we are on is to find a passage west if such exists if we fail to make Baffin's Bay. Now you see the season is too far advanced for either course, and we will head south from the ice and Arctic seas. We shall sail as fast as we can and I advise economy in all things for we shall be back for the season next year . . .

He proposed that they would sail back to New Albion for wooding, watering and replenishment of provisions, then proceed to St Peter and St Paul, the Russian outpost in Kamchatka.

King wrote, not surprisingly, that this announcement was received with 'general joy'. After passing through the Bering Strait – again in bright sunshine – Cook hugged the American coastline, past present-day Nome and thus into another great sound, wider by far than Nootka Sound, but much less productive. Cook did not linger. He had had another change of plan. They would not go to Kamchatka after all, but would winter instead at the Sandwich Islands, where the climate would be more benign and they would find all they wanted. However, he was also going to call at the Aleutian island where they had so nearly run aground on the way north. At Unalaska there was unlimited and varied fish, and friendly inhabitants. As soon as they anchored in their old harbour, boats went out for fish and in a few hours were back with enough for both sloops. One halibut, a particularly tasty fish, weighed 254 pounds.

A few days later two large salmon pies were delivered by an Aleut, along with a letter written in Russian. The pies were delicious, and John Ledyard, the marines corporal, volunteered to take a return gift of wines and spirits to the other side of the island where a Russian settlement had apparently been established. This led to much roistering between the fur traders and the officials and men, both at the settlement and on board the sloops, while the Russian governor arrived one day on board the *Resolution* with charts which Cook studied with the utmost interest. It was a highly profitable and enjoyable visit, but the temperature was falling every day, and they were all happy to be heading south again on 26 October.

Cook celebrated his fiftieth birthday on their second day at sea, although he was too busy to give much attention to it. They had left the Aleutians in rising winds and the following morning sailed into the teeth of a full gale. Three days later, when they could see anything, they were still in sight of Unalaska, just one league distant. Both ships were badly damaged, with lost sails and rigging, and they had suffered casualties among the men, too, Clerke having three men hurt and one – his personal servant, John Mackintosh – killed in a fall down the main hatchway.

When at last on 4 November the storm eased, Cook had to face the fact that, with all their efforts to remain together, the *Discovery* was out of sight. He was furious, but everyone else was cheerful and feeling better for the rising temperature and calmer seas. The *Discovery* would turn up for sure, they were saying. This first separation lasted for just twelve hours. At dawn, there she was, ten miles distant, and when later in the day she resumed station, they could see what a battering she had taken.

The voyage south was uneventful, and it was not until 26 November that there was anything of significance to report. But on that day, with the temperature in the 80s and enjoying an easterly trade wind, land was sighted dead ahead at dawn. It was evidently another Sandwich Island.

In the country was an elevated saddle hill* whose summit appeared above the clouds. From this hill the land fell in a gentle slope and terminated in a steep rocky coast against which the sea broke in a dreadful surf . . . It was not long before we saw people on several parts of the coast, some houses and plantations. The country seemed to be both well wooded and watered. The latter was seen falling into the sea in several places . . .

Their welcome was typically Polynesian, canoes cutting through the surf and paddling at great speed towards their sloops, coming alongside to enable the men to climb nimbly up the side and present themselves on deck with their offerings of fish and fruit and roots. Then, as the word spread, more and more came, some with pigs, then with the young women, displaying themselves provocatively. But Cook was not having them on board, and they resorted to mocking and grimacing.

For a while the *Resolution* and *Discovery* coasted west along the north coast of this island, which they learned was Maui, while the traffic with the island continued, the trading conducted in a friendly spirit. Like the Hawaiians of Kauai and Niihau, it was iron that they were

---

* This was the extinct volcano Haleakala (10,000 feet), with the north side of the lip long since collapsed.

chiefly interested in. This was confirmed when, on 30 November, a chief of great girth came on board with his entourage. His name was understood to be Terreeoboo, and Jem Burney noted that 'he had two long pieces of iron, shaped like skewers, well painted.'

Chief Terreeoboo was not a pretty sight: 'Of indeterminate age, disabled by the effects of drinking kava, eyes red, skin encrusted with scabs, and shaking all over as if from the palsy.' With wondering watery eyes, he stomped about the *Resolution*'s decks, wheezing at the effort, but amiably disposed. Before departing after two hours, he presented Cook with some piglets, then was hoisted out like a piece of awkward cargo.

Soon after Chief Terreeoboo had left on that last day of November, in the evening sun Cook discerned more land to the south, a massive island bigger by far than any he had discovered before in the Pacific. The Chief had left a number of his entourage behind, and one of these told Cook that this island was called Owhyhee.

Cook closed the land during the night, and at first light the spectacular north-east coastline of Hawaii was revealed: the tumbling cliffs, the deep valleys, the numerous waterfalls, the richness of the tilled hinterland rising to the ash-grey slopes of the volcanic summit of Mauna Kea and other peaks, covered with perpetual snow. (The highest peaks are almost 14,000 feet.)

Soon they could make out figures gathered on headlands, staring out to sea and waving white cloths. And then came the inevitable canoes, at their usual racing speed to be the first to trade. These, too, streamed white cloths. Cook ordered his ensign to be broken out in response. The trading of axes for pigs and fruit continued until 6 p.m., when they cheerfully packed up and paddled home.

Cook continued to ply south and then west round this great island, reckoning on trading more fruitfully by moving from community to community. All along this coast they were received with more respect than anywhere else in Pacific Polynesia; and everywhere with the waving of white cloths, many of them large streamers. Then there occurred two events on board the *Resolution* which puzzled and unsettled the officers as well as the people.

First Cook, for no explicable reason, reversed his severe prohibition against women coming on board. The young gentlemen especially were delighted and took full advantage of the relaxation. Second, as if to balance this privilege, Cook imposed a new restriction on an equally sensitive subject, the grog issue. Without any consultation, he rationed it to every second day, serving out in its place a concoction of beer made from their new ample supplies of sugar.

This he tried himself, finding it 'like new malt beer', his officers agreeing, but not the people. They refused to touch it, so Cook cut the grog ration entirely, at the same time summoning everyone for a dressing down.

He was clearly in one of the rages which they had witnessed with increasing unease over the past months:

So you will not drink this beer because it may be prejudicial to your health [he shouted at them]. It is something extraordinary that you should think it unwholesome when I and my officers have been drinking and benefiting greatly from it ... I can help you no more. Every innovation of mine – portable soup, sourkraut, all of them – have been designed by me to keep my people generally speaking free from the dreadful distemper, scurvy. I cannot help it if you choose not to drink this healthful decoction. You will be the sufferers. Had you drunk it, you would have been served grog every other day. Now the grog cask will be struck down in the hold and you can content yourselves with water. This is a very mutinous proceeding. In future you cannot expect the least indulgence from me.

The loss of liquor, exacerbated by the wind driving them far out to sea and far from the obliging women, brought the *Resolution* even closer to mutiny than the forced eating of walrus up in the Arctic. It is highly likely that Gore and King, both sensible officers, were aware of the dangerous mood of the men and prevailed upon their captain to lift the restriction.

By 19 December the wind had brought them back within five leagues of the extreme eastern point of the island. 'I had not a doubt we should weather it,' Cook noted. He then continued in his journal to describe yet one more crisis on this voyage which would never have been allowed to occur in earlier days:

At one o'clock in the morning [the wind] fell calm ... and left us at the mercy of a north-easterly swell which hove us fast towards the land, so that long before daylight we saw lights upon the shore which was not more than a league distant. The night was dark with thunder, lightning and rain ... At daybreak the coast was seen extending from NBW to SWBW, a dreadful surf broke upon the shore which was not more than half a league distant. It was evident we had been in the most imminent danger.

To compound their troubles, 'our main topsail split right in two', added King' ... 'the weather became squally, we split also our main topgallant sail'.

Luckily, the damage to sails and rigging occurred just after they had beaten off from the shore by the narrowest of margins. Fifteen minutes earlier and their fate would have been inevitable. Meanwhile, Clerke had kept the *Discovery* well to the north and well clear of the land, so that he was never in any danger.

During the last days leading up to Christmas, both the *Resolution* and *Discovery* were able to indulge in heavy trading, axes and knives, chisels and adzes, for fruit, vegetables and pigs. But it was a brief interlude; the weather became hostile again, and Cook determined to double the eastern cape, Kumukahi, in order to continue a circumnavigation of the island and find an anchorage. The south-eastern coast was as barren, right down to the sea, as the north-eastern coast had proved abundant in settlements and crops.

The sloops had become separated again, for a reason as inexplicable as the cause that brought them together again on 7 January. When Clerke took a boat to have discussion with his senior officer, he thought Cook looked wearier and revealed a shorter temper than ever before. He was saddened and anxious about this change in his old friend. As for Clerke himself, Cook noted a bad deterioration in his physical appearance. His cheeks were sunk, his skin like grey parchment, and there was much coughing. But not even the advanced stage of his tuberculosis could dim Clerke's spirit, and his conversation was as waggish and engaging as ever, which made the obvious imminence of his death all the more tragic to contemplate.

The chief topics of their talk were the shortage of water and the urgent need for a refit of their sloops. The *Discovery*, for instance, had not had her upper deck swabbed down for weeks because the water filtered straight through to the deck below.

Together, the two ships succeeded in doubling the extreme southerly point of the island, Kalae, and worked their way north along a coast as promising as the north-east of Hawaii, searching for an anchorage.

At length, on the morning of 16 January, 'at daybreak seeing the appearance of a bay,' wrote Cook, 'sent Mr Bligh with a boat from each ship to examine it, being at this time three leagues off. Canoes now began to come off from all parts, so that by 10 o'clock there were not less than a thousand about the two ships'. They had discovered a bay as neatly formed as Adventure Bay in Van Diemen's Land. They learned from the Hawaiians that it was called Kealakekua.

KEALAKEKUA BAY is like a considerable oblique bite into the western coast of Hawaii, providing protection as an anchorage from all but south-west gales, which Bligh judged from their brief experience of the island to be rare. He measured the inner basin of this bay at approximately a third of a league, and about half a league at the opening, Cook Point as it was to be called to the west and Palemano Point to the south.

There appeared to be few navigational hazards, just signs of a reef off the southern point. The bay's most prominent feature was a tall, black cliff which rose from a settlement called Kaawaloa on the north-west side of the bay to the eastern side, where Bligh reckoned it was as high as 400–500 feet. This dark cliff appeared to fall straight into the sea when he first noted it, but he later saw that at low tide a narrow pebble beach was exposed. The name of this bay derived from this dominant cliff, Kealakekua meaning 'path of the gods'. The real historic origin was more prosaic. One had only to look high above the cliff to the summit of Mauna Loa, almost the same height as Mauna Kea on the eastern side of the island. Clearly, the shudder of some volcanic upheaval had caused this landslip.

Close to the eastern end of this cliff, where it gave way to a steep, scrubby slope, Bligh identified what he believed to be a Tahiti-style *morai*, an eighteen-foot-high rectangular structure. He brought his boat close in shore where there appeared to be a safe landing place. He and Edgar, who as the *Discovery*'s master was in charge of the other boat, walked side by side boldly up the slope, followed by the oarsmen and the marines. They were greeted with proffered gifts and girls as at Kauai and Niihau. The two masters returned friendly signs and a word or two in Polynesian. But it was water they were after, and they found it soon enough, in the form of a pure pool fed by a stream, and within cask-rolling distance from the shore.

The light was fading when the two boats returned. Bligh reported to Cook. 'It is a good safe anchorage, sir, 14 fathoms with a sandy bottom where I sounded. There is pure water on the east side, here,' he added, pointing to the rough map he had made. 'And there is plentiful wood not too far inland . . .'

While Bligh and Edgar had been carrying out their survey, the *Resolution* and *Discovery* had been suffering a mass invasion on a scale they had never experienced before. Men and women of all ages swarmed over the waist rails of both sloops in such numbers that the *Discovery* took on a list. The Hawaiians' priorities were all too evident: trading and thieving for the men, seduction for the women, both activities carried on in a spirit of near hysteria. The decks of the sloops became the scene of Babylonian copulation and acquisitiveness.

Those who had nothing to trade resorted to thieving on a massive scale. In no time at all, the *Resolution* lost the lids of the ship's coppers, while other nimble Hawaiian young swimmers discovered the nails securing the hull sheathing and began prising them out.

PAINTED BY Wm HODGES.   ENGRAVED BY J. BASIRE

CAPTAIN JAMES COOK, F.R.S.

William Hodges observes age and weariness in the face of his captain at the termination of his second voyage.

LEFT James (Jem)
Burney, son of
musicologist Charles
Burney and brother of the
novelist and diarist,
Fanny.

BELOW Omai, the
Polynesian from the
Society Islands, brought
to London where he was
too much fêted for his own
good, but was returned
safely to his island home
by Cook on his third
voyage.

Contrasting anchorages on the third voyage:
(ABOVE) Adventure Bay, Bruni Island, Tasmania;
and, (BELOW) far north in Sandwich (Prince William)
Sound, east of present-day Anchorage, Alaska.

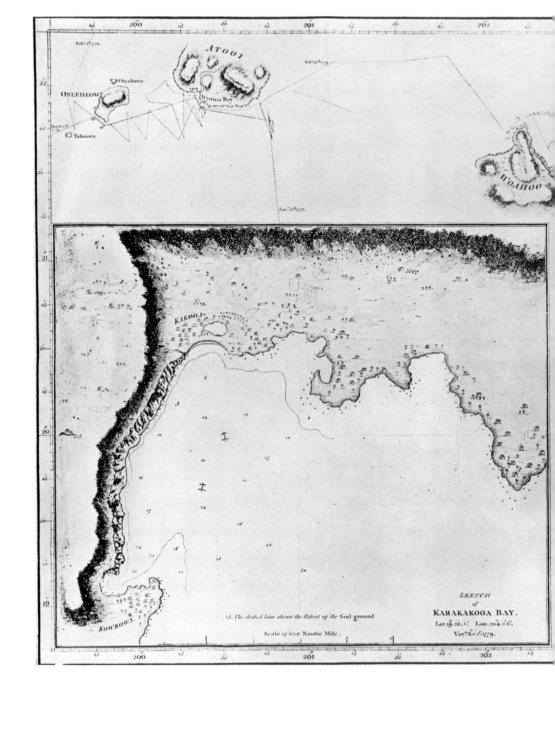

SKETCH
of
KARAKAKOOA BAY.

Lat 19.28.0'. Lon. 204.0'.6'.
Var.º.9.e.E.1779.

S. The dotted Line shews the Extent of the foul ground

Scale of ONE Nautic Mile.

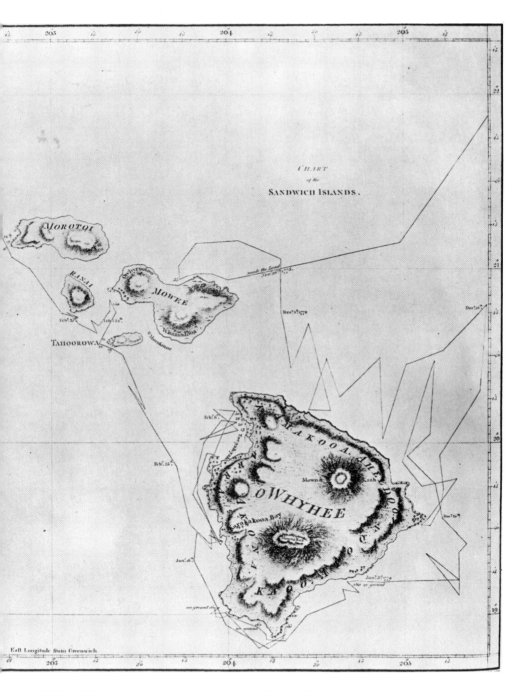

William Bligh's chart of the Sandwich Islands, showing
the course of the two sloops before and after the disaster
in Kealakekua (Karakakooa) Bay. Note the anchorage positions
of the two sloops within the bay.

Webber's drawing of the *Resolution* and *Discovery* off Icy Cape,
their most northerly position in their thwarted attempt
to break through the North-West Passage.

The two sloops at anchor in Kealakekua Bay.

The widow, Mrs Elizabeth Cook, who lost not only
her husband but all her children in the fifty-six years
she survived after Cook's death.

Johann Zoffany's famous rendering of the fight between Cook and his marines and the Hawaiian warriors of Kealakekua Bay, 14 February 1779. Cook fatally wounded lies centre.

Cook's earlier judgment on the honesty of these people was made to look ridiculous.

The marines were ordered to put a halt to the wholesale robbery with small shot. It had little deterrent effect; and it was not until two chiefs came on board, Kanina and Parea, that some semblance of order was regained. They did this by fierce instructions to leave, or, in some intractable cases, by picking up the women and hurling them overboard.

Greater authority was instituted by a holy priest who came on board the *Resolution*, to be received with proper respect by Cook and the officers. Like the chief they had met on the other side of the island, this priest was shaking from kava drinking, his skin peeling. He was introduced as High Priest Koa.

No sooner had the priest and Cook greeted one another than Cook became the subject of an elaborate ceremony, in which it was clear that he was regarded here as a god.

The gestures of respect were too elaborate and awesome for anything less. Koa first presented Cook with a small pig and two coconuts. He then rose from his kneeling position and called one of his aides, who handed over a red cloak. This Koa wrapped about Cook's shoulders, all the while repeating the word 'Orono'.

After Koa had left, Kanina and Parea indicated that Cook should follow them ashore for another ceremony. We can imagine Cook's weary acceptance of the need to suffer the ordeal. He had endured this sort of thing all over the Pacific for the sake of good relations with the inhabitants, but this time there was every indication that it was going to be longer and more elaborate than any before.

With Bayly and King in support, Cook landed at Kealakekua village on the eastern side of the bay and in the shadow of the cliff at its highest point. The first thing that struck them was the quiet with which they were greeted. After the earlier thunderous row on board the ships, this silence of the people was unsettling. All that disturbed it as they advanced towards the village, past hundreds of prostrated Hawaiians, was the repeated word 'Orono', uttered as if whispered on a light breeze.

Inevitably, their destination was the *morai* Bligh had marked on his map. It was bigger than any they had seen at Tahiti or elsewhere. Crudely carved images and human skulls looked down from the tops of numerous poles, and on the altar at one end were a number of sacrifices, including an enormous half-decayed hog. The entire *morai* area was surrounded by a high fence much in need of repair and with more carved images upon it.

Cook's journal ends before this ceremony so we have no account from him. King, however, describes what followed in great detail and over many pages. In brief, it consisted of incantations, murmured 'Orono's from ceremonially dressed sub-priests, the waving of wands tipped with dogs' hair, the sacrifice by Koa of a small pig by hurling it to the ground and then holding it over a fire, and the hazardous ascent to the top of the *morai* by a ladder. Here there was much more incanting and the presentation to Cook by Koa of another hog, wrapped in a ceremonial cloth.

King was greatly admiring of Cook's forbearance:

The captain descended and Koa led him to different images, said something to each but in a very ludicrous and slighting tone, except to the centre image, which was the only one covered in cloth . . . Before this image he prostrated himself, and afterwards kissed, and desired the captain to do the same, who was quite passive and suffered Koa to do with him as he chose.

The ceremony slowly developed into a feast, with much kava chewing and spitting. Finally, Cook gave up when offered pork which he suspected was from the decayed hog. Koa, observing his difficulty, obligingly chewed it for him and then handed it back. But Orono became the god that failed, albeit briefly.

When at last they were allowed to leave, King muttered to Cook, 'With all the encumbrances, sir, I should still have been better pleased to be received by the Friendly Islanders than here.'

Neither Cook nor King nor any other of the voyagers ever learned the reason for the reception at Hawaii as a welcoming-of-god ceremony. In fact, *Orono makua* was the god of Hawaii's season of abundance. Tradition had it that Orono himself would one day appear in a great canoe, to be greeted by the islanders with white banners. Orono would then coast the island from north to east, to south and to west, at the season of greatest abundance, which would be marked by ceremonies of a religious nature, and come to this bay. The *Resolution* and *Discovery* had arrived at Hawaii exactly on time, had processed round the island as legend had predicted and had been received by white banners, to which Orono had replied by breaking out his flag.

Moreover, Orono had come to Kealakekua, 'the path of the gods', and halted before the *morai* as predicted. The coincidence was beyond belief, but true.

THE FOLLOWING DAYS were occupied with the usual trading, ship repair and maintenance, exploring the environs, collecting of plants by David Nelson, and for many consorting with the women, who were as ardent as ever. Even Samwell and the young gentlemen were sexually satisfied.

Hundreds of hogs were salted down in casks for the Arctic six months hence. The greatest single contribution to the sloops' provisions stores arrived with the King of Hawaii, no less. High Priest Koa had given notice of this event and had informed Cook that this monarch wished to perform a ceremony at the shore encampment set up by Bayly and the carpenters.

The King of Hawaii's flotilla of mighty canoes was observed paddling round the headland and into Kealakekua Bay as predicted by one of Koa's priests. In the lead was the King's own sixty-foot-long catamaran. He sat at the rear, a magnificently dressed figure in cloak and elaborate cap decorated with multi-coloured feathers. The second canoe contained High Priest Koa, 'hunched and shaking as always, elaborately attired and surrounded by hideous busts made of basketwork. They were covered with multi-coloured feathers, the eyes represented by pearl oyster shells, the distorted mouths filled with the teeth of dogs.' The third canoe was stacked high with the finest provisions the island produced, from yams to hogs, homage to Orono, and a greater load in one boat than Cook had ever seen.

The King's canoe paused briefly alongside the *Resolution*, the monarch making no effort to communicate, and not even looking up from his crouched stance. It was indicated to Cook that this was merely the signal for him to follow the King ashore in his pinnace. The meeting between Cook and the King took place in Bayly's observatory, amidst all the astronomical clutter. James King, who had made all the arrangements ashore and drawn up a ceremonial guard of Royal Marines, thought it a bizarre venue. The Hawaiians had reasoned that this was Orono's *morai*, the telescopes and quadrants and other instruments sacred holy symbols. The King, flanked by his chieftain sons, and followed by more high chiefs, some of them of a ferocious mien, advanced into Bayly's tent.

It was not until this moment, when in turn the King tore off his cloak and put it around Cook's shoulders, and then lifted his hat and placed it on Cook's head, that he exposed his face for the first time. Like the high priest's, it was peeling and covered in sores, the eyes were red and watery, but the expression through the ravages of kava was happy and benign.

Cook recognised the shaking figure at once. It was Chief Terreeoboo, whom they had met at Maui. However, he was an even more august figure than a mere chief. He was King Terreeoboo of Hawaii and all these islands. They had earlier underestimated his rank.

HAD THIS CEREMONIAL VISIT of the King of Hawaii been more than the paying of obeisance by the supreme secular power of these islands to the recently arrived supreme religious power? It was a question no doubt posed by many of the more intelligent of the ships' companies after the catastrophe that lay ahead. Could it be that the visit was in anticipation of an expected imminent departure of Orono, that immense canoe-load of provisions a final tribute?

In the days that followed there was a marked diminution in the hysteria so evident in their early days in this bay. There was no lack of friendliness, the men felt perfectly safe wandering about ashore on their own; and there was certainly no shortage of willing women. But there was a noticeable increase in thieving. King and Phillips, ashore in the tabooed encampment, lost pewter plates and cutlery one night. Clerke resorted to flogging one persistent offender.

By the last days of January there were more direct hints that they might be overstaying their welcome. When Cook remarked that they hoped to be leaving soon, the King did not attempt to conceal his satisfaction. Several Hawaiians were seen to rub their stomachs on meeting a sailor, and even patting the visitor's stomach, indicating that they had fed well.

Cook was as keen to be away as the islanders were anxious for Orono to return to his heavenly home. Cook intended to stretch westwards to complete his survey of Hawaii and any other islands in the archipelago he had not already discovered, and let it be known on 1 February that he would be leaving in three days.

During those last days several events occurred which led to much speculation later. The first was the death of 'old man' Watman. The condition of his health had been variable throughout the voyage and had caused Cook as well as his many friends much anxiety. He had just been discharged from the tent for convalescents, which had been set up on shore, and pronounced fit for normal duties. Then, almost as soon as he was back on board the *Resolution*, he developed what Samwell diagnosed as a haemorrhage of the brain and soon died.

Priest Koa knew that a warm relationship existed between Cook and Watman and begged King to allow him to be buried at the *morai*, thus assuming he was a priest of some note. On 1 February, then, Cook with his officers and Watman's closest friends came ashore and participated in the Church of England ceremony and burial conducted by Cook. As the grave began to fill, Koa took over, conducting a Hawaiian service of great solemnity, while a dead pig, plantains and other provisions to help him on his last long journey were thrown into the grave. A post was then erected by Watman's shipmates and a board attached to it, by wooden plugs, on which had been carved:

Georgius tertius Rex 1779
Hic jacet Gulielmus Watman

As night fell, the mourners who had returned on board could hear the Hawaiian lamentations for their shipmate, AB William Watman from Reigate, Surrey.

On that same day Cook had conceived the notion of taking away as useful kindling the fencing round the *morai*. King was therefore instructed to ask Koa if he might buy this fencing, which was both extensive and half rotten. King wrote later: 'I must confess I had at first some doubts about the decency of the proposal, and was apprehensive.' Koa, it seemed, treated the request as of no importance and shrugged off the idea of payment. The fence was then rapidly demolished and, with the enthusiastic help of some of the islanders, carted down to the waiting boats, leaving the *morai* unguarded. The *Resolution*'s men included in the booty the carved images, which would be worth something back home. When King pointed out this pillage to Koa, the priest again appeared indifferent, taking back only the one image which both he and Cook had kissed during the earlier ceremony.

On the evening before departure, Koa approached King and asked him if, as the son of Orono – as he had apparently regarded him from the first – he would remain behind. Concealing his astonishment as well as he could, King politely refused – and did so again when Koa insisted that they could conceal him in the forest until Orono sailed to his paradise.

King later learned that Koa had approached Cook himself on the subject. Cook had procrastinated and promised to consider the request carefully when they returned to the bay, which seemed to have appeased the priest.

The last unexpected occurrence took place on the day the sloops sailed. Kitson described what followed:

On the appointed day [of departure] Captain Cook and Mr King were invited to Koa's residence by Terreeoboo, and on their arrival found the things they had given to the natives laid out on the ground, and at a short distance a large quantity of vegetables of every kind, and near them a large herd of pigs. The articles of exchange were then presented to the King, who set on one side about one-third, presumably for his own use, and then the vegetables and pigs were handed over to Cook. Mr King says, 'We were astonished at the value and magnitude of this present, which far exceeded everything of the kind we had seen, either at the Friendly or Society Islands.'

King was understandably astonished. For some time the islanders had made it clear that they had provided all that could be spared of provisions from their limited resources. And now they were being offered yet another great consignment, greater even than King Terreeoboo's offering from his canoe.

When the time came for departure, the ships unmoored and a great armada of canoes put off from the shore, with every show of lamentation from the paddlers and passengers. Ashore, the entire remaining population of the bay lined the rocks and the headlands, many waving white cloths. Koa had begged successfully to be allowed to remain on board with Cook as far as Maui, their next destination.

For Cook's men there was a strong measure of regret at parting after the contentment occasioned by this visit. For the Hawaiians, it had been a strange two and a half weeks, busy, emotional, traumatic even, like no other period in their lives or in their history: an unpredicted divine descent upon the steady round of the seasons; an event of great satisfaction paid for at a great price [in their food reserves].

26

Death among the Rocks

THE EXPEDITION'S DEPARTURE FROM KEALAKEKUA BAY on 4 February was slow, serene and emotional. There was almost no wind, and from among the countless canoes following them, Cook and Clerke were content to allow both priests and women on board, their canoes towing behind the *Resolution* and *Discovery*. Even the King came briefly on board to bid a final farewell to Orono. High Priest Koa was another visitor. He told Cook and his officers that he had changed his name to High Priest Bretannee as a celebration of the visit.

By the early morning of 6 February, when they were approaching the northern tip of the island, Upolu Point, Cook sighted a deep bay which promised to make a good anchorage and provide both wood and water in abundance for future mariners. Cook asked Bligh to take two boats and report on its suitability. Koa insisted on accompanying him as a passenger, to the inconvenience of Bligh, whose men had to half carry the bulky, shaking figure down to the launch, where he sat incanting prayers for their safety.

As events turned out, prayers were soon needed. The wind got up without any warning, as it so often does in these seas, and Bligh could see the canoes towing behind the sloops casting off and hastening back home or heading for this bay. Before Bligh's boats could return to the ships, Koa insisted on being put ashore, evidently lacking confidence in the power of his own prayers.

Bligh battled his way back to his ship through rising seas, picking up an old woman and two men from one upturned canoe. Now it came to blow very hard for thirty-six hours, and the *Resolution* and *Discovery* could do nothing but ride out the storm. But the price paid by the *Resolution* in particular was high. On the morning of 8 February, as Cook's ship was struck by a ferocious gust, the foremast split. Evidently, the Deptford disease had not finished with them yet. It was, by chance, three years to the day since Cook had stood up from his seat at the Admiralty and volunteered for this voyage.

Cook now faced a dilemma, one that he shared with Clerke by sending Bligh over to the *Discovery* to seek his opinion. It was essential that they put in to a safe anchorage and conduct repairs, not only to the foremast but also to an old leak which had reopened in the heavy weather. He could continue to Maui and search for a bay there, or return to Kealakekua, where the Hawaiians could not be expected to understand their problem. This time they might resent their presence after all the provisions that had been supplied only days earlier. Besides, the *reappearance* of Orono, and from the wrong direction, hardly accorded with religious tradition.

Cook decided to take the risk and return to an anchorage where all the facilities were available. 'All hands much chagrined', King noted, 'and damning the foremast.' They were as anxious as Cook was to continue their voyage.

Cook was reassured to see many canoes coming out to greet them as in the past. There was no hysteria to be noted, the atmosphere was generally friendly, and there was some trading. A contrary wind delayed the *Resolution*'s return to her old anchorage, and when she did so all on board recognised a disquieting change. The canoeists had all but disappeared, there was no one to be seen on shore, and a silence had fallen over the area. Samwell recalled later:

Kamehameha, a chief of great consequence . . . but of clownish and blackguard appearance, came on board . . . dressed in an elegant feathered cloak, which he had brought to sell but would part with it for nothing but iron daggers, which they have of late preferred to . . . everything else; and all the large hogs they bring us now they want daggers for, and tell us they must be made as long as their arms . . . Kamehameha got nine of them for his cloak . . .

This same chief had a young boy with him whom he constantly fondled, revealing to Samwell what he called 'a detestable part of his character'.

Adzes, chisels, axes, all once highly valued, now aroused no interest in these Hawaiians: daggers, and as long as possible, were now the sole trading currency. Cook and Clerke could not fail to note this disturbing new tendency. But the repairs, which might take as long as two weeks, had to be started and there were no incidents when the carpenters set up their workshops at the site of their old encampment.

At the same time, the bay, which had appeared so deserted at the time of their arrival, became crowded with Hawaiians again, who were in a restless mood and were provocative in manner, taunting the visitors and stealing without shame or fear for the consequences.

Even King Terreeoboo appeared displeased at the return of the sloops. He arrived one morning, as before in tremendous style in his great catamaran with its upper deck, and heavily escorted. His canoe headed straight for the *Resolution*, and assisted by his sturdy sons, he made his way on board.

The formalities when he met Cook were perfunctory. Held steady by his sons, the King was full of questions. Why had they returned? How long would they be staying? Cook answered as well as he was able, but, according to Jem Burney, 'He appeared much dissatisfied' with the answers. The King next visited the *Discovery*. Clerke was having a bad spell and felt too weak to leave his cabin. After leaving a gift of a cloak and a hog, the King departed and was taken ashore.

The *Discovery* had been suffering from a series of outrageously blatant thefts all morning. The worst was a chisel and a pair of tongs from the forge, which the blacksmith had been using to make the much-needed daggers. The thief was apprehended before he could get away. Hearing of this, Clerke lost his temper and ordered him to be given forty lashes.

This unhappy incident led to the arrival of Chief Parea, who had always in the past been so friendly and helpful. Now he was in a dangerous mood, his tone not in the least deferential: 'You have beaten one of my men,' he accused Clerke. 'You will bring violence upon yourself if you beat my King's subjects.'

There was also a curious and disturbing incident on board the *Resolution* at about this time. A chief arrived and was received courteously by Cook. He wished to know who were the fighting men – the *Tata Toa* – among the white people? Was Cook a *Tata Toa*? Cook judged that this was no philosophical question and answered promptly that, indeed, yes, he was a fighting man. He was then asked to show his wounds, and Cook presented his right hand for examination. The scar between his thumb and forefinger, originating from his time in Canada as a young man, proved the point, and the chief was satisfied. Persisting, the chief made the same demand of James King, who had nothing to prove that he was a *Tata Toa*. The chief then revealed his old scars; he was a *Tata Toa* all right.

Back at the *Discovery*, anchored two cables to the east, Clerke and Parea were still engaged in acrimonious conversation, Clerke suffering from the strain of the occasion. Suddenly there was a cry from the deck above: 'Thief! Thief! There he goes.'

Clerke laboured up the gangway as quickly as he could. One of Parea's entourage had stolen the same chisel and tongs as the previous thief. But this one was already in the water, his swimming seemingly unimpeded by the weight of iron. Marines, with muskets raised, were awaiting orders.

'Open fire!' Clerke ordered without hesitation. But the culprit was already a small and distant target and none of the balls found him. Edgar with Midshipman Vancouver and two men were soon in pursuit in the small cutter, but anyone could recognise that they had no chance of catching up with the canoe into which the thief had scrambled.

Cook was already ashore, intending to visit the carpenters to see what progress had been made on the mast. Unlike the four in the *Discovery*'s small cutter, he was armed, a marine carrying his double-barrelled gun. John Gore, in temporary command of the *Resolution*, saw all that happened, and all that followed, as if witnessing a melodramatic pageant, scene by scene, from the forecastle of his ship.

Another scene of violence on shore was also unfolding. Clerke had earlier ordered a party to the watering place near Kealakekua village. The party was under the command of the ship's quartermaster, thirty-three-year-old William Hollamby from London, a steady man at all times. Like all watering, it was a strenuous business but until now conducted in harmony with the local people, the girls watching and flirting, some of the young men giving a hand in rolling the full casks down for parbuckling into the boat.

This time it was altogether different. There were no witnesses to their activity except a few briefly seen figures wearing protective mats, in the surrounding palm grove. Hollamby was also conscious of a humming sound in the air as from a hive of bees, which seemed to be coming from the village. Next, Hollamby's party became the target for stone-throwing, which these Hawaiians, like most Polynesians, practised with great power and accuracy, often with a sling. At the same time they shouted taunts. Hollamby's men did not have a pistol between them, so the quartermaster hurried off to the encampment and sought out King, who was in command there.

'The rascals are becoming very insolent, sir,' he told the lieutenant. 'They seem only to pay regard to a musket.'

King armed himself with a musket and, in company with an armed marine and Hollamby, also now armed, marched to the watering place. Fearlessly, King walked into the palm grove, sought out the chief and ordered him to desist, or muskets would be used. With equal calmness, the chief ordered his men to drop their stones and led them all back to the village.

'If you have more insults, inform me at once, Mr Hollamby,' King instructed before returning to the encampment. This coincided in time, shortly before 8 p.m., with the arrival of Cook's pinnace. As soon as his lieutenant told him of the affray at the watering place, Cook broke into a rage. 'All day we have been troubled with these Indian thieves,' he complained. 'Please instruct Corporal Ledyard [commanding the encampment marines] to have the muskets loaded with ball instead of shot, and if there is more stone-throwing or insolence, fire upon them.'

Cook's examination of the carpenters' progress was broken by the sound of gunfire from the *Discovery* as the thief escaped with the chisel and tongs. He now observed the thief being picked up by the canoe and the hopeless pursuit by the small cutter manned by the *Discovery*'s master, Tom Edgar, and George Vancouver. Cook's view of these events was diametrically opposite John Gore's from the *Resolution* forecastle, and neither could do anything to correct the situation. Cook did try, however. 'Come with me, Mr King,' he ordered the lieutenant. 'There has clearly been a serious theft and we must endeavour to recover the article.'

Cook and King, with two marines as escort, saw Vancouver standing at the prow of his boat, pointing towards the shore at Kealakekua and shouting. The two officers were running, with their escort, towards the shore where the canoe would land. Not a word could be heard because as the canoe hit the beach, it was surrounded by a roaring mob of Hawaiians welcoming the thief and his loot.

King turned to look back in order to consult with his captain. Cook was still running, but in the opposite direction. King briefly puzzled over the reason for this. Certainly, it could not be fear of this mob. He decided his place was at Cook's side and hastened after him.

Dusk was falling and the lanterns had been lit on the *Resolution* and *Discovery*. What had got into his captain's head, King kept asking himself, while fearful of asking why Cook continued on this southerly heading away from Kealakekua village, where the thief had evidently landed. Still Cook paced on south, his face contorted with anger, his great strides obliging King to break into a trot to keep pace.

Almost at Palemano Point they began meeting groups of inhabitants. There was no prostrating now, nor cries of 'Orono'. The people just looked fearful, as well they might, for as Cook demanded knowledge of the thief, he indicated meaningfully the double-barrelled gun in the hands of one of his marines. They were directed south again by gestures rather than words, and Cook continued in that direction, while King thought that 'they were amusing us with false information'.

At length Cook halted, panting heavily. 'We shall never apprehend the rascal by this means,' he remarked, all too accurately, and so they reversed their direction.

MUCH HAD BEEN HAPPENING, most of it of a disturbing nature, in Cook's and King's absence. First Parea's canoe, in which the thief had escaped ashore, was relaunched and picked up Parea from the *Discovery*. Edgar and Vancouver in the small cutter off Kealakekua, the men's oars at rest, must have witnessed the chief's return. It was followed almost at once by the arrival of a canoe alongside, bearing the stolen tongs and chisel, Parea evidently having ordered their return.

This should have marked an end of the proceedings. They had what had been stolen and there seemed no chance now of apprehending the thief. But Edgar suddenly conceived an idea, a very bad one as it turned out. Seeing Cook's pinnace nearby awaiting the return of the captain, the master ordered it to come alongside. He assumed, wrongly, that some of the men would be carrying arms. His intention was to go ashore, seize Parea's canoe and hold it hostage against the delivery of the thief. It is possible that Edgar felt that this was his duty and, if successful, would gain him much kudos.

In his enthusiasm, Edgar was the first to seize the prow of Parea's canoe and attempt to launch it. But, unsurprisingly, he and Vancouver and the men were spotted before they could get it into the water.

The chief [Parea] began to remonstrate with the Master, who attempted to shrug him aside and complete the launching with the aid of Vancouver. Parea therefore seized him, pinioning his arms behind his back with one hand, and holding his hair with the other. A seaman responded by leaping out of the pinnace with an oar with which he beat Parea about the head and shoulders until he released Edgar. The fighting now became general, the scene tumultuous. Stones began flying, and a great number of natives closed about the unfortunate crew of the pinnace. Parea demonstrated his frightening strength by seizing the oar out of a seaman's hand and breaking it in two as if it were a twig.

Edgar and Vancouver, the first targets of the assault, began wading out to a rock offshore, holding their hands over the back of their heads as some sort of protection from the fusillade of stones following them. At the same time, the cox and crew of the pinnace seized the remaining oars and stretchers from their stranded boat as weapons in an attempt to hold back Parea's men.

The affray was at its height, others beside Edgar and Vancouver were being hurt, when a voice sounded out above the taunts and shouts of Parea's men. It was Parea himself, suddenly fearful of causing a death, and the consequences of it, and commanding a cease-fire. When

Edgar and Vancouver, much bruised and bleeding, returned to the shore, they took advantage of the lull again to attempt to relaunch the pinnace, helped this time by some of Parea's men. The much-abused party paddled away as well as they could with one oar and a broken half of another. They had been utterly humiliated and had revealed to the inhabitants how vulnerable they were without their firearms.

When Cook arrived back at the encampment with King after their fruitless journey, both officers were weary and depressed. Learning of the struggle on the beach, Cook broke into another rage, upbraiding first his cox for getting involved when they had no firearms, and then Edgar and Vancouver, whose injuries spoke for themselves.

Before leaving King for the night, and warning of the utmost vigilance, Cook spoke solemnly to his lieutenant: 'I am very sorry, Mr King, but the behaviour of these Indians must at last oblige me to use force. They must not imagine they have gained an advantage over us by what has occurred today.' It was dark when he stepped into his pinnace to be taken back to his ship.

WHEN AT ANCHOR IN HOT CLIMATES, Cook had for long resorted to having all but one of the ship's boats in the sea overnight, filled to the gunwales with water. This acted as protection against the sun's damaging heat, and also as security against theft. Jem Burney was the officer of the 4–8 a.m. watch on the *Discovery*. It was Sunday, 14 February, the morning after the tumult of Saturday afternoon.

The sun always took its time to rise above the towering peak of Mauna Loa and the other high land, but there was light enough in the sky soon after 5 a.m. and Burney was conducting his regular round of inspection, his eyes glancing over the moored boats. He paused in horror, looked more closely for confirmation, and at once hastened to his captain's cabin. Clerke was awake. His sleeping was bad and he was feeling rotten when Burney burst in. His news reflected his state of agitation: 'The large cutter is missing, sir.'

Clerke got out of his swing bed and asked Burney to call his servant. 'I must inform Captain Cook at once,' he added.

Cook had been signalled that Clerke would shortly arrive to report and was dressed ready to greet him when he came on board the *Resolution*. Clerke told later that Cook, his temper under control but in a very determined state, agreed that this was a serious matter indeed. 'They are set upon doing us every injury and we must not allow them to get the upper hand.'

The strategy was agreed in a minute. Kealakekua Bay was to be blockaded:

Captain Cook proposed that his boats should go to the north-west point of the bay [Clerke reported], and mine to the south-east point to prevent any canoes going away. 'You will please instruct your officers to drive any canoes on shore if they should attempt to go away. We shall fire our great guns if it should prove necessary.'

When Clerke arrived back at the *Discovery*, Edgar, Burney and Second Lieutenant John Rickman were standing by for orders. Peckover had the 4-pounders primed, and the two surviving boats had been drained and made ready. Rickman was put in charge of the launch and Burney was told to man the jolly boat. Every man was to be armed.

The *Resolution*'s launch was to be commanded by Williamson, and Bligh was given the cutter. Bligh was away first, hell-bent on blood. He had always disapproved of Cook's 'softness with the Indians' and was in a mood to shoot on sight. Having no trust in the Marines, he had chosen the men he most trusted, and ordered ball rather than shot in the muskets. All these men, as they rowed away strongly from their ship, were aware of a distinctive humming sound, the same menacing buzz that the watering party had heard of the previous day.

It needed no glass to identify the warriors lined along the black cliff top, hundreds of them, both here and intermittently seen in the forest, all armed and wearing protective mats. The women and children of Kealakekua, Kalama, Kaawaloa and other villages had become refugees in their own land, all hastening inland along the tracks through the forests. There could be no doubt in the simplest sailor's judgment that these Hawaiians were preparing for war on a grand scale.

The opening skirmish was in Cook's favour, thanks to William Bligh. Bligh had seen the launching of several canoes from Kaawaloa and had his eye on the largest, which was already heading fast for the north-west entrance to the bay. Bligh urged on his men in an effort to cut it off and, in typical Bligh style, threatened a dozen lashes for every oarsman if it got away.

The canoe had now hoisted a sail and was travelling at twice their speed close along the coast. A cannon crashed out on the *Resolution*. It was well aimed, the ball making a fine splash ten yards ahead of the canoe's prow. The canoeists continued paddling without a pause, attempting to manœuvre between the black volcanic rock shore and the advancing launch.

Bligh ordered the men to rest on their oars and take up their muskets. 'Fire!' he shouted and the muskets crashed out at close range at the racing canoe. Bligh ordered the reload, but it was not needed, not on this target. Many of the canoeists leaped into the water, the remainder – those who were not dead or badly injured – frantically steering their canoe towards a narrow inlet among the rocks.

Eyewitnesses on the *Resolution* were close enough to the scene of Bligh's fusillade to note its success. John Gore expressed his satisfaction to his captain standing alongside. Cook evidently made no response; instead, he stated his intention of going ashore himself with, as escort, Lieutenant Phillips, Sergeant Gibson, Corporal Thomas and seven marine privates.

'I shall bring back with me the King to detain him on board,' Cook told Gore. 'I believe it necessary to act swiftly against these Indians. We have witnessed the effect of musket fire upon them. So also have the Indians. They will not stand the fire of a single musket now.' He turned to his servant and ordered, 'Fetch my double gun, and look sharp.'

John Gore was horrified at Cook's plan, which seemed suicidal in view of the Hawaiians' mood and the gathering of this mighty army less than a mile away. But he also knew from the expression of grim determination on his captain's hawkish face that it would be futile to protest. Instead, Gore confined himself to saying, 'I trust, sir, that you will not proceed without powerful protection. You may be sure', he added, 'that I will keep all our starboard battery trained on the town.'

At this moment King came on board the *Resolution* from the shore encampment, anxious to know what was happening and what was intended. Cook was loading his gun, one barrel with shot, the other with ball. He repeated his plan. 'Your business, Mr King, is to quiet the minds of the Indians on your side of the bay. Inform them that they will not be hurt. And, Mr King, keep your party together and on their guard.'

'Aye, aye, sir.'

The two officers rowed off in their different directions at the same time. King, who had been as anxious as Gore about Cook's proposed operation, was somewhat reassured when he noted the strength of his captain's escort: besides the marines in his pinnace, he had called in Williamson in the launch. William Lanyon in the small cutter had four young gentlemen, Trevenen, Ward, William Taylor and Charlton, like everyone else armed with pistol and hanger as well as a musket.

Bayly was waiting at the landing point, and King quickly told Cook the details. He next ordered the American corporal of marines to post his men, muskets loaded with ball, and not to hesitate to open fire if provoked. King himself then boldly marched off to High Priest Koa's house in the village. Koa had other priests with him. 'I found that they had already heard of the cutter's being stolen,' King reported later, 'and I assured them that though Captain Cook was resolved to recover it, and to punish the authors of the theft, yet they and the people of the village on our side need not be under the smallest apprehension of suffering any evil from us.'

The carpenters had just begun their day's work on the foremast. They were aware that there was a crisis, but also that it was urgently necessary to complete their repairs. Their muskets were stacked nearby, and they, too, had been ordered not to hesitate to use them if they were in any way provoked. Suddenly, there was a renewed distant outbreak of musket fire, followed by screams and cries. These were not easy working conditions.

Jem Burney in the *Discovery* was in the best position to watch events on both sides of the bay, albeit through his glass. Cook had now landed on the volcanic rocks at the usual place when visiting Kaawaloa and was making his way along the track towards the village. His height made him easily identifiable, with Phillips at his side, then Sergeant Gibson, Corporal Thomas and the seven marine privates. They soon disappeared among the coconut groves, and Burney switched his attention to the launch, small cutter and Cook's pinnace off the landing place, oars dipping to keep them on station.

Again the *Resolution* opened fire at an unseen target, the sound, like thunder, echoing off the great cliff. Bligh was pursuing another large canoe, and Burney awaited the crash of a volley of musket fire. Instead, Burney and Clerke, who had joined him on the forecastle, heard renewed cries from the stationary canoe earlier fired at off the landing place at Kaawaloa. Rickman in the launch was firing another volley.

A small canoe, like a satellite, detached itself from the large one, from which the sound of lamentation arose, and moved rapidly and unimpeded across the bay towards the *Discovery*. Burney instructed the armed guard not to open fire unless ordered. At the same time, Clerke ordered the jolly boat away 'to find out how matters stand with Mr Rickman, and to ask him to bring any seized canoes to the ship'.

There were four men in the canoe, all in an agitated state and speaking so swiftly and angrily that even Burney, who was fluent in the language, could not make out at first what they were saying, only that the words 'Orono' and 'Kalimu' were repeated. At length, Burney told Clerke that he believed they were telling them that Chief Kalimu had been killed. They remembered this thug from earlier proceedings in Kealakekua Bay, and had no doubt that Rickman had been much provoked before opening fire.

Still agitated and dissatisfied, the canoeists paddled off towards the *Resolution*, crying out 'Orono' as if ignorant that Cook was ashore. The canoe did not long delay at the ship, evidently gaining no satisfaction here either. Through his glass, Burney now saw the canoe land at Kaawaloa and the four men run towards the village.

At the same time, the humming sound, which had never ceased, rose in volume as if a new army had arrived, and was joined by the distinctive threatening, echoing sound of hundreds of conch shells being blown.

ASHORE, COOK, PHILLIPS and the other marines were also aware of the sudden increase in volume of sound, and the sudden blowing of the conch shells, a certain prelude to violence. Cook had headed straight for King Terreeoboo's house, an unpretentious thatched dwelling near the centre of the village. He had been met on the way by the King's two young sons, who called Cook 'Toote' rather than 'Orono' and were always cheerful and welcoming. On this occasion, too, they were undismayed and incurious about the armed guard of red-coated marines.

Cook instructed Phillips to enter the house and to tell the King that he was outside waiting to see him. Phillips found Terreeoboo just awaking, and it was some time before the King became aware of Phillips's presence and what he was saying in his halting Polynesian.

At length the King got shakily to his feet, donning a cloak, and made his way to the entrance. Here he expressed pleasure and surprise at the sight of Orono. Cook took him by the hand and at once invited him on board his ship. The King gladly agreed. With a son on each side to keep him steady, Terreeoboo made the first faltering steps towards the landing place. At the same time, Cook told Phillips that the King appeared entirely innocent of any part in the theft of the cutter.

A crowd had gathered about this party, almost all warriors armed with spears, clubs and recently wrought daggers, some with long blades. Cook disdained to notice the crowd, talking with some difficulty but in a friendly fashion to the King. The marines formed a wedge-shaped ram, like the prow of a ship, as a protective shield as they advanced. They did not have far to go through the coconut grove, and in a few yards the black rocks of the shore would be in sight, with the three boats awaiting them.

Two events then occurred almost simultaneously which brought a fatal turn to Cook's intentions. First, the four canoeists landed and spread the word of Chief Kalimu's death at the hands of the visitors. Then, as if fired by this news, one of the King's mistresses broke from the crowd and fell at Terreeoboo's feet, shrieking and begging him not to go farther. Two minor chiefs at the same time held his arms. The King either lost his balance or fell down under the pressure.

Cook roared with anger, his voice heard even above the rabble's shouting, and the King, from his sitting position, assumed an un-regal mien, 'dejected and frightened', as Phillips later described him.

Phillips shouted in Cook's ear, 'Shall I order my men to arrange themselves in order along the rocks by the waterside, sir?'

Cook nodded agreement. 'Yes, do that, Mr Phillips. We can never think of compelling the King to go on board without killing a number of these people.'

David Samwell later provided the most literate and comprehensive account of the next critical phase:

The Indians were now grown very daring and troublesome. They threw several stones at our people, by which one of them was knocked down. One was seen . . . threatening to dart his spear at Captain Cook, who on being shown the man shot at him. The sergeant told him that he had shot the wrong person upon which he ordered him to shoot the right one, which he did and killed him.

The ardour and impetuosity of the Indians were by this a little repressed . . . The body of them fell back. [But] a volley of stones now came among our people on which the Marines gave a general fire and [thus] left themselves without a reserve. This was instantly followed by fire from the boats, on which Captain Cook expressed his astonishment, waved his hand to the boats [and] told them to cease their fire and come nearer in to receive the people . . .

At this point it seemed for a moment that Cook's prediction that these Hawaiians would never stand up to musket fire might be correct. The body of people edged back like a spent wave on a shore. Samwell was of the firm opinion that if the marines had firmly stood their ground, all might have been well. Instead, conscious that they might be overwhelmed before they could reload (about twenty seconds), many turned and fled over the rocks, leaving behind their muskets.

This panic-stricken retreat was observed by all in the boats, and by many with glasses on board the ships. They also saw to their horror that not all of them completed their escape. Corporal Thomas, who, like Phillips, had stood his ground and even completed his reloading, had a dagger thrust into his stomach so that he fell among the rocks; he was not seen to rise again.

Phillips, too, completed a reload, but fell to the ground and was stabbed in the shoulder as he lay there. However, the valiant lieutenant managed to seize his musket and shoot his assailant dead at one yard range.

Other Marines were falling on the rocks or as they began to wade out, tantalizingly close to salvation. Private Harrison appeared to the horrified boats' crews to be literally hacked to pieces. Tom Fatchett went down, too, his head as red from gushing blood as his uniform jacket. John Jackson, oldest of the privates and a veteran who had survived a long campaign in Germany, was struck by a spear in the face, just below the eye. Screaming with pain, he attempted to draw it out, and it broke off. With blood pouring from the wound, he waded out, and fell into the sea, unable to swim, with stones tearing up the water all around him.

Theo Hinks never had a chance of reaching the water, stabbed to death by a dozen screaming warriors. Phillips still struggled on, already badly wounded and now struck on the back of the head by one of dozens of stones slung or thrown at him. He stumbled on the slippery rock, recovered and hurled himself into the sea. He could swim strongly, unlike some of his marines, struck out for the pinnace and dragged himself over the gunwale. But, as he did so, he caught a glimpse of the unfortunate Jackson, half drowned and helpless, and, plunging back into the sea, dragged him to the pinnace, where he was pulled on board. Now recognising that the pinnace was grossly overloaded and might be swamped, Phillips unselfishly, while barely conscious, made for Lanyon's small cutter manned by the young gentlemen.

There was no question of the launch being an alternative refuge. Lieutenant Williamson, noted for his shooting of Polynesians, had chosen to interpret Cook's hand signal as an order to retreat, not to come to his rescue, as everyone else, including his own crew, had read it. So outraged were the crew at this desertion that it was all Williamson could do to keep his men rowing. When one of them stood up and fired his musket at extreme range – more as a gesture than with any hope of hitting anything – Williamson threatened to shoot anyone who followed this example.

At the height of this battle, there was a poignant occurrence which few witnessed at the time. One of Terreeoboo's princes had run ahead during an early stage of the procession to the shore. He had intended to surprise his father by greeting him as he boarded the pinnace, and then to accompany him on board the *Resolution* for a day of fun. Instead, he had found himself involved in the firing of muskets immediately around him, with the fearful noise half deafening him, and then, willy-nilly, becoming the target by his own people of volleys of stones from the land. At once bewildered and terrified, the little prince dived into the sea and swam far out into the bay.

On board the two sloops, eight bells rang out simultaneously, for once an irrelevant background chorus. Everyone who could was on deck, greatly agitated at what they saw, although only those with a glass on board the more distant *Discovery* could follow the sequence of events in detail. Cook appeared to be the only survivor still on the shore among the rocks. All about him were the corpses of his marines, and far more numerous warriors. His tall figure was stooped, a hand at the back of his head as some protection from stones. Why was he walking so slowly, his men asked themselves. Was it because he was hurt? Or perhaps he was continuing to express his disdain by not hurrying?

Even now these warriors hesitated to attack Orono, as if they were supernaturally fearful of the consequences. Then, as David Samwell described the final attack:

An Indian came running behind him, stopping once or twice as he advanced, as if he was afraid that he should turn round. Then, taking him unaware, he sprung to him, knocked him on the back of his head with a large club taken out of a fence, and instantly fled with the greatest precipitation. The blow made Captain Cook stagger two or three paces. He then fell on his hand and one knee and dropped his musket. As he was rising another Indian came running at him, and before he could recover himself from the fall, drew out an iron dagger he concealed under his feathered cloak and stuck it with all his force into the back of his neck. This made Captain Cook tumble into the water where [it] is about knee deep.

Here he was followed by a crowd of people who endeavoured to keep him under the water, but struggling very strongly with them he got his head up, and, looking towards the pinnace which was not above a boat's hook length from him, waved his hands to them for assistance, which it seems was not in their power to give.

It was not yet quite the end of Cook's struggle for survival for he got his head up again and attempted to scramble on the rocks. Then another warrior gave him a shattering blow on his head with a club and Cook went down for the last time. Those who were close by could witness the terrible and frenzied assault on the body when it was laid out on the nearby rocks, warrior after warrior pushing and shoving to bludgeon and knife the corpse.

27

A Lament for Orono

FROM THE BRIEF AWESOME SILENCE that followed the death of Cook and the shock it caused, there developed a faint sigh of fear and lamentation over Kaawaloa, and from the ships, and the boats heading towards them, a kind of hush of disbelief. Lieutenant King expressed the feelings of many when he wrote later that

I, as well as the others, had been so used to look up to [Cook] as our good genius, our safe conductor and as a kind of superior being, that I could not suffer myself – I could not dare to think – he would fall by the hands of the Indians, over whose minds and bodies he had been used to rule with absolute sway.

George Gilbert wrote of it 'appearing to us somewhat like a dream that we could not reconcile ourselves to . . . Grief was visible in every countenance, some expressing it by tears, and others by a kind of gloomy dejection.' In one of the boats coming alongside the *Resolution* a number of the men were crying, 'We have lost our father! Our father is gone!'

As that dreadful day wore on, a wide variety of emotions began to fill the gulf of shock. On board the *Resolution*, where Gore had now taken over command, the rage began to build up and a number of 4-pounders were fired at random at the village without orders. Most of the lower deck expressed violently the need for revenge. Many advocated that the two sloops should be warped close inshore and the village bombarded until not a house was left standing, and not a warrior left alive.

William Bligh was the natural leader of this school, and expressed outrage when more moderate voices were heard, especially that of Gore, whom he had always held in contempt. The contempt for John Williamson was unanimous, however, and many were the threats against his life. He had compounded his crime (as it was seen) of refusing to contribute to the defence of Cook and the marines by denying with equal firmness his duty to recover the bodies lying among the rocks after the massacre was over and the beach lay deserted. At the time, this angered his men and there was a near mutiny in the boat before the lieutenant, musket threatening, prevailed upon his crew to return to the *Resolution*.

Charles Clerke was now expedition commander and would later transfer to the *Resolution*. Meanwhile, he rose nobly to his fearful responsibilities in spite of a physical condition so debilitating that he could scarcely keep the deck. His first concern was for the encampment, for Lieutenant King, William Bayly and the marines, and for the ship's watch, astronomical instruments and the *Resolution*'s foremast. He calculated that a bombardment of Kealakekua village would deter any attack, and soon the *Discovery*'s 4-pounders were blasting out.

This bombardment was still continuing when King was spotted being rowed out to the sloop in the jolly boat. He was waving his arms and was heard to be calling, 'Stop firing!', in a state of great agitation. Clerke ordered the cease-fire, and King came on board. He explained that relations on his side of the bay were still friendly, and that Koa and his priests had all assumed that, as Cook's son, he, James King, was now regarded as Orono.

King might indeed be the new Orono, but he was unable to halt Bligh's assault on Kealakekua. Gore had ordered his sailing master to take a strong party to reinforce the encampment's marines. Being a believer in taking the offensive, in King's absence Bligh had advanced on the village with marines and shot everyone in sight, in spite of Bayly's protests. Bligh could reasonably claim that, for his part, he had cleared the village and prevented any attack on the encampment. But by the time the assault could be called off on King's orders, he had stoked up the warriors' fires of outrage and lust for vengeance.

The complete evacuation of the encampment, including the half-repaired foremast, was now Clerke's first priority, and this was accomplished with such speed, the carpenters and others being spurred on by fear, that by noon the expedition had nothing on shore, except Cook's body and the corpses of the four marines who had died with him.

This dangerous operation was carried out in the face of intermittent attacks by spearmen and stone throwers, countered by musket fire from the marines, which took a number of lives. At 4 p.m. some forty men, sailors and marines had been ordered to form a strong force to attempt the recovery of the bodies, which had long since disappeared from the rocky shore on which they had been lying. Two boats, commanded by Burney and King, headed for the shore, and as they did so the natives, who had earlier fled inland, ran down to the shore from Kaawaloa, the men casting aside their weapons and all making signs of friendship. High Priest Koa, who had evidently canoed from Kealakekua to this side of the bay, was seen to step into the sea, and in spite of his weight and the effects of his addiction to kava, swam out to meet them, holding up a large white flag at the same time.

When asked by Burney about the corpses, Koa replied that he, personally, would return Orono's the next day when he could recover it from far inland. The two officers had to be content with this promise and returned to their ships without responding in any way to the overtures of the Hawaiians.

The following day, 15 February, a parcel was delivered to the *Resolution*, not by Koa but by one of his priests. Clerke, who had now transferred to this ship, began to open it in his cabin. He was curious about what it contained. The mystery turned to horror when he exposed a slab of partly burned flesh from one of Cook's hips, which, bowing deeply, the priest explained was all that was available of Orono, the bones being with King Terreeoboo. High Priest Koa would endeavour to retrieve them tomorrow. This priest was allowed to leave unmolested, but he left behind a feeling of sickening anger and hatred.

WORD OF THE CONTENTS of the parcel soon reached the men of the *Discovery*, who became hell-bent on revenge. This fury was further fuelled by acts of provocation which contrasted with the apparent friendliness of the morning's demonstration. A one-man canoe put off from Kaawaloa and hove to just beyond musket range. Here the occupant stood up and whirled Cook's hat round and round on the end of a pole, then exposed his buttocks, smacking them and jeering.

This same derisive performance was conducted along the shore, too, the men using the marines' scarlet tunics as flags while a large, buttock-exposed crowd cheered. One of them flaunted a hanger, indicating that it was Cook's and that it was Cook's own blood that stained the blade.

At this demonstration, not even Clerke could have held back the gunners from opening fire – not that he had any intention of doing so. The 4-pounder balls scattered the screaming crowds, killing and wounding many of them, to the great satisfaction of all on deck.

Even greater retribution was meted out at Kealakekua when

Rickman's watering party was attacked by stone-throwers, and boulders were run down from the cliff top towards them. Rickman himself led his marines as well as his working party, all armed, in an attack on the village, shooting any inhabitants they met, decapitating several of them, and then taunting the warriors on the cliff edge with the heads on the end of poles.

The effect of this demonstration was fearful. There were screams of terror and anguish, and the hordes fled. The Hawaiians also demonstrated fanatical courage. They would brave any fire to recover the body of a compatriot, dipping their mats in water in an effort to quench what they thought was the fire thrown by the white men's weapons.

In order to clear the natives altogether from the watering area, the nearby houses were set on fire. The fire got out of control, and in a strong wind the flames destroyed hundreds of houses and all the natives' possessions.

In the midst of this mayhem, two young Hawaiians, armed with spears, swam out to the *Discovery*. Jem Burney ordered the guards to hold their fire, and the young men swam under the stern of the ship, where they burst into song, a lament for the god Orono. After fifteen minutes of this song, listened to with much professional interest by Burney, they climbed on board and presented him with their spears in atonement for the great wrong of killing Orono. They then dived into the water from the ship and swam ashore.

As so often in their relations with Polynesians in difficult times, it was the unpredictability of the people that was most unsettling: gifts one moment, a ferocious attack the next. Trevenen reported on the one consistent behavioural factor that could always be relied upon:

Notwithstanding our state of hostility, the women swam off to the ship every night. Having the guard about midnight, and observing an Indian jump on board, I presented my musket and should certainly have fired had not I luckily been prevented in time by being told it was a woman.

On the night after the Kealakekua fire, when flames were still rising from the village, no one on board the ships admired this sight more than these women.

Clerke was reconciled to the loss of the Royal Marines' bodies, but remained determined not to leave Kealakekua Bay without the bones of his captain and friend, and he made it clear to Koa that there could be no peace until these were delivered. In reply, it was explained to

Clerke that King Terreeoboo had distributed Cook's bones among the mightiest of his chiefs, and it was going to be difficult to recover them, so highly were they valued.

At length, on 19 February, a message arrived at the *Resolution* indicating that Orono's remains were at the Kaawaloa landing place, along with gifts of peace. King, now taking over responsibility for the expedition's journal, described what followed:

To show them that we accepted the peace, Captain Clerke went in the pinnace & desired me to go in the cutter, to bring him and the presents as was desired. We refused landing which was not much insisted upon, [the chief] coming with great composure into the pinnace, and he and several others came on board. He gave us a bundle wrapped very decently, & covered with a spotted cloak of black and white feathers, which we understood to be a mourning colour. On opening it we found the Captain's hands, which were well known from a remarkable cut, the scalp, the skull, wanting thigh bones and arm bones. The hands only had flesh on them, & were cut in holes, & salt crammed in; the leg bones, lower jaw, & feet which were all that remained & had escaped the fire . . .

'In the evening [of 22 February],' wrote Clerke, 'I had the remains of Captain Cook committed to the deep, with all the attention and honour we could possibly pay it in this part of the world.' Edgar is a little more specific: 'At 5 both ships hoisted ensigns and pendants half staff up and crossed over yards. At ¾ past the hour *Resolution* tolled her bell and fired ten 4-pounders, half-minute guns, & committed the bones of Captain Cook to the deep. At 6 p.m. squared our yards . . .' It was all over.

THE SHIPS WERE NOW in as good order as they could be. The carpenters had worked long days, and with great difficulty, on the foremast, and with even greater difficulty, as 'our rope is all wore or dry rotten', stepped it. They were loaded with as much fresh fruit and vegetables as would last them until they went rotten. All the last trade had been amicable, and nothing was stolen from either the *Resolution* or the *Discovery*. For their part, the officers assured the chiefs and priests that 'we were entirely their friends', wrote King, '& as Orono was buried all recollection of the affair was also buried'.

Clerke believed that no more time should be wasted in this bay or the news of the troubles there might reach the other islands '& have a bad effect'. Clerke also knew that his health was so bad that he would have to depute the navigation of the expedition. He had seen ample evidence that William Bligh was the finest navigator in either ship. Bligh himself explains:

Captain Clerke being very ill in a decline he could not attend the deck, and thus he publicly gave me the power solely of conducting the ships & moving as I thought proper. His orders were, 'You are to explore the [Sandwich] Isles as much as you can & from thence carry the ships to Kamchatka & thence to do your utmost endeavours to discover the NW Passage.'

EVERY MEMBER of both ships' companies would remember for the rest of their lives both the day they arrived off Kealakekua Bay, and the day they left it, 23 February 1779. What a lot had happened in a little more than five weeks! Every human emotion had been exercised, from wonder to fear, from violent hatred to ardent passion. There were times when they wondered if they would ever survive to see the shores of England again. And there were times when some might have been content to remain among these islands for ever.

The ships' boats began pulling them out of the bay at 8 p.m., all but a few of the women having gone ashore. Shortly before darkness fell, a breeze from the shore having got up, the boats were hoisted in '& we sailed out of the bay, receiving as we passed the shore many affectionate farewells', noted King. '[It was] a place become too remarkably famous for the very unfortunate and tragical death of one of the greatest navigators our nation or any nation ever had.'

Eighteen-year-old Midshipman James Trevenen expressed the emotions of his shipmates when he wrote: 'An universal gloom and strong sentiments of grief and melancholy were very observable throughout all ranks on board the ship on our quitting this bay without our great and revered commander.'

They had good reason to be depressed, for they had lost so much; not just two Arctic seasons, which would mean four years or more away from home, but fine men like Watman and Surgeon Anderson and more than half a dozen of their shipmates. And, above all, they had lost 'their father', their leader who had brought them through so many dangers, had shared the good times and had supported them through bad times.

Charles Clerke, their new commander, was loved, too, and in a more intimate way than Cook, but everyone knew that his span of life was almost exhausted. They also knew that after the benign climate of the Sandwich Islands, they faced again the privations and dangers of the frozen north. On their first voyage north they had been buoyed up by the prospects of discovering a short passage home, with prize money at the end of it. Not a man, this time, believed that they would find anything beyond that impenetrable wall of ice of last summer. But the Admiralty and Cook's instructions were clear and must be adhered to. They must try again.

Warrant Officer William Bligh, sailing master, twenty-eight years old, accomplished his task with consummate skill, from the time he completed his survey of the Sandwich Islands, from end to end, until the two sloops were back in the Thames on 4 October 1780, having been away for four years and three months. However tarnished his reputation may have become in later years, nothing can diminish the sublime nature of his navigating skills from the Arctic to Petropavlovsk, to Macao, thence to the Cape and home via Stromness in the Orkney Islands.

For the last fourteen months, John Gore in the *Resolution* commanded the expedition and worked well with Bligh. Clerke had died on 22 August 1779, aged thirty-eight. Ten days earlier he had managed to dictate a last letter to Joseph Banks:

My ever honoured Friend,
The disorder I was attacked with in the King's bench prison has proved consumptive, with which I have battled with varying success, although without one single day's health since I took leave of you in Burlington Street. It has now so far got the better of me, that I am not able to turn myself in my bed, so that my stay in this world must be of very short duration . . .

Now my dear and honoured friend, I must bid you a final adieu. May you enjoy many happy years in this world* and in the end attain that fame your indefatigable industry so richly deserves. These are the most sincerely and warmest wishes of your devoted, affectionate and departing servant,

Chas. Clerke

---

* Banks died forty-one years later in 1820.

28

'An Everlasting Honour to his Country'

THERE IS A MEMORIAL TO COOK on the volcanic rocks where he fell. It is accurately placed close to the water and thus underlines the fact that by walking at his usual long-legged pace he could have reached the water, been dragged into the pinnace and have escaped death. A number of eyewitnesses testified that he sauntered rather than walked and appeared deliberately to challenge the Hawaiian warriors to attack him, while at the same time taking the precaution of placing his hands over his neck.

These questions will never be answered: Was the captain being deliberately disdainful in the last moments of his life before he was struck down? Or was he acting the part of a man who had become careless of his life, consciously or unconsciously? The voyage had been a disappointment almost from the start, when he had to leave Plymouth alone, and, as he was soon to learn, in a crank ship. He had been deviated by contrary winds and had fallen far behind his own timetable. He had been vexed too often and had rarely enjoyed the elation of earlier discoveries.

The Sandwich Islands experience had at first been satisfying, it was true. But never had he been so burdened by thieving and hostile demonstrations. The blackest disappointment was the failure in the Arctic, the *raison d'être* of the voyage. Until now, all his voyaging had been marked by good luck and success. This time the luck had eluded him and he would be bringing home, by contrast with the two earlier voyages, a tale of failure. Moreover, his expectations had been high that there would be the prize money* to crown the completion of his final voyage, to add to his certain promotion to flag

---

* Cook would have received the lion's share of the £20,000.

rank and a likely peerage, or at least a baronetcy. Like his men, Cook harboured no expectation of success at the second attempt to find an Arctic passage.

There is one consideration above all others to support the possibility that Cook had become indifferent about his survival. It is the steady deterioration of his health. The first hint of health problems became evident on the previous voyage. As early as August 1773, when there were serious difficulties in anchoring in Vaitepiha Bay, Tahiti, and the *Resolution* went aground, Sparrman entered the ward room when the crisis had been resolved to find Cook already there. 'Although he had from beginning to end of the incident appeared perfectly alert and able [he] was suffering so greatly from his stomach that he was', reported the Swede, 'in a great sweat and could scarcely stand . . .' A few months later in December, when they were deep in the Antarctic, Johann Förster noted that Cook 'looked pale and lean and laboured under a perpetual costiveness', and frequently vomited.

Förster again on the approach to Easter Island, when the weather was much warmer than before, claimed that it

proved fatal to Captain Cook's constitution. The disappearance of his bilious complaint during our last push to the south, had not been so sincere as to make him recover his appetite. The return to the north therefore brought on a dangerous obstruction, which the Captain very unfortunately concealed from every person in the ship . . .' [See p. 318]

Surgeon-Admiral Sir James Watt, Medical Director General of the Navy (1972–7), had reason to believe that Cook at this time suffered from a parasitic infection of the intestine, probably of the lower ileum:

Alternative diagnoses are unlikely in the light of his subsequent medical history [he contends]. The parasites would cause inflammation of the wall of the intestine, allowing colonization by coliform bacteria which could interfere with the absorption of the B complex of vitamins and probably other nutrients. Gross effects . . . include prolonged ill health, fatigue, loss of appetite, stubborn constipation, loss of weight, digestive disturbances, loss of interest and initiative, irritability, depression, loss of concentration and memory and change of personality – all symptoms exhibited by Cook during the third voyage and faithfully recorded by eyewitnesses.

If this diagnosis is correct, then the infection seems likely to have developed earlier and on the second voyage, adding to the weariness Cook felt at the conclusion of that voyage. Palliser and Sandwich should never have allowed him to go to sea again, with all the manifold demands of an expedition commander on a voyage of three or more years. Palliser was doubly guilty, for as Comptroller he was directly responsible for the efficiency of Deptford Naval Yard: Deptford, Cook's real killer, as it could be described. All honour is due to Hugh Palliser for acting as patron and instructor of Cook in earlier years, but he was not a sparkling success at the Admiralty, nor later when he was third-in-command of the Channel Fleet at the indecisive action off Ushant in 1778.*

What we know for sure is that Cook was a different man on this third voyage. He certainly hazarded his ship on the first voyage, under unprecedented circumstances. But neither on that voyage nor during the Antarctic voyage that followed were there incidents of careless navigation, indecisiveness, violent swings of mood or periods of irritability leading to downright cruelty. The James Cook of 1774 would never have ordered excessive flogging and ear removals of Polynesians, nor ordered his men to eat walrus meat or make do with ship's biscuit only. It was as if the infection which was eating into his intestine also brought about a change in the organic structure of his brain.

ELEVEN MONTHS PASSED before the news of Cook's death reached London. On 11 January 1780 the *London Gazette* contained the following announcement:

Captain Clerke of His Majesty's Sloop *Resolution*, in a letter to Mr Stephens, dated the 8th of June 1779, in the Harbour of St Peter and St Paul, Kampschatka, which was received yesterday, gives the melancholy account of the celebrated Captain Cook, late commander of that Sloop, with four of his private Marines having been killed on the 14th of February last at the island of O'Why'he, one of a group of new discovered Islands in the 22nd Degree of North Latitude, in an affray with a numerous and tumultuous Body of the Natives.

An obituary in this same newspaper on the same day included:

This untimely and ever to be lamented Fate of so intrepid, so able, and so intelligent a Sea-Officer, may justly be considered as an irreperable Loss to the Public, as well as to his Family, for in him were united every successful and amiable quality that could adorn his Profession; nor was his singular Modesty less conspicuous than his other Virtues. His successful Experiments to preserve the Healths of his Crews are well known, and his Discoveries will be an everlasting Honour to his Country.

* He determined that his c-in-c be court-martialled. Admiral Augustus Keppel was honourably acquitted and Palliser resigned his appointment as a result.

Clerke's letter, written two months before his own death, had come overland from Kamchatka to St Petersburg, thence to Berlin and London, taking six months, 'a very short time if the difficulties of transit that must necessarily have been encountered are taken into consideration'.

The news, and the grief, spread throughout the land, deeply affecting, it was said, King George. Joseph Banks, under a pseudonym, wrote a long and fulsome tribute in the *Morning Chronicle*.

Of those who sailed with Cook on his last voyage, and survived the passage home, William Bligh became much the best known, even notorious in his reputation. For all his qualities as a seaman and navigator, his personality led him into more than the one famous mutiny, and his naval career was spotted with courts-martial. His greatest virtue was his loyalty to his men when circumstances were tough, as during the unsuccessful attempt to double the Horn in the *Bounty*, and the phenomenal 3,600-mile open-boat voyage from Tofua to Coupang. His greatest demerits were the unevenness of his authority and his lack of control over his temper. Bligh fought valiantly at the Battle of Camperdown, 1797, and in 1805 Sir Joseph Banks was instrumental in having him appointed Governor of New South Wales. He was not a success, and enjoyed the singular fate of suffering mutiny on both land and sea.

John Williamson retained his reputation for cowardice, and it remains a mystery how he rose to the rank of captain. On the voyage home under Clerke, and then Gore, he was shunned by all, and when Phillips challenged him to a duel he refused to fight. The Admiralty finally rumbled him at the same battle in which Bligh enhanced his reputation. In short, he refused to engage the enemy after ignoring signals to do so, and at his court-martial was found guilty of cowardice. It was effectively the end of his career.

The American thrice circumnavigator, John Gore, seems to have had enough of voyaging by 1780. On his return, he was promoted post-captain and took up Cook's berth at Greenwich, with his Nancy, where he died ten years later. 'A most experienced seaman and an honour to his profession,' wrote an obituarist in *Gentleman's Magazine*.

Gore's fellow American in the *Resolution*, the marines corporal, John Ledyard, was one of several of the expedition who was drawn back to the fur trade in the north, and its easy profits. Failing to get backing for an expedition in England, he persuaded Thomas Jefferson to support him in an astonishing proposal to walk clear across Russia, thence to Nootka Sound, where he would set up a trading company, and then walk across unexplored North America to Virginia.

Empress Catherine heard of this scheme and put a prohibition order on the American. Ledyard set off anyway and walked 3,000 miles to Yakutsk. Here he fell in with Joseph Billings, one of the *Discovery*'s ABS, now captain in the Russian Navy engaged in surveying further the Bering Strait area. This looked promising, but before the opportunity could be exploited, Ledyard was arrested and taken back to the Polish frontier.

As a last resort, Ledyard appealed to Sir Joseph Banks, now President of the Royal Society. Admiring the American's doggedness, Banks offered him the job of leading an expedition for the Association for Promoting the Discovery of the Interior Parts of Africa. Ledyard agreed enthusiastically, took the expedition to Cairo, but before he could set out he contracted a fatal disease.

The ever-lively Jem Burney continued his successful naval career. We catch a glimpse of him at home, thanks to his sister Fanny. He was just sitting down to cards,

when we were surprised by an express from London, and it brought a 'whereas we think it' from the Admiralty, to appoint Captain Burney to the command of the *Latona* . . . This is one of the best frigates in the navy . . . Jem was almost frantic with ecstasy of joy; he sang, laughed, drank to his own success and danced about the room . . . His hope is to get out immediately, and have a brush with some of the Dons, Monsieurs, or Mynheers, while he is in possession of a ship of sufficient force to attack any frigate he may meet.

This proved to be the case, and Burney conducted several successful actions against the frigates of Admiral Pierre André de Suffren. Four years later Burney's health broke and he retired from the Navy. He embarked on a massive five-volume work, *A Chronological History of the Discoveries in the South Sea*. He mixed with poets like Southey, Coleridge and Lamb, and became an expert whist player, even writing a book about it. On his death, Lamb wrote to Wordsworth: 'There's Captain Burney gone! What fun has whist now? What matters it what you lead if you can no longer fancy him looking over you?'

Several more of the *Discovery*'s company became involved in the opening up of the west coast of North America. Nathaniel Portlock and George Dixon, armourer, were engaged to command the two ships of the King George's Sound Company which was effective in developing the fur trade, 1785–8. In 1791 Portlock, who had been master's mate under Bligh in the *Resolution*, was given command of the brig *Assistant*, which accompanied Bligh's *Providence* on his second, and successful, breadfruit voyage.

That aesthete, James King, did not survive for long after his return. He, too, was promoted post-captain and appointed to command the escort to a large convoy destined for the West Indies. As surgeon he had David Samwell, but Samwell could not save his commander and old friend when he contracted tuberculosis and died in 1784.

The Cornish midshipman, James Trevenen, was another who led an adventurous life after his return and who saw Russian service. He served under James King in the West Indies, when he saw much action. On his return he went on to half-pay, but in 1787 was engaged by the Russian Navy to command another voyage of surveying and discovery in the Bering Strait area. But the war with Sweden the following year intervened. He was mortally wounded in battle and was buried at Kronstadt.

Midshipman George Vancouver was responsible for a voyage which came close to emulating one of Cook's. After serving in the West Indies, participating in Admiral George Rodney's great victory at the Battle of the Saints, he was appointed leader of a two-ship expedition to the west coast of North America. He followed Cook's route to the Cape, thence to south-west Australia, Dusky Bay and Tahiti. In April 1792 he sighted the California coast at Cape Mendocino, coasted north to the Strait of Juan de Fuca, which he entered and surveyed, naming one deep inlet Puget Sound (present-day Seattle) after one of his lieutenants, Peter Puget. Like Cook, he based his expedition for the winter months in the Hawaiian islands. Vancouver sustained a good relationship with the King of Hawaii, who formally ceded his island to King George III. Twice more Vancouver sailed north, accepting the cession of Nootka Sound from the Spaniards, who had occupied it in 1789. The expedition came home via Monterey, Valparaiso and the Horn in 1795, after a longer voyage than any of Cook's.

Among Cook's supernumeraries, John Webber was employed by the Admiralty in making finished drawings for engravings to illustrate the official journal. He became a member of the Royal Academy and continued his landscape painting at home and on the continent until his death in 1791.

Finally, the gardener from Kew, David Nelson: as a botanist on the voyage, he had been as assiduous as Banks on the first voyage, but by contrast with Banks was self-effacing and kept to himself. He was scarcely mentioned in the various journals of the voyage. But William Bligh had noted his efficiency and recalled this gardener when he formed his crew for the *Bounty* breadfruit expedition.

During the mutiny of 28 April 1789, Nelson remained loyal to his captain, and was consigned with him and eighteen others into the ship's launch. The last he and the other loyalists saw of the breadfruit Nelson had cherished with such care was their use in their pots as mocking missiles.

Nelson shared the appalling rigours of the open-boat voyage, and was no weaker than the others when they finally reached Coupang on 14 June. But he rose from his bed of recovery too soon in order to go botanising, developed 'an inflammatory fever' and died a few days later. Bligh, who had valued his friendship during the voyage, felt the loss badly.

ELIZABETH COOK, who had suffered so much grief over the death of her infant children, was deeply distressed by the news of her husband's death. Like most sailors' wives, she had understood the danger of her husband's calling when she married him. They had been together for only a few months at a time since their wedding day in 1762, some four years in all.

Later, the Royal Society had a gold medal struck in honour of Cook. In writing to inform Mrs Cook of this medal, Joseph Banks urged her no longer 'to lament a man whose virtues have exacted a tribute of regret from a large portion of the natives of the earth, and let your best affections continue the task they have hitherto so well fulfilled in training up his sons in the paths of virtue and honour'.

But three more bitter blows were to strike at poor Elizabeth Cook. Of her three surviving sons, Nathaniel died at sea at the age of sixteen, when his ship HMS *Thunderer* was lost in a hurricane off Jamaica nine months after his father had been killed on the other side of the world. The eldest son, James, rose to the rank of commander RN, but was lost at sea in a boat when a strong wind suddenly blew up. That was in 1794. A few months earlier, Mrs Cook lost her youngest son, Hugh, from scarlet fever while up at Christ's College, Cambridge.

Unlike her late husband, Mrs Cook was a deeply religious woman. On four days a year, those marking the anniversaries of the death of her last three boys and her husband, she fasted and spent the day reading the Bible and meditating. Her pride in her husband's memory was evidenced by her collection of Cook's obituaries, including a letter of tribute by Banks, and by the poem composed by AB Tom Perry: 'It is now my brave boys we are clear of the Ice . . .' Besides portraits and paintings of his ships on the walls, there were displayed the Royal Society's gold medal to commemorate the departure of the *Resolution* and *Adventure* on the second voyage, the Copley Gold Medal and the third gold medal struck in his honour after Cook's death, and other souvenirs. Her second cousin, Canon Bennett, described her to Walter Besant as

a handsome, venerable lady, her white hair rolled back in ancient fashion, always dressed in black satin; with an oval face, an aquiline nose, and a good mouth. She wore a ring with her husband's hair in it; and she entertained the highest respect for his memory, measuring everything by his standard of honour and morality. Her keenest expression of disapprobation was that 'Mr Cook' – to her he was always Mr Cook, not Captain – 'would never have done so'. Like many widows of sailors, she could never sleep in high wind for thinking of the men at sea . . .

Elizabeth Cook survived her husband by fifty-six years, living through the loss of the American colonies and the French Revolution, as well as Wellington's and Nelson's great victories. She heard of the collapse of the Spanish empire in America, the establishment of a (penal) colony at Botany Bay, all events which would have deeply interested her late husband. She learned of the possession by the British of the Cape of Good Hope and Cape Town, the construction of

The *Discovery*, convict ship with added upper deck, in the Thames
nearly fifty years after her return from the North Pacific

the first main-line railway in England, and the crossing of the Atlantic by an American steamship in 1819.

Elizabeth Cook may not have recognised it, but these events serve to emphasise what an important key her husband had been in the bridge between the early years of eighteenth-century scientific and geographic curiosity, and the industrial revolution in its full flowering. Queen Victoria was on the British throne within months of Elizabeth Cook's death in her home in Clapham, south London.

For most of Mrs Cook's widowhood she had the company of Isaac Smith, her nephew and a retired admiral, who, all those years ago, had been the first European to land in New South Wales. She kept her faculties to the end, aged ninety-three and with her pension, her sons' inheritance, and her share of the profits of her husband's publications, she was a moderately wealthy woman, able to live in comfort and entertain her friends: she had a dinner party every Thursday at three o'clock.

Appendix 1*

When the *Endeavour* reached Batavia in October 1770, Cook offered a reward, plus fifteen gallons of arrack – alcoholic spirit – to anyone of the ship's company who would name the guilty party. Almost at once Patrick Saunders, a fellow midshipman of Magra's at the time, but subsequently disrated, deserted ship and was never seen again.

This curious incident marks one of the few occasions when the strains and stresses of shipboard life on Cook's voyages became evident. The men of the *Endeavour* had already been at sea for nearly two years, living through the natural hazards of voyaging and the long periods when there was little to do. They were almost one hundred in number, and lived day and night confined in a vessel ninety-seven feet long on her lower deck and some twenty-eight feet wide, of which only a small proportion was available for living quarters.

They were mostly young men whose appetites were well developed. Their standard drink ration was generous, but by one means or another those who wished to could augment this ration, and some of them were half drunk all their waking time. In the ship's hold there was scarcely a cask of wine or spirit which had not been illegally broached. Passions were aroused all too readily. Even Cook admitted that his clerk Orton was 'a man not without faults'. He might well have been the victim of sexual jealousy between these two young midshipmen. We shall never know.

The outstanding aspect of this episode is that it leads to the recognition that there was little violence among the *Endeavour's* men. There is no doubt that there were some unrecorded fights, probably induced by drunkenness as on land, but the record over three years was remarkably free of serious discord, for which much of the credit must go to Cook's steadiness and even-handed discipline.

* See page 144–5.

Appendix 2*

The poem, or song, *The Antarctic Muse*, was first published by the scholarly and normally impeccable Dr Beaglehole in his *The Journals of Captain James Cook*, vol. II, p. 870–1. It is a bowdlerised version, however, and we have no means of discovering its derivation. For example, in the first line of the first stanza, Beaglehole has 'sea' as the last word instead of 'Ice', which not only rhymes but makes more sense. The provenance of the Doctor's version also appears to be awry. My rendering is from what appears to be the original holograph in the Dixson Library.

It appears that after the death of Elizabeth Cook certain furniture, books, pictures and papers, including the original of the *Muse*, were eventually inherited by Mrs Ann Arbery. In 1930 Mrs Arbery drew up an affidavit which clarifies the history of the *Muse*. With the permission of the Dixson Library, I reproduce it here, omitting only some superfluous matter:

ANN MARIA SANFORD ARBERY states
as follows:—

I am 72 years of age and a widow. I was born on 20th September 1858 at The New Inn (now demolished) in the village and parish of Withycombe Raleigh, Devon. My father, William Brooks, was the innkeeper. He married Martha Sanford – as his second wife – of the parish of Combe Raleigh, Devon . . . I had two brothers and two sisters, all now deceased except one brother . . . I lived with my parents until I was 8 years old when I left home to live with one of my aunts at Combe Raleigh. I married James Arbery on 18th March, 1886, at Combe Raleigh, and after my marriage lived at Combe Raleigh. While living with my aunt, Harriet Clapp, my mother's sister, I was always told that certain articles of furniture which my aunt, Anne Salway, possessed, had belonged to Captain Cook, the great explorer. This furniture had come into her possession in this way:—

My great aunt, Sarah Westlake and her husband to be, Charles Doswell, were servants of Mrs Cook, the explorer's widow, and when she died she left . . . the contents of a bedroom to my great-aunt, Sarah.

. . . I have a copy of my great-uncle's will. He lived at Clapham, dying a few

* See pages 253–4.

months after Mrs Cook [in 1836] ... My great-uncle after bequeathing sundry legacies by will appointed his wife as residuary legatee to his estate. She by her will left the portrait of Captain Cook to the family solicitor, Mr Mackrell, [who] also arranged the affairs of my two aunts ... By her will great-aunt Sarah left certain furniture and the residue of her estate to my aunts, Ann Salway and Harriet Clapp.

I received the same articles from Harriet Clapp, my surviving aunt, who by her will left me a two-thirds share in her estate. With the furniture and papers which I received were various books. Several of these items I sold to [a] Dr Shortridge about thirty years ago when he was living at Honiton. He was always pressing me to let him have more but I refused when I found that a table of Captain Cook's which I let him have for £5 in payment of a bill for medicine and attendance was sold again by him at a public auction for £175 ...

My particular desire is that as far as possible the furniture and the articles which I now own and which formerly belonged to Captain Cook ... shall continue to be associated with [his] name. These articles are:—

(1) Captain Cook's bureau of a dark foreign hard wood, inlaid which I have always heard went round the world with him ...

(8) A gold brooch with woven hair inside. On the back of the brooch my great-uncle or aunt had Mrs Cook's name engraved because it had been hers and contains a locket of her hair ...

I gave many of the books and papers to Dr Shortridge, including a song composed by seamen ...

'Dr Shortridge ... seems to have been rather a scoundrel!'wrote R. A. Skelton on behalf of the Hakluyt Society, on 10 December 1954. It is clear that he sold all his Cook material to Sir William Dixson, after whom the library in Sydney is named, for a price we shall probably never learn. Ann Arbery claimed in her affidavit to 'have a copy of my great-uncle's will'. And Elizabeth Cook's will (Dixson Library MSQ 147) confirms Ann Arbery's affidavit.

Source References

All source references preceded by 'Adm' are from the Public Record Office, Kew, London. Those preceded by 'BM' are from the British Museum, London. All published works stem from London unless otherwise shown.

1 The Young Yorkshireman

P.2	L.1	W. T. Stearn, *The Botanical Results of the Endeavour Voyage* (1968), p.3.
P.2	L.12	Fanny Burney, *Diary & Letters*, vol. I (1904), p.318.
P.2	L.20	Stuart Papers, vol. II, pp.41–2; quoted in A. Lang, *A History of Scotland*, vol. IV (1900), p.237.
P.3	L.4	J. Graves, *The History & Antiquities of Cleveland* (1808), p.452.
P.3	L.18	W. Besant, *Captain Cook* (1894), p.5.
P.6	L.10	R. T. Gaskin, *The Old Sea Port of Whitby* (1909) p.238.
P.6	L.20	*Ibid.*, pp.238–9.
P.7	L.1	W. H. Smyth, *The Sailor's Word-Book: An Alphabetical Digest of Nautical Terms* (1867), p.170.
P.7	L.14	G. Young, *Captain Cook* (1836), p.7.

2 'An Ambition to Go into the Navy'

P.10	L.12	Quoted in J. C. Beaglehole, *The Life of Captain James Cook* (1974), p.15 (hereafter cited as Beaglehole).
P.11	L.16	Quoted in A. Kitson, *Captain James Cook* (1907), p.18.
P.12	L.15	J. Hamar Journal, Adm 52/578; quoted in Beaglehole, p.18.
P.13	L.26	Kitson, *op. cit.*, pp.23–4.
P.20	L.3	Cook log, Adm 52/978; quoted in Beaglehole, p.43.
P.20	L.17	*Ibid.*
P.22	L.6	*Ibid.*

3 'Mr Cook's Genius and Capacity'

P.23	L.20	Young, *op. cit.*, p.12. Derived from the narrative of James King, one of Cook's lieutenants and admirers, *A Voyage to the Pacific*, vol. III (1784), p.47.
P.24	L.16	Beaglehole, p.51.

P.24   L.22   Colville Journal,
               Adm 1/482; quoted in
               Beaglehole, p.55.
P.25   L.34   Adm 1/482.
P.27   L.6   Kitson, *op. cit.*, pp.64–5.
P.27   L.34   *Ibid.*, p.66.
P.28   L.11   *Mariner's Mirror*, vol. 40
               (1954).
P.28   L.17   *Ibid.*, p.103.
P.29   L.11   Graves MSS, National
               Maritime Museum
               (hereafter NMM), Graves
               to the Admiralty, 20
               October 1763.
P.29   L.20   NMM GRV/106; quoted in
               Beaglehole, p.74n.
P.30   L.12   *Ibid.*; quoted in
               Beaglehole, p.76.
P.30   L.16   *Ibid.*
P.30   L.27   William Shakespeare, *A
               Winter's Tale*, Act IV.
P.31   L.29   Cook to Navy Board,
               22 January 1765,
               Dixson Library, Sydney,
               MSQ 140, 6; quoted in
               Beaglehole, p.82.
P.33   L.6   Quoted in Kitson, *op.
               cit.*, pp.79–80.

4   Appointment to the *Endeavour* Bark

P.34   L.9   Young, *op. cit.*, p.16.
P.36   L.14   Kitson, *op. cit.*, p.85.
P.36   L.32   *Ibid.*, p.84.
P.37   L.39   *Ibid.*, p.87.
P.38   L.19   *Ibid.*, pp.90–1
P.39   L.5   *Ibid.*, p.92.
P.41   L.16   J. C. Beaglehole (ed.),
               *The Journals of Captain
               James Cook* (hereafter
               cited as Cook Journal),
               vol. 1 (1968), p. XCIIn.
P.41   L.29   Quoted in D. Howarth,
               Tahiti (1983), p.13.
P.43   L.15   Quoted in G. A. Wood,
               The Discovery of Australia
               (1922), p.370.
P.43   L.39   *Ibid.*, p.374.

5   The People and the Gentlemen

P.45   L.25   27 March 1768, Adm
               106/3315; quoted in
               Beaglehole, p.129n.
P.48   L.4   P. O'Brian, *Joseph Banks*
               (1987), p.21.
P.48   L.15   Hunterian Oration to the
               College of Surgeons, 14
               February 1822.
P.49   L.17   J. C. Beaglehole (ed.),
               *The Endeavour Journal of
               Joseph Banks 1768–1771*
               (hereafter cited as
               Banks Journal), vol. 1
               (1962), p.11.
P.50   L.26   J. E. Smith (ed.),
               *A Selection of the
               Correspondence of Linnaeus
               & other Naturalists from
               the original MSS*, vol. 1
               (1821) pp.56–7.
P.50   L.35   21 December 1762;
               quoted in *ibid.*, p.160.
P.51   L.6   Quoted in Kitson, *op.
               cit.*, p.95.
P.59   L.23   27 August 1768; quoted
               in Beaglehole, p.153.
P.60   L.5   *Ibid.*, p.154.

6   'A Nursery for Desperation'

P.60   L.20   Banks Journal, vol. 1,
               p.158.
P.61   L.15   *Ibid.*, p.159.
P.63   L.39   Charles Greene Journal,
               27 September 1768, Adm
               51/4545/151.
P.64   L.22   Forwood Journal, 21
               September 1768, Adm
               51/4545/133.
P.64   L.31   Banks Journal,
               vol. 1, p.177.
P.66   L.9   Sydney Parkinson, *A
               Journal of a Voyage to the
               South Seas* (1784), p.4.
P.66   L.27   Cook Journal, vol. 1,
               pp.22–3.
P.66   L.34   Gore Journal, 14
               November 1768, Adm
               51/4548/145

P.67 L.22 *Ibid.*, 15 November 1768.

P.67 L.37 J. Hawkesworth, *An Account of the Voyages . . . for Making Discoveries in the Southern Hemisphere* (hereafter cited as Hawkesworth), vol. II (1773), p.23.

P.68 L.11 Cook Journal, vol. I, pp.496–7.

P.68 L.36 Parkinson, *op. cit.*, p.4.

P.69 L.3 Banks Journal, vol. I, p.190.

P.69 L.14 Hawkesworth, vol. II, p.31.

P.69 L.26 Adm 51/4545/133.

P.70 L.4 Banks Journal, vol. I, p.207.

P.70 L.35 *Ibid.*

P.70 L.40 Parkinson, *op. cit.*, p.6.

P.71 L.28 Gore Journal, 30 December 1768 and 3 January 1769.

P.72 L.36 *Documents relating to Anson's Voyage round the World 1740–1744* (Navy Records Society, 1967).

P.73 L.1 Gore Journal, 13 January 1769.

P.73 L.7 Cook Journal, vol. I, p.41.

P.73 L.27 Hawkesworth, vol. II, pp.43–4.

P.75 L.7 Banks Journal, vol. I, pp.217–18.

P.75 L.12 *Ibid.*

P.75 L.30 Hawkesworth, vol. II, p.45.

P.75 L.36 Parkinson, *op. cit.*, p.7.

P.75 L.39 Forwood Journal, 16 January 1769.

P.75 L.41 *Ibid.*

P.76 L.5 Gore Journal, 21 January 1769.

P.76 L.32 Banks Journal, vol. I, p.221.

P.78 L.21 *Ibid.*

P.78 L.40 Molyneux Journal, 18 January 1769, Adm 51/4546/152.

P.79 L.10 Forwood Journal, 18 January 1769.

P.79 L.19 Bootie Journal, 18 January 1769, Adm 51/4546/134–5.

P.79 L.19 Cook Journal, vol. I, p.45.

P.79 L.32 Banks Journal, vol. I, p.224.

P.80 L.11 *Ibid.* p.229.

7 Mar del Pacifico

P.81 L.16 Add MS 27944; quoted in Cook Journal, vol. I, p.49n.

P.81 L.19 Hicks Journal, 25 January 1769, Alexander Turnbull Library, Wellington.

P.81 L.26 Parkinson, *op. cit.*, p.11.

P.82 L.5 Cook Journal, vol. I, p.58.

P.83 L.3 Banks Journal, vol. I, p.231.

P.83 L.20 *Ibid.*, p.235.

P.83 L.22 *Ibid.*

P.83 L.25 *Ibid.*

P.83 L.33 *Ibid.*, p.239.

P.84 L.11 *Ibid.*, pp.242–3.

P.84 L.33 *Ibid.*, p.244.

P.85 L.25 *Ibid.*, p.246.

P.85 L.33 Gore Journal, 6 April 1769.

P.87 L.2 Banks Journal, vol. I, p.257.

P.87 L.12 Parkinson, *op. cit.*, p.13.

P.89 L.27 *Ibid.*, p.14.

P.90 L.17 Cook Journal, vol. I, p.78.

P.90 L.29 Gore, quoted in Cook Journal, vol. I, p.76n.

P.91 L.24 Banks Journal, vol. I, p.322.

P.91 L.35 *Ibid*, p.253.

P.92 L.3 *Ibid.*, p.254.

P.93 L.26 Cook Journal, vol. I, p.79.

P.94 L.25 *Ibid.*, p.80.

8 Venus Observed

P.96 L.11 Cook Journal, vol. I, p.81.

P.96 L.28 Molyneux Journal,
Adm 55/39.

P.98 L.1 Cook Journal vol. I,
p.82.

P.98 L.24 Banks Journal,
vol. I, p.260.

P.98 L.38 Cook Journal, vol. I,
p.95.

P.99 L.6 Molyneux Journal.

P.99 L.16 Banks Journal,
vol. I, p.264.

P.99 L.25 Molyneux Journal;
quoted in Cook Journal,
vol. I, p.554.

P.100 L.2 Molyneux Journal.

P.100 L.8 Banks Journal,
vol. I, p.266.

P.100 L.20 Variant draft of *Endeavour*
log, BM Add MS 27955.

P.101 L.3 Banks Journal,
vol. I, p.266.

P.101 L.11 *Ibid.*

P.102 L.4 *Ibid.*, pp.266–7.

P.102 L.22 Molyneux Journal.

P.102 L.31 Hawkesworth, vol. II,
p.97.

P.103 L.4 Parkinson, *op. cit.*, p.17.

P.103 L.25 Parkinson, *op. cit.*, p.21.

P.103 L.41 *Ibid.*, pp.25–6.

P.104 L.29 Cook Journal, vol. I,
pp.94–5.

P.104 L.40 Gore Journal, 1–2
June 1769.

P.105 L.5 Molyneux Journal.

P.105 L.18 Cook Journal, vol. I,
p.97.

P.105 L.30 Hawkesworth, vol. II,
p.140.

P.106 L.18 Molyneux Journal;
quoted in Cook Journal,
vol. I, pp.560 and 562.

P.107 L.2 Cook Journal, vol. I,
p.101.

P.107 L.30 *Ibid.*, p.110.

P.108 L.28 *Ibid*, p.114.

P.109 L.5 Molyneux Journal;
quoted in *ibid.*, p.563.

P.109 L.21 *Ibid.*, p.115.

P.109 L.39 Banks Journal,
vol. I, p.313.

P.110 L.36 Gore Journal, 19
July 1769.

P.111 L.9 Cook Journal, vol. I,
p.157.

P.111 L.16 Gore Journal, 14
August 1769.

P.112 L.2 Banks Journal,
vol. I, p.388.

9 'These People are Much Given to War'

p.113 L.2 Parkinson, *op. cit.*,
pp.85–6

p.113 L.8 Official log of the
Endeavour, Alexander
Turnbull Library FMS 55.

p.113 L.15 Banks Journal,
vol. I, p.399.

p.113 L.17 Cook Journal, vol. I,
p.262n.

p.114 L.18 *Ibid.*, p.168.

p.114 L.30 J. A. Mackay, *Historic
Poverty Bay* (Gisborne,
1949), citing Polack's
visit in 1836.

p.115 L.3 Bootie Journal, 9
October 1769.

p.116 L.5 Cook Journal, vol. I,
p.169.

p.116 L.16 Gore Journal, 9
October 1769.

p.116 L.26 'The Poverty Bay
Encounter', Mitchell
Library MSS, drafts
and variant versions;
quoted in Cook Journal,
vol. I, p.535.

p.117 L.1 Banks Journal,
vol. I, p.401.

p.117 L.16 *Ibid.*, p.402.

p.117 L.38 *Ibid.*, p.403

p.118 L.8 *Ibid.*, p.402

p.118 L.14 F. Wilkinson Journal,
10 October 1769, Adm
5L/4547/149.

p.118 L.33 Gore Journal, 10
October 1769.

p.119 L.5 Cook Journal, vol. I,
p.172.

p.119 L.12 *Ibid.*, p.172n.

p.119 L.26 *Ibid.*, p.174n.

p.119 L.40 *Ibid.*, p.173.

p.120 L.8 *Ibid.*, pp.175–6.

p.120 L.28 *Ibid.*, p.178n.

p.120 L.34 *Ibid.*

p.121 L.1 Hicks Journal, 31 October 1769.

p.121 L.9 Cook Journal, vol. I, p.186.

p.122 L.19 *Ibid.*, p.196.

p.122 L.37 *Ibid.*, p.202.

p.123 L.1 Banks Journal, vol. I, p.438.

p.123 L.9 *Ibid.*, p.439.

p.124 L.1 *Ibid.*, p.449.

p.125 L.36 *Ibid.*, p.452.

p.126 L.10 Cook Journal, vol. I, p.233.

p.126 L.20 *Ibid.*, pp.234–5.

p.126 L.30 Banks Journal, vol. I, p.453.

p.126 L.34 *Ibid.*

p.128 L.14 Wilkinson Journal, 20 January 1770.

p.128 L.22 Hicks Journal, 31 January 1770.

p.129 L.3 Cook Journal, vol. I, p.238.

10 'The First Discoverer'

p.130 L.10 Cook Journal, vol. I, p.243.

p.130 L.25 Hicks Journal, 5 February 1770.

p.131 L.13 Cook Journal, vol. I, p.250.

p.131 L.40 Grey MS 51, Auckland Public Library.

p.132 L.3 Cook Journal, vol. I, p.253.

p.132 L.28 *Ibid.*, p.263.

p.132 L.38 Banks Journal, vol. I, p.470.

p.133 L.4 *Ibid.*, p.471.

p.134 L.15 Cook Journal, vol. I, p.270.

p.134 L.37 *Crozet's Voyage to Tasmania*, trans. H. L. Roth (1891), p.22.

p.135 L.10 Cook Journal, vol. I, p.271.

p.138 L.39 R. A. Skelton, 'Captain James Cook after Two Hundred Years', address to the Hakluyt Society, 18 July 1968.

p.138 L.10 Cook Journal, vol. I, p.301.

p.139 L.16 *Ibid.*, p.304.

p.139 L.39 Banks Journal, vol. II (1962), p.54.

p.140 L.35 Parkinson, p.134.

p.140 L.33 Cook Journal, vol. I, p.305.

11 'Insane Labyrinth'

p.142 L.3 Banks Journal, vol. II, p.59.

p.142 L.8 Cook Journal, vol. I, p.305.

p.142 L.26 Cook Journal, vol. I, p.307.

p.142 L.27 Wood, *op. cit.*, p.422.

p.143 L.13 *Ibid.*, pp.310–11.

p.143 L.34 *Ibid.*, p.320.

p.144 L.14 Banks Journal, vol. II, p.62.

p.144 L.40 Cook Journal, vol. I, p.323.

p.145 L.11 *Ibid.*, p.324.

p.145 L.20 *Ibid.*, p.325.

p.145 L.30 Banks Journal, vol. II, p.67.

p.145 L.34 Cook Journal, vol. I, p.326.

p.146 L.10 *Ibid.*

p.146 L.32 Hicks Journal, 8 June 1770.

p.146 L.36 Pickersgill Journal, 3 June 1770, Adm 51/4547/140–1.

p.147 L.8 Cook Journal, vol. I, pp.343–4.

p.147 L.24 Banks Journal, vol. II, p.77.

p.147 L.31 Parkinson, *op. cit.*, p.142.

p.148 L.8 Cook Journal, vol. I, p.344.

p.148 L.11 Hicks Journal, 11 June 1770.

p.148 L.15 Cook Journal, vol. I, p.345.

p.148 L.38 *Ibid.*, p.345.

p.150 L.14 *Ibid.*, p.346.

p.150 L.21 Banks Journal, vol. II, pp.78 and 81.

p.151 L.11 Cook Journal, vol. I, p.350.

P.151 L.40   *Ibid.*, p.354.
P.152 L.18   *Ibid.*, p.357.
P.152 L.27   *Ibid.*, p.362.
P.154 L.14   *Ibid.*, p.365.
P.155 L.30   Banks Journal, vol. II,
             p.106.
P.156 L.1   *Ibid.*, p.107.
P.156 L.4   Cook Journal, vol. I,
             p.380.

12   Paradise to Stinking Hell

P.157 L.12   Cook Journal, vol. I,
             p.385.
P.157 L.25   *Ibid.*, p.387.
P.158 L.12   Banks Journal, vol. II,
             p.145.
P.159 L.10   *Ibid.*, p.147.
P.159 L.18   *Ibid.*, p.148.
P.159 L.36   *Ibid.*, p.150.
P.160 L.33   *Ibid.*, p.169.
P.161 L.25   *Ibid.*, p.152.
P.162 L.35   *Ibid.*, p.154.
P.163 L.33   Cook Journal, vol. I,
             p.421.
P.165 L.1   L. Palmier, *Indonesia*
             (1965), p.45.
P.165 L.41   Cook Journal, vol. I,
             p.501.
P.166 L.21   *Ibid.*, pp.437–8.
P.167 L.25   Parkinson, *op. cit.*, p.182.
P.167 L.38   Banks Journal, vol. II,
             p.191.
P.168 L.2   *Ibid.*
P.169 L.11   Cook Journal., vol.
             I, p.448.
P.169 L.29   *Ibid.*, p.451.
P.169 L.34   *Ibid.*, p.453.
P.170 L.17   *Ibid.*, p.465.

13   'A Voyage Such as Had Never Been Made Before'

P.171 L.13   Banks Journal, vol. II,
             p.251.
P.172 L.25   Cook Journal, vol. I,
             p.458.
P.173 L.1   *Ibid.*, p.467.
P.173 L.4   *Ibid.*, p.466.
P.173 L.11   *Ibid.*, p.467.
P.173 L.42   *Ibid.*, p.489.

P.174 L.12   *Ibid.*, p.470.
P.174 L.24   Banks Journal, vol. II,
             p.275.
P.174 L.26   *Ibid.*, p.274.
P.174 L.38   Cook Journal, vol. I,
             p.474.
P.175 L.14   *Ibid.*, p.475.
P.176 L.3   Kitson, *op. cit,*
             pp.211–12.
P.177 L.18   Beaglehole, p.273.
P.177 L.36   O'Brian, *op. cit.*, p.148.
P.178 L.11   Adm 3/78; quoted
             in Cook Journal,
             vol. I, p. 635.
P.178 L.26   Adm A/2645, index
             10704/17; quoted in
             ibid., p.634.
P.178 L.35   Kitson, *op. cit.*,
             pp.216–17.
P.179 L.4   *Ibid.*, p.217.
P.179 L.13   Adm 1/1609; quoted
             in Cook Journal,
             vol. I, p. 637.
P.181 L.11   Cook to Captain
             Hammond at Hull, 3
             January 1772, Whitby
             Museum.
P.181 L.32   Young, *op. cit.*,
             pp.120–21.
P.181 L.38   *Ibid.*
P.183 L.16   Cook Journal, vol. I,
             p.288.
P.184 L.1   *Ibid.*, p.479.
P.184 L.7   Cook Journal, vol. II
             (1969), p.XIX.

14   'Disgracing the Country'

P.186 L.27   Beaglehole, p.292.
P.186 L.42   BM Add MS 27888, f. 5.
P.187 L.28   *Ibid.*, ff. 4–4v.
P.187 L.37   Cook Journal, vol.
             II, p.XXX.
P.188 L.7   *Ibid.*
P.188 L.7   *Gazetteer & New Daily
             Advertiser,* 11 June 1772;
             quoted in Cook Journal,
             vol. II, p. XXXIII.
P.188 L.38   Banks Journal, vol. II,
             p.335.
P.189 L.4   *Ibid.*, pp.343–4.
P.189 L.20   J. R. Förster to
             Thomas Pennant, 13

P.191 L.13   August 1771; quoted in Beaglehole, p.274n.

P.191 L.13   Intro. to *The Diary and Letters of Madame D'Arblay* (Fanny Burney) (1931 edn), p.3.

P.192 L.36   G. S. Ritchie, *The Admiralty Chart* (1967), p. 29.

P.195 L.11   Clerke to Banks, 31 May 1772; quoted in Cook Journal, vol. II, p.936.

P.196 L.8   *Ibid.*, p.9.

P.205 L.33   *Ibid.*, 9 February 1773.

P.205 L.40   Kitson, *op. cit.*, p.251.

P.206 L.14   Cook Journal, vol. II, p.95n.

P.206 L.31   *Ibid.*, p.99n.

P.207 L.12   Kitson, *op. cit.*, p.251.

P.207 L.17   Cook Journal, vol. II, pp.98–9.

P.207 L.32   *Ibid.*, p.100.

P.207 L.41   Clerke Journal, 6 March 1773.

P.208 L.16   Cook Journal, vol. II, p.106.

15 'Such a Long Passage at Sea'

P.197 L.9   Cook Journal, vol. II, p.17.

P.197 L.27   *Ibid.*, p.688.

P.198 L.21   Royal Archives, Windsor Castle, Georgian Papers 1359; quoted in Cook Journal, vol. II, p.685.

P.199 L.4   *Ibid.*

P.199 L.35   Cook Journal, vol. II, p.21.

P.199 L.37   *Ibid.*

P.200 L.7   W. Wales, *Remarks on Mr Förster's Account of Cook's Last Voyage* (1778), p.20.

P.200 L.12   Clerke Journal, 19 September 1772, Adm 55/103, vol. I.

P.200 L.18   *Ibid.*, 30 October 1772.

P.200 L.21   *Ibid.*, 2 November 1772.

P.200 L.35   Cook Journal, vol. II, p.51.

P.200 L.40   *Ibid.*

P.201 L.20   *Ibid.*, p.755.

P.202 L.19   *Ibid.*, p.53.

P.202 L.28   Clerke Journal, 16 December 1772.

P.203 L.16   Cook Journal, vol. II, p.58n.

P.203 L.34   *Ibid.*, p.77.

P.204 L.2   Mara Journal; quoted in Cook Journal, vol. II, p. 75n.

P.204 L.13   *Ibid.*, pp.80–1.

P.205 L.3   Clerke Journal, 6 February 1773.

P.205 L.28   *Ibid.*, 8 February 1773.

16 Queen Charlotte Sound Rendezvous

P.209 L.3   Clerke Journal, 2 May 1773.

P.209 L.8   Cook Journal, vol. II, p.131.

P.209 L.13   A. Sparrman, *A Voyage round the World with Captain James Cook* (1953), p.43.

P.209 L.21   *Ibid.*, p.46.

P.209 L.26   Beaglehole, p.323.

P.210 L.13   Cook Journal, vol. II, p.112.

P.210 L.19   *Ibid.*

P.210 L.24   Sparrman, *op. cit.*, p.52.

P.210 L.41   Clerke Journal, 29 March 1773.

P.212 L.4   J. G. A. Förster, *A Voyage Round the World . . .*, vol. I (1777), pp.137–8.

P.212 L.13   Cook Journal, vol. II, p.116.

P.212 L.27   *Ibid.*

P.212 L.36   *Ibid.*, p.118.

P.213 L.7   *Ibid.*, p.122.

P.213 L.16   *Ibid.*

P.213 L.22   Clerke Journal, 19 April 1773.

P.216 L.11   Cook Journal, vol. II, p.145n.

P.216 L.20   *Ibid.*, p.155n.

P.216 L.38   *Ibid.*, p.148n.

P.217 L.24   *Ibid.*, p.173.

P.218 L.13   *Ibid.*, p.175.

P.218 L.24   *Ibid.*

P.218 L.29   Cook Journal, vol. II, p.177n.

P.219 L.10   Sparrman, *op. cit.*, p.57.
P.219 L.31   Clerke Journal, 9
             July 1773.
P.220 L.6   *Ibid.*, 29 July 1773.
P.220 L.15   Cook Journal, vol. ii,
             p.187.
P.220 L.39   Clerke Journal, 6
             August 1773.

17   Horrors of Grass Cove

P.222 L.5   Cook Journal, vol. ii,
             p.202.
P.222 L.19   *Ibid.*, p.201.
P.223 L.27   *Ibid.*, p.207n.
P.223 L.40   *Ibid.*, p.206.
P.224 L.35   *Ibid.*, pp.238–9.
P.225 L.10   *Ibid.*, p.211n.
P.225 L.16   Clerke Journal, 1
             November 1773.
P.225 L.35   *Ibid.*, 5 November 1773.
P.225 L.39   Wales Journal; quoted
             in Cook Journal,
             vol. ii, p. 801.
P.226 L.6   Sparrman, *op. cit.*, p.93.
P.226 L.30   Clerke Journal, 17
             September 1773.
P.227 L.3   Cook Journal, vol. ii,
             p.241.
P.227 L.27   *Ibid.*, p.245.
P.228 L.4   *Ibid.*, p.246.
P.228 L.23   Wales Journal; quoted in
             ibid., p.812.
P.228 L.39   *Ibid.*, p.813.
P.229 L.32   Cook Journal, vol. ii,
             p.292.
P.230 L.30   R. Furneaux, *Tobias
             Furneaux* (1960), p.141.
P.231 L.7   *Ibid.*, pp.142–3.
P.231 L.23   *Ibid.*, p.144.
P.231 L.28   Cook Journal, vol. ii,
             p.743.
P.232 L.10   Furneaux, *op. cit.*,
             pp.145–7.
P.233 L.18   *Ibid.*

18   From Icebergs to Tropical Heat

P.234 L.13   Cook Journal, vol. ii,
             pp.299–300.
P.235 L.6   *Ibid.*, p.302n.

P.235 L.18   *Ibid.*, p.310n.
P.235 L.26   Kitson, *op. cit.*, p.272.
P.236 L.5   Cook Journal, vol. ii,
             p.315.
P.236 L.12   *Ibid.*, p.315n.
P.236 L.17   *Ibid.*, p.316n.
P.236 L.20   *Ibid.*, p.321.
P.236 L.24   Clerke Journal, 26–27
             January 1774.
P.236 L.33   Cook Journal, vol. ii,
             pp.322–3.
P.237 L.19   *Ibid.*, p.326.
P.237 L.27   *Ibid.*, p.333.
P.237 L.30   Kitson, *op. cit.*, p.276.
P.240 L.4   Cook Journal, vol. ii,
             p.763.
P.241 L.37   Cook Journal, vol. ii,
             p.569.

19   'The Most Horrible Coast in the World'

P.243 L.14   Cook Journal, vol. ii,
             p.571.
P.243 L.24   *Ibid.*, p.572.
P.245 L.23   *Ibid.*, p.578.
P.246 L.16   *Ibid.*, p.583.
P.246 L.22   Quoted in R. Hough,
             The Blind Horn's Hate
             (1971), p.102.
P.247 L.10   Cook Journal, vol. ii,
             p.592.
P.247 L.27   *Ibid.*
P.248 L.3   *Ibid.*, p.601.
P.249 L.8   *Ibid.*, p.602.
P.249 L.19   Clerke Journal, 30
             December 1774.
P.249 L.24   Cook Journal, vol. ii,
             p.604.
P.250 L.19   *Ibid.*, p.617.
P.250 L.24   *Ibid.*, p.615n.
P.250 L.33   Clerke Journal, 16
             January 1775.
P.251 L.8   *Ibid.*, 18 January, 1775.
P.251 L.14   Cook Journal, vol. ii,
             p.622.
P.251 L.37   *Ibid.*, p.629.
P.252 L.28   Clerke Journal, 3
             February 1775.
P.253 L.7   Cook Journal, vol. ii,
             pp.637–8.
P.255 L.3   *Ibid.*, p.643.
P.255 L.24   *Ibid.*, p.652.

P.255 L.34   *Ibid.*, p.653.

20 'A Communication between the Atlantic and Pacific Oceans'

P.257 L.19   Cook Journal, vol. II, p.655.

P.258 L.22   *Ibid.*, p.655n.

P.258 L.36   Sparrman., *op. cit.*, p.204.

P.261 L.32   Adm 1/1610; quoted in Cook Journal, vol. II, p. 694.

P.262 L.28   Cook Journal, vol. II, p.682.

P.263 L.2   *Ibid.*, pp.694–5.

P.264n   J. Boswell Private Papers, XI, p.218.

P.265 L.23   Cook Journal, vol. II, p.960.

P.266 L.3   Kitson, *op.cit.*, p.323.

P.268 L.14   J. Boswell, *The Life of Dr Johnson* (April 1776).

21 A Stalled Departure

P.273 L.3   Dixson Library, Sidney; quoted in Cook Journal, vol. III (1967), p.1488.

P.273 L.30   *Ibid.*, p.1486.

P.275 L.15   R. Hough, *The Murder of Captain James Cook* (in USA *The Last Voyage of Captain James Cook*) (1979), p.19.

P.276 L.10   *Ibid.*, p.20.

P.277 L.38   Cook Journal, vol. III, p.500n.

P.277 L.42   *Ibid.*, p.499n.

P.278 L.14   *Ibid.*, p.500n.

P.278 L.26   Hough, *op. cit.*, p.22.

P.280 L.2   Cook Journal, vol. III, p.1464.

P.280 L.31   Samwell Journal; quoted in Cook Journal, vol. III, p.501.

P.281 L.20   Cook Journal, vol. III, p. CCXXI.

P.281 L.34   *Ibid.*, p. CCXXII

P.282 L.24   *Ibid.*, p.3n.

P.282 L.33   *Ibid.*, p.4.

P.283 L.32   Boswell private papers,

XL 218–19; quoted in Beaglehole, p.475.

P.284 L.20   Dixson Library, Sydney, MSS MS92. Sandwich papers; quoted in Beaglehole, p.507.

P.284 L.30   Young, *op. cit.*, pp.304–5.

P.285 L.6   Cook Journal, vol. III, p.5.

P.286 L.32   Hough, *op. cit.*, p.37.

P.287 L.5   Cook Journal, vol. III, p.8n.

P.287 L.11   *Ibid.*

22 Delays and More Delays

P.288 L.16   Anderson's Journal; quoted in Cook Journal, vol. III, p.736.

P.288 L.30   Cook Journal, vol. III, p.12.

P.289 L.29   *Ibid.*, p.15n.

P.289 L.40   Beaglehole, p.509.

P.290 L.17   Anderson's Journal; quoted in Cook Journal, vol. III, p.757.

P.290 L.28   Cook Journal, vol. III, p.23.

P.291 L.14   *Ibid.*, p.26n.

P.291 L.15   *Ibid.*, p.25.

P.292 L.9   *Ibid.*, p.27.

P.293 L.12   *Ibid.*, p.32.

P.295 L.39   *Ibid.*, p.53n.

P.296 L.4   *Ibid.*, p.56.

P.297 L.3   *Ibid.*, p.63.

P.297 L.21   *Ibid.*, p.66.

P.298 L.5   *Ibid.*, p.77.

P.298 L.8   *Ibid.*, p.77n.

P.298 L.35   *Ibid.*, p.98n.

P.299 L.8   *Ibid.*, p.132n.

P.299 L.23   *Ibid.*, p.133.

P.300 L.12   Hough, *op. cit.*, p.94.

23 Farewell Omai

P.302 L.16   Samwell Journal, 20 September 1777; quoted in Cook Journal, vol. III, p.1062.

P.303 L.19   Cook Journal, vol. III, p.213.

P.304 L.30   Samwell Journal, 9

October 1777; quoted in *ibid.*, p.1068.

P.305 L.14 Cook Journal, vol. III, p.231.

P.305 L.29 *Ibid.*, p.232.

P.306 L.15 *Ibid.*

P.307 L.13 King Journal, 11 October 1777; quoted in *ibid.*, p.1383.

P.309 L.11 Cook Journal, vol. III, p.257.

P.309 L.25 C. Lloyd (ed.), *A Memoir of James Trevenen* (Navy Records Sty, 1959), from marginal notes by T. in his brother's copy of Cook's third voyage.

P.309 L.38 Clerke Journal, 1 January 1778; quoted in Cook Journal, vol. III, p.259n.

P.311 L.5 Cook Journal, vol. III, p.261.

P.312 L.25 Quoted in Hough, *op. cit.*, p.124.

P.312 L.30 *Ibid.*

P.313 L.10 Clerke Journal, 20 January 1778.

P.313 L.15 Quoted in Hough, *op. cit.*, p.125.

P.313 L.20 King Journal; quoted in Cook Journal, vol. III, p. 1391.

P.314 L.6 Cook Journal, vol. III, p.269.

24 'Very Nice Pilotage'

P.318 L.1 David M. Cooney, *A Chronology of the US Navy* (New York, 1965), pp.7–8.

P.316 L.22 Cook Journal, vol. III, p.289.

P.318 L.37 D. J. Weber, *The Spanish Frontier in North America* (1993), p.237.

P.320 L.19 Cook Journal, vol. III, p.292n.

P.320 L.26 *Ibid.*, p.293n.

P.321 L.25 King Journal, 30 March 1778, quoted in Cook Journal, vol. III, p.1393.

P.322 L.19 Lloyd (ed.), *op. cit.*, p.20.

P.325 L.12 Cook Journal, vol. III, p.389.

P.326 L.32 Quoted in Hough, *op. cit.*, p.155.

25 The Great Island

P.329 L.7 Cook Journal, vol. III, p.427n.

P.330 L.21 *Ibid.*, pp.473–4.

P.331 L.5 Hough, *op. cit.*, p.171.

P.332 L.7 Quoted in *ibid.*, pp.172–3.

P.332 L.24 Cook Journal, vol. III, pp.481 and 481n.

P.333 L.29 *Ibid.*, p.489.

P.334 L.27 Quoted in Hough, *op. cit.*, p.184.

P.336 L.11 Cook Journal, vol. III, pp.504–5.

P.337 L.14 Hough, *op. cit.*, p.190.

P.337 L.33 *Ibid.*, p.191.

P.339 L.33 Kitson, *op. cit.*, p.465.

P.340 L.14 Hough, *op. cit.*, p.200.

26 Death among the Rocks

P.342 L.22 Samwell Journal, 10 February 1779; quoted in Cook Journal, vol. III, p.1190.

P.346 L.22 Hough, *op. cit.*, pp.209–10.

P.348 L.1 Clerke Journal, 14 February 1779; quoted in *ibid.*, pp.213–14.

P.350 L.1 King Journal, 14 February 1779; quoted in *ibid.* p.218.

P.352 L.16 Samwell Journal, 14 February 1779; quoted in Cook Journal, vol. III, p.1197.

P.353 L.4 Hough, *op. cit.*, p.225.

P.354 L.18 Samwell Journal, 14 February 1779; quoted in Cook Journal, vol. III, p.1198.

27 A Lament for Orono

P.355 L.6 Lloyd (ed.), *op. cit.*, p.23.
P.355 L.1 Gilbert Journal, 14 February 1779; quoted in Hough, *op. cit.*, p.229.
P.355 L.14 Samwell Journal, 14 February 1779; quoted in Cook Journal, vol. III, p.1200.
P.358 L.7 Hough, *op. cit.*, p.235.
P.358 L.30 Lloyd (ed.), *op. cit.*, p.24.
P.359 L.8 Cook Journal, vol. III, p.566.
P.359 L.20 *Ibid.*, p.548n.
P.359 L.37 *Ibid.*, p.567.
P.360 L.3 *Ibid.*, p.567n.
P.360 L.19 *Ibid.*, pp.567–8.
P.360 L.24 Lloyd (ed.), *op. cit.*, p.25.

28 'An Everlasting Honour to his Country'

P.363 L.10 Sparrman, *op. cit.*, p.52.
P.363 L.19 Cook Journal, vol. II, p.334n.
P.363 L.26 R. Fisher and H. Johnston, *Captain James Cook and His Times* (1979), p.155.
P.366 L.19 *Diary and Letters of Mme. D'Arblay*, vol. I, (1834), p.370.
P.369 L.4 Kitson, *op. cit.*, p.508.

Appendix 1

P.371 L.18 Cook Journal, vol. I, pp.323–4.

Index

Index

Index